Empathy and Agency

Empathy and Agency

The Problem of Understanding in the Human Sciences

edited by

Hans Herbert Kögler
University of North Florida

Karsten R. Stueber
College of the Holy Cross

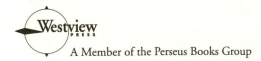

Westview PRESS

A Member of the Perseus Books Group

Published in 2000 in the United States of America by Westview Press, 5500 Central Avenue, Boulder, Colorado 80301–2877, and in the United Kingdom by Westview Press, 12 Hid's Copse Road, Cumnor Hill, Oxford OX2 9JJ

Find us on the World Wide Web at www.westviewpress.com

Library of Congress Cataloging-in-Publication Data
Empathy and agency : the problem of understanding in the human
  sciences / edited by Hans Herbert Kögler and Karsten R. Stueber.
     p. cm.
  Includes bibliographical references and index.
  ISBN 0-8133-9120-2 (hc).—ISBN 0-8133-9119-9 (pb)
  1. Psychology—Philosophy.   2. Science and psychology.
3. Empathy.   I. Kögler, Hans Herbert, 1960– .   II. Stueber,
Karsten R.
BF64.E67   2000
128'.4—dc21   99-35722
                                                                                                          CIP

The paper used in this publication meets the requirements of the American National Standard for Permanence of Paper for Printed Library Materials Z39.48–1984.

10   9   8   7   6   5   4   3   2   1

Contents

Preface

In philosophy of mind and cognitive psychology, we have recently witnessed a revived interest in empathy, or simulation, as a cognitive tool for understanding others. By focusing on the question of how we gain knowledge of other minds, and whether we use simulation/empathy or theory as a means for this task, philosophy is rediscovering a topic that has been at the center of controversy in the philosophy of social science. "Simulation," as presented in recent cognitive psychology and philosophy of mind, is a challenge to the established orthodoxy that the understanding of others is based on theory or rationality. Evidence about the cognitive development of young children suggests that instead of using a "theory" to predict and understand others, we rather imaginatively put ourselves into the other's situation. In this vein, the role of emotions and motivations for making sense of others is emphasized. Understanding human agency is thus not the same as explaining how something in the material world occurs. This idea dovetails well with the conception of empathic understanding, or *Nacherleben* (reliving), of some paradigms in the philosophy of social science. In early hermeneutic thought, "empathy" was construed as a special method of access to historical and cultural phenomena due to the psychological similarity between interpreter and interpretee. It has been taken to break the monopoly of explanatory methods established by the natural sciences. Instead of just explaining and constructing external phenomena, interpreters in the human and social sciences "understand" the social or cultural world, that is, they relive and reexperience its meaning.

Yet in light of the cognitive revolution, linguistic turn, and what we might call "the unchallenged orthodoxy of the interpretive turn," philosophers of social science from almost all traditions tend nowadays to be skeptical and negligent about the role of empathy for understanding human agency. We believe that the new and overwhelming evidence from cognitive psychology and the philosophy of mind challenges the methodological status quo in the human and social sciences. We have conceived this anthology in the belief that the contemporary discussion justifies a renewed investigation of empathy within the realm of philosophy of social science by taking into account the current arguments for empathy/simulation in cognitive psychology and the philosophy of mind. At stake are issues like the relation between everyday and social-scientific interpretation, the role of empathy or simulation in understanding human agency, the scope and adequacy of attributing theoretical or rational assumptions in the course of interpretation, and the nature of rational and/or causal explanations in the human and social sciences.

This anthology is intended to be accessible to a broad audience. In order to facilitate this goal, the introduction outlines the main features of both the current debate and the traditional debate about empathy's role for understanding human agency. Our introduction will serve two purposes in particular. First, it will provide a systematic survey of the most important debates that have shaped the contemporary field of the philosophy of social science. We are focusing on the debate among Collingwood, Dray, and Hempel about the function of laws in social-scientific explanation, the controversy about rationality and relativism triggered by Winch and MacIntyre, the debate between Schleiermacher, Dilthey, and Gadamer on the empathetic or dialogical nature of hermeneutics, and on the *Erklären/ Verstehen* debate in the social sciences. Second, the introduction will clarify the importance of the simulation debate for the methodological problems in the social sciences. We will point out many connections that exist between earlier models of empathy and recent simulation theory, and discuss those correspondences in light of their relevance for a methodology concerned with understanding human agency.

The various contributions presented here will explore the role of empathy for understanding agency from different perspectives. It is the editors' hope that such "cooperation" among various philosophical traditions is beneficial to both the philosophy of mind and the philosophy of social science, and that it will allow us to get a precise understanding of our epistemic relation to other minds and agents. The chapters in this book also show that the shared interest in simulation (or empathy) as a method for interpretation has organically produced a convergence of philosophical interest of formerly rather separated philosophical fields. The methodological paradigms presented here include the philosophy of mind, simulation theory, social theory, naturalized epistemology, Davidsonian theory of meaning, Wittgensteinian, Diltheyan, and critical-hermeneutic approaches to understanding, and normative-pragmatic and antirealist positions. They thus encompass a wide range of methodological perspectives that are relevant for the disciplines of cognitive psychology and cognitive science, for sociology, anthropology, and history, and, of course, for all interested in the philosophy of the human and social sciences.

Philosophical writing in general tends to be the result of intellectual cooperation and conversation. This is even truer for *Empathy and Agency: The Problem of Understanding in the Human Sciences,* which approaches contemporary simulation theory from a variety of different perspectives in the philosophy of human and social sciences. The editors are grateful to numerous people who helped us bring this project to completion. We would like to thank the contributors for their enthusiastic cooperation. Similarly, thanks are due to our editor, Sarah Warner, of Westview Press for her generous support. We are particularly grateful to Rosa de Jorio and Manisha Sinha for their intellectual companionship and for their comments on the introduction. In the end we would also like to express our gratitude to our academic institutions, the University of North Florida and the College of the Holy Cross, who supported this project through a summer research grant and a faculty fellowship, respectively.

Hans Herbert Kögler and Karsten R. Stueber

Introduction:
Empathy, Simulation, and Interpretation in the Philosophy of Social Science

HANS HERBERT KÖGLER
KARSTEN R. STUEBER

How do minds understand other minds? On what grounds and with what methods do we understand, predict, or explain how other human beings think, feel, and act? Based on our commonsense intuitions, it seems that we solve this task by empathizing with another person and by utilizing theoretical knowledge about how people in general act. When we hear that an airliner has crashed, when we are told that a friend has lost a job or a colleague has received a promotion, we can understand how the persons affected by such events feel and why they act as they do by empathizing with them and by putting ourselves in their situation. No theory seems to be necessary in order to understand their reactions in such situations. But we are also able to predict and explain another person's behavior by taking a more detached perspective and by appealing to everyday and scientific knowledge about why people act in a certain manner. We know, for example, that people under the influence of alcohol drive erratically and are prone to be involved in car accidents and that people who do not prepare for exams tend to do badly on them. Theoretical knowledge seems to be sufficient to fully account for people's behavior in these cases.

Common sense alone does not tell which one of these methods is more fundamental for dealing with other people and what psychological mechanisms are utilized for such purposes. It also does not tell us whether our ability to explain and predict another person's actions is fundamentally different from the manner in which we predict and explain events in the natural sciences. Questions like these are at the center of the traditional philosophical debate about methodology in the human and social sciences. They have been vigorously discussed under the banner of *Erklären* versus *Verstehen* ("explanation" versus "understanding"). Yet these issues are hardly resolved. For that reason, it is worth noticing that similar questions are being pondered with renewed rigor, in light of new empirical findings, in the contemporary debate between simulation theory (ST) and theory theory (TT). This interdisciplinary debate, which has seen participation by philosophers and child psychologists, is concerned with the question of whether our interpretations of other agents are implicitly guided by a psychological theory, as theory theorists maintain, or whether we interpret them by empathetically putting ourselves in their shoes, as simulation theorists assert. However, even though the proponents of this contemporary discussion are in general quite aware of the old debate they tend not to pay much attention to it, since most of them favor a more empirical approach to the topic.

This anthology attempts to bridge the gap between these very related but still isolated philosophical conversations by taking a closer look at the proposal for simulation theory from the perspective of the philosophy of social science. We focus on simulation theory because the simulation position prima facie strengthens the claim that our study of other human beings is methodologically different from the study of the physical world. It challenges the hermeneutic and positivist orthodoxy associated with the work of Gadamer and Hempel, who dismiss empathy as a viable principle of interpretation or scientific explanation. We feel also that the integration of the simulation position into the philosophy of social science will considerably broaden the scope of the discussion and its evaluative framework. In the end, the simulation proposal can gain widespread acceptance only if one can plausibly show that simulation is the central mechanism of understanding for the human and social sciences, since it is here that we supposedly use our ordinary strategies of interpretation in the most disciplined and reflective manner.

The purpose of the anthology is thus twofold. We hope to invigorate a traditional debate in the philosophy of social science by providing it with a new perspective. At the same time, we intend to make a contribution to a contemporary philosophical discussion by making it aware of certain aspects of the more traditional debate. This introduction will provide the reader with the philosophical background knowledge necessary for a proper understanding of the various contributions. We will briefly outline the traditional "explaining versus understanding" debate in the analytic and continental-hermeneutic traditions of philosophy and we will broadly describe the relevant aspects of the debate between simulation theory and theory theory. However one views the contemporary debate, it is our hope that a dialogue with the simulation position and its attempt to clarify the psychological mechanisms of folk-psychological interpretations will allow us to better characterize the structure of interpretation involved in the understanding of other agents.

1. Two Philosophical Camps

Ever since the attempt to construct the study of human actions and human affairs in analogy to the successful natural sciences, philosophers, historians, and social scientists have worried about the plausibility of understanding the human and social sciences on such a model. In this regard, one commonly distinguishes between two philosophical camps taking opposing views on the question of whether or not there is a principal methodological difference between the natural and the social sciences. The view that denies such a distinction is called either positivism or more generally naturalism, whereas the position that maintains a principal difference is variously called idealism, methodological separatism, or, in more contemporary terms, interpretivism or hermeneutics.

Naturalists base their position on an ontological intuition. For the naturalist, Cartesian dualism is not a viable ontological option, given what modern science and evolutionary theory tell us about how the human species evolved. Human beings, like any other biological organism, are part of nature and are constrained by the same physical forces. They have to be primarily conceived of as physical entities. Accordingly, all their properties, including mental ones, have to be understood as being in some way dependent or supervenient on the basic physical properties and mechanisms of the physical world. Yet if human beings cannot sensibly claim to inhabit a noumenal world in the Kantian sense, it is hard to understand why the study of human affairs should be radically different from the study of the natural world. For naturalists, it is the aim of both the natural and social sciences to develop empirically well supported and comprehensive theories that have high predictive powers for certain domains of investigation. Such theories enable us to explain causally the occurrence of a certain event by appealing to an empirically well supported body of knowledge that is integrated by the articulation of causal mechanisms underlying the observed macrophenomena. Naturalists might allow that natural sciences and social sciences differ in the specificity with which the laws of the respective disciplines are articulated. But, for them, this does not indicate any essential difference in the method according to which one has to proceed in the construction and the empirical testing of theories. It might merely indicate the less developed nature of the relatively young social sciences, or it might indicate a subject matter of such complexity that it surpasses our computing and calculating powers. Whatever the reasons for these differences, it does not validate the conclusion that there is anything qualitatively special about the human sciences.[1]

It is difficult to characterize the hermeneutic position in such general terms, but it is best understood in its opposition to naturalism. For the proponent of the hermeneutic position, the above arguments have the character of a *non sequitur*. Admitting that human beings are part of the physical world does not imply that the relationship between the researcher and his or her object in the human or social sciences is identical to the relationship of the natural scientist to his or her domain. Such a claim is taken to be as absurd as the claim that our interaction with other human beings is not different from our interaction with inanimate physical things. Rather, in order to investigate the realm of human action and interaction, the researcher has to adopt an attitude and a method of investigation that is appropriate to the study of human beings by another human being and allows one to recognize their unique individuality. And that method and attitude, it is maintained, is radically different from the method of study in the natural sciences. The aim of the so-called human sciences is not so much to develop a comprehensive and predictively accurate theory as to understand human actions and affairs.

Yet understanding, or *Verstehen,* is much more than a mere battle cry against the perceived shortcomings of naturalism. In the preceding paragraph, the claims of the hermeneutic position were mainly characterized in the negative. A more positive characterization of the tradition requires a detailed discussion of the arguments for the above negative claims. As we will see, one can distinguish very different forms of such arguments prevalent in the hermeneutic or interpretivist tradition that depend on very distinct conceptions of understanding and its object. One can nevertheless distill a core argument for the hermeneutic opposition to the naturalist conception of the human sciences.

According to the hermeneutic position, human beings differ essentially from inanimate organisms because human beings interpret the world from a specific point of view. They not only react to their environment but have a subjective perspective on their natural and social surroundings. It is such a point of view that is constitutive for the unique individuality of each person. In order to study the action and affairs of human beings appropriately, one has to reconstruct that perspective. Otherwise one is unable to grasp the significance that members of a society attribute to particular practices in their society. But the conception of objectivity that is embedded in the methods of the natural sciences is a detached or external conception of objectivity, according to which an entity can be accepted as real only if it can be subsumed under a general concept of a nomological theory.[2] As long as we are constrained by the methodological principles of the natural sciences, we try to transcend our merely subjective point of view and try to describe the world from a perspective that is "external to a specific point of view."[3] Hermeneutic theorists therefore contend that it is inherently paradoxical to study human beings, who have a particular subjective point of view, from a detached and external perspective. It is the attempt to study human beings who have a subjective point of view from a perspective that cannot admit the reality of somebody having a distinct point of view.

It is exactly this insight that drove philosophers like Dilthey and Collingwood into opposition to a positivist conception of the human sciences. It motivated them to conceive of the human sciences as being methodologically autonomous and to argue for specific versions of empathy as the appropriate method to gain objective knowledge in this domain, especially in the historical sciences.[4] In contrast to natural scientists, historians cannot restrict themselves to a mere external description of historical events by proceeding from a perceptual acquaintance with individual events to the recognition of laws of nature under which such events can be subsumed.

> The historian, investigating any event in the past, makes a distinction between what may be called the outside and the inside of an event. By the outside of the event I mean everything belonging to it which can be described in terms of bodies and their movements. . . . By the inside of the event I mean that in it which can only be described in terms of thought. . . . His work may begin by discovering the outside of an event, but it can never end there; he must always remember that the event was an action, and that his main task is to think himself into the action, to discern the thought of its agent.[5]

Only historians who are able to discern the thoughts that are expressed in human actions can find them intelligible and can understand them as rational activities of particular agents.[6] But one cannot understand how a historian could ascertain the objectivity of a thought, whose existence depends on the mental activity of an agent having a subjective point of view, on the model of the natural sciences and its perceptual basis. Understanding a thought in its subjectivity cannot be identified with the perception of an object in the external world. Grasping the peculiar objectivity of a thought can only be accomplished by integrating the thought of another thinker into one's own subjective cognitive system. Yet if such integration is successful, it is not necessary to appeal to laws of nature in order to grasp a thought's effects on other thoughts and actions. For Collingwood, the integration of another person's thoughts into one's own cognitive systems seems all that is required for such recognition.[7] In order to understand the action of another person one therefore has to be able to think the thought expressed in that action and has to know that one is thinking such a thought.

The act of thinking, then, is not only subjective but objective as well. It is not only a thinking, it is something that can be thought about. But because . . . it is never merely objective, it requires to be thought about in a peculiar way, a way only appropriate to itself. It cannot be set before the thinking mind as a ready-made object, discovered as something independent of that mind and studied as it is in itself, in that independence. It can never be studied 'objectively' in the sense in which 'objectively' excludes 'subjectively'. It has to be studied as it actually exists, that is to say as an act. And because this act is subjectivity . . . or experience, it can be studied only in its own subjective being, that is by the thinker whose activity or experience it is. This study is not mere experience or consciousness, not even mere self-consciousness: it is self-knowledge.[8]

Collingwood calls this integration of another person's thought into one's own cognitive system reenactment.[9] He insists that the described historical method is not only the appropriate method to study the past but the right method to study other minds in general.[10] We do not use reenactment or simulation only to grasp the thought of Caesar but also to recognize the thoughts of our friends and neighbors, as well as our own past thoughts. In this respect Collingwood's method of reenactment can be regarded as a precursor to contemporary simulation theory. Nevertheless, Collingwood leaves a lot of questions unaddressed that have to be answered for his position to be plausible. Even if one grants that the nature of subjectivity might constitute a challenge to the naturalist's position, does this imply that we can gain knowledge of another person only by actually reenacting his or her thought processes? Collingwood has never conclusively argued that reenactment is the only possible method for grasping the subjective perspective of another person. Why shouldn't a psychological theory be of any help in this context? Furthermore, how exactly does the process of reenactment function psychologically? It seems absurd to assume that we can completely identify ourselves with the other person. But if that is not possible, how can anyone claim to have adequately grasped the inside of an event? Even if reenactment should work for a person I know very well, this does not automatically show that reenactment is possible for a person from a very different social and cultural context. Collingwood was quite aware of certain limitations of the method of reenactment, since he realized that not every generation of historians is able to relate appropriately to all historical periods. Our own cultural context might set some boundaries within which reenactment is possible. Understanding can break down. Hence, the writing of history and history itself has to be regarded as an open-ended endeavor. More importantly, as Collingwood emphasizes, reenactment is only possible insofar as the act of thinking and its object are concerned. It cannot re-create the immediacy of a qualitative episode of consciousness that another person has experienced in a certain situation. Reenacting such thoughts does not necessitate re-creating the exact cognitive context of another thinker. I can reenact another person's thoughts if I am able to integrate them into an appropriate cognitive context.[11] Yet one is certainly justified to wonder what exactly makes a cognitive context appropriate for such a reenactment and how one can determine whether the reenactment was successful and whether it provides knowledge of other minds. Fortunately, these questions are addressed in more detail by contemporary simulation theory.

2. Simulation Theory Versus Theory Theory

The debate between simulation theory and theory theory is primarily a debate about how one can explicate our folk-psychological capacity to interpret, predict, and explain another person's actions and thoughts. Proponents of both positions attempt to provide a psychologically realistic account of these capacities in terms of their underlying psychological mechanisms. For that very reason the discussion focuses on empirical questions regarding the cognitive development of young children, since one can argue for a psychologically realistic account of our interpretive capacities by showing that we acquire certain cognitive mechanisms as children.

The main focus of the debate between ST and TT then is the question of *quid facti* in the tradition of Locke's and Hume's analysis of the mind. One is interested in how the mind works in understanding other minds, independent of the question of whether or not these mental procedures are epistemically justified. Interwoven within this debate, especially on the side of simulation theory, are more traditional epistemological issues concerning the question of whether or not these psychological mechanisms provide genuine knowledge of other minds and questions regarding our grasp of psychological concepts. Even though these concerns are not shared by all proponents of the debate, they connect it to the traditional discussion in the philosophy of social science. Philosophers of social science were never just interested in answering the question of how researchers causally produce an interpretation of another culture. Rather, they tried to show how one would justify such an interpretation. Simulation theorists would, however, insist that such epistemic concerns cannot be addressed independent of an investigation of the psychological mechanisms that we actually use to interpret another agent.

For the purpose of this introduction, it will be sufficient to analyze one version of the theory theory position, proposed by Alison Gopnik, Andrew Meltzoff, and Henry Wellman.[12] According to them, children's cognitive development is characterized by the acquisition of a body of knowledge about various domains in the physical realm and the mental realm. They claim also that this body of knowledge is organized very much like a scientific theory. A theory is not the mere storage of unconnected pieces of information; it provides an explanatory account of observed macrophenomena in terms of underlying "lawlike" regularities that are postulated to hold between "unobservable" theoretical entities. Our folk theory of mind might, for example, include the *ceteris paribus* principle that somebody will do x if he desires y and believes that x is a means to y.[13] In contrast to an adult scientist, however, the child is not reflectively aware of its theoretical activity and of its final theoretical product, that is, the end product is a tacit theory of mind.

According to TT, we predict another person's behavior analogously to the way a natural scientist would predict the occurrence of any event. We would use relevant information about that person in conjunction with our tacit folk-theoretical knowledge in order to predict what he will do next. If we know that somebody wants to drink a cold beer and we know that he believes he has to go to the kitchen in order to satisfy his desire, we will predict that he will go to the kitchen in light of the above tacit belief-desire principle.

The proponents of this version of TT do not claim that children are born with a full-blown adult theory of mind.[14] Rather, children acquire such a theory after going through various paradigmatic theoretical stages characterized by various different conceptions of belief and desires. Only such a dynamic conception of tacit theory construction is able to account for the various experimental results in child psychology, such as the so-called false-belief task. It is by now a very well known and established experimental fact that children under the age of four are not able to pass this task. In its classic conception by Heinz Wimmer and Josef Perner,[15] children were asked to predict the behavior of a specific character, Maxi. They see a play in which Maxi observes that a piece of chocolate was put away in the kitchen. While he is away and without his knowledge, the chocolate is hidden in another location. Children are now asked where Maxi will look for the chocolate when he comes back and wants to eat the chocolate. Only children over the age of four seem to be able to consistently answer this question correctly. Younger children tend to predict that Maxi will look at the location where the chocolate was actually hidden, not where he thought the chocolate was. For theory theorists, this shows that children under the age of four do not have the same theory of mind as adults. Their concept of belief does not allow for the possibility that a belief could misrepresent facts in the world. Children at that age rather have something like a "copy" conception of belief, according to which the beliefs of a person directly mirror the facts in the world.[16]

But TT is not the only game in town. Proponents of ST claim that the above phenomena can be easily explained in a simpler fashion and without the need to postulate a tacit theory of mind. According to simulation theorists, children under the age of four do not lack an adult theory of mind. They lack the ability to simulate another person and look at the world from the perspective of that person. For them, understanding another person does not primarily involve any appeal to a body of knowledge about human psychology. It involves only our own cognitive system that we normally use to deliberate about what to do next. In predicting the action of another person, we put ourselves in his shoes, imagine the world "as it would appear from his point of view," and "then deliberate, reason and see what decision emerges."[17] Simulation theorists typically claim that simula-

How about habit — the "theory" & "simulation" occur in the non-personal subjective. I thought consciously "think" is habit.

tion is the basic procedure for predicting the actions and thoughts of another person. It is not a mere heuristic that we use instead of appealing to a theory. Simulation theorists can allow for the possibility that we sometimes do indeed appeal to certain psychological generalizations in such an endeavor. But for the simulation theorist such an appeal is a mere heuristic shortcut, since these generalizations are derived from prior simulations of other persons.

With Stephen Stich and Shaun Nichols one can distinguish two basic types of simulative procedures, that is, one can distinguish between an "actual situation simulation" and a "pretense-driven-off-line-simulation."[18] In the first kind of simulation, we predict the action of another person by putting ourselves in a situation very similar to the one he or she is in and by observing how we would react in these circumstances. We predict, in this manner, how another person might solve an arithmetic problem by solving it ourselves, that is, we predict another person's behavior in light of thoughts we have. In the pretense-driven simulation, on the other hand, we feed our own decision system with pretend beliefs and desires and run it "off-line." Using this method, I am able to predict how a person will act when he or she believes that the earth is flat even though I do not share that belief and I will not act on that belief. I just feed my cognitive system with such a belief and see what happens while disallowing it to make any real decisions. Both types of simulation are, in Goldman's terms, not theory driven but process driven. For that reason, simulation theorists do not find it necessary to distinguish always between these two types of simulation.

There are three very different conceptions of the simulation theory proposed by Alvin Goldman, Robert Gordon, and Jane Heal. For Goldman, knowledge of other minds acquired by simulation is a form of analogical inference. I infer the other person's thoughts by using myself as a model for his psychological processes and by introspecting my own thought processes while simulating him. But as an epistemic externalist and reliabilist, Goldman does not require that I have access to reasons that would provide a justification for such an inference. My inference from me to you is solely justified[19] if simulation is in fact a reliable procedure and I have mapped your psychological processes isomorphically. I do not have to be able to provide evidence for the assumption that I am on the whole psychologically similar to you.

Gordon opposes Goldman's model conception of simulation, since he is concerned that such a view falls prey to Wittgensteinian worries about analogical inference.[20] In simulating another person I do not use myself as a model for the other person in Goldman's sense. Rather, simulation has to be understood as "personal transformation" through a "recentering of my egocentric map" in which I make "adjustment for relevant differences."[21] In order to know what another person would do in a specific situation, I have to ask myself what I would do while simulating the other person. But this is no inference from me to you because the "I" does not possess its ordinary reference but refers to the simulated character.[22]

Gordon's conception of simulation is best illustrated with the help of a spatial example. Imagine that you walk with a friend who is approached by a fierce-looking dog. Assume that your friend is as afraid of dogs as you. In such a case you will be able to predict his or her behavior and emotional state by just reacting to the environmental clues, since you share almost the same spatial perspective. This is a case of total projection, as Gordon calls it. Simulation requires more effort if total projection is not possible and you have to adjust for relevant differences between you and the simulated person. If you, for example, notice that your friend, who is walking five hundred feet away from you, is approached by a dog, you will have to imaginatively shift your spatial perspective in order to share your friend's egocentric outlook toward the environment. Things obviously become more complicated if your friend likes dogs and you are afraid of them. In this case you will also have to make adjustments to account for these differences. For Gordon, however, these adjustments are not based on any general psychological theory. They are based on information or evidence regarding differences in cognitive and emotional dispositions between specific individuals.[23]

Heal defends the most limited version of simulation theory.[24] In contrast to Gordon and Goldman she is not concerned with the question of how simulation is realized on the subpersonal level. She also follows Collingwood closely in asserting that simulation is basic for the prediction of another person's thoughts with a specific propositional content, given that we know his or her other thoughts. Our only option to accomplish such a task is to simulate or co-cognize his or her thoughts by thinking about the same subject matter. Yet for Heal psychological theory plays a greater role in our effort to predict other people's actions than Gordon and Goldman admit. She argues that the attribution of a psychological state to another person in a certain environment requires some tacit and theoretical understanding of the workings of our sensory organs. Furthermore, theory also plays a role in the prediction of mental states without propositional content. No amount of simulation would allow us to predict how somebody will feel or act after drinking a bottle of scotch.[25]

In this introduction we will not focus on the question of which version of simulation theory is most plausible. We are more interested in the question of why one should prefer simulation theory to a theory theory position. Theory theory presents simulation theorists with a serious challenge. The strength of theory theory position lies in its comprehensiveness in explaining the cognitive development of children in various areas. If TT is right, children do not just acquire a theory of mind but they construct theories about various domains of the world. If this is true, a simulation theorist has to explain why children's cognitive development proceeds so differently when other minds are concerned. Why should not children also acquire a theory of mind if they acquire a folk theory about physics? The problem for ST is in this respect analogous to the challenge the interpretivist or hermeneutic position faces in the philosophy of social science. They are asked to explain what is so special about the explanation of human affairs and actions that it justifies a claim of methodological separatism.

In our opinion, a number of important arguments have been made on behalf of simulation theory, which seem to address these questions directly and are further discussed in some of the contributions to this anthology. These arguments go beyond the claim that simulation theory can account as well for the various experiments in child psychology as the theory theory position. Such a claim would not be able to respond to the above challenge. Whether or not these arguments are sufficient to establish simulation as the sole procedure for understanding another person might be doubtful, as various contributors in this anthology argue. But these arguments seem at least to suggest that simulation has to play a central role in interpreting another person.

First, it has been pointed out, especially by Robert Gordon, that simulation theory postulates a hot methodology in predicting another person's behavior, which engages our own motivational and emotional system. In contrast, theory theory only requires a cold and merely intellectual methodology that presupposes a certain conceptual sophistication. But the theory theory is hard-pressed to explain why we at times show an emotional response in trying to understand the perspective of another person. It also has difficulty in accounting for the fact that we can predict another person's actions in light of his emotions even though we do not have concepts or names for the relevant emotions.[26]

Second, it is very unlikely that we possess a theory precise enough to allow us to predict and explain the behavior of other people. The folk-psychological generalizations that are mostly cited by proponents of TT are very abstract, vague, and inaccurate because their application is extremely limited by an infinite number of ceteris paribus clauses.[27] Even if one admits that we tacitly store these vague and abstract generalizations, like the earlier mentioned belief-desire principle, we have to appeal to our simulative capacities in order to know when the ceteris paribus clauses are satisfied. Only because of our simulative abilities can we predict that somebody who is worried because his child is very sick might forget to take an umbrella, even if it is raining outside and he does not want to get wet. Furthermore, it is very implausible that we possess psychological generalizations for all types of human behavior. We do not have a general theory about what people find funny. It is more plausible that we use our own judgment and simulative capacities to predict how somebody will react to a joke.

Third, Goldman and Gordon claim that ST is best suited to explain why we do not have any difficulty in understanding some irrational behavior or attributing inconsistent belief sets to particular persons. Irrationality does not constitute an interpretive problem as long as we ourselves are prone to such irrationalities and would simulate such irrational responses.

Whereas Goldman and Gordon tend to stress that simulation allows us to deal with irrationality, Heal emphasizes that only simulation also allows us to grasp the rationality of thought processes, since it is not very likely that we possess a tacit theory of rationality. She claims that without such a theory, our only means to understand how one thought follows rationally from another is to think these thoughts ourselves.[28] In emphasizing rationality as the principal criterion of action and thought, Heal situates the simulation proposal squarely in the traditional debate about whether or not rationalizing explanations of actions are radically different from causal explanations in the natural sciences.

3. The Debate About
the Logical Structure of Action Explanations

The problem of rationality and the question of how reasons explain actions has been the central focus of the debate between naturalists and interpretivists in the last forty years. It still defines to a large extent how contemporary philosophers of social science, especially in the analytic tradition, conceive of the difference between explanation and understanding. Within this debate, two very different strands are discernible. On the one hand, one is concerned with an analysis of the logical structure of explanation in general and of action explanation in particular. This strand derives from the interest of logical positivism in providing a logically precise characterization of scientific theories and practices. The other strand of the debate focuses more on epistemological or methodological questions concerning the justification of interpretations of other cultures. It derives especially from an anthropological debate regarding the explication of "primitive" cultures and the possibility of radically different conceptual schemes. The proponents in this debate did not sufficiently distinguish between these very different concerns because they tended to take opposing views regarding the logical and the epistemological or methodological questions. But it is important to hold both strands apart. It is theoretically possible to be a monist in regard to the logical structure of explanations in the natural and social sciences but a methodological separatist insofar as the justification of such explanations is concerned. In this section, we focus exclusively on the question of the logical structure of action explanations. In the next, we will emphasize its epistemological side.

The work of Carl Hempel on the structure of scientific explanation defined for a long time the parameters of this debate. Hempel understands explanation and prediction in epistemic terms. An event is explained if and only if we are justified to expect the occurrence of that event because of certain explanatory facts. For that reason, Hempel conceives of scientific explanations as arguments with a certain form. He distinguishes between the deductive nomological and the inductive statistical model of explanation.[29] According to the deductive nomological model, an event is explained iff a sentence describing the occurrence of the event (the explanandum) can be logically derived from the explanans, that is, a set of sentences containing singular statements asserting the occurrence of particular events and universal sentences describing universal and deterministic laws of nature. Hempel requires that the explanans is true, has empirical content (i.e., it is susceptible to test by experiment and observation), and none of the sentences of the explanans can be derived from the explanandum. Not all laws however are deterministic laws; some of them describe mere statistical regularities. If the explanans contains laws of a merely probabilistic character, the explanandum does not logically follow from the explanans. It only follows inductively, that is, the truth of the explanans makes the truth of the explanandum probable to a certain degree. In the inductive statistical model of explanation, an event is explained iff the explanandum follows inductively with high probability from the explanans.[30]

In the beginning, Hempel regarded the above conception of explanation to be applicable without modification to both the natural and the social sciences, including history. For him, the historian implicitly appeals to certain lawlike regularities in order to account for a specific historical event and in order to show that its occurrence was not merely a matter of chance. These lawlike regularities do not necessarily have to be specific historical laws. Specific historical laws might not even exist. The historian could also help himself to laws found in other disciplines such as psychology or sociology. Yet Hempel is aware of the fact that the historian is rarely able to articulate these regularities precisely. Historians normally provide only explanation sketches that would require more "filling out" before they could be regarded as "full-fledged" explanations. [31]

With this account, Hempel puts himself squarely in the tradition of Mill's account of the moral sciences. He explicitly rejects claims like Collingwood's that the social sciences are characterized by a special "method of empathetic understanding."[32] Empathy can play a role only within the context of discovery as a heuristic device for finding the generalizations that one appeals to in a scientific explanation or prediction. It does not have a place in the context of justification. Recognizing how I would have acted in a specific situation does not in itself verify or confirm a lawlike regularity about how persons in general act under such conditions. Empathetic identifications can only suggest certain formulations for behavioral laws that have to be submitted to further empirical testing.[33] According to Hempel, empathy's scope is also limited because it cannot provide explanatory insights for all situations, especially if we are asked to put ourselves in the shoes of a person who is psychologically "abnormal."

The last objection to empathy has to be taken seriously, even by contemporary simulation theorists. It would severely limit the scope of empathy as a general method in the social sciences. To take a more recent historical example, one might indeed wonder how empathy is possible as a tool for predicting or explaining the actions of concentration camp guards. It seems that we are only able to explain such behavior through theoretical knowledge, which we gain from experiments such as Stanley Milgram's obedience study or Philip Zimbardo's prison experiments.[34] One has to point out, however, that Hempel's first objection cannot be directly applied to the contemporary simulation position because simulation theorists are committed to epistemic externalism or reliabilism. Hempel seems to be an epistemic internalist who does not just require that we appeal to true generalizations in the explanation of an event but demands that we have reasons for the correctness of such generalizations.[35] As epistemic externalists and reliabilists, simulation theorists regard a belief to be justified if it is produced by epistemically reliable mechanisms. They do not require that we also have to recognize the reliability of these mechanisms or be able to justify such claims. Consequently, a psychological prediction is justified if all human beings are psychologically structured in the same manner and our simulative processes function reliably in predicting other peoples thoughts and actions. We do not have to be able to justify or provide further reasons for these claims about the reliability of our simulative capacities. On Hempel's behalf one might want to respond that the strict standards for scientific explanations require an adherence to epistemic internalism. Empathy then could be allowed to play a role in our ordinary folk-psychological explanations with their lower justificatory standards, but not in scientific predictions and explanations. Yet even such a move would imply the acceptance of a form of prediction and explanation that does not fully correspond to the above described Hempelian model.[36]

Nevertheless, Hempel's account of historical explanations did not go unchallenged. As especially William Dray[37] has pointed out, Hempel's analysis does not fit the historical task of explaining the actions of individual agents. Dray emphasizes that Hempel's objection against Collingwood's position misses its central point and misconceives the logic of action explanations. Hempel's account of explanation as involving essentially an appeal to a law is adequate only if we provide an explanation from the viewpoint of an external spectator. In our explanation of actions, we try to pay attention to the agent's own perspective by citing his or her reasons (belief and desires) for acting in a certain way. In explicating an action in this manner we do appeal implicitly to certain general "principles of action,"[38] like the principle mentioned before, that somebody will do y if he or she desires x and believes that y is a means to x. According to Dray, such principles do not have the character of descriptive, empirical laws. They have to be better viewed as normative, prescriptive principles that articulate what would be the appropriate action for any rational agent in a certain situation.[39]

In response, Hempel modified his original model to take into account the appeal to rationality that seems to be essential for action explanation.[40] According to Hempel, action explanations have the following form:

A was in a situation of type C.
A was a rational agent.
(Schema R) In a situation of type C, any rational agent will do x.
Therefore, A did x.

Hempel conceives of general statements having the form of schema R as empirical generalizations and he views rationality as "a broadly dispositional trait."[41] He assumes that one could articulate objective and empirical criteria for deciding whether or not somebody is rational in a certain situation. Hempel maintains therefore that reason explanations correspond broadly to his general conception of scientific explanation, given these modifications.

The debate between Dray and Hempel, which is still continuing in contemporary philosophy of mind and social science, concerns the question of whether schema R does have empirical status or whether it should be regarded as analytically true. If the latter were the case, schema R would merely articulate our concept of agent rationality and could not be empirically tested, as Dray and others maintain.[42] According to their line of reasoning one cannot decide whether or not somebody is rational independently of his or her fulfilling schema R. Consider any of our ordinary folk-psychological generalizations in terms of belief and desires. It could be argued that we are not justified in attributing any beliefs and desires to a person if such generalizations are not true of him or her. The folk-psychological generalizations would therefore lack empirical content because they cannot be tested and further refined. Empirical testing would require that we could ascertain the existence of a belief and desire independent of the generalizations that we want to test. If these arguments hold up, then one could argue that rationalizing explanations, which play a central role in the human and social sciences, have to be distinguished from explanations in the natural sciences.

The opposing side in this controversy points out that beliefs and desires enter into a variety of specific generalizations. Although it is true that we cannot test all of them at once, it is indeed possible, as advances in cognitive psychology show, that some of them can be empirically refined and tested while holding onto the others. In this respect our psychological or folk-psychological theory cannot be distinguished from other scientific theories. Testing can only proceed piecemeal. This implies also that certain generalizations are viewed as having a more central status for our accepted theory than others.

Even if this issue has not been completely solved, it is important to distinguish the arguments for the analytic character of schema R from very similar neo-Wittgensteinian arguments against the causal character of social scientific explanation, that is, the so-called logical connection argument.[43] According to this argument, reasons cannot be causes because causes and their effects have to be two distinct events that are contingently and not logically related. But in explaining actions in terms of reasons, Wittgensteinians claim that we do not refer to different events. Rather, we are redescribing certain observed behavior. If we say that somebody writes on a piece of paper because he has the intention of signing a check and paying his debts, we are not referring to a mental event distinct from the behavior. We are identifying the writing behavior as the signing of a check. In order for a behavior to be the signing of a check, it internally or logically requires that the agent has certain intentional states and that the behavior takes place within the context of certain social institutions with certain conventions and rules. In using the intentional idiom, we do not causally explain the behavior; rather, we recognize its significance by tracing its "internal relations"[44] within a broader social context. "Explanations" in the human sciences are hence more similar to linguistic interpretations of a speaker's utterances than to causal explanations in the natural sciences.

However, as Davidson has pointed out in his seminal article "Actions, Reasons, and Causes," this argument does not hold water because it does not sufficiently distinguish between events and their linguistic descriptions. Whether or not two events are causally related does not depend on the way we describe these events. To assert that the cause of B caused B is certainly analytically true because of the way we choose to describe the cause and the effect. Yet describing B and its cause in this manner does not imply that we are not referring to two distinct events in the world that are causally related.[45] Similarly, the description of a certain behavior might be logically related to describing a person in intentional or mental terms. But this does not exclude that the description of the behavior and our intentional idiom indicate different events that are causally correlated. Recognizing the significance of a form of behavior with the help of the intentional idiom is logically not incompatible with a causal explanation of that behavior.

And, as Davidson has made clear, our ordinary practice of interpretation commits us to a causal understanding of mental states. The attribution of mental states to an agent makes his or her behavior intelligible by showing it to be rational behavior. But rationalizing the behavior of the agent is not a sufficient condition for the correctness of an interpretation of the specific behavior at a particular time and place. There are many ways of rationalizing the behavior of an agent and many ways to recognize it as behavior of an arbitrary type. But if we attribute reasons that do not cause the agent to act at this particular time, then we fail to make this particular behavior intelligible to us. We would also fail to correctly describe its significance for the agent. Thus our interpretative stance relies implicitly on a causal understanding of mentality.

Even though these arguments prove that the logical connection argument is not valid, they do not show how we can philosophically conceive of such explanations to be real causal explanations. In order to resolve this issue, one would need to answer the above question of whether generalizations using mental terminology have empirical or analytic status. One would also have to find a solution to the metaphysical problem of how mental properties qua mental properties can be causally efficacious, given the assumption of physicalism with its claim that causal powers rest primarily on physical properties.[46] In light of the above considerations, we have to conclude that the discussion of whether or not explanations in the human sciences have a radically different logical form has proven to be inconclusive, at least until now.[47]

4. Rule Following and Understanding a Primitive Society

We leave the question of whether and how one can conceive of rationalizing action explanations as causal explanations unresolved. Yet even if one regards them as causal explanations, it does not automatically imply that there is no significant epistemic difference between the natural and the social sciences. In order to provide an adequate explanation of an action in intentional terms, one has to describe the beliefs and desires of a certain agent in terms of concepts that characterize his or her outlook on the world. To characterize a person from twelfth-century Europe in terms of the conceptual repertoire available to us today would be a pure anachronism. Even if we could rationalize actions in such a way, such a rationalization could not provide the reasons that moved the agent, that is, it would be a purely external characterization of the agent's perspective. It was because of such problems that Collingwood proposed his version of empathy as the method central for the human sciences. But Collingwood did not sufficiently discuss the question of how empathy is to be applied in situations in which the researcher encounters a different cultural context and different conceptual schemes. The question of how to interpret persons from radically different cultural environments is more than a practical problem for anthropologists. It raises philosophically important issues about the nature of conceptual schemes and the possibility of radically different forms of rationality. The discussion about the structure of such interpretations has ramifications regarding the methodological distinction between the natural and social sciences and the question of the scope of empathy. For these reasons the topics just mentioned were discussed with great virulence in the late 1950s and the 1960s, especially in Great Britain.

A particularly influential position is represented by the work of Peter Winch, whose outlook is shaped by a specific interpretation of Wittgenstein's rule-following considerations. Wittgenstein analyzed the notion of rule following in order to provide an account of linguistic meaning and mental content, since meaning constitutes the normative standard that guides both linguistic behavior and its evaluation by others. Winch extends Wittgenstein's analysis to the investigation of all social phenomena because social-scientific investigations are, in Winch's opinion, mainly concerned with revealing the significance or meaning that agents associate with their actions.[48] For him, Wittgenstein's private language argument implies also that one has to regard the practice of rule following as an essentially social practice. As Wittgenstein supposedly has shown, the distinction between being objectively right and wrong—and thus between "being objectively right" and only "seeming to be right"—cannot in principle be conceived of on the Cartesian model, in which meaning is constituted by private mental acts or entities. Wittgenstein argues, or at least Winch and many other of his interpreters take him to suggest,[49] that the distinction between being objectively right or wrong makes sense only within the context of a social form of life in which public criteria for the evaluation of the correctness of an action are available and accessible to the members of the community. Knowing how to follow a rule is only possible if one participates in a particular social practice or a particular form of life.

For Winch, these considerations have strong methodological implications regarding the investigation of social institutions and other cultures. Like Collingwood, Winch rejects a merely external description of social organizations that he sees exemplified in a purely statistical and quantitative approach in sociology. Such an approach would make as much sense as the attempt to study another language by merely recording how many times the speakers of the language use a certain word. It does not allow one to recognize what is most important for the study of another language, that is, the fact that linguistic expressions have a meaning in specific contexts of use. Using such methods in the study of social affairs means that one is unable to discern the web of rules that are constitutive for social institutions

Excellent distinction. Apply it to Turner!

and for agents attributing significance to their actions. As a consequence, one is unable to recognize the nature of the social institution under investigation from such an external and "scientific" perspective.

The aim of sociological study consists primarily in gaining an understanding of the rules of a social form of life that guide its participants. This does not necessarily imply that the agent himself is able to formulate precisely the rule he or she is following. To regard behavior as rule following requires minimally that "it makes sense to distinguish between a right and a wrong way of doing things in connection with what he does."[50] Yet for Winch to justifiably apply such normative distinction to behavior implies that the agent has some conception of the fact that his behavior is normatively evaluable and that he can stand corrected in light of his obligation toward these rules. It is exactly this possibility of reflective and conceptual awareness of one's obligation toward the rule that distinguishes rule following from a mere habit and custom. To be more concrete, living by the rule of honesty does not require that one is able to define the concept of honesty in terms of necessary and sufficient conditions, but one has to have some comprehension of this concept and its alternative, that is, dishonesty.[51] Accordingly, Winch does not insist that the researcher has to use only the concepts that the participant in a social practice would use to articulate the rules he or she is following. But he demands that the explication of the researcher "must necessarily presuppose, if it is to count as genuine understanding at all, the participant's unreflective understanding" and his or her theoretical concepts must be "logically tied" to "concepts which belong to the activities under investigation."[52] As an example one might think of Weber's category of innerworldly asceticism, which he uses to analyze Calvinism in order to show its affinity to the spirit of capitalism. Even though "innerworldly asceticism" might not be a category a Calvinist himself would use to describe his or her own religious and social practice, Weber justifies its usage in terms of concepts Protestant writers themselves used to describe their form of life.[53]

Although Winch aligns himself with Collingwood in arguing against a scientistic and for an interpretivist conception of the social sciences, he does not endorse empathy or reenactment as the principal method of the social sciences. He explicitly rejects an "inner sense" conception of *Verstehen* that views it primarily as the grasp of the mental content of the agent's mind.[54] Such a psychological understanding of empathy does not take into account sufficiently the Wittgensteinian contention that mind and meaning are constituted within the realm of a social form of life. If one would like to speak of empathy in regard to Winch, one can only conceive of it with von Wright as "the ability to participate in a 'form of life.'"[55] To a certain extent this characterization of Winch is misleading. It tells us only half the truth, since it indicates that a Winchean would reject a theory theory position of inter-

a piece of "true"? collective subject

pretation. If, as Winch believes, Wittgenstein's rule-following considerations are correct, then no general theory could provide any help for deciding which rule a person is following. To grasp a rule requires participation in a form of life in which one follows a rule as a "matter of course."[56] Thus there cannot be a general rule book of how to participate in a form of life. Such a hypothetical rule book could not be understood except within the context of a particular form of life. But this would contradict the claim that it provides guidelines for studying every form of life.

It is also important to recognize that Winch could not wholeheartedly endorse the simulation position either. He would object to the naturalistic conception of the mind that simulation theorists presuppose. The simulation theory assumes that human beings are psychologically similar because of our shared biology. For Wittgenstein, on the other hand, the conceptual scheme of a particular culture that one needs to grasp in order to correctly characterize the psychological states of persons within this culture is constituted by a certain social practice. Winch argues in "Understanding a Primitive Society" that there can be radically different practices with their own rules for the evaluation of what is real and what is rational. The concept of rationality and reality cannot be understood except in relation to the rules of a very particular social practice and cultural context. Winch not only objects to certain anthropological interpretations that implicitly evaluate so-called "primitive" cultures by our standards of scientific rationality.[57] He also objects to Edward Evans-Pritchard's claim that the Azande are objectively wrong in believing in the reality of witchcraft. Since there are no universal principles of rationality to which each culture has to adhere, each culture has to be judged by its own local standard of rationality and sense of reality. Such relativism, however, would not only curtail the theory theory position but would also limit the claim of simulation theory. Simulation supposedly proceeds by taking into account relevant differences, by feeding our own cognitive system with a few pretense beliefs and desires, and by "replicating" the cognitive processes of the other person. But this model presupposes that we share the same organization of our cognitive mechanism and that our thoughts are processed in the same rational manner. If Winch's relativism is right, just feeding our own cognitive system with a few pretense beliefs would not get us very far in understanding the radically different rule-following practice of another culture. Our only option is to immerse ourselves in the practices of that culture and rewire our own cognitive system in the process. For Winch, such immersion in a different cultural context is possible because all cultures share deep human concerns for "birth, death, sexual relations,"[58] even though they might conceive of their significance very differently. Such immersion is certainly atheoretical but it is not a form of simulation. Immersion into another culture has to be seen in analogy to learning how to speak another language. Yet learning another language cannot be conceived of as simulating that language within the context of English grammar. If conceptual relativism à la Winch is true, the claims of theory theory and simulation theory can be seen to have very limited scope. They would only seem to argue about how we understand other people within our own culture. But such a debate would not be worth all the fuss.

There are principally two ways of countering the above relativistic position, which would also reestablish the relevance of the TT and ST debate for the interpretation of other cultures. One could point to certain empirical research that claims to show that as a matter of fact people are not as different as a radical conceptual relativist supposes them to be. This might be a line of thinking that is particularly compatible with the empirical justification of the simulation position that Gordon and Goldman favor. It is, however, not clear whether such a merely empirical line of thought addresses sufficiently the concern raised vis-à-vis the tremendous cultural gap between our modern form of life and the witchcraft practices of the Azande, which do in fact seem to exist and motivated a relativistic position in the first place.

There is another way of countering conceptual relativism that has been particularly influential in this debate. It was articulated by Martin Hollis within the context of the philosophy of social science and by Donald Davidson within the context of the philosophy of language.[59] According to this line of reasoning, a Winchean form of relativism cannot be consistently maintained. Winch assumes implicitly that an interpretation of Azande culture is empirically possible while at the same time claiming that their and our concepts of reality and rationality are incommensurable. Davidson and Hollis argue that we can for a priori reasons conceive of an interpretation to be possible only if there is sufficient overlap and agreement between the interpreter and interpretee regarding the perception of reality and adherence to certain norms of rationality. Without such overlap no interpretation would be able to get off the ground. For Hollis, such agreement between interpreter and interpretee constitutes the condition of the possibility for anthropology, while for Davidson it is the necessary presupposition for conceiving of something as a conceptual scheme or language. He claims that interpretation is only possible if it is constrained by the principle of charity. According to his position, it is required that the interpreter "optimizes" agreement between himself or herself and the interpretee. More concretely, Hollis insists that we could not conceive of another agent as being interpretable unless his reasoning adheres to modus ponens and the law of noncontradiction.[60]

This introduction is not the place to engage in a close textual analysis of either Davidson or Hollis or to debate in detail the various counterarguments against the charitable approach to interpretation.[61] For our purpose, it is more important to emphasize that the rejection of conceptual relativism by Quine, Hollis, Davidson, and others has allowed for a certain revival of the notion of empathy in the context of interpretation theory. If radically different forms of rationality are not conceivable, empathy can again be considered as one method of interpretation. As Quine asserts, "Practical psychology is what sustains our radical translator all along the way, and the method of his psychology is empathy: he imagines himself in the native's situation as best he can."[62] The interpreter is thus able to guess what features of the environment are salient for the interpretee by simulating him or her and taking his or her perspective in order to come up with an interpretative hypothesis. Richard Grandy uses an appeal to simulation as the pragmatic method of translation in order to argue for his principle of humanity as a pragmatic constraint of translation. According to this line of reasoning, we have to translate others so that "the imputed pattern of relations among beliefs, desires and the world be as similar to our own as possible."[63] Otherwise any translation would be useless, since it would not allow us to predict the behavior of other people while simulating them.

Whether or not one finds this appeal to simulation in the discussion of interpretation theory fully persuasive is certainly another matter. Interpretation theorists à la Quine do not even seem to consider the alternative theory theory position. Yet the mentioning of empathy by interpretation theorists indicates that it is time to take simulation as an interpretive method seriously again and to discuss simulation theory more thoroughly and broadly. For that very reason, it is helpful to consult the continental hermeneutic tradition in which a discussion of the scope of empathy has always been crucial for conceiving of the structure of interpretation adequately.[64]

5. Empathy as the Method of the Human Sciences?

The basic goal of this anthology is to explore the fruitfulness and relevance of the simulation approach for the human and social sciences. If ST is right in its claim about atheoretical forms of understanding and interpretation, this fact must have implications for the methods used in the interpretive disciplines. Furthermore, whether ST can contribute to those methodological debates provides itself a test for its theoretical veracity, since it is those sciences that systematically and methodically practice the understanding of human agency and meaning. It is thus all the more apt that we now turn to early, often mentioned but rarely examined predecessors of ST like Friedrich Schleiermacher and Wilhelm Dilthey. The turn to the hermeneutic debate concerning empathy is most relevant because the empathetic transposition into the other, seen as a method to allow the first-personal reexperience of the other's original thoughts and intentions, is here explicitly introduced as a methodological principle of the human sciences. Whereas ST presents its different versions of an empathetic and transpositional approach as mechanisms of everyday social understanding, the hermeneutic tradition sees the empathetic reconstruction of the other's experiences as a privileged method of human-scientific interpretation. Empathy is both taken to do justice to the intuition of a unique relation between interpreter and interpretee *and* to yield a method of access to the other's meaning that can match the ideal of objectivity of the more established and successful natural sciences.

The method of "transposing yourself into the other" is conceived as providing the human sciences with a methodological equivalent to observation in the natural sciences. The conception of empathetic transposition is thus driven by the ideal to reach some objective ground, to discover the true object of understanding.[65] In this vein, the transposition into the other and/or her situation is conceived as diminishing or even eliminating any cultural or historical distance so as to overcome any obstacle to direct or immediate understanding. The elimination of contextual differences should allow the interpreter to see and experience a situation exactly as the author or agent did. Putting yourself in the other's shoes is taken to enable the reexperiencing or "reliving" of the *original intentions* that stand behind the expressions that make up the text, work, or action. Interpretation thus finds its scientific object in the intention that has inspired and driven the author or agent, and it employs the transposition into the other's context and mind-set as a method to engage in the immediate and first-personal reconstruction of that intention.

Although the hermeneutic discourse is, especially in its most influential nineteenth-century representatives, driven by the ideal of matching the natural-scientific standard of objectivity and truth, the uses of empathy to accomplish this goal are haunted by deep methodological tensions. In fact, the reflection on the preconditions of interpretation in the human sciences can be seen as both dominated by the will to demarcate empathy as a true *scientific* method and by being forced to acknowledge that objectivity and determinacy of interpretation cannot be achieved on such a basis. On the one hand, the reexperience of original intentions is taken to provide the realizable goal of capturing the truth vis-à-vis the meaning of the text, work, or action; on the other hand, the more detailed analysis of how such intentions are constituted and how they can actually be reexperienced is recognized as threatening the very possibility of ever reaching the ideal of objective interpretations. As we will see, the dynamics of this reflection on empathy as a method in the human sciences ultimately leads to the rejection of the natural-scientific ideal of objectivity and truth for interpretation.

In Schleiermacher,[66] we are facing a deep tension between the methodological orientation at the reexperience of the original intention of an author on the one hand and his belief in the codependency of thought and language on the other. The immediate object of interpretation is the text. The text is given in linguistic symbols that express its meaning. The meaning is taken to be the expression of the thought of the author. In order to understand what the author "had in mind," the interpreter has to reconstruct what the author thought or intended to say while writing the text. By focusing on the main thought, the interpretive process culminates in the reexperience of the author's initial intentions; it thus reestablishes the "objective" (since immediate and original) meaning of the text.[67]

The tension we see in Schleiermacher has its origin in the fact that Schleiermacher aims at the reexperience of the original thought and yet emphasizes that thought is necessarily mediated by language by asserting that "speaking is the medium of for the commonality of thought. . . . Indeed, a person thinks by means of speaking. Thinking matures by means of internal speech, and to that extent is only developed thought."[68] Schleiermacher concludes from this premise that interpretation must be a twofold process combining both *grammatical* and *psychological* interpretation. In one sense, any expression of a text (or historical context) is mediated and determined by the symbolic and cultural conventions of its time. In order not to miss the meaning of the text thus requires familiarity with the specific usage and content of these linguistic meanings and conventions. Schleiermacher calls the reconstruction of this semantic context, including the analysis of language use and common terms and concepts, "grammatical interpretation." However, a text must similarly be conceived as an act of thought expressed by the author, and as such belongs as a *Lebensmoment* to the life context of that specific individual. Insofar as the symbolic expression is constructed by a real living subject, its understanding requires a sense of the intentions and motives that have found their expression in the linguistic medium. Entering into these subjective dimensions of the meaning defines "psychological interpretation."[69]

With regard to the psychological interpretation, empathetic reexperience of the original thought is understood to be the essential method. However, due to the relationship between language and thought, we can conceive of empathetic reconstruction in two different ways. On the one hand, empathy can be understood as the gaining of access to a pure psychological and presymbolic dimension of "thought," which is conceived of as being prior to its expression in words and sentences. The linguistic, historical, and cultural conventions and their understanding through grammatical interpretation are thus nothing but preparatory stages toward the ultimate goal—consisting of the pure and immediate grasp of the authorial intention. On the other hand, we can see the original intention as a thought that is itself necessarily mediated and shaped by linguistic and cultural conventions. The reconstruction of the original thought is thus not an attempt to get through to some pure and ideal meanings but rather the understanding of symbolically mediated intentions and thoughts that are expressed in the text. Indeed, if thought is necessarily intertwined with language, then the grammatical reconstruction of linguistic meaning does not just pave the way to a pure psychological experience but rather already entails the true understanding of meaning. Equally, the grasp of the supposedly pure subjective intention can never aim at something immediate and presymbolic because the very "object" of such an aim is symbolically mediated and thus is intrinsically connected to the understanding of linguistic and cultural forms.

What are the consequences of these reflections for the usefulness of empathy to achieve objective interpretations? How can the empathetic reexperience yield some objective meaning, if meaning itself is seen as intrinsically intertwined with linguistic and cultural expressions? It is obvious that Schleiermacher understands the antiobjectivistic implications of his insights, since he explicitly designates interpretation as an "art."[70] The imputation of meaning, which is grounded in the attempt to reexperience the other's original intentions, can never be more than a projective and hypothetical, in short, an interpretive act, which Schleiermacher thus calls a "divination." Even though the interpreter's use of empathetic transposition is supposed to reach the other's original intentions, the determination and articulation of such intentions and thought remains bound to a hypothetical inference vis-à-vis the other's thought. Its final truth can never be fully redeemed. According to our reading, this is not so much because Schleiermacher buys into a metaphysics of the deep and obscure individual, which takes the self to be never fully expressible in shared public terms.[71] Rather, the fact that the individual expression of thoughts is intertwined with language, and thus presents in each case a novel and creative act of meaning constitution, makes any fixed and exhaustive interpretation of meaning impossible. Schleiermacher's idea of the empathetic "reconstruction" of an author's original "construction" of meaning thus does justice to the unavoidable indeterminacy that inheres in any act of interpreting meaning expressed in linguistic symbols. Although the reconstruction of the contextual conventions in grammatical and historical interpretation is supposed to rule out arbitrary anachronistic and ethnocentric impositions onto the other's intentions, the "final assessment" of that very intention is a divinatory, that is, interpretive act.[72]

In Dilthey, the tension between empathy as an objective method and the interpretive nature of cultural and historical meaning reaches its fullest and most succinct expression. Writing under the influence of positivism and historicism, Dilthey attempts to give an epistemological foundation to the historical and cultural sciences (the *Geisteswissenschaften*), which both captures their methodological uniqueness *and* grounds their scientific claims to objectivity. In order to put the diverse disciplines concerned with human behavior on a common ground, which is intended to unify as well as justify their assertions, Dilthey suggests to go back to the *Erlebnis*, the lived experience. According to Dilthey, actual self-experience can epistemically ground the human sciences because it is immediately given in experience and thus does not produce a problematic and possibly skeptical distinction between subject and object: "In the case of lived experience, there is no difference between an object that is perceived and the eye that perceives it."[73] The epistemic certainty vis-à-vis one's own immediate self-experience can be carried over to other meaning and thus allows for epistemic certainty vis-à-vis the understanding of other meaning, since this meaning is equally based in human lived experience: "Accordingly, even the understanding of others is founded upon a reconstruction of the unity of experience within which each individual expression is experienced. Whereas the unity of external nature is imposed on the appearances by applying abstract concepts, the unity in the spiritual world is a lived one, it is experienced and understood."[74] While natural processes are ontologically alien to the human understanding and thus require an imposed construction of models and laws, human expressions, since deriving from a ground that is given immediately within ourselves, allow for the emotional-volitional-cognitive reexperience of their underlying unity and meaning. Empathy as a method is thus based on the assumption of the immediate self-givenness of my own spiritual or mental experience, which enables me to extend this certainty in analogical fashion to other human agents. The objectivity of such attributions of meaning to human expressions and behavior is thus grounded in the epistemic certainty of my own mental states.

To be sure, for Dilthey the designation of *Erlebnis* and empathetic reexperience as epistemological basis ultimately make sense only because it is the human subject, defined as psychophysical unity, from which the world of history and culture emerges. The epistemological argument for lived experience draws on the ontological assumption that the human individual expresses and objectifies itself in the historical and cultural world, which in turn allows us to take our subjective experience as a methodological gateway into the fabric of historical meaning. In his first systematic attempt at the grounding of the human sciences, the *Introduction to the Human Sciences*,[75] Dilthey suggests the recourse to the basic fact of *Erlebnis* because history and culture are built up from the interactions of individual psychophysical beings. Dilthey conceives the epistemological grounding of the human sciences in terms of a "descriptive psychology" that reconstructs the basic traits of what he calls the *Urzelle der Geschichte,* the basic unit of history. According to Dilthey, the knowledge of the being that makes history provides us with the key to understanding history in its manifold concrete expressions, manifestations, and objectifications: Every historical or cultural meaning, or so this early project assumes, can be traced back to general psychological traits.[76]

In the context of assessing the relevance of ST for the social sciences, it is instructive to see how Dilthey is finally led to abandon the psychological position in favor of a hermeneutic grounding of the human sciences. In a first step, Dilthey rejects both a positivistic approach to *Erlebnis* (since mere observation would simply miss its first-personal givenness) and an introspective approach (since this would ignore the cultural embeddedness and historical influence regarding the "immediate" self-experience). Sticking to his historicist inclinations, Dilthey consequently objects to introspection as a psychological method because it can only reach an already culturally and socially formed individual. Accordingly, accepting one's own psychic unity as an expression of universal human traits, without checking the extent to which historical and cultural influences have shaped one's inner experiences, might lead one to falsely generalize and misconstruct the universal psychological structure.[77] Descriptive psychology must thus be accompanied and checked by a "comparative psychology" that analyzes and compares the manifold forms through which psychophysical beings have expressed and objectified themselves throughout history and culture. The very grounding of historical and cultural meaning in a psychic sphere is thus, due to the cultural influence on the self, referred back to the understanding and interpretation of historical and cultural forms.[78]

As a consequence of this, Dilthey abandons in a second step the project of a psychological grounding altogether. In his second major work on the grounding of the human sciences, the *Construction of the Historical World in the Human Sciences,* Dilthey opens himself to the full implications of the individual's situatedness in cultural and historical contexts. Instead of grounding interpretation in the Cartesian self-evidence of *Erlebnis,* he now suggests *Leben* as a more broadly conceived foundation. Life is not defined in terms of a psychological relation alone but includes the triadic and complex structure *Erlebnis* (lived experience), *Ausdruck* (human expression and cultural objectification), and *Verstehen* (understanding and interpretation). Although *Erlebnis* is still part of the whole picture (so as to preserve the unique first-personal relation of all understanding), the dimension of *Ausdruck* (as expression, manifestation, objectification of meaning) is now explicitly introduced in order to emphasize the universality of cultural and historical mediation. However, it is the third category, *Verstehen,* that now becomes the most central feature of social and historical life. Given the universality of cultural expressions that mediate our self-understanding or lived experience, it is actually *Verstehen* as the mode of making sense of ourselves through the manifold expressions and manifestations that always already define our everyday meaning. Meaning in the human sciences is thus not grounded in some "psychic inner sphere" but rather exists from its inception in a commonly shared and understood historical world. Agents make sense of their individual acts and expressions in terms of a shared background, a common sphere of signs, assumptions, and practices in which they always already understand themselves. Instead of conceiving of the social and historical world as being com-

posed and built up from individual beings and interactions, subjective meanings and intentions are rather embedded in and constructed from within a
sphere of common understanding and interaction:

> Every individual expression of life represents something shared in the realm of
> objective spirit. Every word, every sentence, every gesture or convention of po-
> liteness, every work of art and every historical deed are only comprehensible
> since there is a unity that binds the one who expresses himself with the one who
> understands the expression; the individual experiences, thinks, and acts solely in
> a shared sphere of common meanings, and it is on its basis that he understands
> at all. Everything that is understood has as it were the mark of being known
> from such a sphere of common meanings. We live in such an atmosphere, it sur-
> rounds us constantly; we are immersed in it; we are everywhere at home in such
> a historical and understood world, we understand meaning and significance of
> all its aspects, we are ourselves woven into those commonalities.[79]

The human and cultural sciences, then, are seen as reflexive differentiations
that emerge from the concrete needs and purposes of social and historical
life. Although the hermeneutic disciplines always remain tied to this context of life and are thus defined by experiential concepts such as purpose,
meaning, intention, and significance, the meaning of those terms cannot
any longer be construed in a narrow psychological context. It now has to
be defined in terms of the shared "objective spirit" within which all individual understanding is embedded.[80]

The turn to a broader and hermeneutic basis of understanding makes
Dilthey become aware of three essential limits of the psychological and empathetic approach to interpretation. The first limit of a psychological
grounding consists in the fact that the understanding of meaning is really
misconceived if rendered in psychological terms. When we interpret an art-
work, apply a law, reconstruct an action plan, or analyze a philosophical
argument, we are not aiming at the psychological states of the author but
rather at the objective meaning and validity that is expressed in such symbolic expressions. We are aiming at what the author had in mind in his or
her intentional orientation at the subject matter, which found its expression
in a certain cognitive structure defining and expressing a more general
meaning. According to the late Dilthey, "this knowledge is not psychological knowledge, but the reference to a cognitive form with its own structure
and lawfulness."[81]

The second limit of the empathetic approach emerges if we consider that
the self is now situated in the shared realm of cultural and social meanings; as
such, it is intrinsically shaped and influenced by its social and cultural surroundings.[82] Yet if this is the case, then the reconstruction of the meaning of
those symbolic and social institutions can no longer be based on empathetic
experience either. Dilthey himself put the finger on the wound: "The individ-

ual is nothing but a nodal point for cultural systems and organizations into which its whole existence is embedded; how could those institutions then be understood by reference to the self?"[83]

Finally, we should recall that the recourse to empathy implies immediacy of self-knowledge, which is essential for the ideal of a complete and objective knowledge of meaning. Yet if the self is now placed in the historically and culturally shifting sands of shared social meanings, which are part of an essentially open and never completed historical context, the idea of an objective and completed meaning of history must be recognized as an unrealizable goal. With regard to complete historical understanding, Dilthey invokes the analogy to individual life, which would fully comprehend its meaning only in the hour of death. Yet the essential openness of history prevents even this possibility from ever becoming real:

> It is a relation which is never fully completed. One would have to await the end of a life and could only, in the hour of death, overlook the whole which would give each part its definite meaning. Similarly, one would have to wait for the end of history in order to possess the complete materials to determine the meaning of all of its parts. At the same time, however, the meaning of the whole can really only be understood by understanding the parts. Understanding oscillates permanently between those two perspectives. Our conception of the meaning of life changes constantly.[84]

It constitutes both Dilthey's greatness as well as his limits that he clearly saw the hermeneutic consequences of his reflections and yet never gave up the project of achieving objective knowledge in the human and social sciences. Even though Dilthey recognizes the constraints that haunt an approach based on the inner reexperience of other lived experiences, he never fully overcame his orientation at reexperience as the paradigmatic form of understanding meaning; in the same vein, Dilthey never abandoned his intention at objective knowledge in the human and social sciences. If, however, the basis of empathetic reexperience is revealed as too narrow a platform to account for the understanding of historical and cultural meaning, we have to ask how and based on which alternative the interpreter can understand meaning in the human sciences. Gadamer's philosophical hermeneutics is an important first step toward an answer to these questions.

6. Philosophical Hermeneutics and the Turn from Empathy to Dialogue

Gadamer's theory of interpretation can be best introduced by showing how it rejects the approach of an empathetic reexperience of original intentions. The methodological reflections aimed at overcoming an empathetic approach attempt to establish the need to take one's own cultural and social situation reflexively into account and to conceive of the interpretation of other texts, documents, actions, and practices in terms of a dialogue between interpreter and interpretee. Instead of conceiving of meaning as a fixed object, that is, the "original intention" that we need to rediscover underneath the symbolic expression, the text is rather seen as presenting us with a meaningful and potentially valid view concerning some subject matter or purpose.[85] By attempting to understand the text, we are thus attempting to grasp what it has to say to us concerning an issue or question. Interpretive understanding can be seen as a "fusion of horizons" whereby the understanding of the interpreter and the meaning of the text merge into a new, meaningful insight concerning something. Interpretation is thus a dialogue in which the interpreter brings his or her own beliefs productively into play and relates them to the subject matter or purpose that is expressed by either text or action. Since some versions of ST defend a psychologistic reading of human understanding based on empathetic reexperience, we have to carefully consider the arguments that philosophical hermeneutics presents against any such view.[86]

To begin with, the idea of understanding as the reexperience or reconstruction (as enabled by transposition into the other's situation) of an original intention is misguided inasmuch as it identifies, falsely, the meaning of the text with the intention of the author. Everyone agrees that it is the meaning of the text, document, action, and so on, that we want to understand, but it is misguided to assume that this meaning represents the original intention of an author or agent. According to Gadamer, the meaning of the text cannot be identified with the original intention at all:

> Our understanding of written tradition per se is not such that we can simply presuppose that the meaning we discover in it agrees with what its author intended. Just as the events of history do not in general manifest any agreement with the subjective ideas of the person who stands and acts within history, so the sense of a text in general reaches far beyond what its author originally intended. The task of understanding is concerned above all with the meaning of the text itself.[87]

The assumption of an identity between meaning and intention is idealistic and wrong because it assumes the undistorted realization of action plans in history as well as the historical unaffectedness of the meaning of beliefs and assumptions expressed in texts and symbolic expressions. Such an assumption attempts to abstract from what Gadamer calls the *Wirkungsgeschichte* or "history of effect," that is, it attempts to abstract from precisely that meaning of the text or action that historical and cultural mediation has rendered *significant* for us. As Arthur Danto's thought experiment regarding the concept of an ideal chronicler of all events has shown, historical knowledge is intrinsically defined by the significance that we attribute to events from within our present situation and thus cannot be identified with a true description of objective events as such. Since even a complete list of "everything that happened" would still fall short of providing anything like historical knowledge, we must recognize that the significant selection and interpretation of past events from the perspective of subsequent and contemporary events is an unavoidable and substantial part of historical knowledge.[88] Research concerning historical events and phenomena like the "First World War," the "Presocratics," or "new German expressionism" convey already in their concepts the retrospective perspective from which they are undertaken; distinctions as to what actually happened can only be made from within the construction of a relevant object and perspective that necessarily constructs the historical world from our point of view. The attempt to reestablish the original context of the pure authorial intention thus involves the paradox of denying one's own position vis-à-vis the historical meaning one attempts to understand.[89]

Furthermore, as Gadamer points out, the interpretation of the past through text or action is oriented at the meaning of text or action itself. What is available and needs to be made intelligible in interpretation is the concrete symbolic and practical expression. To define interpretation as the reexperience of an original intention thus orients understanding at something only indirectly given. Gadamer phenomenologically contends that the mere understanding of the textual or practical expressions requires first and foremost an orientation at the subject matter or purpose of the expression.[90] Such a content-related orientation is taken to be an unavoidable first step to make sense of the utterances or actions at all. In turn, to orient ourselves at the subject matter or purpose of the other's behavior implies that we draw on our own conceptions and assumptions as to what makes sense regarding the issue at stake instead of attempting to unearth some hidden original intention in the other's psyche. We rather assume that what the other has to say or intends to do makes sense vis-à-vis the subject matter or purpose at hand and that it is basically plausible or true. Accordingly, what gets invoked in the act of interpretation is not so much a psychological theory or inquiry into the specific motives and intentions "behind" the symbolic or practical expression but rather the rationally motivated assumption that what the other says or does is reasonable and meaningful. What Gadamer calls "the fore-conception of completeness" implies that we are always oriented at a content that we take to be coherent and plausible and not at a psychological state or intention of the other:

> The fore-conception of completeness that guides all our understanding is, then, always determined by the specific content. Not only does the reader assume an immanent unity of meaning, but his understanding is likewise guided by the

constant transcendent expectations of meaning that proceed from the relation
to the truth of what is being said. Just as the recipient of a letter understands
the news that it contains and first sees things with the eyes of the person who
wrote the letter—i.e., considers what he writes as true, and is not trying to understand the writer's peculiar opinions as such—so also do we understand tra-
ditionary texts on the basis of the expectations of meaning drawn from our
own prior relation to the subject matter.[91]

Accordingly, the relation between meaning and subject matter or purpose is
an intrinsic one, and as such requires a hermeneutic assumption of rationality in order to gain access to the meaning itself; the turn toward a psychological *explanation* can thus be only seen as a second and less "natural" attempt that sets in once our initial expectations concerning the truth and
plausibility of the text or action are disappointed.[92]

What both arguments establish is that the reconstruction of symbolic and
practical acts as original intentions misconceives how we actually understand meaning. This in turn points to the fact that the reference to an objective intention in understanding destroys a fruitful and productive relationship with the past or other cultures. Since the psychological orientation
aims at the understanding of a fixed object, it does not engage in a mutual
dialogue regarding a shared subject matter or purpose. The artificial construction of the other as object thus fails to open the interpreter to the specific claims and perspectives that the other, grounded in his or her different
historical, social, or cultural perspective, has to offer to her. The ideal of the
original intention as "object of interpretation" is in truth a construction
that follows the natural-scientific ideal of objectivity according to which the
object should be represented in subject-independent terms.[93] It tends to ob-
struct and even eliminate the sense in which the tradition could appear as a
meaningful object: "*A person who reflects himself out of a living relationship to tradition destroys the true meaning of this tradition.* . . . real historical thinking must take account of its own historicity. Only then will it
cease to chase the phantom of a historical object that is the object of pro-
gressive research, and learn to view the object as the counterpart of itself
and *hence understand both.*"[94]

In contrast to the natural scientific ideal of objectivity, Gadamer's alternative interpretive theory takes as its point of departure the unavoidable
dependency of the interpreter on his or her own beliefs and assumptions.[95]
As we have seen, what is really understood with regard to a text's or an action's meaning is the subject matter or purpose—what it is about. We have
also seen that we approach the views expressed concerning the topic at
stake with the expectation of truth and plausibility. However, what needs
to be emphasized according to Gadamer is that such a rational attitude is
not guided by a formal theory or a universal conception of rationality;
rather, it emerges from the concrete, historical, and cultural assumptions

and practices in which each interpreter is embedded. In order to understand a text's subject or an action's purpose, we have to reconstruct how the subject views the subject matter or purpose. We could even say that in order to do this, we must take the perspective of the subjects or participants that express or intend something with their speech act or social act.[96] In this sense, we could see a true analogy to the positions of Collingwood or Winch, who urge us to understand the meaning from the participant's point of view, to reenact the thoughts that the authors or agents themselves thought. However, and this is Gadamer's unique contribution to the debate, in order to take such a perspective, we have to draw on our own culturally and historically situated beliefs and assumptions. The thoughts and rational beliefs of the other are not just given as such but can only be reconstructed in relation to what we ourselves deem rational and plausible. Interpretation has to draw on the whole, often unconscious assumptions regarding a subject matter or purpose; it is thus essentially tied back to one's own linguistically mediated and culturally situated background.[97] Since the understanding of others has to disclose their rational orientation toward some issue, and since such orientation can only be explicated by bringing into play our own situated and finite preconceptions, interpretation is for Gadamer a never objectifiable and never finished dialogue with the other.

Yet, instead of seeing the radical finitude and situatedness of human understanding as a limit or constraint of interpretation, Gadamer draws on the linguistic mediation of all experience in order to show that interpretive truth and objectivity, albeit understood differently than in the natural-scientific paradigm, are nonetheless possible. For Gadamer, interpretation is grounded in language, since our whole experience is ultimately mediated and articulated in linguistic concepts. Furthermore, language itself is seen as essentially defined by communication and dialogue, which enables him to draw a structural analogy between the understanding of texts and the conversation between two subjects. Since both phenomena are oriented toward a shared subject matter, it makes sense to apply the model of interpersonal communication to the relation between an interpreter and the text or action:

> When we try to examine the hermeneutical phenomenon through the model of conversation between two persons, the chief thing that these apparently so different situations—understanding a text and reaching an understanding in a conversation—have in common is that both are concerned with a subject matter that is placed before them. Just as each interlocutor is trying to reach agreement on some subject with his partner, so also the interpreter is trying to understand what the text is saying.[98]

The microstructure of that interpretive dialogue can then be further clarified by what Gadamer calls "the logic of question and answer." Instead of trying to reexperience an original psychological state, we should try to uncover the basic question that a text attempts to address. Gadamer draws here explicitly on Collingwood, yet only by giving the idea of reenactment a very specific turn. Discovering the question, accordingly, cannot simply mean to reconstruct an objective (and thus "dead") question of a historically closed context. Gadamer rather argues that in order to fully understand what a text questions, we have to adopt the attitude of questioning ourselves. Thus, by reconstructing a question that the text asks and that we thus address to us, we are truly entering into a dialogue concerning the subject matter—and thus don't fall into an objectifying and unproductive form of description. The necessity to rethink the subject matter ourselves pushes us toward what the text deems to be essential, which in turn draws our own thinking and reasoning into the process of asking that question ourselves. Only in such an engaged attitude, Gadamer contends, is authentic hermeneutic experience possible. It seems clear that if such a reconstruction of the interpretive process holds water, the result of such interpretations will not just produce another "historical fact" but will actually continue to ask the questions that define the very core of the tradition to which the text belongs. Interpretation, very much in the spirit of Michael Oakesshott's "conversation of mankind," will be productive if it leads us to understand and be part of our cultural heritage. The truth of interpretation and its objectivity thus consist in the plausibility and significance that such historical and cultural readings can achieve for our own self-understanding.

The essential difference of this dialogical view in comparison to alternative interpretive theories is that it is not oriented at thoughts or intentions for their own sake but consciously emphasizes the need for and productivity of bringing one's own assumptions into play. Indeed, the belief that one can abstract from oneself and one's context when interpreting, say, by attempting to reconstruct the position of the original reader, denies the essential connection between the other's meaning and our own perspective.[99] Yet this does not entail that we should assimilate the other's meaning naively to our context, nor that we can ignore the essential alterity that a historically and culturally situated other represents for us. Historical and cultural interpretation is thus defined by the seeming paradox that it has both to emphasize and articulate the other's difference to ourselves *and* to overcome that very distance so as to have the text speak to us. For Gadamer, the paradox is ultimately an illusion, since the articulation of difference falls within our own horizon of meaning and is thus a reconstruction of the other view against the background of a shared and not altogether alien understanding of the subject matter. Ultimately, the view of the other and our own views are mediated or, better, premediated by the underlying unity of a shared tradition that continues to shape our understanding of everything we can possibly understand. Gadamer sees the differentiation of sameness and difference, understood as the demarcation between "the past" and "the present," as a superficial abstraction that is grounded in the deeper unity of preunderstanding and tradition. It is only against such a background that our own as well as the other's "horizon" can come to be understood:

> Hence the horizon of the present cannot be formed without the past. There is no more an isolated horizon of the present in itself than there are historical horizons which have to be acquired. *Rather, understanding is always the fusion of these horizons supposedly existing by themselves.* . . . Projecting a historical horizon, then, is only one phase in the process of understanding; it does not become solidified into the self-alienation of a past consciousness, but is overtaken by our own present horizon of understanding. In the process of understanding, a real fusing of horizons occurs—which means that as the historical horizon is projected, it is simultaneously superseded.[100]

The projection of another context of meaning is thus at best a necessary phase to avoid a hasty or ethnocentric assimilation to our own situated expectations; in any event, it has ultimately to be dissolved into the mediated immediacy of an understanding of the truthfulness and plausibility of the view regarding the question at stake. The plausibility of an interpretation is thus grounded in the plausibility of the beliefs it can articulate as being expressed in the text, which in turn is seen as engendered by a shared and substantive continuity of beliefs and values in our historically grounded self-understanding.

Gadamer's philosophical hermeneutics has been highly influential for the methodological self-conception of the human and social sciences, both in the Anglo-American and the Continental-European context. Introduced into methodological debates by philosophers like Charles Taylor, Jürgen Habermas, Richard Bernstein, and Richard Rorty, the hermeneutic rejection of natural-scientific objectivity together with an acceptance of the dialogical and open-ended nature of human interpretations has gained momentum. Yet, in the present context of discussion, we want to draw attention to four problem areas that have not yet been adequately addressed by philosophical hermeneutics. All four issues question the hermeneutic claim to universality (i.e., the claim that all understanding is interpretive in the sense indicated by Gadamer) and thus represent currently pressing issues in the philosophy of the social sciences.

1. The first aspect concerns the methodological difference between the natural and the human sciences. Hermeneutic theorists have long contested the ideal of scientific objectivity as applicable to the human sciences based on the difference between the interpretive nature of human science and the objective-explanatory character of natural science. In a somewhat surprising turn, those theorists suddenly found themselves confronted by the claim that there is no difference between the natural and the human sciences be-

cause both are essentially socially situated activities, and thus both are interpretive. True, after Kuhn one cannot easily assert that scientists try to encounter the world by freeing themselves from all prejudices. Even natural scientists encounter the world within the context of certain paradigmatic matrixes that guide their research and allow them to interpret their experiments. From this perspective, science itself is revealed as a particular human point of view reflecting the cultural context of a specific time. Interpretation is therefore not special to the human sciences. It seems to be at the core of the natural sciences also. One who accepts this postempiricist picture of science might wonder whether the interpretivist's claim—that the methods of the natural sciences with their detached conception of objectivity cannot grasp a subjective point of view—is valid.

Admittedly, the hermeneutic position developed traditionally in opposition to a positivist conception of the natural sciences has failed to do justice to the interpretive dimension of natural science. But its recognition alone does not constitute an automatic repudiation of the argument for methodological separatism. It can still be maintained that the human sciences are special because only their object of investigation includes another subjective point of view. Nothing that Kuhn has shown changes anything in this respect. The postempiricist claim that interpretation plays an important role in the natural sciences is equivalent only to a rejection of an empiricist conception of the foundation of the sciences. Postempiricism, however, does not conceive of interpretation as the attempt to reconstruct another point of view from the subjective perspective of the researcher. The various paradigms in physics, for example, suggest that each of these paradigms instantiates a detached perspective of objectivity that is inappropriate for the human sciences. If we follow Gadamer's basically convincing account that portrays the understanding of a text or a practice as the encounter with another's view concerning a subject matter, we have to accept that what is understood here is another meaningful perspective vis-à-vis a shared issue. The hermeneutic experience can be taken to reveal the existence of another symbolic and meaningful perspective, and thus it involves a different kind of reconstruction than the one practiced in the natural sciences. Since the interpreter is oriented toward something that is in itself interpretive and symbolic, the interpretation implies something like a "double hermeneutic"; as such, it can also become reflexive knowledge for the interpreted subjects themselves.[101]

2. As for the issue of intercultural understanding, Gadamer's hermeneutic theory faces another challenge regarding its claim to universality. Philosophical hermeneutics replaces the historicist reconstruction of the intended or objective meaning with a truth-oriented fusion of horizons that establishes the most plausible account concerning the subject matter as the best possible interpretation. Yet if the underlying traditions, cultural contexts, or symbolic and evaluative perspectives are radically different, a true

merger into one shared and true understanding is impossible. Every interpretive theory that correlates truth and meaning is thus faced with the question of how to interpret different perspectives that cannot be considered "true" according to the interpreter's own standards. Gadamer's "fore-conception of completeness," just like Davidson's "principle of charity," argues in response that we have to establish some kind of shared understanding or agreement, against the background of which meaningful differences in worldview and belief can alone be established.

Because Gadamer bases his interpretive theory on the model of dialogue, which implies a mutual taking into account of the perspective of the other, interpretation here is designed along the lines of recognizing the other's possible truth. Understanding is not so much conceived as a charitable extension of only one's own taken-for-granted perspective but rather as the mutual expansion of our own as well as the other's horizon. However, since Gadamer ultimately identifies understanding with agreement on truth, successful and productive interpretations might be limited to the cultural traditions in which the interpreter herself is placed. Gadamer is certainly correct in arguing that meaning has to be understood against the background of one's own beliefs and assumptions; yet one might still emphasize the multiplicity of perspectives on a shared subject matter, given the different cultural and historical contexts, as well as the changing relevance of what seems true and significant, which can emerge from intercultural interpretive encounters. In light of radical cultural and historical difference, the dialogical approach might have to open itself to a pluralistic rather than a consensual conception of truth. Since ST suggests that we understand meaning by taking the attitude of the other, without arguing that this implies a teleological orientation at consensus, it might help to further the cause of a pluralistic conception of interpretive truth.

3. Philosophical hermeneutics defines the structure of interpretation fully through the analogy with linguistic communication. It sustains this claim with the thesis of the fundamental character of the symbolic mediation of experience. While accepting that there are indeed many nonlinguistic aspects of experience and reality, those dimensions must ultimately be seen as an integrated part of "that conversation of the soul with itself" (Gadamer). Especially in light of ST, the linguistic turn in interpretation faces the challenge that there might be more primordial and prelinguistic dimensions of mutual understanding. For instance, emotional experiences, together with bodily gestures expressing such states, might indicate a level of immediate emotional understanding that exists relatively independently from linguistic and social influence. Such a thesis was stated earlier in the twentieth century by Max Scheler, Ernst Cassirer, and Helmut Plessner, and more recently has been revived by simulation theorists like Robert Gordon and Alvin Goldman.[102]

The debate around the status of emotional experiences and their understanding presents one of the most promising and novel aspects of the extension of the debate between ST and TT to the philosophy of the social sciences. We hope that the full understanding of the relevance of emotions and motivations for interpretive understanding may lead to a more complex and rich hermeneutic theory. It appears to us that Gadamer's critique of empathy, which correctly addressed the misguided objectivism attached to the idea of original intentions, has thrown out the baby of emotions with the bathwater of scientific objectivism. Yet the challenge that a theory of linguistic mediation faces vis-à-vis emotions might not lead backward to a theory of prelinguistic and basic emotions but rather pave the way for an understanding of how emotions and motivations are related to and intertwined with linguistic meanings and conventions. We might just stand at the verge of a new and complex theory regarding the interplay between emotional and linguistic factors for interpretive understanding.

4. Hermeneutic theory attempts, just as much as the empathetic model it replaces, a reconstruction of the agent's perspective on the world. It thus aims at the other's symbolic perspective and its meaning. While an empathetic reliving of the original intention is discarded as misguided and illusionary, interpretation still aims at the reconstruction of the valid understanding of an issue or subject matter from the agent's point of view. Thus a fourth, and with regard to the social sciences perhaps most pressing, challenge holds that such a perspective still gives an undue privilege to the self-understanding of the author or agent. Such an understanding is now mediated by our own horizon, but the goal and orientation of interpretation is nonetheless the first-personal understanding of the subject matter or purpose, and thus it remains essentially bound up with the subjective view of the world. In contrast, one can also insist that the goal of a social-scientific analysis of meaning is to challenge the situated and limited self-understanding of agents and to transcend their naïveté through an objective explanation of the social factors that define their meaning and agency.

At this point, we would say that any objectifying and explanatory method, whatever its ultimate success in identifying such factors, can never claim to fully bypass or ignore the self-understanding of subjects and agents. Since the interpretation of human agency aims at an understanding of human expressions and actions that imply a subjective self-understanding, the self-understanding of those agents represents an integral part of the very "object" of inquiry and cannot be disregarded. Even an explanation of the meaning of authors and agents through objective factors needs to identify this meaning in order to account for it in some more structural or objective terms. However, it is also true that taking the self-understandings of agents into account does not mean that all the factors and structures that go into its definition are transparent to the subjects themselves. The agents might lack the repertoire of reflexive attitudes as well as the concepts and theories that could capture the functions and structures of those implicit and objective factors of meaning. Hermeneutics as much as ST thus face a fourth challenge suggesting that its focus on first-personal and truth-oriented understanding implies a "hermeneutic idealism" that naively takes the agent's self-understanding at face value by assuming it to be the only causally effective force in the constitution of meaning. Since our anthology discusses ST and interpretive theory in the context of the social and human sciences, we have to focus on this aspect regarding the understanding or explanation of meaning in more detail.

7. Simulation Theory and the *Erklären-Verstehen* Debate in the Social Sciences

The challenge that ST poses to theories of understanding based on a general theory or formal rationality involves at least two aspects, both of which dovetail well with insights gained from philosophical hermeneutics. On the one hand, simulation theorists argue that the understanding of human agency requires no theoretical understanding of psychological processes such as belief and desire. In order to make sense of others, it suffices to imagine ourselves in their situation or to orient our own thought at the same subject matter. This echoes Gadamer's claim that we do not understand by applying a theory of language or mind, but rather from within a content-oriented linguistic preunderstanding of the subject matter itself. Interpretation is misconceived if not understood as oriented at the subject matter from within some traditional preconception. On the other hand, ST also challenges the idea that explanations of human actions and expressions have to invoke some lawlike, nomological assumptions and generalizations. No one denies that reasons can function as causes, but the assumption that the commitment to the causal efficacy of intentional concepts also implies a commitment to laws is rejected as ungrounded.[103] Similarly, hermeneutics dismisses the need for lawlike generalizations as an unjustified imposition of the concept of "explanation" as used in the natural sciences to the realm of the human sciences. For hermeneutic theorists, it is simply artificial to ask for such a requirement, since it is clearly discredited by the historically open and changing nature of human and cultural understanding. If one now considers that these are the two major challenges raised against the theoretical approaches to understanding, and that the psychological and rational *theories* of explanation base their analysis equally on intentional concepts, one might be inclined to think that there really is no deep issue concerning the nature of interpretation as *Verstehen* (understanding) or *Erklären* (explanation). Since all approaches aim, in one form or another, at a reconstruction of *intentional* concepts, the debate seems to concern different modes of *Verstehen,* that is, which method or approach is right with regard to the theoretical or nontheoretical implications of the application of such intentional concepts.[104]

However, the fact that all these theories of interpretation focus on intentional concepts and thus remain related to the agent's self-understanding brings up the issue of *explanation* from an entirely different angle. The question arises whether human actions and expressions can fully be understood (or "explained") through the reconstruction of the subject's orientation at the situation or subject matter, or whether we have to include a perspective that allows us to explain the influence of objective and nonintentional factors on first-personal meaning. The issue has been at the core of the debate between hermeneutics and ideology critique, and it is relevant here because of the intentional orientation that all parties share that are thus far involved in the debate concerning simulation.[105] The *Erklären–Verstehen* debate in the human and social sciences concerned the idealistic assumptions that are involved in the hermeneutic conception of interpretation. According to Habermas and Apel, philosophical hermeneutics remains, in spite of its criticism of empathy as interpretive method, bound to the agent's self-understanding. Hermeneutic reconstructions of the meaning attempt to capture the other's historically mediated understanding of the subject matter or purpose, if not the original intention of the author or agent. Understanding is here seen as mediated by the historical efficacy of the *Wirkungsgeschichte,* which effects a fusion of horizons by opening our preconceptions to the truth and plausibility inherent in the text. Yet such an identification of the meaning of interpretation with the subject matter that is discussed assumes that both author and interpreter are capable of making transparent all relevant features of the meaning at stake. In other words, it assumes that the meaning that is reconstructed through such an intentional interpretation captures all the relevant aspects that define the meaning itself. Accordingly, such an identification of the interpreter's perspective with the intentional orientation of the other fails to investigate whether any nonconscious and nonintentional factors shape the understanding of the agent. Putting these methodological concerns in the form of a positive counterthesis, Habermas concludes that this hermeneutic conception of meaning rests on a "linguistic idealism," since it does not realize the extent to which power and economy shape the social institution of language. Although language is seen correctly as the privileged medium through which any self-understanding must pass, the hermeneutic claim to universality nevertheless comes down to the exclusion of nonintentional factors for language formation and thus for individual understanding and meaning. To remedy this arbitrary decision, the claim to universality must be restricted in order to allow for an analysis that can *explain* the impact of objective social structures on subjective self-understanding.[106]

We have just outlined the argument for an explanatory approach to the realm of human culture and agency. Yet it should be emphasized that this approach still considers meaning to be defined by human intentions and concepts. Indeed, the basic distinction between *Verstehen,* as an interpretive and first-personal approach to the self-understanding of agents, and *Erklären,* as an explanatory analysis regarding the objective factors that have influence on those intentions and concepts, is not an either/or matter. What critical social theory objects to in the hermeneutic approach is that *all* interpretation can be based on first-personal understanding. As an alternative, it is not suggested that an explanatory approach to the objective social causes of meaning can altogether replace the interpretive approach. Such a methodological attitude would in fact be reductionist vis-à-vis the meaningful claims and assumptions that are expressed and manifested in human expressions; it would thus miss the necessary relatedness of understanding to such first-personal meanings, which are deemed essential to disclose the "object domain" of the human and social sciences in the first place. What critical social theory argues for instead is a combined or double-edged approach that takes both the first-personal self-understanding and the third-personal objective background into account. In order to do so, it has to conceive of a methodological matrix that allows the interpreter to understand how both modes or levels of meaning can be correlated in one approach.

In the debate between hermeneutics and critical theory,[107] both Apel and Habermas suggested an extrapolation of the idea of psychoanalysis to the social sphere. Psychoanalysis can indeed be seen as combining an interpretive with a theoretically objectifying approach in order to yield a deeper and reflexive understanding of meaning. The pathological phenomena that are first experienced and described in the first-personal attitude are here transformed and analyzed with the help of a nonintentional, theoretical framework; finally, those explanations, say, of neurotic or psychotic behaviors and distortions, are again understood and accepted by the patient. Thus the hermeneutic and reflexive reappropriation of the theoretically explained life history by the individual is seen as crucial for the explanatory success of the theory.[108] The goal of the explanation of hidden factors of meaning is thus a *reflexive* insight, which is intrinsically related to the self-understanding of the subject and yet only possible through a theoretical break with her immediate comprehension of events and symbols. Similarly, the hidden and pervasive functions of power and economy in modern society, which usually escape the awareness of agents lacking the conceptual tools for their analysis, need to be made explicit through a methodical detachment from their immediate first-personal perspectives. The objectifying impact of social macrostructures on interpersonal and experienced microstructures requires a theory that detaches the self from its embeddedness into situated and interpretive contexts. Yet such a critical theory of culture and society remains nonetheless bound to the hermeneutic premise that what such an objective analysis tries *to explain* is a historically and culturally *understood* world. Accordingly, it is never forgotten that the very identification of the meaning to be explained is tied back to our own first-personal understanding. This holds true also in the case of the understanding of ideologies, since their assessment *as ideologies* can only be undertaken in comparison to our own true and rational assumptions. Ideologies are defined as sets or systems of beliefs and assumptions that (1) are shaped by social practices and institutions without the conscious awareness of the agents, (2) distort and misinterpret relevant aspects of reality that are intentionally understood as such and such by the agents, and (3) are functional in maintaining a certain set of (unjust and unjustifiable) social institutions and practices. The intended result of such theoretically mediated analyses (i.e., of the ideology critique) is not the production of factual and objective knowledge per se; it is rather the creation of reflexive scientific knowledge that allows a deeper and more comprehensive understanding of the objective factors that shape meaning so as to create critical reflexivity of the agents themselves.[109]

In the current context of discussion, three distinct theoretical models that attempt a mediation between understanding and explanation have been influential.[110] The first, now classic attempt to combine a conception of reflexive agency with the analysis of social power structures was developed by the early Frankfurt School. In this approach, defended by Max Horkheimer, Theodor W. Adorno, Herbert Marcuse, and others, psychoanalysis is not so much invoked as a model for critical theory but is itself used as a substantial part of the realization of the new theoretical framework.[111] The Frankfurt School argues that the economic and administrative power structures of late capitalism can only be fully understood if their impact on the consciousness of individual agents is reconstructed. However, in order to understand how agents are related and determined by economic and state-related practices, their impact on the agent's unconsciousness needs to be analyzed. This is because of the obvious unreason and irrationality that govern the thinking and acting of the overwhelming number of subjects in late capitalism. Horkheimer and Adorno are convinced that the susceptibility of the masses to fascism, Stalinist socialism, and cultural consumerism requires a theoretical frame that can explain the lack of rational thought and political resistance.

In the model of an explanatory social theory that Horkheimer and Adorno propose, the lack of rational thought is explained by a weakening of the capacity for autonomous thinking and self-determination that is brought about by a change in the general social conditions that formerly allowed rational selves to develop. In order to understand this complex process, psychoanalytic theory of the self is invoked to mediate between the individual agent and the socioeconomic structure. In classic capitalism, the family with clearly defined roles of father and mother allowed for the development of a strong ego with an equally strong internalized superego, which in turn allowed for the control of the forces of the id. In late capitalism, the rational control through the ego is weakened due to the inability to internalize a strong superego, which is due to the weakening of the authority of the father due to new economic constellations.[112] The lack of internal control of the id makes it possible for these drives and desires to be ruthlessly exploited by fascist leaders and consumerist capitalists. In addition, the amount and nature of aggression toward victims such as the Jews asks for methods that draw on psychoanalytic categories. Anti-Semitism, for example, can in part be explained by a process of projection whereby the anti-Semite attributes traits onto the other that are both felt and denied within himself. Similarly, the conception of an authoritarian personality type presents a model that tries to explain the crystallization of certain aggressive and nonreflexive modes of self-understanding as emerging from specific social conditions.[113] Yet the introduction of the intermediary psychoanalytic dimension is intended not only as an explanation for the pervasive success of social power over rational agency. Indeed, the existence of such a dimension has been mainly conceived as a critique of a narrow economic determinism, and as such rejects the simplistic idea of a monodimensional causality between economy and individual consciousness. In other words, the existence of a psychological sphere of mediation between thought and society also entails the relative autonomy of the individual agent; it represents a potential for reflexive criticism and rational self-determination.[114]

However, Horkheimer and Adorno ultimately argue that late capitalism dissolved the classic structure of psychic mediation, thus delivering the agent's id (desires, needs, etc.) directly to social engineering and political manipulation. This assessment of the lack of internalized self-control has two dramatic consequences for the project of a critical theory. First, it now might seem that resistance and reflection can only be conceived if the agent internalizes some external authority (a strong father figure), while the lack thereof undercuts the development of a self-controlled rational self. This, however, involves the paradox that the resistance to power seems to require a power-based structure of socialization.[115] Second, critical theory now loses any concrete political connection to the social world, since there simply is no more potential for reflexive thought and critical agency. This involves a further paradox because critical theory is explicitly defined as a reflexive project and is thus determined by the success of the theoretical explanation with regard to the agent's enlightened self-understanding.

The so-called communicative turn in critical theory suggests that the impasse of the old Frankfurt School can be avoided if we do not conceive rationality as a capability of the individual agent but rather as an intrinsic feature of communicative social practices. As Jürgen Habermas argues in his major opus *The Theory of Communicative Action,* the foundation and possibility of critical reflection and democratic self-determination is then not to be found in the autonomy of the subject but in the rationality assumptions that are built into the everyday use of language.[116] In modernity, a general public sphere emerges in which agents can articulate the validity claims raised in communication in theoretical, practical, and aesthetic discourses. While Habermas presents us thus with a more positive assessment of postfascist democratic institutions, his interest remains in a theory that can also analyze the causal impact of social institutions such as late capitalist economy and state on the intentional communicative attitudes. The relation between structural social power and individual intentional agency has now shifted toward an analysis of communicative social spheres, which he calls the "lifeworld," and functional social subsystems, which are organized around the codes of money and power. What Habermas refers to as "the colonization of the lifeworld" occupies the theoretical space of the impact of ideologies and power on the subject. The intermediary dimension between the communicative agent and social power structures (such as capitalistic economy and state bureaucracy) is now defined as the communicative contexts that allow situated selves to define and articulate their interests and self-conceptions. Inasmuch as communicative spheres like the family, school, or public political sphere are subjected to noncommunicative "functional" imperatives such as efficiency and power, their inner orientation at intentional or rational dimensions such as equal recognition and truth get distorted, which is taken to result necessarily in social pathologies. However, since it is communicative action that first defines the possibility of social life and interaction, the systemic functionalization of communication and self-understanding can never be total. Built into our communicative existence are counterfactual assumptions and ideals that always contain the seeds for a critical and rational public sphere. Its realization presents the very challenge for the modern form of life.

The third influential paradigm for mediating social power with individual agency (without reducing one to the other) can be seen as a response to problems inherent in the paradigm of communicative action. As we mentioned earlier, implied in the communicative perspective is a very positive assessment of the existing public sphere. Precisely such an understanding of modern rationality and democracy leaves undiscussed the extent to which practices of power and exclusion have permeated modern life even in its supposedly communicative forms. As Michel Foucault points out in works like *Discipline and Punish* and *History of Sexuality,* our contemporary society is not so much defined by the rise of freedom and equality that would then be endangered by the rise in economic and bureaucratic powers.[117] Rather, complex power practices that establish highly diversified regimes that discipline, observe, and evaluate in order to produce the modern individual are what holds agents in their grip. Through temporal and spatial arrangements in institutions like the prison or the school, in conjunction with objectifying human sciences, subjects are subjected to endless control and supervision. These micropractices of power neither occupy the unconsciousness nor distort communicative reason through functional imperatives; rather, they impact the body, the gestures, the whole habitus of situated agents. While the so-called dispositives of modern power have to be traced back to diverse micropractices addressing the concrete body and self, they nonetheless form a general and encompassing tendency in contemporary Western societies to mold agents into socially conditioned subjects.

Accordingly, in the third model the analysis focuses on social practices as mediators between the self-understanding of the agent and objective social structures, which are taken to produce "docile bodies" and "subjected subjects" through the structuration of the self through society. Yet even this model attempts to play out the true dialectic between understanding and explanation in that it conceives practices not as fully defined by power but also as a source of social resistance and individual self-determination. The very nature of power as exercised through micropractices is ultimately taken to imply the possibility for inverting and resisting domination in specific contexts, to develop counterdiscourses and counterstrategies against power, and to generally engage in subversive as well as self-developing practices that can oppose and challenge practices of subordination.[118]

By briefly introducing these three basic paradigms in the cultural and social sciences, we attempt to point out yet another challenge for ST as a social-scientific methodology. All the approaches that address the distinction between *Verstehen* and *Erklären* in the human sciences distinguish a level of individual consciousness and agency, a level of objective social structures that require specific tools for their analysis, and a level of mediation whereby the impact of those spheres onto each other can be reconstructed.[119] All these approaches share an interest in reconstructing objective structures with regard to their power-related impact on the agent's self-understanding, and accordingly take that self-understanding more or less explicitly into account. Simulation theory, just as much as hermeneutic theory, defines the agent's self-understanding as a situated and nonnomological experience that can sufficiently be understood through the first-personal relation between interpreter and interpretee. What the debate between hermeneutics and critical theory makes clear is that such a relation is not sufficient for capturing all relevant factors that define an agent's self-understanding. The first-personal approach falls short of addressing the complex combinations of first-personal and third-personal perspectives that are used in social and cultural studies today.[120] Subsequently, the paradigms on which the bulk of those studies rest are defined by a combination of both approaches, and can thus not be grounded with reference to the first-personal experience of understanding alone. If ST wants to make good on the claim to ground a social-scientific methodology, it has to clarify its relation and relevance to the explanatory dimension of understanding.

At this point, however, we are well advised to recall Gadamer's defense against Habermas's call for an objective social-scientific perspective.[121] According to Gadamer, every attempt at understanding, including the one by critical social theorists, has in some form to draw on beliefs and preconceptions that are handed over from tradition; accordingly, the interpreter is always placed in a concrete perspective from which he or she understands. The interpretation can thus never claim to be absolutely objective or neutral. We have seen how this view echoes the claim of ST that understanding other human agents has to begin from our own mental experiences, which are employed to bridge from our situated perspective to the situation of the other. If ST can plausibly argue for the primacy of first-personal experience with regard to social understanding, it will be relevant *for any approach* that attempts an understanding of meaning and agency. Although critical social theory has shown that a first-personal approach needs to be complemented by third-personal methods, the reconstruction of the impact of those objective factors on intentional concepts nonetheless presupposes a first-personal understanding of their meaning. Inasmuch as ST presents us with a renewed and forceful claim regarding the methodological significance of the first-personal approach to understanding, it requires a careful consideration of its relevance for the methodology of the human and social sciences. The following chapters present the first systematic attempt to take up this timely discussion.

8. Simulation Theory and Social Science: The Current Debate

Our outline of the main aspects of the *Erklären–Verstehen* debate and the various conceptions of understanding should clearly show why a discussion of ST is necessary for the human and social sciences. The chapters in this anthology indicate why it can be expected to be a fruitful endeavor. The survey offered in this introduction has analyzed an intricate assembly of arguments for and against empathy or theory as the fundament for predicting, explaining, or interpreting the behavior of other agents. It has also shown that rejecting empathy as the sole basis for understanding does not automatically imply the adoption of a full-blown theory theory position. In addition, it has revealed the need for clarifying the exact nature of the contribution of empathy and theory for understanding agency. Simulation theory raises these issues with renewed vigor, and the authors of this volume discuss them in their chapters from a variety of philosophical backgrounds and perspectives.

Robert Gordon directly addresses the issue of the logical structure of explaining actions by reasons in Chapter 1, "Simulation and the Explanation of Action." He develops an account of reason explanations that acknowledges, contrary to some predecessors of contemporary simulation theory, that actions depend on the reasons for which they are performed. At the same time he challenges squarely the orthodox conception of reasons in terms of beliefs and desires. For Gordon, reasons should be understood as facts that one appeals to in considering a particular course of action and not as specific mental states of the agent. "It is not sentences that ascribe a belief that argue for the action, but rather sentences that express the belief. . . . It is the certainty of getting drenched, not the agent's being in a state of certainty about it, that is a genuine reason."[122] The orthodox view rests on the mistaken assumption that reasons have to be identified with an agent's mental states because only such events or states can be viewed as covered by natural laws. Through a detailed analysis of a legal court case, Gordon shows that one should better view the dependence of actions on reasons as a counterfactual relation that is supported by nonaccidental correlations between situation types and action types. Such generalizations are very different from laws of nature. Nevertheless, Gordon agrees that reasons have to be within the epistemic horizon of the agent, as the orthodox view suggests. Facts can only be reasons insofar as the agent is aware of them. Yet he points out one can easily account for this assumption within the context of ST. Furthermore, ST allows one to understand how small children are able to understand ordinary action explanations without having any concept of belief and knowledge.

In Chapter 2, "The Theory of Holistic Simulation: Beyond Interpretivism and Postempiricism," **Georg Vielmetter** continues to make the case for ST. He argues for a hybrid version of ST that conceives of simulation as a naturalistic basis of the interpretive process but admits that appeal to theoretical information is unavoidable at later stages of the interpretive process. Simulation is best seen as a prelinguistic and biologically based capacity that allows us to recognize the emotional responses of other humans and mammals to their environment. This empathetic capacity constitutes the necessary starting point for all interpretative attempts of other agents. Yet in order to complete a successful interpretation that takes into account the relevant differences between individuals, the simulative process also needs to be complemented by knowledge of holistically constituted linguistic and theoretical discourse. "'Readiness for simulation' comes in a prepacked, biologically fixed module, but not the successful result. . . . the simulation process is penetrated by a kind of knowledge that is very different from the one gained by automatic mechanisms and is more exposed to traditional epistemological and semantic problems."123 The bulk of Vielmetter's chapter attempts to show how the pretheoretical and the theoretical factors must work together in order to allow for an understanding of human actions. Furthermore, Vielmetter does not want his claims for ST to be misunderstood as arguing for a strict dualism between the natural and the social sciences. Even though simulation is required for understanding other agents, understanding is only one of the goals of the social sciences. In order to achieve the other goal—prediction, it might be helpful to use the explanatory models developed in the natural sciences.

Stephen Turner's chapter, "Imitation or the Internalization of Norms: Is Twentieth-Century Social Theory Based on the Wrong Choice?" (Chapter 3), takes up the issue of basic emotions as a pretheoretical starting point for understanding and expands it to a global critique of rule-governed models of mind and culture. According to Turner, psychological mechanisms like imitation, simulation, and role taking are entirely sufficient to account for our ability to understand others. For mainstream twentieth-century sociology, culture is an internalized set of rules and norms, which parallels in interesting ways the theory theory conception of the mind as rule governed. However, the hitherto neglected "hard facts" regarding prediscursive psychological mechanisms of social cognition suggest otherwise. Building on G. H. Mead and Max Weber, Turner argues that acknowledging the crucial role of such mechanisms invites a paradigm shift toward an "emulationist" position. Understanding is thus not norm governed but based on an internal mental device, a "private shorthand," that allows one "to take the attitude of the other in the relevant stereotypical ways and to employ the significant symbols in this activity of attitude taking. . . . Acquiring a culture, in this approach, is nothing more than acquiring the ability to take the attitude of others with respect to stereotyped roles and significant symbols. "Culture" is thus not a system that needs to be "inherited" but a set of learned capacities organized around objects such as symbols, ritualized actions, and so forth."124 Turner backs up his antitheoretical stance by showing how the theoretical conception of culture is entangled in the conflict between the universal claim to a mental theory and the cultural relativity of some of its major concepts, like belief.

David Henderson and Terence Horgan's "Simulation and Epistemic Competence" (Chapter 4) evaluates the scope of our simulative capacity within the context of a naturalized conception of epistemology. Henderson and Horgan are interested in addressing the question of whether and to what extent simulation is a necessary ingredient in our epistemic competence to produce what they call reliable, systematic, and robust knowledge of other agents. Henderson and Horgan agree with Heal that simulation has to be seen as an essential element in such an epistemic endeavor, since it is highly implausible that we have a theory of relevance or can solve the so-called frame problem in terms of a theory specifying the exact character of transitions between discrete psychological states. As they point out, the same arguments that Heal puts forward to support ST are central for rejecting a computational model of the mind in favor of a connectionist model. According to their conception of connectionism, we can only expect very broad psychological generalizations that contain ineliminable ceteris paribus clauses. Thus the application of any psychological theory requires the use of our off-line cognitive capacities similar to the ones described by simulation theorists. Yet, as Henderson and Horgan emphasize, our simulative capacities face significant "blind spots" if not used in conjunction with theory. Only a joint application of both theory and simulation can be judged to be epistemically robust and reliable. "Insofar as both simulation and theory can be reliable, each within its own somewhat varying range, applying them jointly . . . should be reliable in yet a greater range of cases than applying either of them in a maximally exclusive fashion."[125] Henderson and Horgan conclude by emphasizing that one should not conceive of their view as implying an interpretivist conception of the social sciences. For them, interpretation and explanation are central for both the social and the natural sciences.

In his "Understanding Other Minds and the Problem of Rationality" (Chapter 5), **Karsten Stueber** discusses simulation theory within the context of the controversial debate of whether interpretation forces us to conceive charitably of other persons as rational agents. He shows that, even though Heal's argument for simulation does not depend logically on the assumption that agents are strictly rational in a formal sense, simulation is, pace Goldman, fully compatible with a charitable conception of interpretation. He argues that the principle of charity is best understood as constraining the interpretive process globally or holistically. Charity, understood holistically, needs simulation as a mechanism, which provides the interpreter with concrete interpretive hypotheses. This conception of charity implies also, as he maintains, that agents have to be conceived of as minimally rational persons. Stueber, however, emphasizes that simulation theory fails to describe the full range of interpretive strategies and is of limited use as far as interpretations of agents from very different cultural frameworks are concerned. According to his account, interpretation of other agents is best understood as the interplay between projection and cognitive extrapolation. Central for our interpretive success are also our second-order capacities to recognize differences between our and the interpretee's basic cognitive and cultural presuppositions and not merely first-order simulative capacities. Yet Stueber's account should not be seen as a theory theory version but as an alternative to current versions of ST and TT. As he shows finally, his position is fully compatible with the hermeneutic claim about the open-ended and prejudicial nature of interpretation.

Theodore Schatzki's chapter, "Simulation Theory and the *Verstehen* School: A Wittgensteinian Approach" (Chapter 6) sets the stage for the hermeneutic discussions of ST. Schatzki's distinction between a mentalistic paradigm of understanding, according to which meaning is reconstructed through recourse to mental entities, and a social-pragmatic paradigm, according to which meaning is practical, social, and public, puts the hermeneutic response to ST in focus. Schatzki argues that ST can be understood as a version of the mentalistic paradigm in hermeneutics. While his Wittgensteinian approach acknowledges the importance of referring to intentional concepts in understanding, he argues that intentional concepts and meanings are grounded in "social matrices of meaning" composed of language, social practices, and bodily expressions. Schatzki expounds a pluralistic methodology according to which interpreters grasp the meaning of an act or expression either by directly capturing its content ("reading") or by reconstructing its conceptual assumptions ("inferring") or by hypothetically putting themselves in the other's shoes ("imagining"). Even though there is no single method of understanding, all understanding is nonetheless embedded in contextual life conditions and practices that always already shape interpretation: "Reading, inferring, and imagining require familiarity with social practices. One reason for this is that these operations presuppose the grasp of mental concepts, and the relevant concepts are those woven into the practices that the actors to be understood carry on."[126] According to Schatzki's analysis, ST appears to be limited on three accounts. First, ST focuses on mental concepts alone without emphasizing the social-pragmatic background as a source of meaning; second, ST privileges simulation as the only method by ignoring other means of access to meaning; and third, ST identifies understanding with first-personal approaches without doing justice to the technical vocabularies used in the social and cognitive sciences.

"From Simulation to Structural Transposition: A Diltheyan Critique of Empathy and Defense of *Verstehen*" by **Rudolf Makkreel** (Chapter 7) pursues the same problematic from a Diltheyan perspective. In a systematic reading of Dilthey's theoretical development, Makkreel shows how Dilthey came to realize the limits of the mentalistic or psychologistic paradigm of understanding and how he advanced toward a position that acknowledges the deep and pervasive embeddedness of meaning in historical and cultural contexts. While the method of this chapter is an interpretation of Dilthey's views regarding interpretation in the human sciences, the upshot is a set of systematic claims with high relevance for the social-scientific debate concerning ST. Makkreel argues, first, that understanding can never be direct and immediate but is always based on mediation through historical and cultural expressions. Second, interpretation is not mainly oriented at the mental content of the author but rather is concerned with the "intentions" and "meanings" of characters and expressions in the text or document. Accordingly, the task of the human sciences has to be the explicit articulation of historical and cultural meanings, which find a more objective and determinate form through human-scientific interpretation. According to Makkreel, the method of the human sciences consists in the "structural transposition" of the interpreter into the other cultural and historical context, which alone does justice to the social and nonpsychological nature of meaning: "Merely to change some facts about myself and my situation (as in ST) may suffice to predict certain general patterns of behavior in people from other cultures. But to understand what that behavior means, I need to recognize the more pervasive structural ways in which experience is framed by a historical and cultural context."[127] Makkreel's chapter seems to suggest that ST, in order to work as a method for the human sciences, has to travel a path similar to the one of Dilthey's development.

Hans Herbert Kögler in his "Empathy, Dialogical Self, and Reflexive Interpretation: The Symbolic Source of Simulation" (Chapter 8) explores how such a hermeneutic amendment of ST as a method of social sciences would look. By distinguishing a psychological model of empathetic understanding from a hermeneutic conception of taking the perspective of another, he suggests that the basic intuition of ST—that interpretation consists in taking the attitude of the other—can only be defended in a paradigm based on the symbolic mediation of experience. In a first step, Kögler shows that psychological attempts at grounding historical and cultural understanding in some form of immediate understanding must fail: Neither basic emotions nor simulated or analogical inference from the interpreter to the other can bypass the pervasive cultural and historical embeddedness of meaning. Yet in a second constructive step, he acknowledges that simulation and role taking are effective in acquiring cultural and historical meanings, since they are mechanisms involved in the process through which agents develop a symbolically mediated and conscious sense of self. By revisiting the debate concerning the false belief task in light of a hermeneutic conception of language, the first-person standpoint of the interpreter reveals itself to be grounded in linguistic dialogue and communicative practices. Several consequences follow for a social-scientific methodology. First, the interpreter is seen as radically situated in symbolic and cultural contexts and he or she cannot bridge over to the other context without reflective interpretation of background assumptions and practices. Second, the method of attitude taking fully develops only in the symbolic medium, which in turn allows for the methodological attitude of reflexivity vis-à-vis the cultural and historical perspectives of all agents involved (instead of orienting interpretation at prediction or at rational consensus). Finally, linguistic mediation allows for a theoretical detachment from one's particular dialogical encounters, which can become functional in correlating theoretical perspectives to the first- and second-person perspectives. Since such a detachment allows for a structural analysis of background assumptions and practices, it can reveal hidden power relations and arrangements that usually remain woven into the intentional meaning perspectives.

James Bohman's chapter, "The Importance of the Second Person: Interpretation, Practical Knowledge, and Normative Attitudes" (Chapter 9), introduces the normative-pragmatic perspective to the debate concerning ST. Agreeing with a general hermeneutic perspective, Bohman conceives of interpretation as a holistic and culturally embedded activity, and he defines social science as a reflective explication and articulation of the meanings of cultural and historical contexts. Bohman's contribution to the debate consists in pointing out what kind of normative implications are built into a dialogical approach to interpretation. He first shows how all understanding is intrinsically normative, since the grasp of meaning depends on an understanding of the reasons that someone could give for her beliefs and actions. Since we can, according to this argument, conceive reasons only by evaluating them as valid or invalid, interpretation is essentially normative. Bohman can then proceed to the core of his argument, which shows that the normative implication of understanding can only be grounded in a dialogical approach that bases interpretation neither on the first- nor on the third- but rather on the second-person perspective. Both ST and TT fail to see that the indeterminacy of interpretation can only be overcome by taking the other's understanding of herself (or of our understanding of her) systematically into account: "It is not *I* or *we* that must be satisfied; the interpretive situation is one in which an interpreter is interpreting someone else, who in turn can offer an interpretation of his own actions and the interpretation of the other's interpretations. The I who is an interpreter is a *you* as a participant in communication, and thus no account of the hermeneutic circle can do without the second person."[128] Bohman's essay thus completes the hermeneutic discussion of ST by focusing on the normative dimensions of the dialogical approach.

In Chapter 10, "The Object of Understanding," **Paul Roth** addresses the metaphysical assumption that is the basis for the claim that methodologically the human and social sciences must be distinguished from the natural sciences. Such separatism presupposes implicitly that the human sciences have their own special domain—meaning, intention, or rules—which requires a special method of investigation—understanding or empathy. Roth focuses his discussion on the question of whether one should conceive of historical explanations on the model of narrative realism or narrative antirealism. In opposition to the narrative antirealist, the realist maintains that historical explanations are correct because they represent an independently existing past. Roth argues for a position of narrative antirealism by showing that recent attempts to argue for the coherence of the notion of an ideal chronicle to which all historical narratives contribute are philosophically incoherent and cannot be made sense of, given actual conflicts between various historical interpretations. For him, narrative realism can also not be maintained by suggesting that the intentional structure of action itself implies a specific narrative form for historical explanations. Even if it is admitted that intentions provide some narrative structure to the lived experience, intentions alone do not suffice to answer the question of which narrative structure is explanatory for a certain historical event. Moreover, it is not always the case that intentional agency provides such narrative unity. Roth concludes that our desire for understanding does not imply the existence of any special object of understanding or that there is any interesting metaphysical or methodological distinction between the natural, human, and social sciences. As he proclaims, "We seek understanding. But from this it does not follow that there is a thing to be sought—the object of understanding."[129]

Simon Blackburn's "Reenactment as Critique of Logical Analysis: Wittgensteinian Themes in Collingwood" (Chapter 11), based on a lecture given at Oxford, concludes the volume by placing Collingwood's holistic theory of interpretation in the current context of the philosophy of mind and language. Blackburn enlists both Wittgenstein and Collingwood in a criticism of the Frege-Russell paradigm concerning the objectivity of propositional content. Collingwood is shown to reject the idea of a "science of the mind" modeled after the natural sciences on the grounds of the reflexive, holistic, and normative aspects of thought. By rediscovering the largely neglected Collingwood, Blackburn introduces the doctrine of the reenactment of historically embedded questions (instead of the formal-logical reconstruction of propositional content) as an alternative to observation- or theory-based approaches to meaning and content. "To know what someone is thinking, it is never sufficient to conduct an 'objective' investigation modeled on either observation or theory in natural science. There is no telling what you think except by thinking for myself the same thought, reliving the problem as you saw it and then reenacting the process with which you met it."[130] Collingwood's emphasis on the question as the focal point of understanding is made plausible on epistemological grounds. Only by reconstructing the historical problem context of the other can we hope to identify the determinate meaning and content of the other's statements and thoughts. Observation-based approaches overlook the interpretive and holistic background of attributing meaning, especially with regard to supposedly public linguistic meaning, but theory-based models invoking hardwired mental frameworks fail to understand the contextually contingent and conscious nature of grasping historical thought. Only by reenacting authentic responses to concrete questions can we specify the objective content of a statement or a thought. Although both Wittgenstein and Collingwood rightly reject the poverty of logical analysis, it is Collingwood's concept of historical reenactment that points to a viable and constructive alternative.

Taken all together, the chapters in this volume indicate a new stage in the methodological debate concerning the human and social sciences. The following analyses regarding the relevance of simulation and empathy for understanding force us to rethink the precise scope and implications of what has been called the "interpretive turn" in the philosophy of social science.[131] For one, while all contributors agree on the basically holistic and interpretive nature of understanding, the issue of pretheoretical and prelinguistic dimensions such as emotions and motivations has certainly come to the fore as an important methodological issue. The "interpretive turn" thus cannot be rendered as a "linguistic turn" per se but needs to be reevaluated in light of recent evidence. Furthermore, the long-standing debate between a unified science account on the one hand and methodological dualism on the other has at last been overcome. The articles in this anthology are rather interested in delineating the precise and complex nature of interpretation in the human and social sciences, instead of being concerned with a priori arguments for or against *Erklären* or *Verstehen*. Accordingly, the rich and diverse contributions in this volume mark, we believe, the beginning of a more pluralistic and less dogmatic discourse on the adequate methods and approaches that are concerned with understanding human agency.

Notes

1. Richard Rorty espouses an interesting position of pragmatic naturalism. Like all naturalists, Rorty does not think that there is a notable ontological difference between human beings and the rest of nature. For that reason, it might in principle be possible to develop a predictive science of human beings on the model of physics. Rorty, however, allows that the hermeneutic and intentional vocabulary might be more useful for moral considerations. Yet this does not indicate that we have to prefer it for predictive and explanatory purposes. See Rorty 1979; 1983; 1991a.

2. For the following, see Thomas Nagel, "Subjective and Objective," in Nagel 1979, pp. 196–213; and Nagel 1986. Charles Taylor (1980) argues similarly.

3. Nagel 1979, p. 209.

4. That is, they did not object to the idea that an objective science of human affairs is possible. See, for example, Collingwood 1946, p. 9: "Science is finding things out: in that sense history is a science." For a further elaboration of this theme in Schleiermacher and Dilthey, see section 5 of the Introduction. For Dilthey, read also the essay by Makkreel, Chapter 7 of this anthology. Simon Blackburn further explicates the relevance of Collingwood for contemporary philosophy of language and mind in his contribution (Chap. 11 of this anthology).

5. Collingwood 1946, p. 213.

6. For Collingwood's insistence that the historian studies the rational activities of agents, see pp. 231, 316ff. In Collingwood one also finds another major theme of the interpretivist tradition—the claim that human sciences do not provide causal explanations supported by natural laws. Insofar as the historian understands the inside of an event, he or she does not have to ask for any further regularities in order to justify the explanatory power of his or her descriptions. "After the historian has ascertained the facts, there is no further process of inquiring into their causes. When he knows what happened, he already knows why it happened" (p. 214). The historian who uses causal terminology uses them in a special sense (i.e., non-Humean sense) because the thought that "causes" the event is not "something other than the event, it is the inside of the event itself" (p. 215).

7. Robert Gordon argues similarly within the context of contemporary simulation theory. See Gordon 1995c, p. 116f. For a further elaboration of this topic, read his essay in this anthology, Chapter 1.

8. Collingwood 1946, p. 292.

9. Only because the historian is capable of such a reenactment is he or she able to evaluate the authority of particular historical sources. Collingwood compares the historian in this respect to a detective trying to solve a murder. See pp. 266ff.

10. Collingwood 1946, pp. 209, 219.

11. Collingwood, pp. 284ff. See also pp. 300–301.

12. See Alison Gopnik and Andrew Meltzoff 1997; Henry Wellman 1990; Alison Gopnik and Henry Wellman 1995. For a description of the various versions of the theory theory, see the introduction by Davies and Stone (1995a). Another model of the theory theory is proposed by Josef Perner 1993.

13. For a very useful articulation of the adult folk theory of mind, see Wellman 1990, chap. 4.

14. Jerry Fodor claims that our folk-psychological theory is innate.

15. Heinz Wimmer and Josef Perner 1983. The contemporary debate about whether children acquire a theory of mind was motivated by research in animal psychology and the question of how one could experimentally test whether chimpanzees have a theory of mind. Consult the influential article by Premack and Woodruff 1978.

16. See Wellman 1990, p. 257f.

17. Heal 1995a, p. 47; Goldman 1995a, p. 85.

18. Stephen Stich and Shaun Nichols 1997.

19. See Goldman 1995a, pp. 92–93; 1996, p. 190.

20. Gordon and Goldman differ also in regard to the question of whether simulation plays any role for our understanding of psychological concepts. Gordon holds such a thesis, whereas Goldman vehemently denies it and opts for a first-person account of psychological concepts. Insofar as we focus here on certain methodological questions in the philosophy of social science, these differences are not important for our purposes.

21. See Gordon 1995b, p. 56; 1995a, p. 63.

22. See Gordon 1995c, p. 119.

23. Gordon also subscribes to the "principle of least pretending." It seems to suggest that one should prefer that simulation that allows one to predict the actions and thoughts of another person correctly with the least number of necessary adjust-

ments. This principle shows some similarity to Davidson's principle of charity. But Gordon seems to prefer an empirical justification for this principle. See Gordon 1987, p. 142; 1995a, p. 65.

24. See especially Heal 1996b; 1998.

25. Heal would allow for the possibility that our psychological concepts are constituted by being embedded in a general psychological theory. For that very reason she does not seem too concerned with whether or not simulation should be regarded as a form of analogical inference.

26. See especially Gordon 1996a. For further discussion of this aspect, see the chapters by Georg Vielmetter and Hans Herbert Kögler in this anthology.

27. See especially Goldman 1995a and Gordon 1995c.

28. Heal 1995a, p. 52. Goldman and Gordon would agree with this aspect of Heal. See Goldman 1995a, pp. 78–79 and Gordon 1995c, pp. 116–117. Both, however, tend to stress the problem of irrationality in order to argue against TT and Davidson's principle of charity. For a further elaboration of Heal's argument, see the chapter by David Henderson and Terence Horgan in this anthology. For a discussion of the issue of rationality and irrationality in relation to simulation theory and action explanation, see the chapter by Karsten Stueber.

29. For Hempel, see especially "Studies in the Logic of Explanation" and "The Function of Laws in History." Both articles are in Hempel 1965, pp. 245–290, 231–244.

30. For Hempel, a scientific prediction has the same logical form as an explanation. However, in a prediction the "explanandum" is a sentence that describes the occurrence of an event in the future. Even though Hempel's model was for a long time the received view on explanations, this is not the case anymore. For an overview about the debate and different conceptions of explanations, see Salmon 1989 and Ruben 1990.

31. Hempel 1965, p. 238.

32. Hempel 1965, p. 239.

33. For a witty statement of this position, see also Neurath 1973, p. 357: "Empathy, Understanding (Verstehen) and the like may help the research worker, but they enter into the totality of scientific statements as little as does a good cup of coffee which also furthers the scholar in his work." Popper argues similarly in Popper 1957, p. 138. For the most detailed rejection of empathy along those lines see Theodore Abel 1948.

34. Milgram 1963; Zimbardo 1972.

35. For a good introduction to the contemporary debate about epistemic internalism and externalism, see especially Bonjour 1985 and Alston 1989, chaps. 8–9.

36. This might be a position that Goldman would find very plausible, since he explicitly restricts the simulation proposal to the domain of interpreting other people within the context of folk psychology. He does not want to deny that a scientific and nomological explanation of human phenomena is possible. Goldman 1995a, p. 92.

37. Cf. Dray 1957, especially chap. 5. Similar points were made in the flood of "little red books," as Davidson is fond of saying. Among them are Winch 1958; Melden 1961; Peters 1958.

38. Dray 1957, p. 132.

39. Dray himself did not directly deny the causal character of action explanations. He seemed to agree with Collingwood that if we speak of causation in the context of rationalizing action explanations, we have to conceive of causation in a special sense. See Dray 1957, pp. 150ff.

40. For the following, see Hempel 1965, pp. 471ff.

41. Hempel 1965, p. 472.

42. For example, Davidson, "Hempel on Explaining Action," in Davidson 1980; 1987. See also Rosenberg 1995. For an example of the opposing view see Henderson 1993, chaps. 4–7.

43. For the following, see especially Davidson "Actions, Reasons, and Causes" in Davidson 1980; Rosenberg 1995, pp. 43ff.

44. For this, see Winch 1958, chap. 5. For a contemporary formulation of a Wittgensteinian conception of the social sciences, see Schatzki 1996.

45. Davidson 1980, p. 14.

46. For this debate, see the articles in Heil and Mele 1995; Kim 1993; 1998. For an overview of the debate, see Stueber 1997a.

47. Notably, Winch no longer insists on the noncausal character of the explanations in the social sciences. See the preface to the second edition of *The Idea of a Social Science,* xi. Nevertheless, he rejects a Humean account of causation.

48. See Winch 1958.

49. For an influential analysis of Wittgenstein's rule-following considerations, see Kripke 1982. Nevertheless, at least one of the editors of the anthology strongly disagrees with this interpretation of Wittgenstein. See Stueber 1994b; 1993, chap. 4. For a critique of Winch on these grounds, see also Hollis 1972.

50. Winch 1958, p. 58.

51. Winch 1958, pp. 57–65.

52. Winch 1958, p. 89.

53. In this respect Winch's analysis of the social scientist's explication of rules differs from the project of theoretical linguistic à la Chomsky. The linguist's analysis of the grammatical or semantical rules of English is not bound by concepts that are familiar to most users of the English language and that they would use to explicate their intuitions of the grammaticality of certain linguistic expressions. His rule formulations only have to reflect the actual grammatical intuitions of normal users of the English language, including his own. The linguistic theory is correct only if it allows construction of linguistic expressions that normal users judge to be grammatically well formed.

54. Winch 1958, p. 119. For this problem, see also Chapter 6 in this anthology, by Ted Schatzki.

55. Von Wright 1971, p. 29.

56. Winch 1958, p. 30.

57. For a nice, short overview of the various positions in the anthropological field regarding the issue of different forms of rationality, see Lukes 1970.

58. Winch 1964, p. 107. It is interesting to note that Winch somehow modified his strong conceptual relativism of that article later on. In "Nature and Convention" (Winch 1972) he claims that one cannot intelligibly conceive of a society that does not adhere to the norm of truth telling.

59. For Hollis, see especially Hollis 1970a; 1970b. For Davidson, see his articles on radical interpretation in Davidson 1984, especially "On the Very Idea of a Conceptual Scheme." As both authors acknowledge, they owe a great debt to Quine in this respect, especially the first two chapters of Quine 1960.

60. Davidson and Quine claim furthermore that meaning and reference are objectively indeterminate and inscrutable. They assert that there is no fact of the matter that allows us to decide between various incompatible interpretation schemes. Paul Roth discusses the implications of this thesis for the philosophy of social science in Roth 1987. For a discussion and critique of Davidson's indeterminacy thesis, see Stueber 1993, pp. 156ff.

61. For a further discussion of these issues, see Chapter 5 in this anthology, by Karsten Stueber.

62. Quine 1992, p. 46.

63. Grandy 1973, p. 443.

64. For an explication of certain similarities between Davidsonian and Gadamerian interpretation theory, see Stueber 1994a.

65. For a thorough critique of methodologies that assume a fixed "object of understanding," see the chapter by Paul Roth in this volume.

66. Schleiermacher's hermeneutics took its departure from problems in biblical exegesis, which he extended in his methodological lectures to the first general theory of interpretation. See Schleiermacher 1977; Ormiston and Schrift 1990; Frank 1990.

67. The implied theory of meaning is congenial to Paul Grice's intentionalistic semantics and is also expressed by Husserl's phenomenological conception of intentional meaning. In the context of hermeneutic theory, E. D. Hirsch Jr. has forcefully defended a conception of interpretive objectivity based on the author's intention. See Hirsch 1967.

68. Schleiermacher 1977, p. 97.

69. The understanding of subjective motives and intentions requires an understanding of the whole life, which itself can only be understood from making sense of the individual acts and expressions. Also, the understanding of the whole life requires a grasp of the general cultural context, which again is only possible by understanding the concrete lives and practices. This back-and-forth between the whole and the part that seems to characterize human interpretation is often called a "hermeneutic circle."

70. Schleiermacher 1977, pp. 100ff.

71. This is the major point of Hans-Georg Gadamer's criticism of Schleiermacher's "romantic" hermeneutics. As Gadamer sees it, interpretation is here fully oriented at the disclosure of the productive process that has led to the expression of some meaning in the text. Understanding is thus the reconstruction of an original construction, which requires a reliving, a reexperiencing of what the author experienced while producing the work or act. This, on the one hand, orients understanding fully at the model of the aesthetic process. The author or agent is seen as a creative agency of meaning constitution who can be disclosed only by reconstructing the creative path "within" the other self. On the other hand, this requires in turn that the interpreter enters, as it were, into the mind-set of the other, that she makes herself similar and immediate with the author and her original intentions. According to Gadamer, both assumptions are misguided and impossible, which renders

Schleiermacher's hermeneutics useless. The idea of a "metaphysics of individuality," which implies the assumption of a deep and inexplicable self, is shared by many romantic writers, famously expressed by Goethe's statement: "Individuum est ineffabile." See Gadamer 1989, pp. 184ff.

72. By means of this peculiar combination, Schleiermacher can both claim that interpretation is divination and yet that the interpreter might understand an author better than he or she understands him- or herself. Since the interpreter has to make explicit what is taken for granted for the other, she also grasps more clearly assumptions and premises that are involved in her thought.

73. See Dilthey 1982a, p. lxxx.

74. See Dilthey 1982a, pp. 263–264.

75. See Dilthey 1989.

76. This argument goes back to G. Vico's claim that with regard to history *verum et factum convertuntur,* which is taken to make a truthful and objective account of history possible. Even late Dilthey refers to this idea when he states, "Only that which the human spirit has created can he understand," in Dilthey 1981, p. 184.

77. Dilthey exemplifies his point with reference to Nietzsche, whom he takes to have falsely generalized his own obsession with power into a universal psychology that makes the will to power the essence of all human behavior.

78. In other words, the hermeneutic circle extends to the very grounding of interpretation itself.

79. Dilthey 1927, 3:146–147.

80. The late Dilthey takes this the concept of "objective spirit" from Hegel and redefines it for his own purposes. Dilthey makes his Hegelian turn by situating the self in a shared social and historical context, which he designates as the "objective spirit" of the age and culture. Yet Dilthey radicalizes Hegel's historicism by downgrading the "absolute spirit" (philosophy, religion, art) to aspects of the "objective spirit." While the early Dilthey receives his major motives from Schleiermacher, the late Dilthey orients himself more toward Hegel.

81. Dilthey 1981, p. 96. See the chapter in this anthology by R. Makkreel, who develops the antipsychologism of Dilthey and interprets his methodology in terms of a "*structural* transposition" into the other.

82. Dilthey distinguishes with regard to that environment "cultural systems" that express the objective realms of meanings aimed at shared values such as truth, beauty, law, and education; and "social organizations" that fulfill a specific and important social function, such as the family, political parties, or the state. Dilthey argues that neither the meaning of shared symbolic values nor the function of social organizations can be derived from the individual psyche; they are rather posited prior to individual psychic life.

83. Dilthey 1927, 7:251.

84. Dilthey 1927, 7:233. Translated by Kögler and Stueber.

85. The reference to concepts like purpose, or even "the subject matter," might seem to refer back to the intention of an agent or author. Yet it must be emphasized that such an intentional state can only be understood by reconstructing in light of which beliefs and assumptions a purpose or subject matter is viewed, which in turn requires a rational orientation at the issue itself and not a psychological reconstruction of some hidden motives or "intentions."

86. This seems true for Gordon and Goldman; Heal, however, seems to come very close to a Gadamerian understanding of interpretation; see the chapter in this anthology by Karsten Stueber, who discusses her concept of co-cognition regarding a shared subject matter.

87. Gadamer 1989, p. 372.

88. See Danto 1965.

89. This does, of course, not deny the need to avoid simplistic assimilations to our current context. For a discussion of Arthur Danto's model in this context, see the chapter by Paul Roth.

90. Purpose is not a psychological concept but a rational concept expressing a truth-related intention.

91. Gadamer 1989, p. 294.

92. This is the point at which Gadamer would allow for an explanatory and theoretical attitude, one that would explain why agents do not express plausible views and attitudes. The basic idea is that we only need to turn to psychological motives or historical explanations once the initial attempt at a rational reconstruction of the beliefs and assumptions has failed. For a further discussion of this sense of psychological explanation, see section 7 below.

93. See section 1 above, "Two Philosophical Camps."

94. Gadamer 1989, pp. 360, 299. To understand the expressions and actions of others thus involves a basic openness toward their claims to validity and meaningfulness, which we have to attend to not fully miss what is entailed as meaning in their statements and actions. Any methodology that attempts to construct an *object* of understanding is accordingly conceived as a destructive force to the interpretive dialogue.

95. For an encompassing analysis of Gadamer's hermeneutic theory in the context of recent philosophy of language and interpretation, see Kögler 1996a.

96. Again, this is not to be understood as a psychological process but rather as a cognitive reconstruction of the plausible reasons that make someone say or do what he or she says or does.

97. The relevance of an implicit and holistic background understanding for the constitution of explicit linguistic meaning has recently received much attention in the philosophy of language and interpretation. See Dreyfus 1980; Searle 1979; 1989; 1995.

98. Gadamer 1989, p. 378.

99. See the discussion of Danto's thought experiment above.

100. Gadamer 1989, pp. 306–307.

101. The chapter by Schatzki discusses the difference between natural and human sciences; the chapter by Kögler focuses on the reflexive nature of interpretations in the human and social sciences.

102. The chapters by Vielmetter, Turner, and Kögler explicitly address the relevance of emotional experience and their bodily expressions for interpretations in the human and social sciences.

103. See the chapter by R. Gordon.

104. See the chapter by Henderson and Horgan.

105. See Apel et al. 1971; Ormiston and Schrift 1990.

106. Habermas 1990. Subjective self-understanding is taken to be mediated by language, but language is not identical with the intentional understanding of its meaning alone. Social practices and institutions influence symbolic forms as well and thus indirectly the understanding of the agents.

107. For the relevance of this debate to the discussion of simulation theory, see the chapter by James Bohman.

108. This reading of psychoanalysis stems from Frankfurt psychoanalyst A. Lorenzer, on whom both Apel and Habermas draw; see also Habermas 1971.

109. The assumption is indeed that any supposedly "objective" or "neutral" social science fools itself about its connection to underlying assumptions and interests, and thus remains blind with regard to its most guiding premises and research perspectives.

110. In what follows we will sketch the theoretical ideas behind most of the critical social sciences and cultural studies practiced nowadays. It goes without saying that we have to forgo any more detailed discussion of differences in models and applications.

111. See Horkheimer and Adorno 1996; see also Jay 1973.

112. Horkheimer 1987.

113. See Adorno et al. 1982.

114. Since the self is taken to normally develop a psychic triad of ego, superego, and id, the rational self (or ego) is capable of controlling its desires and needs rationally and thus of resisting aggressive power drives and instincts.

115. The issue of the extent to which modern subjectivity is connected to mechanisms of authority and power has driven related projects such as the work of Michel Foucault, and more recently Judith Butler.

116. Habermas 1984; 1987.

117. See Foucault 1979; Foucault 1978.

118. See Foucault 1985; Dreyfus and Rabinow 1983.

119. For an analysis of these three dimensions in the context of the sociology of knowledge, see Kögler 1997a; 1997b.

120. See Grossberg, Nelson, Treichler 1992.

121. Gadamer 1990.

122. Gordon, p. 67 in this volume.

123. Vielmetter, p. 88–89 in this volume.

124. Turner, p. 112 in this volume.

125. Henderson and Horgan, p. 136 in this volume.

126. Schatzki, p. 176 in this volume.

127. Makkreel, p. 192 in this volume.

128. Bohman, p. 223 in this volume.

129. Roth, p. 264 in this volume.

130. Blackburn, p. 282 in this volume.

131. See Hiley, Bohman, Shusterman 1991.

Chapter One

Simulation and the Explanation of Action

ROBERT M. GORDON

Although simulation theory (ST) was developed as a solution to problems in the philosophy of mind, it bears obvious affinities to theories that particularly concern the aims and methodology of the social sciences, most notably those centered on the concepts of *Verstehen,* or "empathetic understanding," and historical reenactment.[1]

These older cousins of ST do not enjoy the best of reputations, however. Among analytically oriented philosophers, at least, they are best known for their antinaturalist portrayal of ordinary, everyday *reason explanations*, that is, explanations of actions in terms of the reason (or reasons) for which they were performed. A major thesis of some *Verstehen* theorists was that, whereas the natural sciences attempt to explain *(erklären),* so-called explanations in the social sciences, as well as ordinary "commonsense" reason explanations, are really not explanations at all, but merely attempts to interpret, that is, to understand *(verstehen)* actions, to indicate how they might have been seen by the agents themselves. In the 1950s and 1960s, several analytic philosophers, influenced by Wittgenstein as well as by continental views, claimed that what I am calling reason explanations have merely a justificatory, or normative, aim.[2] According to William Dray's account, for instance, they involve an attempt to view the world and the agent's situation as the agent saw them at the time of action, and to pick out those aspects the agent saw as justifying the action. They portray the action as a reasonable thing to have done, given what the agent was aiming at and what the agent believed to be the relevant facts.

Does ST share these views? It would be presumptuous of me to speak for ST generally, for the term "simulation theory" has a broader coverage than just the theory I intended to be putting forward in my 1986 paper, "Folk-Psychology as Simulation,"[3] and in subsequent elaborations. My own version of ST definitely shares some of the antinaturalism of its predecessors, in ways I hope to make clear. Most important, it denies that reason explanations must be interpreted against a background of laws, or at least that they imply, presuppose, or entail that there is a relevant causal law. Yet this antinaturalism does not deny that they are explanations and that they perform an explanatory function beyond merely portraying the action as reasonable from the agent's point of view. They surely do answer "Why?" questions, and they may have the form "A X'd *because* p," where "p" states a reason of A's for X'ing. How they do this is the topic of this paper.

1. A Shortcoming of Predecessor Views

A major shortcoming of the predecessors of ST was pointed out by Donald Davidson in his classic 1963 paper, "Actions, Reasons, and Causes."[4] One way to describe the problem is that there is a logical gap between having a reason for X'ing and actually X'ing *for* that reason. That there is such a gap is most obvious where the agent has more than one reason for doing something yet is actually moved to action by only one. (The problem of filling that gap I will call the *mixed motives* problem.) For example, Sam, out for a stroll, is caught in a sudden rain and also finds himself in a dangerous district. Sam runs. Is Sam running because it is raining (and he will get drenched if he doesn't) or is he running because he is in a dangerous district (and he will be in danger if he doesn't)—or for both reasons? If one says,

1. Sam is running because it's raining,
or
2. Sam is running because he is in a dangerous district,

one is saying something that answers this question. One is not just specifying a fact that made the action appear to the agent reasonable, rational, justified, or attractive; one is more particularly specifying a fact that is *a reason for which* Sam is running.

Davidson's solution to the mixed motives problem is that what differentiates those reasons that are reasons for which (or because of which) the action was performed from those that are not is a *causal relation* between the reasons and the action. The "because" in "he did it because . . . ," where we go on to name a reason, signifies a causal relation, and the explanation is construed as a causal explanation. What makes it not just an "accident" that A X'd, given that A had reason R for X'ing, is that reason and action are linked, under some description of each, by some law of nature—though the explainer may not know what law this may be. Reason explanation thus not only requires something beyond *justification* from the agent's point of view; the further ingredient is a naturalistic one, having to do with the way nature operates rather than with the way the agent sees things. This is not to say that Davidson's account of mind, of "the way the agent sees things," is naturalistic; far from it. What is naturalistic—and adds to his account the tension expressed patently in his doctrine of anomalous monism—is his view, to be discussed shortly, that if mental events are to explain actions, they must be token-identical with events that are covered by laws.

Davidson does not explicitly discuss reasons such as,

It is raining.
I am in a dangerous district.

He does not claim that reasons such as these, reasons or considerations that one might put forward in *arguing for* running, are causes of the action for which they are reasons. It would not be his position that (1) entails,

Sam's running was caused by its raining (or by the fact that it is raining, by the precipitation, etc.).

and that (2) entails,

Sam's running was caused by his being in a dangerous district.

This is just as well. Reasons for acting, some of which are the reasons for which people act, are in fact a motley lot. It would require a broad under-standing of what a causal relation is to allow *being in (or entering) a dangerous district* as a cause of anything. If this is not convincing, consider the following:

Joan flew to Hawaii, because *there will be a solar eclipse there tomorrow*.
Max abandoned his thesis, because *it was contradictory*.
I bought thirty-two feet of fencing, because I'm enclosing a ten-foot di-
ameter, *and pi is just under 3.2*.

Davidson's conception of the relevant causal relation is not broad enough to accommodate these reason explanations as they stand. Central to his conception is the Principle of the Nomological Character of Causal-ity: that two events are causally related only if they are covered, under some description of these events, by a law of nature, that is, that there is a law of nature that correlates the occurrence of events of the one description to the occurrence of events of the other description.[5] Davidson further claims that these must be strict, exceptionless laws. Tomorrow's solar eclipse is no doubt covered by such laws, but these are not laws that "predict" Joan's flying to Hawaii today. That pi has the value it has is a necessary truth, which is not covered by any laws of nature; likewise, that Max's thesis (taking "Max's thesis" as a rigid designator) is contradictory.

2. The Move to Mental Explanation

To maintain his causal analysis without compromising his nomological conception of causation,[6] Davidson must claim that the *real* explanans in a reason explanation is not in general those reasons or considerations in favor of the action for which the agent acted, but rather *something that can plausibly be held identical with an event covered by a law of nature*. Thus he holds that a reason explanation is always, at least implicitly, a *psychological* explanation. When made fully explicit, it is always an explanation in terms of *a property of the agent*, specifically, the agent's having certain beliefs and desires. This is a point that has in recent years become dogmatically "obvious" to many philosophers. In the case of,

1. Sam is running because it's raining (and if it is raining, running helps avoid getting drenched),

the more explicit version would be,

1B. Sam is running because he *believes* that it is raining (and that if it is raining, running helps avoid getting drenched).

Further, it is the standard view—and Davidson's—that 1 and 1B are enthymematic. Reason explanations are said to portray the action as a reasonable thing to have done, *given* (a) what the agent believed to be the relevant facts and also (b) what the agent was aiming at. It is because of qualification (a) that mention is made of the agent's beliefs; and it is because of qualification (b) that mention is made of the agent's desires or, generically, pro-attitudes. Davidson thus identifies a "primary" reason with a pair of propositional attitudes, namely, a belief and a pro-attitude, adding that typically in giving an explanation one would not need to mention explicitly both the belief and the pro-attitude.

The question, "Why is Sam running?" is for Davidson chiefly a matter of which of two belief-desire pairs actually caused his running: (a) the one consisting of his belief that he will get drenched unless he runs and his desire not to get drenched or (b) the one consisting of his belief that he will be in danger unless he runs and his desire not to be in danger. Or, in a case of causal overdetermination, each pair *a* and *b* independently causes his action. In short, a reason explanation represents an action, that is, an instance or token of some general action type T, as *caused by* beliefs and desires that correspond to premises of a practical syllogism that *provide a basis for* performing an action of type T. Thus, even though reason explanations aim at a kind of understanding not sought in explanations of other events, showing the action to be rational from the agent's point of view, a causal component had to be present as well. Not only are rational and causal explanation compatible, according to Davidson: Reasons explain why an action is performed *only if* they—that is, the relevant beliefs and desires—are causes of the action. To assert that an agent acted because of a particular reason is to give a causal explanation of a special kind.

Summing up so far: An apparent advantage of analyzing reason explanations as belief-desire explanations rather than as simple nonmental explanations is that the former, but not the latter, seem to be the sorts of entities that might be held identical with events that are covered by laws. The reason for preferring entities that might be held identical with events that are covered by laws is that (given the nomological conception of causation) this is required for a causal relation. A causal relation, in turn, seems to give us a solution to the mixed motives problem.

3. Why Causation Rather Than Counterfactuals?

It is not clear why Davidson insists on a *causal* relation between reasons and action, rather than merely a *counterfactual* relation. It would appear that a counterfactual difference between primary reasons a and b would be enough to fill the gap between having a reason to X, and X'ing for that reason. Suppose the following:

> If Sam did not have belief-desire pair a, then he would not be running—that is, he would not, even if he had belief-desire pair b, and other things were "equal."
> However, it is not the case that, if Sam did not have belief-desire pair b, then he would not be running—that is, he would not, even if he had belief-desire pair a, and other things were "equal."

If there is this counterfactual difference between the two belief-desire pairs, then it would seem that Sam is running for just one reason, namely, that it is raining. (In saying this, I am ignoring problems that are common to a causal account of reason explanation and a counterfactual account. For example, just as there is a problem of "deviant causal chains," so there would be a problem of deviant counterfactual chains. Sam's running may counterfactually depend on a belief-desire pair, but in the "wrong" way, a way that does not make this a reason for which he is running.) Not only does the counterfactual difference seem to fill the gap just as well as a causal relation does; it is plausible—though I will not argue the point—that it is only because the causal relation has these counterfactual implications that we are inclined to give credence to a causal account of reason explanation. In other words, what makes the causal account seem compelling, at least in my example, is that it would yield the counterfactual difference I have indicated between a and b.

If counterfactuals suffice to solve Davidson's mixed motive problem, however, then haven't we eliminated the need to think of reason explanations as belief-desire explanations? One problem with understanding reasons as belief-desire pairs is the fairly obvious one that it is not Sam's believing it is raining that is a reason of his. It is not sentences that *ascribe* a belief that argue for the action, but rather sentences that *express* the belief, for example, "it's raining" or "I will get drenched if I don't run." It is the certainty of getting drenched, not the agent's being in a state of certainty about it, that is a genuine *reason for* running, a *consideration in favor of* running. Likewise, in the case of desires or other pro-attitudes: Apart from special cases, it is the sentences that express them, not those that ascribe them, that are premises of practical arguments, for example, "It would be awful to get drenched now," not, "I have a desire that I not be drenched now." Can't we, then, let reasons be reasons, that is, considerations that might be raised in arguing for the action, rather than states of the agent for whom they are reasons? Suppose:

> If it were not raining, then Sam would not be running—that is, he would not, even if he were in the dangerous district, and other things were "equal."
> However, it is *not* the case that: If Sam were not in the dangerous district, then he would not be running—provided it were raining, and other things were "equal."

If this is so, then it would seem that Sam is running for just one reason, namely, that it is raining. (In saying this, I am again ignoring problems that are common to a causal account of reason explanation and a counterfactual account.)

If we assume that counterfactuals suffice for the mixed motive problem, then perhaps we need not abandon the "motley lot" I spoke of. We need not worry whether being in or entering a "dangerous district" can plausibly be identical with an event covered by a law of nature—much less, whether a necessary truth can be. This may allow us to pick up all the fallen dominoes. If we don't need a causal relation to solve the mixed motives problem, then perhaps we don't need to limit the explanans in a reason explanation to something identical with an event that is covered by laws. And if this is so, then we don't need to insist that the real explanans in a reason explanation must always be a mental state rather than a reason proper, a consideration that might be raised in arguing for the action. Indeed, we may not even have to abandon causality if, as some philosophers think, causality itself may be understood in terms of counterfactuals: for example, that event c caused event e provided that, if c had not occurred, e would not have occurred.

4. But Don't Counterfactuals Rest on Laws?

There is a problem, however. For it is widely held that counterfactuals themselves rest on laws. Using a simplified possible-world approach to counterfactuals, Jaegwon Kim[7] explains clearly why this is supposed so:

> The counterfactual "If P were the case, Q would be the case" is true just in case Q is true in the [possible] world in which P is true and that . . . is as much like the actual world as possible (to put it another way: Q is true in the closest P-World). . . . Let's see how this works with the counterfactual "If this match had been struck, it would have lighted." In the actual world, the match wasn't struck; so suppose that the match was struck . . . but keep other conditions the same as much as possible . . . it was dry, and oxygen was present in the vicinity. Did the match light in that world? In asking this question, we are asking which of the following two worlds is closer to the actual world:
>
> W_1: The match was struck; it was dry; oxygen was present; the match lighted.
> W_2: The match was struck; it was dry; oxygen was present; the match did not light.
>
> We would judge, it seems, that of the two W_1 is closer to the actual world. But why do we judge this way? Because, it seems, we believe that in the actual world there is a lawful regularity to the effect that when a dry match is struck in the presence of oxygen it ignites, and W_1, but not W_2, respects this regularity. . . .
>
> Consider a psychophysical counterfactual: "If Brian had not wanted to check out the noise, he wouldn't have gone downstairs." . . . Consider the following two worlds:
>
> W_3: Brian didn't want to check out the noise; he didn't go downstairs.
> W_4: Brian didn't want to check out the noise; he went downstairs anyway.
>
> So why should we think that W_3 is closer than W_4? . . . The only plausible answer, again, seems to be this: We know, or believe, that there are certain lawful regularities and propensities governing Brian's wants, beliefs, and so on, on

the one hand and his behavior patterns, on the other, and that given the absence of a desire to check out a suspicious noise in the middle of the night, along with other conditions prevailing at the time, his not going downstairs at that particular time fits these regularities better than the supposition that he would have gone downstairs at that time. . . .

Again, the centrality of psychophysical laws to mental causation is apparent. . . . the laws involved in evaluating these counterfactuals . . . are rough-and-ready generalizations tacitly qualified by escape clauses. . . . Laws of this type, often called ceteris paribus laws, seem to satisfy the usual criteria of lawlikeness: . . . they seem to have the power to ground counterfactuals, and our credence in them is enhanced as we see them confirmed in more and more instances. . . . it seems beyond question that they are the essential staple that sustains and nourishes our causal discourse.

The ceteris paribus laws Kim mentions are different from the strict laws Davidson requires, and they may seem to support psychological counterfactuals of the sort Kim mentions. But the choice is not just between two sorts of law. For laws are not the only generalizations that satisfy the criteria of lawlikeness: There are others that support counterfactuals and are confirmed by their instances. Moreover, contrary to the widely held conviction that Kim articulates, it appears to be these others, not laws, that sustain and nourish our explanations of action and in particular our determinations of the reason or reasons for which the agent acted. To illustrate my alternative view, I will use a historical example.

5. A Court Case

Mixed motive questions, concerning which of the agent's reasons are reasons for which the action was performed, are often of considerable practical, moral, and legal import; they are not just philosophers' questions. In lawsuits concerning discrimination in employment, the crucial issue, typically, is whether illegitimate considerations of gender or race, for example, swayed a decision to reject a candidate for hiring or promotion, rather than just job-relevant considerations. Was candidate x chosen rather than candidate y because x was the better person for the position, or was this consideration one among others, such as race or gender?

The difficult cases are those in which a case is made that both types of consideration point in the same direction, and the possible influence of biases is masked by the possible presence of legitimate, job-relevant considerations. In a case decided by the U.S. Supreme Court in 1989, a female employee of Price Waterhouse, a major accounting firm, highly regarded for her competence and intelligence, had been turned down for promotion to a partnership in the firm. She sued on the grounds that the decision was discriminatory.[8] The firm admitted that there had been widespread sex stereotyping: She had been held "too assertive for a woman," her behavior too masculine. She had been advised that to improve her chances for partnership, she would have to become more "feminine" in the way she walked, talked, and dressed.[9] But the firm argued that there were also legitimate, nondiscriminatory grounds for denying her the position, such as a "lack of leadership qualities," and it claimed that the decision was influenced only by these latter considerations. They further maintained that it was the burden of the employee to show that the decision had been due *solely* to the unallowable, discriminatory consideration; that, "but for" the gender factor, the decision would have gone the other way.

The Court ruled to the contrary.[10] The relevant statute forbids an employer to "deprive any individual of employment opportunities . . . because of such individual's . . . sex." Congress, the Court plurality notes, had specifically rejected a qualifying amendment that would have replaced "because of" with the more restrictive phrase "*solely* because of." Therefore, the employee plaintiff has only to prove that gender was one of the factors on the basis of which the decision was made, not that it was a "but-for" cause in the absence of which the decision would have gone the other way. It then becomes the burden of the defending employer to prove (by "a preponderance of evidence") the contrary, that it is *false* that,

> If it had not taken the illegitimate factor, the employee's gender, into account, it would have decided in favor.[11]

Or, in other words, the burden is to prove that the decision was gender independent, where the criterion of gender independence is the counterfactual,

> GI. The partners would have made the *same* decision irrespective of gender—even if the candidate had been a male with like credentials.

6. The Importance of Policy Invariance

For earlier and later decisions to count as evidence of the influence of particular reasons on the promotion decision under examination, a crucial assumption must be made: that the firm did not change its *standards* for promotion to partnership; or, more broadly, its *policy* with regard to such promotions. Price Waterhouse certainly had no official policy requiring that female partners act in a "feminine" way. But, given the behavior pattern discerned in other employment decisions and given internal communications, there appeared to be an operative policy, a de facto standard, permitting such considerations to count in evaluations of a candidate. Assuming that there was no change in policy, then one may infer that in the case under examination such considerations were again allowed to influence the decision. The charge of sexism in this case may be confirmed or disconfirmed by examining other decisions, given the assumption that the underlying policy does not vary.

The Court was quite clear about this assumption. Despite substantial evidence of a *general pattern* of discrimination in Price Waterhouse's past promotion decisions, the Court reaffirmed an earlier decision that in adjudicating an individual claim, as opposed to a class action, it is not sufficient to establish that such a pattern existed. For the relevant statute "does not authorize affirmative relief for individuals as to whom, the employer shows, the existence of systemic discrimination had no effect."[12]

In an individual case, it was argued, the focus is on the influence of particular reasons on a particular hiring decision. Thus, Price Waterhouse was given the opportunity to show that, despite the general pattern, in this case the counterfactual GI was true: They would have made the same decision even if they had not taken the plaintiff's gender into account. If there had been a general policy, it may not have been applied in this particular case. The Court evidently had an insight that was not granted at least some of the philosophical behaviorists, namely, that, where the concern is to explain a particular decision or action, the relevance of a general pattern of behavior is merely evidential. It is evidence, but not conclusive evidence, that the corresponding counterfactual conditional held in the particular case in question. They left it open to the firm to show that in the particular employment decision in question, the outcome was just what it would have been had they not been systemic discriminators.[13]

It is crucial to assume consistency of policy, not only when we move from the general to the particular but also when we move from the actual to the counterfactual. Applying Kim's possible world analysis, consider the following two possible worlds:

W5: The candidate was a male with like credentials; the partners decided in favor of the candidate.
W6: The candidate was a male with like credentials; the partners decided against the candidate anyway.

Why should we think that W5 is closer than W6? According to Kim's view, the only plausible answer is that we know, or believe, that there are certain lawful regularities governing the wants, beliefs, and so on, of the voting partners and their behavior patterns; and W5 better fits these regularities. A law, of course, covers any member of a set of individuals and ignores differences among these individuals. For a law to be applied to a given individual *i*, it must be complemented with specific parametric data concerning *i*. Thus, in the case of Price Waterhouse, the differences between a company that is influenced by sexist considerations and a company that is not would be counted as differences in *data*, whether these concern propositional attitudes or physical or computational states; the laws themselves are invariant from one individual or company to another.

There is, however, another answer, and one that seems to me far more plausible. There are lawful regularities of a sort, but they concern not relations among physically described events nor the invariant formal relations between wants, beliefs, and actions, but rather *substantive relations between situations and actions,* mapping types or descriptions of situations onto types or descriptions of actions, and varying across agents and, within a single agent, over time. In the case of Price Waterhouse, for example, on the basis of prior decisions, internal correspondence, and other evidence, we know, or believe, that the firm, or a sufficient number of the voting partners, was *in this particular decision* applying a certain standard for promotion to partnership; or, more broadly, implementing a policy with regard to such promotions. And, *once we take away the gender factor* (with other conditions remaining as they were), *it better fits this standard or policy* to decide in favor of a candidate with such credentials than to decide against.

If the agent is successfully implementing the same policy in a number of decisions, then there will be a corresponding correlation between descriptions of the situations in which the agent acted and descriptions of what the agent did in those situations. This will be a *nonaccidental correlation.* The statement that at a particular time period a particular agent is implementing a certain policy is of course not the statement of a law of nature. Yet one may express a *policy* as a lawlike principle: for example,

JG. If x is a candidate for promotion, x is promoted if and only if x is both job qualified and gender qualified.

JG would be confirmed by promotions of job-and-gender-qualified candidates and by denials of promotion to candidates who are either not job qualified or not gender qualified. JG is *dis*confirmed by promotion of candidates who are either not job qualified or not gender qualified, or by denial of promotion to a job-and-gender-qualified candidate. In addition, if JG is the expression of a general policy, it clearly *supports counterfactuals,* specifying whether purely hypothetical candidates would have been promoted and also whether a particular actual candidate would have been promoted if, counterfactually, she had been gender qualified.

The Court, as I mentioned, held that a record of systemic discrimination was not decisive if it could be shown that in the case in question the defendant would have made the same decision even if they had not taken the plaintiff's gender into account. However, the Court failed to note that the counterfactual may be false *for reasons having nothing to do with sexism.* For example, suppose that, if the partners had not considered gender, their decision would have been favorable—*but only because the meeting would have been shorter.* Suppose it is a psychological law that the longer a meeting runs, the less likely it is that the discussants will vote in favor of the matter under discussion. If the partners' meeting had been shortened either because gender was not considered or because other business was expedited, the decision might have been favorable. Likewise, the decision would have been *un*favorable even if the gender issue had *not* been taken up, provided other business had extended the meeting. In such a case, where the relevant fact is not the issues discussed but the length of the meeting, what should the Court decide? Strictly, the partners would fail the counterfactual test: They would *not* have made the same decision if they had not taken the plaintiff's gender into account. And yet, although the decision was influenced by an "extraneous" factor (meeting length) that was affected by a discussion of gender-related matters, the decision is not, intuitively, an instance of gender discrimination.[14] In short, what should be held determinative of a discriminatory decision is not the truth[15] of the counterfactual conditional but the truth of a gender-discrimination *generalization* such as JG, which in this case was true because a corresponding company policy was in force and being implemented in that employment decision.

However, if we are interested in a general characterization of what must be assumed constant when projecting from actual behavior patterns to future or counterfactual behavior, "policy" isn't the concept we want. Even systematic race or sex discrimination may reflect not a policy but a general sense of what is appropriate or right, even morally right. Or it may simply be the unprincipled expression of a general attitude, socially sanctioned or not. And yet, given a general attitude or a general sense of what is right, and no countervailing reasons, one's behavior may resemble that of a person carrying out a policy. There will be a corresponding correlation between situations and actions, *and it will not be an accidental correlation.* That is, the lawful regularity JG will characterize the substantive relations between situations and actions, and one would be warranted in projecting from actual behavior to future or counterfactual behavior. JG will be confirmed by positive instances and disconfirmed by negative.

Turning to my other example, suppose that Sam does not start running until he enters a dangerous district, although it had been raining for some time before. Further, he continues to run well after it stops raining. He stops running only when he has left the district. The evidence regarding Sam may be summarized as follows:

Phase 1: Raining but not in dangerous district: Sam does
   not run.
Phase 2: Raining *and* in dangerous district: Sam runs.
Phase 3: Not raining but in dangerous district: Sam runs.

We want to discover the answer to the following question: In phase 2, is Sam running because (a) it is raining (and he will get drenched if he doesn't run) or is he running because (b) he is in a dangerous district (and he will be in danger if he doesn't run)—or is he running for both reasons? It seems reasonable to infer from the evidence that in phase 2, Sam was running because (b) he is in a dangerous district, and that he was *not* doing so because (a) it was raining.

To warrant this inference, however, we must assume that in the relevant respects *Sam acts consistently* in all three phases. Suppose that Sam does *not* act consistently in the relevant respects throughout the three phases. Suppose that in phase 1 Sam was indifferent to getting drenched, or even thought it a great idea. But, just as he entered the dangerous district, he suddenly became (perhaps through a quasi-religious experience) a rain avoider. Consequently, he started running. Thus, in the ambiguous phase 2, Sam was in fact running *because it was raining;* this was the sole *reason* for which he was running. Further, suppose that, just as it stopped raining, he suddenly came to see, by an equally obscure process, *being in a dangerous district* as a reason for running. So, although his original reason for running—the rain—was no longer applicable, he continues to run. Then, despite Sam's behavior before and after phase 2, we were mistaken in inferring that in phase 2 Sam was running because he was in a dangerous district. Our inference is warranted only if Sam was not inconsistent in the way described; if, on the contrary, it is lawful or nonaccidental that in all relevant respects he *would have acted similarly in similar situations* in each of the three phases.

What I have been discussing are reason explanations in the strictest sense: explanations of action in terms of the reasons, the favorable considerations or arguments, for which they were performed. These are probably the most common form of explanation of action, and they should be of particular interest to friends of simulation theory. For they are the explanations we give, typically, of our own actions, either current or in the recent past: Why am I running? Because it's raining; because I'm late; because I'm training for a marathon; because I'll live longer if I do.[16] These answers not only indicate something about the world that explains why one so acted, but indicate that it explains it because to the agent this was a consideration favorable to so acting.

Other people, of course, or the agent at another time, might not find the reason a good one; they might not view the consideration as favorable to this action. We have only to think of an employer explaining that an employee was turned down for promotion "because she wasn't feminine enough." One might recognize the explanation as successfully *explaining* the action, even if it fails to *justify* it, to show it in a favorable light, or even to make minimal "sense" of it. To be informed that Sam is running because, say, "there's a gibbous moon" is to learn why he is running, but such an explanation is likely to introduce a question that leaves one more perplexed than before. We needn't be told this by Sam. By noting the occasions on which he runs without any other evident reason and by applying Mill's methods, we may even discover for ourselves that (apparently) Sam is running because there's a gibbous moon. We surmise that there is a longer story to be told or unearthed that will cause his running to make sense at least from Sam's point of view: that gibbous moons have certain astrological influences, for instance, affecting those who do not run.

It is here, *within* our commonsense thinking about action, that the traditional distinction between *explanation* and *understanding* appears to have its place. Simulation in the light of Sam's background and his behavior at other times may help us overcome our perplexity, enabling us to answer the question, What does a gibbous moon have to do with it? But we have an *explanation* nevertheless, even if it is one that doesn't make the action make sense. In the case of a perverse or evil action, in fact, one just might not *want* to make it make sense; one doesn't want "understanding," even in the context of pretend play or biography. So too in the case of an unobjectionable action done for a wrong or perverse reason, such as an act of "charity" performed solely because it will make the recipient feel inferior: One might not wish to make doing it *for that reason* make sense. Someone might insist that an explanation in terms of the agent's reasons cannot be a *genuine* explanation if the explainer lacks empathetic understanding. However, I do not think that the concept of explanation will bear the weight of a "genuineness" test. I do want to note, however, that it is sometimes very important to get such an explanation *right*. To know that Sam is running because the moon is gibbous may rule out other explanations and, like an explanation in the physical sciences, may help in the prediction and control of future behavior.

7. Simulation and the
Implicit Ascription of Knowledge

Although I have been stressing that reason explanations are explanations in terms of facts that count as considerations in favor of so acting, I fully appreciate that, where the explanans in a reason explanation is a fact, it must be a fact of which the agent is *aware,* a fact that is *known* to the agent; thus, the agent must have the corresponding *belief.* This distinguishes, for example, the explanation,

1. Sam is running because it's raining,

from noncognitive brute-cause explanations such as the following:

1a. Sam is running because he is on amphetamines.
1b. The sewer is running because it's raining.

The accepted view (at least, the view *I* once accepted, taking it to be the accepted view) is that reason explanations and the corresponding counterfactuals are peculiarly complex sorts of explanations and counterfactuals. We understand from (1) that Sam's running is counterfactually dependent[17] on the fact that it is raining, *by way of Sam's belief*—indeed, his *reliable* belief, constituting *knowledge*—that it is raining. Likewise, the partners' vote was counterfactually linked to the candidate's being a woman, by way of their belief that the candidate is a woman. With this understanding, when we consider counterfactual possibilities, we restrict possible worlds to the agent's horizon of knowledge, excluding worlds in which the agent does not know or believe that the antecedent, or the explanans, is true. This account would shore up and be shored up by the general picture of reason explanations as, at least implicitly, belief-desire explanations.

Such an account seems natural, given the commitments I once shared. However, to restrict possible worlds to the agent's horizon of knowledge would seem to require, on the accepted account, considerable conceptual sophistication. If (1) exemplifies a relatively complex form of explanation, excluding worlds in which the agent does not know or believe that p, then why do young children—three-year-olds—seem to use and understand this form, even though they lack the concepts of knowledge and belief, or at least the capacity to use them explicitly in explaining actions? Must we conclude that young children really do not understand reason explanations as distinct from brute, noncognitive explanations such as (1a) and (1b)?

I will briefly sketch an alternative account that shows how, even if one lacks the concepts of knowledge and belief, one can give and understand explanations, such as,

Sam is running because it's raining,

that implicitly confine the explanans to the agent's epistemic horizon. According to my account, even the young child explains actions in terms of full-fledged reasons, not in terms of a generic noncognitive explanans that befits a flood sewer just as well as a person. What takes conceptual sophistication, requiring explicit use of the concepts of knowledge and belief, is *inclusion* of possible worlds beyond the agent's epistemic horizon. Only the *older* child is capable of giving and grasping such explanations.

My alternative account rests on simulation theory. To introduce the account, I begin by considering first-person, present-tense explanations. Suppose that among the partners at Price Waterhouse who voted against the female candidate there was a particularly scrupulous individual who asked himself, "Would I be making the same decision if the candidate had been a male with like credentials?"

To answer this question, he need only imagine the decision to concern a male candidate with like credentials. (This requires adjustments to accommodate the new premise—most obviously, denial that the candidate is a woman.) That is, he assimilates the *if*-clause into his own *practical* knowledge base, taking its content, or what it asserts, as *a possible datum for decision making*. It becomes available as a possible reason, as something that may be taken into consideration. He follows the procedure I described in the first of my "simulation" papers:

> To simulate the appropriate practical reasoning I can engage in a kind of *pretend-play*: pretend that the indicated conditions *actually obtain,* with all other conditions remaining (so far as is logically possible and physically probable) as they presently stand; then—continuing the make-believe—try to "make up my mind" what to do given these (modified) conditions.[18]

I am not suggesting that this is always a reliable way to answer questions about one's actions in hypothetical situations. The crucial point for the present paper is this: If the fact that p is assimilated into one's *practical* knowledge base, as something that may be taken into consideration, then it is not beyond one's epistemic horizon. Where this is done "off-line," as in entertaining a counterfactual possibility, it excludes possible worlds in which one does not know or believe that p. Whatever I introduce as a possible premise for decision making, as a fact that may be taken into consideration, I introduce as something *of which I am aware,* as something *known to me* and

therefore *believed by me*. I implicitly restrict possible worlds to my horizon
of knowledge simply by milking the counterfactual premise for its practical
consequences: by thinking, for example,

> Supposing the candidate to be a male, other things being equal: *How
> shall I vote?*

Purely theoretical inference from counterfactual premises does not restrict possible worlds in this way. One may consider, for example, what
would happen if the food one is eating were heavily contaminated with sal-
monella. Using background theoretical beliefs, one might trace the natural
sequelae in one's body without supposing oneself to be aware of them as
they progress.[19]

To milk counterfactual premises for their practical consequences is
child's play. Children's pretend play sets up counterfactual premises for
the main purpose of acting on them—unlike the pure *mind* play of, say,
hypothetico-deductive reasoning. A child engaged in pretend play—a
young child, at least—*always, unavoidably*, restricts possible worlds to her
projected horizon of knowledge. Simply by allowing the explanans, or
the counterfactual antecedent, as input to practical reason, she treats it as
something of which she is aware, thereby excluding possible worlds in
which it lies beyond her horizon of practically available knowledge. She
does so, whether or not she possesses the *concepts* of knowledge and belief. Thus, even a young child explains her own action in terms of a full-
fledged reason, not in terms of a generic noncognitive explanans that befits a flood sewer just as well as a person. What does take conceptual
sophistication is, rather, inclusion of possible worlds *beyond* one's current
horizon of practically available knowledge, that is, worlds in which, as
far as *theoretical* reason is concerned, it is the case that p, even though, so
far as *practical* reason is concerned, it is not (or, epistemically, may not
be) the case that p. To consider such worlds, the pretend-player must engage in a compartmentalized *double* pretense. The child keeps two tracks
going. One of them makes its premises available to practical as well as
theoretical inference, for example, "these globs of mud are tasty pies."
The other confines its premises to a purely theoretical compartment:
"These pies have secret magical powers: Eating such a pie immediately
transforms one into a donkey." The children innocently "eat" their pies;
then, acting out the sequelae of unseen forces, they begin to walk on all
fours and bray.

It is the same with counterfactual thinking and reason explanation. A
double pretense is required—with a corresponding conceptual sophistication, I believe—to include possible worlds beyond one's current horizon of

practically available knowledge, that is, worlds in which, as far as *theoretical* reason is concerned, it is the case that p, even though, so far as *practical* reason is concerned, it is not (or, epistemically, may not be) the case that p. In contrast, simply by *not* running a double pretense, we treat the explanans in a reason explanation as a fact that is known to the agent. We treat the explanans as something known, simply in treating it as something not limited to theoretical reasoning—as something of potential practical significance.[20] This we may do in utter innocence, without using or even possessing the concepts of knowledge and belief. We do it, as I said, just by *not* running a double pretense, thus excluding possible worlds in which there is a divide between fact and belief.

What about explaining the actions of others? You know, of course, what a simulationist will say about that: In the third-person case just as in the first person, one treats the explanans or the counterfactual antecedent as accessible to practical reason. If I conceive the other's situation in its practical aspect, as a situation in which one is to *act*, then I conceive it as a situation of which the other—the individual I am simulating—is aware. Thereby, I exclude possible worlds in which there is a divide between fact and belief—worlds, for example, in which it is not raining but Sam thinks it is, or worlds in which the Price Waterhouse candidate is really *a male candidate successfully passing as female*. Not to exclude these possibilities calls for a double pretense: One track of the pretense (it is really *not* raining, the candidate for promotion is really a male passing as female) is milked only for its theoretical (i.e., nonpractical) consequences: Because it is not raining, poor Sam, needlessly running, *would not get wet* even if he were not running; because the candidate is really a male, the employer has unwittingly exercised his gender bias against *someone of his own sex*. In short, in reason explanations such as,

1. Sam is running because it's raining,

the implicit ascription of a complex epistemic state (e.g., Sam's knowledge that it is raining) is a consequence of *not* performing a certain complex act, that of making some counterfactual premises available to theoretical reasoning but not to simulated practical reasoning.

What I have briefly put forward in this final section is a new account of the *cognitive* dimension of reason explanation, an account I will develop further in another place.[21] The main thrust of this chapter has been to free ST from a stigma earned by some of its predecessors: their failure to recognize that actions *depend on* the reasons for which they are performed. Because this dependence pivots on general features, reason explanations must be implicitly general, a trait they share with explanations in the physical sciences. However, I have argued, against Davidson and many other writers, that the generality that is pertinent to reason explanations is not the generality of a scientific law, which assigns common causal properties to all entities, states, or events of certain kinds. In the Price Waterhouse case, we assume the invariance, not of *law* but of the partners' *general standard or policy*. What is relevant, in general, is the nature of the situation and the nature of the act, and we assume consistency of content, situation types being linked to action types. This provides the rails along which projection rides, from past to future and from actual to counterfactual.[22]

Notes

1. On *Verstehen*, see Schutz 1962; 1967; Von Wright 1971, chap. 1. On reenactment, see Collingwood 1946.

2. Among the more prominent of these philosophers are Dray 1957; Winch 1958; Melden 1961; Anscombe 1957; Taylor 1964; Von Wright 1971. I steer clear of the more common philosophical term "rational explanation" to avoid both its congenital ambiguities and the legacy of refined or technical senses introduced by others. I also avoid Davidson's term "rationalization."

3. Gordon 1995a.

4. Davidson 1963.

5. Davidson further argues that there can be no *psychological* or *psychophysical* laws at all, on the grounds that the assignment of content to beliefs and desires obeys a normative constraint of maximal rationality, which has no place in the application of objective laws of nature.

6. One might accept Davidson's view that reason explanations are a species of causal explanation but deny that all causal relations are backed by laws. I will not be taking a stand here on either question: I will not be denying that reason explanations are causal or that causal explanations are always nomological. (I do deny the conjunction, however; in a later section, I argue that the implicit generality that underlies reason explanations is not nomological.)

7. Kim 1996, pp. 141–142.

8. *Price Waterhouse v. Hopkins*, 490 U.S. 228 (1989).

9. A lower court judge had remarked, "It takes no special training to discern sex stereotyping in a description of an aggressive female employee as requiring "a course at charm school." Nor . . . does it require expertise in psychology to know that, if an employee's flawed "interpersonal skills" can be corrected by a soft-hued suit or a new shade of lipstick, perhaps it is the employee's sex and not her interpersonal skills that has drawn the criticism."

10. They write: "To construe the words "because of" as colloquial shorthand for "but-for causation," as does Price Waterhouse, is to misunderstand them. But-for causation is a hypothetical construct. In determining whether a particular factor was a but-for cause of a given event, we begin by assuming that that factor was

present at the time of the event, and then ask whether, even if that factor had been absent, the event nevertheless would have transpired in the same way."

11. This standard with respect to mixed motive cases was later modified (to plaintiffs' advantage) by the Civil Rights Act of 1991.

12. Thus the Court allowed neither the agent's self-understanding nor the objective behavior pattern to be decisive. Like Davidson, the Court appreciated the logical gap between having a reason one sees as justifying one's action, and acting for or because of that reason. The fact that sexist considerations were allowed to enter into the deliberations may have been symptomatic of the attitudes of many of the partners, attitudes that probably affected the way they "saw" and justified to themselves their decision not to promote. But establishing this leaves open the question whether sexist considerations, or indeed gender considerations of any sort, actually *made a difference* in the decision itself; or whether, on the contrary, legitimate, gender-blind considerations alone would have led to the same decision.

13. I should add that they overstate this position. They say that if legitimate, nondiscriminatory considerations were strong enough to have led to exactly the same decision, then "the existence of systemic discrimination had no effect." As in other cases of overdetermination, it is not correct to say "had no effect"; what would be correct to say is that it had no *differential* effect. For if it had no effect, then it would be equally correct to say that the *legitimate* considerations (lack of leadership qualities, for example) had no effect either; whence, from the conjunction, it follows that *no* considerations had any effect on the decision!

14. Except on a broad construal, perhaps, encompassing what might be called de facto discrimination. That is, there might be a bias toward exclusion of females, or "unfeminine" females, just because a small minority of sexists draws out what would otherwise be an open-and-shut case.

15. Or substitute whatever term is appropriate for counterfactuals, if not "truth."

16. Each of these responses may be put in terms of a desire: because I want to avoid getting drenched/to avoid arriving too late/to be in good shape for the marathon/to live longer.

17. For reasons similar to those given earlier, we should not think of this as a *causal* link.

18. Gordon 1995a, p. 62.

19. This needs qualification. I might infer, for example, from the counterfactual premise that most automobiles are powered by fuel cells, that Sam believes that most automobiles are nonpolluting. I may infer this by a purely theoretical (e.g., nonpractical) inference from "most automobiles are powered by fuel cells" to "most automobiles are nonpolluting." If this inference occurs within the scope of simulation, then an ascent routine yields, "I believe most automobiles are nonpolluting," where "I" refers to Sam, the individual simulated. In that case, I am implicitly restricting possible worlds to Sam's horizon of knowledge, that is, it is implicit that in all possible worlds considered, Sam is aware that most automobiles are powered by fuel cells. In general, a question of scope arises whenever a counterfactual or hypothetical supposition is combined with a simulation—a topic I intend to take up in future work.

20. A very naive animist might do the same, of course, in explaining the sewer's behavior, but few people are likely to reverberate emotionally and motivationally to a sewer's "situation."

21. To be published in the journal *Protosociology*, special issue, "Mental Representation, Ascription of Attitudes and Interpretation: On Contemporary Philosophy of Mind and Language." Forthcoming.

22. Comments by the following people helped me see the need to write the last section of this chapter: Fred Adams, Larry Davis, Joel Anderson, Philip Pettit, Piers Rawling, Carol Slater, Dona Warren, and the editors of this volume.

Chapter Two

The Theory of Holistic Simulation: Beyond Interpretivism and Postempiricism

GEORG VIELMETTER

One of the chief goals of social science is understanding other people's behavior. What is disputed, however, is the question of whether there is some special "operation called Verstehen" and—if so—whether this operation distinguishes the social sciences fundamentally from the natural sciences.

The current competitors in this old *Erklären/Verstehen* debate are interpretivism and postempiricism. Interpretivism holds that understanding other people is a very special operation that separates the social sciences from the natural sciences. Postempiricism regards *all* sciences basically as interpretive and does not find a specialized discipline for interpreting humans. Thus postempiricism holds a new version of scientific monism, whereas interpretivism stubbornly defends a scientific dualism.

I will argue for a position beyond postempiricism and interpretivism. In the main part of this chapter, I will introduce the theory of holistic simulation—a version of simulation theory—as a new and promising account of how we understand human behavior, demonstrating that there is something special about interpreting humans.

However, the fact that understanding is a special way of gaining knowledge about people's behavior does not motivate a strict dualism between the natural and the social sciences. This is so because simulation theory permits a naturalized account of the process of interpretation. In later parts of this paper, I will show some of its consequences for the theory of social science.

In detail, I will proceed as follows: (1) I will introduce simulation theory. (2) I argue that simulation theory allows us a naturalized understanding of the basic mechanisms of interpretation. (3) I then distinguish between dif-

ferent forms of simulation. (4) In light of this account, I introduce the doctrines of both epistemic and semantic holism and elucidate their relevance
for simulation. (5) The outcome is a new version of simulation theory,
which I dub the theory of holistic simulation. Holistic simulation rests on
an "empathetic" method. (6) The theory of holistic simulation regards interpretation as a kind of empathetic observation and enables us to distinguish between two kinds of evidence we use in the process of interpretation. (7) Finally, I argue that this account in interpretation theory blurs the
distinction between observation and participation and thus (8) situates the
theory of understanding beyond interpretivism and postempiricism.

1. Simulation Theory

According to simulation theory (ST), the process of interpreting other
people's behavior rests neither on the (even tacit) application of a theory
nor on rationality. ST claims to give a psychologically much more realistic
and plausible account than theory theories or rationality theories of interpretation,[1] since they concentrate on what people are actually doing in interpreting others.[2] So the basic question simply is: What are they actually
doing?

The answer ST provides is that we exploit *all* our natural and socially acquired resources in interpreting (and predicting) the others' behavior. This
is an informative and discriminating answer, for the alternative theories are
more restricted and emphasize primarily our intellectual and linguistic capacities. Robert Gordon recently dubbed this difference as one between
"cold" and "hot" methodologies:

> Concerning the "theory of mind," or more broadly the methodology by which
> people anticipate and predict another's actions, there are basically two kinds
> of theory. One kind holds that we use what I call a cold methodology: a
> methodology that chiefly engages our intellectual processes, moving by infer-
> ence from one set of beliefs to another, and makes no essential use of our ca-
> pacities for emotion, motivation, and practical reasoning. . . . The other kind
> imputes to us a hot methodology, which exploits one's own motivational and
> emotional resources and one's own capacity for practical reasoning.[3]

In this sense, ST is a hot methodology. It does not focus on theories or rational calculi that we are supposed to apply but primarily on emotional,
motivational, and practical features of the simulator. Note that this does
not imply that theories or rationality play *no* role in interpretation.[4] What
it means is that neither is *basic* to interpretation. Thus understanding interpretation as simulation involves two major shifts. First, it emphasizes the
role of practical and emotional skills and, second, it relativizes this process
to the very person who is actually and currently interpreting.

But why do we call the deployed activity simulation? It is because we simulate the other's situation and behavior, that is, we put ourselves in the other's situation—imaginatively, of course—or, in computerese, off-line.[5] In other words, I project the behavior *I would* show in this situation onto the other, the simulatee (and not the behavior *someone should* show according to some normative standard).

How does it work? Many simulation theorists implicitly or explicitly hold that simulation is based on an implicit inference from simulator to simulatee.[6] The simulator must first identify her own—actual or imaginative—mental states and then concludes that the simulatee is in similar states. According to this position, simulation is finally based on Mill's argument by analogy and thus is characterized by, as Gordon puts it, three central features:

1. an analogical inference from oneself to others
2. premised on introspectively based ascriptions of mental states to oneself
3. requiring prior possession of the concepts of the mental states ascribed[7]

It is my impression that the relativization of the process of interpretation (or at least the emphasis) to the person who is actually and currently interpreting leads many simulation theorists to such a view.[8] Obviously, the implications of the inference by analogy understood this way are extremely problematic; they contradict almost every lesson we learned from philosophers such as Wittgenstein, Ryle, and Quine, among many others. Not surprisingly, some critics branded ST a new version of Cartesianism.[9] Since I think that the arguments against subjectivist and introspectionist views are indeed overwhelming, I will not try to fix what seems to be a hopeless case. Instead, I want to sketch another version of simulation theory that avoids the traps of the analogical inference. In doing so, I will basically rely on Robert Gordon's writings on ST, since Gordon explicitly opposes introspectionist views. My strategy is this: I will demonstrate that in order to interpret other people's behavior by simulating them, interpreters employ neither introspectively based ascriptions of mental states nor concepts of these mental states. Without these suppositions, the inference by analogy becomes unproblematic. This can be shown by an analysis of the role of similarity in the process of interpretation, an aspect Gordon has not yet written about.

2. Naturalizing Similarity

According to simulation theory, we are able to project the behavior we would show in the other's situation and thus simulate her behavior. How can we understand this operation without making use of the dubious inference by analogy? By naturalization. If we were able to show that simulation does not primarily rest on analogical inferences of the simulator but on natural, preconscious capacities due to features of mammalian biology, the core of the interpretive process would be naturalized. Do we have evidence for this?

We have. Let's take one of Gordon's examples to demonstrate the point.[10] Suppose you are hiking in the mountains and your partner suddenly blurts out, "Go back!" She herself immediately and cautiously turns around and you follow her, searching the relevant, which is to say near to middle distant environment especially, for frightening and menacing features. As you then face the grizzly standing at the curve, say, twenty yards away, you instantly realize what's going on—and interpretation ends.

This is an ideal, although common and very easy in the case of intentional, explanation of another's behavior. What the hiker is doing is projecting his own beliefs about the environment on his friend (neglecting the small spatial distance between them). In this sense, he supposes her to perceive the environment in a very similar, ideally identical way. And this yields projective understanding because her behavior would be his given her situation.

Two features of this description are central; first, what we are looking for are not theoretically identifiable but "practically or emotionally relevant features."[11] This search engages the simulator's own practical and emotional responses to features of the environment, thus distinguishing this hot methodology from a cold one deployed, for example, in explaining why a tree in a forest is split. In both cases beliefs about the environment are important, but in the latter we neither project them onto the tree nor connect them with emotional responses.

Second, the supposition that the other hiker perceives the environment in a similar or even identical way need not be interpreted in the inference-by-analogy way. At least, and this is decisive, the simulation process does not basically rest on the analogical assumption. It depends on the similarity of the motivational and emotional responses between simulator and simulatee. Complex beliefs about the world need not necessarily be similar.[12]

A great deal of empirical research in developmental psychology backs the claim that the basic emotional similarity actually exists.[13] We find *imitative mechanisms* already in infants, for example, the smiling response to a smile. There seem to be at least six emotional facial expressions that are universal.[14] Human beings seem to have a natural inclination to reproduce facial expressions they are exposed to, and even partly the correlating emotion.[15] Some other imitative mechanisms may even play a role in content ascription:

> One such mechanism is mimicry of perceptual orientation, especially gaze mimicry: When conspecifics are seen gazing intently in a particular direction, especially with a display of emotion, human beings—like other primates, apparently, and many other mammals—tend to look in the same direction, where 'same direction' may have to be determined by triangulation. By getting us to see 'through the other's eyes', this imitative mechanism facilitates identifying the situational cause or 'object' of the other's action or emotion: 'Ah, there's something moving through the bushes, *that's* why he is running.' *The existence of such automatic aids suggests that the readiness for simulation is a prepacked 'module' called upon automatically in the perception of conspecifics and perhaps members of other species.*[16]

Of course, imitative mechanisms of that kind are not actions presupposing language, rationality, or theories, but biologically fixed, automatic mechanisms. Nonetheless, they seem to be able to yield the kind of similarity that ST needs to be right.[17] Similarity is no longer argued for by the dubious analogical argument, but *naturalized:* Interpretations as simulations get started simply due to the biological fact that humans and other primates are similarly constructed. Similarity thus refers to *neurobiologically fixed mechanisms of perception.* That makes it possible for humans and other higher mammals to *automatically identify* and *empathetically understand the (expressive) situation of conspecifics.* This is an interesting result, since it gives concepts such as empathy, or *Nachbildung,* which have been unduly slighted by purely linguistically oriented philosophy, a naturalistic basis.[18]

Therefore, the basis of the process of interpretation is an activity, a skill, or a capacity that has its foundation in the contingent but factual biological constitution of humans and other higher mammals. In this sense, ST is a *naturalization of interpretation.* Nature simply provides us with the capacity for projective changes of perspectives and empathetic, imitative duplications of (emotional) situations of others. This basic *empathetic method,* and not theories or laws, is what yields the explanatory understanding we are looking for and makes us—as Gordon notes[19]—see the connection between explanans and explanandum.

Note that even if simulation is basically a *first-person method,* the above explication enables us to see why it is *not a one-person method.*[20] This distinction is most important, since it allows us to flee the solipsistic trap. Gordon refers to it when he speaks of a "shift on the egocentric map" the simulator is performing.[21] The simulator does *not* infer—neither theoretically nor analogically nor rationally—to mental states of the simulatee but *evokes* them, the other's most basic mental states in himself, by deploying the empathetic method. In this sense, the simulator *becomes,* off-line, of course, the other person, or, more precisely, he becomes his *Doppelgänger.* And in the easiest, the routine cases of interpretation, that's all the simulator has to do.

3. The Forms of Simulation: Total and Partial

These easy cases may be dubbed situative simulation or—as Gordon calls them—"total projection."[22] Situative simulation, because we examine only the simulatee's situation without paying attention to particular, especially deviant personal traits; total projection because we project without any adjustments.[23] Theoretically more complex are personal simulations or partial projections, in which we must care about personal features of the simulatee. In general, in these simulations our expectations are not satisfied. If, for example, the friend on the hike neither looks scared nor starts to flee but appears interested, sits down, and takes out her notebook, and we again connect this behavior to a grizzly standing twenty yards away, most of us would find this behavior strange. The environmental features we suppose caused her behavior don't seem to fit. In other words, the states we evoke in ourselves with the help of the empathetic method do not make much sense to us *automatically* as a reaction to facing a grizzly. In order to obtain an understanding of the simulatee's behavior we need to deploy *further knowledge.* I will argue later that we do *not* face *any* restrictions here. Let us assume first that we know our hiker to be an intrepid naturalist. If we activate that knowledge, we will easily understand why she shows interest, sits down, and takes notes.[24] We will not have a problem supplying ourselves with the relevant intrepid-naturalist beliefs, desires, and emotions and thus performing an intrepid-naturalist simulation.

Gordon emphasizes that even in partial projections semantic knowledge need not play a role within simulations. The fact that we evoke in the one case interest and attention but in the other fear and fright makes no difference in the process of simulation. This is right and important. In both cases I deploy the empathetic method to identify relevant states of the other. We do not need "conceptual sophistication" for this task.[25] This is the basic reason why ST cannot be reduced to a theory theory.[26]

Whereas Gordon focuses on biologically fixed features of the simulation process, I would like to shed some light on social and semantic components. We have seen that the natural and basic part of simulations—what I called the empathetic method—is not sufficient for a successful simulation. Especially in the case of partial simulations we have to deploy further knowledge, and this is, at least in important parts, social and semantic knowledge. "Readiness for simulation" comes in a prepacked, biologically fixed module, but not the successful result. In order to use the information that our hiker is an intrepid naturalist, the least we have to know is the *meaning* of the words "intrepid" and "naturalist." We need this kind of information as *evidence* in higher forms of simulation. And with this, the simulation process is penetrated by a kind of knowledge that is very different from the one gained by automatic mechanisms and is more exposed to traditional epistemological and semantic problems.[27]

4. Holism

The most important doctrine that comes into play now is *holism,* both epistemic and semantic. This is not the place to go into details regarding the problems and obscurities of holism, and so I just want to introduce some distinctions I regard as crucial in this context. By doing this, I confine myself also to forms of holism that are less disputed than others (or so I hope).[28]

By "semantic holism" I intend two doctrines: the holism of meaning identification and the holism of meaning ascription. The latter holds that we are just able to ascribe the meaning of an utterance to a speaker if we are able to relate this utterance to other utterances and other behavioral evidence. The former claims—at a more basic level—that we are only able to identify the meaning of a sentence with reference to other sentences of that language.

Epistemic, or verification, holism consists in the well-known Quinian thesis that we are unable to test a single sentence of a theory in isolation. Instead, we always verify at least "a block of theory as a whole," since we are always able to save a specific sentence in the light of recalcitrant experience by reinterpreting this sentence or giving up others.[29] The basic argument for verification holism is the claim that observation sentences are theory-laden.[30] If the meaning of sentences is identifiable only by its place in a theory, or language, then sentences are interpretable in various ways. There is no direct method for either verification or falsification. This makes clear that the distinction between epistemic and semantic holism is purely heuristic; both derive from the same argument. Therefore, we are allowed to use "language" and "theory" interchangeably in this context, as Quine often does.

5. The Theory of Holistic Simulations

Holism is important in this context because the process of simulation is not restricted to the empathetic method. We need to deploy further knowledge, which is basically linguistic or linguistically couched and thus holistic. As a consequence, simulations become underdetermined and have to be interpreted antirealistically, or so I will argue.

As already mentioned, the employment of further knowledge is crucial, particularly in partial projections. If my companion coolly sits down after facing a grizzly, I have a problem: I am puzzled and do not know exactly how to go on and how to treat her. Simulation as intentional explanation or interpretation is in the first place a problem-solving activity or, as John Passmore puts it, "the explanation sets out to resolve my puzzlement."[31] Whereas in total projection the problem of understanding another's behavior is solved immediately after it appeared, in partial projection the situation is more complicated when the behavior of the simulatee turns out to be unexpected and is not easily connectable to potential causes in the environment.

Thus in partial projection we need further *evidence* to understand the other's behavior. Such evidence could be the preceding knowledge that the hiker is an intrepid naturalist. But even then we have multiple possibilities of how to go on. We can, for example (and probably most likely), tell the typical belief-desire story: She wants to do some research on grizzlies and/or become famous, believes grizzlies are not as dangerous as is commonly supposed, has a vocational interest, and so on. We could also substitute the process of interpretation by the application of a (in a more narrow sense) scientific theory. Imagine I recently read a new book called *Why Naturalists Are Weird: A Neurobiological Explanation* and learned that we have overwhelming evidence for the thesis that naturalists automatically pull out notebooks and sit down as soon as they face a grizzly because of a rare and peculiar brain anomaly. Nearly all naturalists' brains are anomalous in this way, and neurobiological theory tells us that sitting down and pulling out something is due to this defect. Having this information, I can (and I probably will) stop further simulation and substitute it for this theory.

Most importantly, note that we do not substitute simulation *as a whole* for a theory, that is, we do not give up the first-person perspective in favor of a third-person perspective right from the beginning. Even in those cases, learning about the most basic mental states of the simulatee by deploying the empathetic method remains fundamental. This is the reason for this approach's being a version of a simulation theory: Knowledge gained by the empathetic method is regarded as the entering wedge of interpretation; it is a necessary, though not sufficient, condition of understanding others. Depending on the case, this knowledge plays a bigger or smaller role, but it can never be neglected in order to get the interpretation started. However, I think it is right to regard this version as a hybrid one, since semantic and/or theoretical knowledge definitely plays a role in the interpretive process.

The most interesting consequence of this structure of the simulation process epistemically is that the outcome of a simulation should be understood in a *nonrealistic* way. As I see it, simulations are not able to yield realistically understood knowledge and understanding of another's behavior because of the second component of each simulation process, namely, the (implicitly or explicitly used) empirical, semantic, or theoretical knowledge. The genetically first component, prelinguistic knowledge of another's states delivered by the empathetic method, can be understood realistically. This knowledge is "biologically fixed" in a way that makes it reliable by nature. However, the second component, the further needed knowledge, is not fixed in an analogous way but rather is dependent on culture and language—if our doctrines of holism and theory-ladenness of observation sentences are taken for granted.[32] This distinguishes my version of ST from many others that interpret simulation in a more or less realistic way. I want to dub this version the theory of *holistic simulation.*

6. Two Kinds of Evidence

Simulation theory enables us to explain central conditions and the basic process of interpretation naturalistically. Interpretation does not start with a theoretical description of another's mental states but with an empathetic *Nachbilden* or *Nachempfinden* of them with the help of genetically fixed, automatic mechanisms. Doing this does not require either mental concepts or explicit knowledge of mental states. We are just doing what comes naturally. This pretheoretic praxis or capacity makes it possible for us to understand which situation the other is in. Since the empathetic method is a first-person but not a one-person method, it is able to bridge the gap between simulator and simulatee without deploying either a theory or a linguistic (and therewith again a theory-laden) discourse. This entails the following: *If* pretheoretic evidence is possible, then it is possible only with the help of the empathetic method.

Certainly, simulation is not able to avoid the behavioral circle we encounter in every bit of interpretation. Beliefs, wants, goals, and their connections are identifiable or attributable only with reference to the other's behavior (including speech behavior, of course). We simply lack a direct link to his mind. But the naturalization of the empathetic method allows us a direct, imaginative identification of at least simple wants and emotional expressions. *And these states are able to serve as direct, pretheoretic evidence.* Being afraid, startled, interested, concentrated, curious, or escape seeking, for example, are states we are able to "observe" directly—we can "read them in the other's face"—insofar as we instantly evoke them in ourselves and thus understand them immediately—noninferentially and nonintrospectively but rather naturally and imaginatively. These data are the most objective evidence we have in understanding and explaining other people's behavior. And we also need these data, for example, in order to apply our neurobiological naturalist–grizzly theory: If this theory is to explain anything at all, we must know in advance that this is a case the theory applies to. So these empathetically acquired data are the first and most natural evidence for the explanation of behavior. I will call it evidence$_1$. Evidence$_1$, the basic feature and condition of interpretation, is due to the biological constitution of higher mammals. So interpretation is basically a *natural process* controlled by our hard wiring.

But note first and most importantly that evidence$_1$ is, though necessary, not sufficient for interpretations. In and of itself it cannot yield the connections we need in order to understand behavior. I can see that my companion runs away frightened or sits down full of interest. I can recognize, via gaze mimicry, that in either case she first stared at this specific object. So I will automatically establish a connection between these events and consider the perception of this object the cause of fear. And depending on what reaction the perception of that object evokes in me, I will either successfully stop (total projection) or actually just (re)start (partial projection) my effort of understanding.

This is the place at which social contingencies come into play. For it is all but natural that the grizzly causes fear. We learn that bears are (supposed to be) dangerous, and probably it is a natural reaction of sorts to run away from danger. If things are dangerous, we tend to run away. The crucial question is when the antecedent is true. There may be some more or less universally frightening events like fire, but these are exceptions. Nigel Barley remarks that the Dowayos, a mountain tribe in northern Cameroon, show great fear toward chameleons and owls but are unafraid of scorpions and snails.[33] Crucial for understanding another's behavior is not its objective but its social or subjective adequacy, respectively. We have empirical and theoretical evidence (which belong to a group I will soon call evidence$_2$) for claiming that owls are actually harmless, whereas scorpions and grizzlies are more harmful. But this is irrelevant in this specific explanation of behavior, since humans do not at first and at most believe true sentences.

The fact that I stop further interpretive efforts if my companion demonstrates fear in facing this object is simply due to the fact that *I* am afraid of grizzlies (subjective adequacy) or that *I* know that most people are afraid of grizzlies (social adequacy). So I *expect* spontaneously the other's fear. The simulator's expectations serve as evidence in interpretations and decide whether a simulation can be performed *easily* or not. But (as I will explain below) expectations are different in structure from evidence$_1$, so we may dub them evidence$_2$. Interpretation succeeds easily in case we have specific expectations because evidence$_1$ and evidence$_2$ together are sufficient for explanations of behavior. Evidence$_1$ allows a basic identification of mental states, and evidence$_2$ connects them in a sense-making way with events in the world, which are considered causes of that specific behavior.

But the set of applicable evidence$_2$ does not just consist of expectations. Together with evidence$_1$, the latter are in fact sufficient but *not* necessary for an understanding of another's behavior. This is because expectations can be substituted. Only evidence$_1$ is necessary and is therefore most important. In many cases, expectations as evidence are not even available, namely, always if our expectations are contravened. I expect neither the cool, relaxed naturalist nor the panicky Dowayo facing an owl. As already noted, in such a case I need to activate further external knowledge. This knowledge may consist of *everything*—from biographical material about my companion to highly complex theories about kinship relations of the Dowayos, from diaries to results of experimental brain research. This material belongs to the set of all possible evidence$_2$ as well.

Why do we distinguish between these two kinds of evidence used in the interpretive process? Because they are different in structure. Evidence$_1$ is acquired by using the first-person, empathetic method. But since this is not a one-person method, that evidence is *transsubjective,* anchored in human nature, biologically understood. What on the one hand privileges it epistemically makes it on the other hand more complicated: its atheoretical and prelinguistic character. Evidence$_1$ is contingent just in the narrow sense: Phylogenetically everything could have run differently. But it hasn't, and so this contingency does not play any role here—possible worlds do not help comprehend how real people do understand other real people. Since evidence$_1$ is prelinguistic, it is free of holistic problems. But this privilege has its obscurity. Its prelinguistic character makes it *as* evidence$_1$ *incommunicable;* an evidence$_1$ does not even have truth-value. I as simulator evoke these evidential states in myself in this specific situation. Though evidence$_1$ is *trans*subjective, it is not *inter*subjective in a common sense: I cannot argue for it in a discursive process. In some sense, it is bound to me *personally*.

Contrary to evidence$_1$, evidence$_2$ is contingent in a social sense. Exactly which expectations we have depends on our preknowledge. This again depends partly on individual cognitive competencies and partly on socially acquired knowledge. Whether I interpret this object over there as an evil grizzly or a good-natured god of the forest, a fascinating endangered species, a grizzly hood, or an undetached grizzly part, is in principle an open question. All we know is that I will interpret it *as* something. We are able to perceive objects in the world as similar; in this sense there are sensually perceivable similarity structures in the world, which also make it possible for us to learn a language.[34] Yet the meaning of the words that we use to refer to these objects is not determined by these structures, but holistically by language–internal references. Thus the expectation of an adequate reaction to a dangerous grizzly or a good-natured goddess is dependent on socially acquired and holistic meaning knowledge. It then follows that expectations which serve as evidence in interpretations (allow-

ing us to establish a connection between evidence₁ and further features of
the situation) show an epistemic problem complementary to the one of
evidence₁: On the one hand, they are social and linguistic in character and
thus underdetermined and probably indeterminate (on my interpretation
of holism). But on the other hand, they are communicable and thus open
in principle for intersubjective argumentations.³⁵

The knowledge we need to use when our expectations are contravened is
of the same epistemic character. It is different from expectations simply in
light of the fact that we did not assume that it would be relevant in this specific simulation or that we even have to acquire it; this may be a psychologically, but not an epistemically relevant, difference, especially since we will
incorporate this knowledge in future expectations. Relying on this material,
we now either perform a simulation with modifications in attitude and
facts ("I am an intrepid naturalist. What will I do?" "Over there stands the
good-natured god of the forests. What will I do?") or we substitute the interpretation process—*after* deploying the empathetic method—for a theory.
Note, first, that at this point of the simulation process the path that we take
is absolutely open and, second, that modifications within simulations may
be guided by theories. The factual modification that, for example, a specific
tribe considers, say, scorpions good-natured goddesses of the mountains is
part of a cultural anthropological theory based on interpretations of behavior. Here we face a nesting phenomenon: Simulations of behavior of these
people lead cultural anthropologists to (holistic) theories, which again can
serve as material within other simulations.³⁶

So simulators are able to both modify simulations through every form of
knowledge and substitute them for a theory. What they are going to do is
free in principle. The answer to the question of when a simulation may be
regarded as successful depends on the criteria for success. I can see two different ones: correct prediction and understanding. Whereas the first is relatively easy to operationalize and confirm, the second is more complicated.
This is due to the fact that understanding via simulation is a function of a
simulator's own expectations, knowledge, beliefs, emotions, and psychic
structure. In everyday life, a simulator gains understanding of another's behavior if he is able to connect evidence₁ with evidence₂ in a way that is similar to things he already knows, whereas in social science, we seek an adequate and not merely familiar understanding.³⁷

7. Beyond Observation and Participation

What are the consequences of holistic simulation theory for interpretation
in social science? We saw that interpretation as holistic simulation is a practical ability, or a competence, rather than a theory. We gain knowledge of
expressions, simple wants, and maybe simple opinions empathetically in-

stead of by deploying a rational calculus. Starting with them, we ascribe at first behavioral similarity, not rationality. Such ascription distinguishes interpretations with respect to humans and maybe some primates from every other explanatory strategy. If one is—like Daniel Dennett[38]—inclined to call this a "stance," then it is the natural, biologically conditioned stance. From that follows a genetic priority of ST that also has, I suggest, some epistemological consequences. Only simulation is able to access evidence$_1$, which is the basis for interpreting and thus understanding other people. Neither physical nor functional explanations are able to do so. Since evidence$_1$ is transsubjective, simulation gets an objective component that the other strategies lack.

Contrary to most other approaches, simulation is an explanatory strategy that does not proceed from a purely third-person observer perspective but is performed from an empathetic first-person perspective. Though this may look like the old methodologically dualistic distinction between observer and participant, it actually is not. For empathy is not participation, as it is understood by adherents of participatory approaches, that is, as an intersubjective, or communicative, in any case first-person plural or second-person singular enterprise. So simulation elides the traditional participant-observer distinction. It merely exploits the fact that the object under scrutiny shares many features with us scrutinizers, so that we are able to understand it in part directly and have some evidence we lack in other cases. This is of course not to say that a participatory approach is worthless in principle but that it is neither basic nor unavoidable. In any case, we do not need it to gain the necessary knowledge of basic mental states, as many of its adherents claim.

We may understand interpretations/holistic simulations as *empathetic observations*. Of course we need some descriptions in intentional terms in order to understand the other's behavior, but these we get quasi-automatically by deploying the empathetic method. It enables us to interpret behavioral states directly as specific mental states without more ado. This is why I speak of empathetic observation: We get this information more or less for free, by empathetically observing the other. Nothing more is needed.

The dualist might raise an objection at this point: But don't we *in fact* speak with the other? Don't we *actually* "participate in discourse"? No doubt we do, even fairly often. But what follows from that? Philosophically, the relevant point is that it is not required for coping with, explaining, and understanding another's behavior. In many cases, it would be a waste of time (and even foolish) to neglect such a source of information, but such comments of every kind of the persons under scrutiny is, in my terminology, "just" evidence$_2$. So utterances of the person we attempt to understand serve as evidence but do not enjoy a special, epistemically privileged status. Although important, they are not more important than any other type of evidence. In this respect, self-description or communication is on a par with neurobiological theories.

Let me briefly demonstrate the force of the theory of holistic simulation and the role of empathetic observation by a now well known example: Renato Rosaldo's analysis of head-hunting, which the Ilongot men of northern Luzon, Phillipines, used to practice. Rosaldo reports that when you ask an Ilongot man why he cuts off human heads

> his answer is a one-liner on which no anthropologist can really elaborate: he says that rage, born out of grief, impells him to kill his fellow human beings. The act of severing and tossing away the victim's head enables him, he says, to vent and hopefully throw away the anger of his bereavement. The job of cultural analysis, then, is to make this man's statement plausible and comprehensive. Yet further questioning reveals that he has little more to say about the connections between bereavement, rage, and headhunting, connections that seem so powerful to him as to be self-evident beyond explication. Either you understand it or you don't. And, in fact, for the longest time I simply did not.[39]

Rosaldo studied the Ilongot for many years and tried to do what a scientific anthropologist is obliged to do: give a narrative explanation of the Ilongot men behavior, constructing a "thick description" in Clifford Geertz's sense, that is, telling a coherent story of the other's action by relying on observation, participation, communication, and theories, and therewith searching for the cultural meaning and relevance of the natives' behavior. But Rosaldo failed; he was simply not able to deliver the expected story.

Things changed after a devastating loss that Rosaldo experienced. His wife, anthropologist Michelle Rosaldo, died during field research. For the first time in his life, Rosaldo was in a situation emotionally close to that of the (older) Ilongot men: He was enraged and learned what grief and bereavement really consist of. As a consequence, Rosaldo's explanatory problem changed dramatically. He no longer had to understand a behavior that was totally strange to him and even explicated in a very obscure way. All of a sudden, Rosaldo was able to empathize with the Ilongot, at least in some fundamental respects. To put it in the jargon of ST, Rosaldo was no longer forced to rely (unsuccessfully) on theories, communication, and observation (evidence$_2$) but was able to perform a partial projection using mental (especially emotional) states he could identify in the other and now evoke in himself (evidence$_1$). This is evidence for my claim that a specific similarity is needed in order to understand another's behavior. And obviously, some parts of this similarity—for example, in case of grief and bereavement—are acquired in later years.[40] Due to the cultural difference, Rosaldo could not of course perform a total projection let alone perform the Ilongots' behavior. But this is not necessary to get an interpretation started. What is necessary is the ability to empathize; knowledge and theories about the structure and culture of the Ilongot society come second.

8. Beyond Postempiricism and Interpretivism

My argument leads me to the conclusion that there is no absolutely privileged method for the social sciences—pace interpretivism—and furthermore, that the distinction between social and natural sciences is blurred, even if—pace postempiricism—simulation based on the empathetic method is fundamental.[41]

The empathetic method is fundamental because it is based on the biological constitution of higher mammals. As far as I see, the only reliable way to gain knowledge of mental states is thus prelinguistic and therefore noncontingent. Moreover, it allows us to understand the process of interpretation in a naturalized, empirical, nonnormative, and nonidealistic way.

I started with the premise that understanding the behavior of human beings is one of the two chief goals of what we call social science (the other chief goal is prediction). If I am right that simulation based on the empathetic method is what we regularly and reliably apply in understanding fellow human beings, then there is indeed something special about this ability. At the very least, simulation is the first method because it comes quasi-naturally and yields a specific kind of evidence. Since we normally prefer to do what comes naturally, why not in this case?

However, this is not to be read as contradicting postempiricist morals, especially its antidualism. I offer three arguments why this is so. First, understanding and predicting are two different kettles of fish. No doubt, we have seen that simulation can also predict human behavior, but there is no reason why it does so exclusively. Dennett is right that we are able to treat humans as physical or functional systems, if we regard that as useful. And in any case, a good reason for doing so is the ability to predict.

Second, though ST is based on a similarity between simulator and simulatee, it does not hypostatize this connection—as many interpretivists do—to a subject-subject relationship, as opposed to a subject-object relationship, and thus conclude that every other method is wrong. Though simulations gain something objective (or transsubjective) by relying on evidence$_1$, I claimed that the output of a simulation is not to be understood realistically to the extent that evidence$_2$ works holistically. Other methods, which do not take evidence$_1$ into account but concentrate instead on, say, physical or biochemical features or pure behavior, do in fact miss something objective. But this is not a problem in principle. In order to regard these methods as simply wrong, one has to hold one of two claims: (1) that one method is capable of grasping an object, phenomenon, or system in its *totality* or (2) that specific features *have to* be dealt with. I have no idea how to understand the first claim if we don't want to invoke entities like the *Weltgeist* or the God's-eye view. The second claim is wrong as well, at least taken unqualifiedly. From an epistemological perspective, it depends on one's epistemic purpose. A social scientist who wants to predict behavior should, in my opinion, at least begin with a simulation—chances are high it will provide a head start. Should that social scientist object, I have no epistemic reason to think that he will fail. Things are different if gaining understanding is the aim, for here starting with simulation seems to be unavoidable. In order to make sense of a conspecific's behavior, we exploit the natural (minimal) similarity between them, thereby gaining knowledge of basic emotional and other mental states. At least this seems to be epistemically necessary. To construct the other as maximally similar beyond that is again a pragmatic matter.

Finally, there is a third reason why this approach does not contradict postempiricism: When simulation may be applied is an open empirical question. Of course, humans are the natural target of simulative activities. But note that "humans" is much broader than "persons" in the ordinary sense, which excludes such individuals as babies and some mentally disabled conspecifics. Moreover, since the capacity to simulate is a feature of the biological constitution of higher primates, we may apply simulation also to some nonhumans, if they demonstrate the necessary expressive similarity. It is even conceivable to address artifacts that way, again if we find enough expressive similarity. Grant, counterfactually, the robot Lt. Commander Data, an officer of Star Trek's Next Generation crew, who is hardly distinguishable from humans (except for his phenomenal memory and somewhat clumsy way of speaking). Since his expressive, verbal, and other behaviors are alike, we are able to simulate him holistically and observe him empathetically. Biological constitution yields an argument for why ST works, but it is not restricted in principle to biologically similar systems. Simulation theory works with all behaviorally similar systems.

9. Conclusions

Given that understanding is a chief aim of social science, simulation comes naturally. The reason is simple: Like their conspecifics, social scientists are simulators, which means that humans don't start with a theory or with standards of rationality for understanding other human beings but proceed most fundamentally in an empathetic and imaginative way. However, since simulation consists of two parts—knowledge gained by deploying the empathetic method and further, external knowledge that goes holistic—the result of simulations is not realistically true. Moreover, theories can play an important role within simulations, after having deployed the empathetic method. But the latter part seems to be unsubstitutable in order to yield understanding.

Simulationism, however, does not reinvoke the old distinction between natural and social sciences. Even if we hold that it is basic for understanding, simulations may be applicable to nonhumans that show enough expressive similarity as well. This alone blurs the distinction between social sciences and natural sciences, for simulation may be applicable in, for example, biology, especially zoology. Moreover, though simulation comes naturally, this is not to say that other methods are wrong. Especially for the predictive goal of social sciences, functionally and theoretically, even physical explanations developed in natural sciences may be helpful. Holistic simulation blurs both sides of the old distinction.[42]

Notes

1. I discuss this in detail in Vielmetter 1998, chaps. 2–5.

2. Goldman 1995a; 1993.

3. Gordon 1996a, p. 11.

4. For this reason my version of simulation theory may be called a "hybrid" one: It contains theoretical and discursive elements, even if simulation is basic. I will elaborate on this point below.

5. Actually, both of these terms are slightly incorrect, since, as I will explain below, in simulating we mostly evoke some emotional states in ourselves.

6. Cf., for example, Goldman 1995a; 1995c; Heal 1995a; Harris 1989; 1992.

7. Gordon 1995b, p. 53. Gordon characterizes this view but opposes it, as will become clear in the next sections.

8. Versions of this inference can be found, I think, for example, in Goldman 1995a; 1995c; Heal 1995a; Harris 1989; 1992.

9. Cf. Perner and Howes 1992.

10. Gordon 1995c.

11. Gordon 1995c, p. 103.

12. Gordon wants to include beliefs in the basic simulative process. I think this is right insofar as we simply project our beliefs on the simulatee in easy cases of interpretation. However, in general I am skeptical about this claim due to epistemological considerations I will discuss in sections 5–6. It will become clear that the epistemic status of (at least most of our) beliefs is different from that of emotions.

13. Cf. in general Harris 1989; for the role of imitation Meltzoff and Moore 1983; Meltzoff and Gopnik 1993; Meltzoff 1995. For a good overview about newer psychological research on empathy cf. Eisenberg and Strayer 1987.

14. Cf. Harris 1989, chap. 1.

15. For this reason "off-line" or "imaginative" is slightly incorrect.

16. Gordon 1995c, p. 113; emphasis on the last sentence is mine.

17. These mechanisms allow us to identify differences as well. Differences play an important role in partial projections, which I will discuss in the next section.

18. I am aware of the fact that such a claim is disputed. James Averill, for example, is of the opinion that emotions are social constructions (cf. Averill 1980). Yet there is empirical evidence that a basic expressive similarity actually exists. Cross-cultural studies do at least back up Darwin's claim that feelings are often visible in the face. Paul Ekman demonstrated that for certain facial emotional expressions (happiness, sadness, anger, disgust, surprise, and fear) the case for universality is hard to resist (cf. Ekman 1973; Ekman and Friesen 1971). Research in developmental psychology supports this claim (cf. Harris 1989, pp. 10–25). Averill himself concedes that there are some biological determinants of emotion and that "standard emotional reactions vary along a continuum, one end of which is anchored in biological systems, and the other end of which is anchored in sociocultural systems" (Averill 1980, p. 64). This statement at least relativizes a radical constructivist claim, and I do not see that it necessarily opposes a more nativist claim toward *some* basic emotions.

19. Gordon 1995c, p. 115.

20. Note that talking of a first-person method or perspective should not be understood exactly the way this expression is meant in the hermeneutic tradition, for example, in Schleiermacher or Dilthey. For these authors, a first-person perspective presupposes a developed, self-conscious subject that understands a similar structured subject by analogical inferences.

I mentioned earlier that this version of ST does not interpret the empathetic process in an analogical way. However, talking of a first-person perspective with regard to children may be misleading, for children are not yet able to perform what Robert Gordon calls "comprehending self ascriptions" (cf. Gordon 1995c; 1996a); they are not able to realize that ascripted beliefs, desires, and emotions may be false. I cannot follow this point here. Nevertheless, I want to mention that simulation theorists are not in a worse position than rationality theorists or theory theorists—on the contrary. The latter are confronted with what Paul Churchland calls the "problem of the early stages": How do babies acquire rationality or theories (cf. Churchland 1979, sec. 19)? Contrary to their opponents, simulation theorists have some promising ideas for answering these psychogenetic questions. Cf. Gordon 1995b; 1995c; 1996a; Vielmetter 1998, pp. 238–250.

21. Gordon 1995b, p. 56; 1995c.

22. Gordon 1995c, p. 102.

23. This is, of course, idealized. We always need to adjust a little bit, primarily spatial perspectives. But this is without any further theoretical relevance, especially because the distinction between total and the soon-to-be-introduced partial projection is a gradual and not a principled one.

24. This example also makes clear why the difference between total and partial projection is a function of preceding expectations. If I had turned myself into an intrepid naturalist in advance, a total projection would have been sufficient to understand the simulatee in this case. Therefore, the form and outcome of simulations is heavily dependent on the particular person who performs it.

25. Gordon 1995c, p. 114f.

26. In this sense, the empathetic method as the basic part of simulations is not—to use Pylyshyn's term (1984, p. 133)—"cognitively penetrable." Stich and Nichols (1992, pp. 66ff.) hold that simulation-based accounts are cognitively impenetrable,

that is, not dependent on the interpreter's knowledge or ignorance of the domain, whereas information-based accounts like theory theories are. This is clearly a misunderstanding. As I will argue soon, simulations consist of two parts; only the first, the empathetic method, is cognitively impenetrable.

27. To be sure, total projections—the easy cases of simulation—rely on this kind of knowledge as well. We just do not use it explicitly or problematize it in these cases because our expectations are absolutely fulfilled. Therefore, the empathetic part of simulation is most crucial in those cases.

28. My impression is that a vast majority of both analytic and continental philosophers subscribe to holism in one form or another. However, there is a stubborn and sophisticated critique, most influentially by Jerry Fodor and Ernest Lepore (1992). Cf. also (the, to my mind, more thorough) chap. 3 in Fodor 1987. Other critics are, for example, Adolf Grünbaum 1976 and Michael Devitt 1993.

29. Quine's two best-known pieces in this respect are Quine 1963; 1971. Even Fodor does not object to this thesis (Fodor 1987, p. 64f.).

30. I hasten to add that this is oversimplified, as are these passages in general. Quine himself does not subscribe to a full-fledged holism but tries, as is well known, to rescue his "holism cum empiricism" by deploying observation sentences that are conditioned to stimulary situations. He later introduced the distinction between "holophrastic" and "analyzed" observation sentences; the latter are supposed to be theory-laden, whereas the former are not (cf. Quine 1986; 1992). As I see it, this distinction is important to solve what Paul Roth called "the paradox of language learning," but I cannot follow this discussion here (cf. Roth 1978; 1987). So if I speak of "observation sentences," I mean analyzed ones in Quine's sense, which are theory-laden.

31. Passmore 1962, p. 107.

32. I am aware of the fact that Quine himself (who is the chief reference for these theses) would not subscribe to an antirealistic interpretation of holism and theory-ladenness. I developed these claims in Vielmetter 1998, esp. chap. 4, relying on Paul Roth's Quine interpretation (cf. Roth 1978; 1984; 1987) and on Mary Hesse's resemblance theory (cf. Hesse 1980, chaps. 3, 7). Anyway, if someone does not accept an antirealistic interpretation of holism, the theory of holistic simulations is not touched in a negative way. The structure of the theory is neutral concerning the realism–antirealism debate.

33. Barley 1986, chap. 10.

34. Cf. Mary Hesse's resemblance theory; cf. Hesse 1974, pp. 46ff.; 1980, pp. 66ff.

35. The different epistemic status I attribute to evidence$_1$ and evidence$_2$ does not imply a different epistemic dignity. It is at least misleading to interpret that evidence$_1$ is "real" because it is biologically fixed, whereas evidence$_2$ is "unreal" due to its social and linguistic origin. All I hold is that evidence$_1$ is a natural phenomenon due to phylogenesis, and evidence$_2$ is a cultural phenomenon delivered by enculturation, socialization, and theory. To conclude from this that evidence$_2$ is unreal presupposes a reductionist version of naturalism or materialism I don't want to be associated with.

36. One may ask why this theory is naturalistic, given that evidence$_1$—pretheoretic knowledge gained by genetically fixed mechanisms—is in any case transformed

by culturally acquired knowledge (evidence$_2$). As I mentioned above, I think that evidence$_1$ is the entering wedge to interpretation. So the starting point of interpretation is due to phylogenesis: the naturally given similarity between systems of the same kind. This is naturalistic in at least two respects: Interpretation is given a materialistic, biological basis, and interpretation can be understood in an antidualistic way. For details, cf. Vielmetter 1998, introduction, chap. 5.

37. For details, cf. Vielmetter 1998, chap. 5. There I also show that we can derive a new principle of interpretation from this structure of understanding, which I call *the principle of maximal similarity*.

38. Dennett 1987.

39. Rosaldo 1984, p. 178.

40. Obviously, this analysis has interesting consequences for the epistemic situation of social science, for it allows personal experience and emotion to become part of the scientific process. Cf. Vielmetter 1998, pp. 321–333.

41. Postempiricism is a position developed in philosophy of science, of knowledge, and of language and is primarily due to W. V. Quine, Thomas Kuhn, and Mary Hesse, among others. From empiricism, it takes the belief that there is no interesting split between social and natural sciences, that is, the subject matter of the two is not considered intrinsically and substantially distinct. From interpretivism, postempiricism learned to appreciate the important role of interpretation in science. In this sense, postempiricism is a combination of empiricism plus interpretivism: *All* sciences are regarded as basically interpretive. Therefore, postempiricism holds a *new* scientific monism (which does not imply a methodological monism). Due to space limitations, I will just mention the doctrine of holism, understanding it as implying both the thesis of underdetermination of empirical theories by data and the thesis of theory-ladenness of observation sentences, as the basic argument for postempiricism. For details, cf. Hesse 1980; Vielmetter 1998, chaps. 4–5.

42. For helpful criticism of previous versions of this article I am indebted to Joel Anderson, Jim Bohman, Larry Davis, Bob Gordon, Bert Kögler, Paul Roth, and Karsten Stueber.

Chapter Three

Imitation or the Internalization of Norms: Is Twentieth-Century Social Theory Based on the Wrong Choice?

STEPHEN TURNER

The dispute between simulation theorists and theory theorists follows a basic pattern in philosophical discussions of cognitive science: Various theoretical principles pertinent to mind, which commend themselves to us for some reason, conflict and must be reconciled, both with one another and with some partially understood or stable domains of fact (such as the empirical phenomenon of language learning) that are taken to be especially significant or problematic. For the most part this has been psychological and linguistic material. The theory theory–simulation dispute, as well as the dispute over connectionism and rule/computational models of the mind, have handled conflicts over such "empirical" linguistic and psychological findings in the following way. One side shows that its account is capable of "explaining," or at least of being consistent with or of excluding the opposite of some experimental or linguistically observed finding, and it argues that the alternative explanation either could not account for or was inconsistent with the finding. Sometimes the argument takes the more limited form of showing that a given approach would face particular novel explanatory burdens in attempting to explain something; the response is often to show how these burdens might be lightened.

To be sure, there are findings, such as the psychological experimental findings that make up the core of the discussion, that need to be accommodated by a successful theory. What this means in practice is that the focus of debate is on, so to speak, each side's efforts to explain the same things. This tends to narrow the discussion. This chapter, like some other contributions to the debate, will attempt to broaden the range of relevant phenomena, and in this way to alter the balance of explanatory burdens. There is nothing sacred about the list of domains taken to be relevant. In this chapter I will extend the discussion to some different incompatibilities between principles and some different domains of "stable, partially understood facts."

My perspective is social theoretical, and my aim in this chapter is to bring some of the topics of social theory into the discussion. I proceed from a specific thought that not all social theorists share: that certain standard accounts of culture, namely, those that treat culture as a shared tacit theory, are problematic pseudoexplanations.[1] The theory theory has a peculiar relationship to these standard views of culture, which I will explain in the chapter. It appears to be compatible, but on examination, and in relation to some more or less stable facts, it turns out that it is not. The incompatibility is so difficult to resolve that it suggests that an alternative approach to mind, such as simulationism or some variant of it, is more plausible, and also that the standard account of culture is not viable. These issues become particularly apparent when we examine a set of stable, partially understood facts about the differences between psychological language in different cultures.

1. Enculturation

Appeals to the notion of enculturation frequently arise in the theory of mind literature, though they are rarely pursued. One very interesting suggestion, made by Peter K. Smith, indicates the reason these issues might be much more relevant than hitherto imagined. Smith notes that the best evidence for mind reading by chimpanzees "comes from those exposed to a symbolic language code," and he observes that "if the labeling of IVs [i.e., the intervening variables in behavior that correspond to what were traditionally called "mental states"] is a crucial step, this might suggest that the presence of words (or symbolic codes) for mental states, such as desires and beliefs, in the language of parents and care-givers may be crucial." He goes on to argue that "the availability of such codes is crucial for the developing individual to develop mind-reading abilities. . . . Various aspects of the care-giving environment will facilitate their use." Having a theory of mind, in this view, is dependent on being part of a "theory of mind"—possessing community.[2]

This formulation quite directly poses several problems that are common to social theory and the theory theory–simulation debate. What is "enculturation," and what is "culture?" Is a theory of mind a cultural artifact, and is acquiring one thus socialization into a community and its culture? Suppose that it is. Smith himself thinks "that the explicit use of such codes by care-givers is likely to be important." But the specific language of mental states—belief, intention, desire, feeling, and so forth—varies quite extraordinarily among cultural communities. And the language of "facilitate," "crucial steps," and so forth is open to interpretation: Is the culture merely an aid to the more rapid acquisition of a capacity that would in the course of time be reached independently? Are the various languages for mental states just different expressions of the universal human theory of mind that would be arrived at or is in some sense already possessed by the normal human? Do different cultures possess different theories of mind, or merely different modes of expression of a common underlying tacit "theory"? Are the variant "codes" constitutive or descriptive? If descriptive, what are they descriptions of? If they are descriptions, could one culture's theory, or mode of expressing a universal underlying theory, be said to be better than another's? These are not idle questions, for there is a serious problem about the universality of the folk psychology and theory of mind that the theory theory is concerned with: The terms of the folk psychology do not have translational equivalents in all the languages and cultures of the world, an issue whose significance and relevance will become evident in later sections of this chapter.

2. Understanding and Norms: The Conventional View

Questions about the nature of understanding are not entirely the product of the debate over theories of mind: Social theorists and philosophical writers on interpretation have long written on these topics. The discussion of the problem of understanding in social theory has developed in two traditions: *Verstehen,* or empathy, the German tradition of Dilthey and Weber, and in taking the role (or attitude) of the other originating in the thought of G. H. Mead. Each regards understanding as both an activity of theorists (or historians and other analysts) and of human beings themselves in the course of their dealings with one another. The problem of culture or norms takes two basic forms as well. The dominant one, rooted in Durkheim and Parsons, treats norms, or culture, as a shared body of rulelike cognitive objects that are understood to be tacit.[3]

The connection between the problem of norms and the problem of understanding, though close, is rarely discussed. Stated as a thesis, the conventional view is this: Understanding, properly speaking, presupposes the sharing of norms. Usually this is stated even more strongly as the claim that communication (or some other feature of human interaction) would be impossible without the sharing of norms. There is also a close and rarely discussed affinity between the problem of norms and cognitive science models of mind that treat the mind as a rule-governed machine. To the extent that norms are thought of as akin to linguistic rules, and rule-governed models of mind as the best approach to explaining the way in which individuals are able to master and follow rules of grammar, tacit social norms may be thought of in the same way. The connection is implicit in the commonplace analogy between tacit societal norms and tacit linguistic norms.

Some social theorists have been skeptical of the "culture as rules" model, and a few have provided alternatives to it. One skeptic was Durkheim's main French rival, Gabriel Tarde, who proposed a theory of "imitation" to explain most of the same phenomena. The basic idea behind this alternative is present in Nietzsche as well. Children, Nietzsche observed, were natural apes, and primitive human beings were, he argued, the same. A herd instinct rooted in, or taking the form of, a horror of difference was the psychological basis of morality, whose specific contents were acquired by childish imitation. Tarde's notion of imitation was more complex and included various kinds of imitation, such as "rational imitation." Weber, who was unenthusiastic about the norms model, accepted "imitation" as a genuine phenomenon and also suggested that morality was, if not rooted in, buttressed by a biological urge to conform—a model that was not so different from Nietzsche's.

These alternative approaches are very interesting in connection with the questions raised above about the nature of a "theory of mind." They deal with the phenomenon of social norms without appealing to any notion of an underlying set of rules or rulelike shared mental contents, such as a shared tacit theory. Imitation is wholly external: One can imitate only what one can see or hear, that is to say, the externals of an act, thus the content of imitation, are limited by our ability to identify something to copy. We may imitate unconsciously, but this does not mean that we have special powers of unconscious discernment that allow us to discern anything other than the external aspects of what we imitate.

3. Fundamental Psychological Mechanisms: The Alternative Approach

"Imitation" is a basic psychological mechanism, so approaches to culture based on imitation proceed by first taking a backward step to the following question: What are the basic psychological mechanisms for such things as understanding, which is to ask what is the basic mechanism that children use to build an understanding of minds, and what internal givens and external data do they build with? Mead gave a distinctive answer to this "basic mechanisms" question that conflicts with the theory theory.[4]

Mead's approach is similar enough to simulation and an older "imitation" theory that Mead began his work by criticizing the idea that the three might be assimilated to one another. I will ignore the differences between the three approaches in what follows, though obviously they were crucial to Mead, and call this family of theories the "emulationist" approach. The common idea of the three theories is that social interaction and "understanding" is the result of the workings of basic psychological mechanisms that enable an individual to emulate other people in thought, for example, to guess what they are going to do, and to refine their expectations and responses to others on the basis of the external data given by the responses and conduct of others.

Mead's variant on this basic idea arose out of a critique of the notion of imitation with which he attempted to account for the problems with the notion of imitation and, more interesting for the purposes of this chapter, to replace it as the fundamental mechanism needed for an explanation of certain key facts about individual social psychological development.[5] The topic of imitation became important in American psychology for reasons quite separate from its role in social theory. James Mark Baldwin wrote an influential work based on observations of his two young daughters.[6] He observed that young children imitate, something that was not controversial then or now. We may take it as a "stable domain of fact" that young children imitate. We may also stipulate the following: Children role-play, and do so endlessly and without apparent motives. They also do various other things, such as repeat, endlessly ask "why" questions that adults find nonsensical, repeat the answers to them, initially without "understanding" them, and apply and alter the answers in new settings, and so forth. Moreover, children vary a great deal in what they do.

The issues between Mead and Baldwin were conceptual, not empirical. Mead argued that one problem with the notion of imitation as a *fundamental* mechanism is that it presupposes what it needs to explain, namely, conscious agency, since imitating is already an intentional act. This of course is an arguable point. Psychological research on imitation establishes that unconscious imitation does in fact occur. But the issue points to a more fundamental problem for theories of mind about the causal or genetic *priority* of particular psychological mechanisms or phenomena. If we attribute a given capacity to the mind prior to its development through external inputs and attempt to explain other capacities as derivative (e.g., by showing how they are produced by the initial capacity operating on inputs, such as experiences, of various particular kinds), we must be careful not to sneak into our account of the fundamental mechanism features of the phenomena to be explained. In the case of consciousness or, alternatively, of intentionality, the temptation is always present, though usually in a concealed form.

Typically this problem arises through, so to speak, reading motives appropriate to developed minds into undeveloped minds. For Mead, imitation was a paradigm case of this problem. People, like the proverbial monkeys, do "copy" the external behavior of others. But the language of copying and imitating is already intentional. We would not say that the accidental repetition of one action by another person or monkey under similar conditions and in close contact was imitation, but we would want something more, some additional mental element to distinguish the accidental from the genuine case. When we begin to describe this additional element, for example, in terms of awareness of what the other is doing, we already have imported a minimal notion of intentionality, namely, the capacity of the imitator to recognize something as a doing or an action. If we add to this something like self-awareness of copying, we have imported a notion of conscious behavior as well. We no longer have a fundamental mechanism but a mechanism that presupposes a developed mind.

Simulation, imitation, and taking the attitude of the other are similar in a key respect. They are presented as fundamental mechanisms, that is to say, as mechanisms that can explain various mental capacities but do not presuppose or require a great deal of prior mental equipment. Simulation differs from imitation in the directionality of the relationship. Imitation, as I have noted, operates by an external pattern being reproduced by an individual. In simulation, the individual has a capacity to think hypothetically, or off-line, about the individual's own behavior or experiences and to project the results of this thinking to the outside world, for example, in the form of expectations about the behavior and responses of others, and to get feedback about the success of these projections. To understand the anger of another person, for example, it is not necessary for the person doing the understanding to have a theory but only to be able to place him- or herself imaginatively in the other person's shoes and to monitor his or her own reactions to the imagined situation. This capacity enables learning in that one can act on one's understanding and then "test" it by acting on it, and modify one's simulative capacities accordingly.

In each of these accounts, the fundamental mechanisms, plus learning by experience through the employment of the fundamental mechanisms, do the explanatory work. Baldwin argued that infants were endowed with a capacity and drive to imitate and that they developed mentally through attempts at imitation. Mead, as I have noted, objected to this on grounds that at the time must have seemed too persuasive, namely, that imitation presupposed what it aimed to explain—capacities for recognizing people and consciously copying.[7] The issue is important for our purposes because what Mead is talking about here is precisely the issue raised by simulation theory, namely, whether interacting with other people requires those who interact to have a so-called theory of mind already or whether one's conceptions of other people and capacities for reasoning about their mental processes derived from some prior act, such as simulating the attitudes of others from which one generates, through a process like hypothesis testing, a set of expectations and capacities that are the functional equivalent of a theory of mind.[8]

4. Explaining Our Capacity to Understand

One reason the question of what is prior is especially important relates to understanding: If the way in which individuals acquire the capacity for understanding others resembles the acquisition of a theory, such as a theory of mind, and if, in the cultural case, it requires the acquisition of some set of normative rules that are interiorized or internalized, the things acquired are assumed to be essentially the same for everyone, and the condition for interaction and mutual understanding is the fact that each of us shares the same theory. Empathy, understanding within a culture, normative action, and so forth are, on this view, like the situation in which two scientific observers in possession of the same instruments and theory are able to make the same calculations and communicate them to one another precisely because they have the same theory. But this describes the case in which people already possess the same theory. The developmental question is, How do they acquire it (or its functional equivalent)?

One problem with the "shared theory" account, from a developmental point of view, is that individuals' experiences in the course of growing up are extremely diverse. In the case of language, the massive quantity of data overwhelms and obliterates individual differences, at least with respect to such things as basic grammar. But for the sorts of things that people have in mind when they talk about empathy, individual differences are bound to be of greater significance. G. H. Mead's account of development holds that children take the attitude of others and grants that children imitate. What distinguishes children from one another is *content*: the roles that they take and the things that they imitate. And here experiences are in some respects common and in other respects very diverse. Little boys in the United States a half-century ago took the role of cowboys, and little girls took the role of mommies and role-played with dolls, though obviously not all little girls and little boys did these things, and some did both. But in the course of their development children take quite different roles primarily because they are in different social environments and are compelled to master interaction through this role-playing with people who are themselves taking different kinds of roles. Roles are themselves stereotypical, a point to which I will return shortly.

Role taking understood as a mode of acquisition of competencies (as well as imitation understood in the same way) falls into a category that for convenience I will label *diversifying*: The same mechanisms, applied in the actual situations in which individuals find themselves, lead to diverse capacities of understanding. The differences bear very directly on the problem of intercultural comparison and understanding, and they provide a simple explanation of the main problems in this domain. The reason we don't have empathy for, say, historical figures in ancient Rome is that we simply do not understand the roles that they are enacting because we never enacted these roles ourselves. Thus we are inclined to reinterpret empathically the activities of Caesar or Cleopatra in the stereotypic forms of the roles that we have in excess, so that Cleopatra presented on the big screen consists of historical figures behaving in stereotypic ways associated with lovers and statesmen of our own era.

These movies are, so to speak, hypotheses about these historical figures in which we, living in the present, make the historical record conform to expectations about attitudes and the like, which we have acquired in the course of our own role-taking and role-playing activities. Not surprisingly, it is usually only possible to make these stories psychologically compelling if we fill in the historical record in a way that better fits our expectations— to make Cleopatra behave in familiar ways, with familiar emotions and attitudes. But in real history and archeology, matters are much more difficult: The conduct of the ancient Romans, especially with respect to sexuality, is a constant challenge to our powers of empathy. It is simply difficult for us to make heads or tails out of their attitudes and motivations because we do not share them, and we do not share them, not because we are some sort of fundamentally different human type but because they acquired their capacities from a pool of stereotypic courses of action that we no longer possess; they are essentially irrecoverable for us because the social world in which they acquired them has disappeared.

The Meadian view of understanding is that understanding another person consists of taking the attitude or the role of the other. Indeed, social interaction and its continued enactment and operation depends very heavily, in the view of Mead's followers, on the fact that people can rely on various stereotypic expectations. If I go into a doctor's office I know how to behave as a patient and the physician knows how to behave as a doctor. By virtue of these roles we understand one another by imaginatively projecting ourselves into the role of the other. If the doctor asks me a personal question, I respond to it by understanding that it reflects and is meant in terms of the role of the physician and not, say, the role of a new acquaintance or a clerk.

In what I have said here I have vacillated between the "stereotypic" aspects of this process and its "diversifying" ones. The literature itself tends to vacillate in this way, and in one sense the notion of role is extremely congenial to the notion of a culture as a set of normatively defined roles; it is in this form that it entered the thought of Parsons. Roles are simply understandable as enactments of normative expectations, and norms can be understood as a notion correlative to roles. If you are sick, for example, you must conform to the sick role in order to be "understood." Parsons, indeed, studied precisely these expectations. But everything depends on how one thinks of the stereotypes. One might think of them as common possessions, as a kind of theory that each member of a group acquires. Or one might think of them as internal mental devices, as a *private* shorthand (consisting, perhaps, of expectations) that is partly structured by public codes, that is to say, by language, or what Mead called significant symbols. Weber seems to have thought of what he called ideal-types in this way as well: as a private set of simplifying cognitive devices, whose employment, consciously or unconsciously, is demanded by the economy of thought in the face of the infinity of perceptual material. But he also recognized that one could be trained, as a lawyer is trained, in the use of conventional ideal-types, such as those of legal categorization, and that one communicates scholarly findings by constructing such types for others.[9]

This "private shorthand" model preserves the personal or diversifying character of stereotypes. We may each use the same terms in describing a "sick" person, and the practical necessities of communication provide feedback; a kind of public disciplining of our usage occurs through the various encounters in which we use the term. But the mental content of the term for us is our own, the product of our experiences, and it could hardly be otherwise, since language learning is done through experience and feedback like any other learning.

Two points should be made here to forestall any misunderstanding and to prepare the ground for the final discussion. Nothing in what has been said here to characterize the "emulationist" approach conflicts with the thought that, among the basic psychological possessions or starting points of individuals, along with a basic mechanism such as simulation or imitation are some basic emotions, perhaps associated with basic facial expressions. Indeed, it helps this approach if the basic material with which "understanding" develops includes some common starting points, so that children do not have to learn what pain is and what expresses it but can instead use this capacity in interpreting others. Common starting points are sometimes called basic emotions, and there is important evidence that there are some universal feelings with universally correlated facial expressions.[10]

If there are some such common (and noncultural or universal) starting points, it makes it possible for us to create a bridge into another language or into the emotional experiences of others by linking our "hypotheses" about the feelings of others with a set of facts, namely, the facts conveyed by facial expressions. There might also be "nonbasic" emotions that are not indicated by facial expressions. These might well arise through various transformations and training out of (or building on) basic emotions. Patriotic feeling, for example, is perhaps rooted in fellow feeling and pride, but it is the product of training or the experience of participating in specific rituals and is nonuniversal and nonbasic. There is no guarantee that such emotions will be accessible to those who have not shared the experiences or analogous ones. Feelings of sexual attraction, though certainly rooted in something "basic," may also develop in very different and mutually incomprehensible ways, depending on the experiences of the individual.

With these various distinctions in mind, we can consider the question of what is it that people "acquire" through feedback from their experiences with others. One answer would be what might be called the "culturalist" one—that people acquire a culture, in a specific sense of this term. Clifford Geertz, himself a student of Parsons, famously defined culture as "an historically transmitted pattern of meanings embodied in symbols, a system of inherited conceptions expressed in symbolic forms by means of which men communicate, perpetuate, and develop their knowledge about and attitudes toward life."[11]

We will shortly reconsider this definition with respect to the notion of "inheritance." The feature that is crucial here is the notion of a "system of ... conceptions," which is to say a theorylike intellectual object. In an earlier part of this discussion I asked whether the theory of mind was such a system of inherited conceptions but delayed answering it.

Another answer to the question, What do people acquire? would be this: All that understanding another person means to "understand" is to be able to interact, and this means to play the relevant roles, to take the attitude of the other in the relevant stereotyped ways, and to employ the significant symbols in this activity of attitude taking. What we "acquire" is no more than the results of our own attempts to interact on the basis of our hypotheses about the attitudes of others, and the feedback that enables us to improve our attempts to take the attitudes of others is the success and failure of our interactions. There is no more than this to understanding, and specifically nothing in the way of "a system of conceptions" that must be "inherited" in order for us to understand.

This "emulationist" account of mutuality is also an account of culture or, rather, an alternative approach to the phenomena that are usually explained as "cultural." Acquiring a culture, in this approach, is nothing more than acquiring the ability to take the attitude of others with respect to stereotyped roles and significant symbols. Culture is thus not a system that needs to be "inherited" but a set of learned capacities organized around objects such as symbols, ritualized actions, and so forth. The capacities are individualized in the sense that personal history of learning is not irrelevant, but disciplining, mutual interaction, and experiences around particular symbols may tend to make people respond in ways that are outwardly uniform.

5. Culture Versus Psychological Universals

Linguistic psychologist Anna Wierzbicka, who works on the problem of the language of emotions, imagines the following dialogue between psychologists and linguists:

P: Fear and anger are universal human emotions.

L: Fear and anger are English words, which don't have equivalents in all other languages. Why should these English words, rather than some words from language X, for which English has no equivalents, capture correctly some emotional universals?

P: It doesn't matter whether other languages have words for fear and anger or not. Let's not deify words.

L: Yes, but in talking about these emotions you are using culture-specific English words, and thus you are introducing an Anglo perspective on emotions into your discussion.

P: I don't think so. I am sure that people in these other cultures also experience fear and anger, even if they don't have words for them.

L: Maybe they do experience fear and anger, but their categorization of emotions is different from that reflected in a standard English lexicon.[12]

P: Let's not exaggerate the importance of language.

This conflict is important for the theory theory, but for a reason that is difficult to explain. The conflict between the linguist and the psychologist is closely analogous to a conflict between a "culturalist" interpretation of the "theory" involved in the kind of reasoning about the minds of others that is learned by children, and a "psychological" one.

How is the diversity of emotion terms in different languages to be explained? Wierzbicka considers angst, an emotion that has no proper English equivalents. The problem with angst is that it is widely reported as an emotion among Germans but is not reported widely in other cultures; indeed, it is not part of the language at all in most other cultures. This emotion, then, is "cultural." The psychological theory is that there are certain common basic emotions that all people have. Angst is therefore not "basic." So there is no direct conflict here. But there is a conflict nevertheless, and it is a profound one.

Both theories attempt to explain the same kinds of facts—emotions. The linguistic or culturalist explanation suggests that emotions are in some sense cultural, dependent on the things that language is dependent on. The psychological explanation holds that at least some emotions, and perhaps all real emotions, are universal and are explicable by features of human psychology, biology, and development that are themselves universal. Neither can be completely right. Either the "culturalist" explanation is specious for some emotions, such as anger, or the psychological account is false, a mistaken attempt to turn a cultural fact into a universal feature of psychology. There is a burden on the psychological account to explain emotions such as angst that apparently are not universal. And there is a burden on the culturalist account to explain why some emotions appear to be cultural and others appear to be universal or noncultural, even though there is no apparent reason that the same cultural explanations that are invoked for angst could not also be invoked for anger.

Of course, there are a variety of possible solutions here. But the important point about these "solutions" is this: They impose additional burdens on the explanation, burdens that are not apparent from the initial explanation. The same point holds in the case of the theory theory, in its relationship to culturalist explanations of "folk psychology," in which there is a similar problem about language, a problem that is in some respects more serious. Folk psychological language is theoretical, and for this reason even more varied than emotion language. Four examples can be given. The term "believe," in which the "false belief" problem is itself defined, lacks good equivalents in some languages—a problem discovered at a practical level, as Rodney Needham has observed, by Bible translators.[13] In many languages, it is impossible to describe sensations. The locutions for description are literally translated in forms like "object x stands in relation y with me." In classical Chinese, it is impossible to formulate statements taking a form analogous to "X believes P," where P is a proposition. To translate "X believes the moon is red" one might say "X uses the moon and deems it red."[14] In short, many of the elements of folk psychology that make up the false belief problem and the conventional theory of mind are *not* linguistically or culturally universal.

This kind of variation poses a problem for enterprises like the theory theory that can be understood by analogy with the difficulties that arise with emotions. They come down to this. The theory theory is an account of developed intentional thinking, complete with an ability to solve the false belief problem. Its answer is that people, all people (with the exception of people with genuine psychological abnormalities, like autistics), somehow acquire this theory. The theory, incidentally, is false, that is to say, it is a part of "folk psychology" and cannot be developed into a scientific theory of mind. If normal people do not acquire the theory, the theory theory is itself false. If they appear to acquire different theories of mind, as the surface differences in language suggest that they do, then these differences need to be shown to be irrelevant to the validity of the theory theory as an explanation.

It would be convenient for the theory theory if the language of folk psychology were the same or more or less completely and easily intertranslatable the world over.[15] If so, it could be said that children are aided to acquire this theory (which it is agreed they do not have from birth, since there is a stage in which they cannot solve the false belief problem) by maxims, codes, and the like—the stuff of culture. If all cultures were uniform with respect to these maxims and codes, it would be possible to list them among the universals of culture, and perhaps even to theorize that the reason they are found in the same form in all cultures is that they reflect a universally acquired psychological "theory" that is in some sense not linguistic but is prior to language or in the language of the mind itself. In this case the surface differences of language could be dismissed, in the manner of P above.

The fact that the diversity of mental language is apparently greater than this is inconvenient, since it imposes additional explanatory burdens. It could mean that people in different cultures have different mental terms and thus genuinely different theories, each of which happens to enable them to solve the false belief problem, but differently, which is to say that the theories are cultural artifacts. This would mean that the theory theory is gratuitous for its main purpose, explaining "folk psychology," because the specific folk psychologies of particular groups are already explained as distinct cultural facts, as something acquired with and as a part of a culture. But this leaves the explanation entirely at the level of culture and cultural adaptation and treats acquisition as a matter of acquiring culture, which of course does not occur in one developmental step.

So a new explanatory burden is created by the "cultural" explanation, namely, a problem of explaining the apparent universality of the solution of the false belief problem. Perhaps it is not such a difficult one. It does seem odd that all cultures should develop a false theory, and more or less the same false theory, and that this is the adaptive theory. But perhaps this is merely odd. One can deny that the commonalities amount to much more than the result: the common ability to solve the inferential problems referred to in English as the false belief problem. If the whole business of mental language and "theory" is cultural and culturally relative, it is perhaps surprising that all cultures have the equipment to solve the false belief problem in the form in which it can arise in that culture. But perhaps it is not. Perhaps it is simply analogous to the fact that all cultures can in some sense think "causally" without all having precisely verbally equivalent concepts of causation. Both ways of thinking are profoundly adaptive (as a culture of autism would not be), so there simply is no extant culture that lacks them.

There are alternatives that can save the theory theory from reduction to culture, but these create some even more peculiar explanatory burdens.[16] If the universal features of the developmental process explain acquisition of the theory theory, and the theory is false, then one must explain the cultural and linguistic diversity of folk psychological idioms. But how does one explain cultural differences if the mechanisms of acquisition of the theory are themselves general and psychological? The problem is analogous to the problem of emotion terms but not precisely analogous, since the terms in question are not primary descriptions but theoretical terms about nonobservable facts. Why would people hold the same "theory" tacitly and non-linguistically but articulate it in different ways? One could say "error" and see the folk theory of different cultures as bad theory, like bad science or ethnoscience. But this is overly complicated. It is more plausible in this case, in contrast to the emotions case, to drop the hypothesis of a universally shared tacit folk psychology entirely. Yet dropping that hypothesis leaves the process by which children develop these cognitive capacities, the empirical findings that have motivated much of the discussion, unexplained, and apparently inexplicable.

What this suggests is that both the culturalist and the psychological universalist approach to theories of mind bring in their train serious explanatory burdens. A combined approach would have its own burdens. Chomsky's linguistics is often the model that thinkers in cognitive science have in mind when they consider the nature of the mechanisms they study. But Chomsky's approach carefully avoids this problem, by modeling the relation of the universal claims it makes to the actual diversity of languages on the relation between language and dialects: All human languages, it is claimed, are dialects of the universal language. This is not an option open to theory theorists. Theories are the same only if the terms of the theory are the same, and the problem here is that the terms of folk psychology are not the same, and some of them do not even appear in other languages.

6. Congeniality and Explanatory Burdens

What sort of argument is this? What we have arrived at is a very crude result. The alternatives of the theory theory and simulation have been extended to deal with some more or less stable facts that are usually of concern to social theory. Various lines of development of the basic idea of the theory theory turn out to run into peculiar explanatory burdens, like explaining the actual cultural diversity of terms for beliefs, intentions, and so forth. When we arrive at these issues, the difficulties mount up. The contrast between "cultural" concepts and a "universal but tacit" folk psychology turns out to produce particularly serious problems, problems of compatibility between explanations. Put simply, the problem is that two "theory theories," a universalistic psychological one and a relativistic culturalist one, attempt to explain the same thing and thus conflict. Neither can be reduced to or made easily compatible with the other. Neither is implausible.

Simulation and related fundamental mechanisms, however, appear to avoid these problems. They don't rely on "possession of a theory" as an explanation, and consequently there is no conflict between two theories of different kinds, each of which explains some of the same things. The problem is to see if the basic mechanisms, together with some plausible starting points, such as emotions and recognition of emotions expressed on faces, can account for the things one wishes to account for. And in this case it is plausible, at least for a broad range of things. Actual experience, notably the empirical experiences gained in role-playing, imitation, and simulation tested by experience, provides a great deal of the kind of psychological content that is needed to have the capacity to interact socially.[17] And the capacities thus understood are congenial with an alternative account both of understanding and of culture itself—not necessarily an account in which a culture is a kind of a theory and in which understanding is by virtue of sharing this theory.

I use the term "congenial" for a reason. Though the relationships here are relationships of a particularly loose kind, they are nevertheless meaningful. The relations between the "stable domain of fact" I have appealed to and the very abstract models at stake in the discussion are not so well defined as to make the facts into very persuasive tests of the models. More importantly, the models can be developed in various ways, on the basis of the internal resources of the models, to account for the findings or facts that are claimed too problematic for them. But difficulties do arise, and the conflict between the culturalist notion of the "theory" that explains intentional language and the psychological notion of the "theory" that underlies the inferences needed to solve the "false belief" problem is a significant one. The less burdened path in the face of this conflict is to avoid the notion of "theory" in either the cultural or the psychological context, and this is congenial with the path I have labeled the "emulationist" model, which avoids appealing to shared tacit theory, psychological or cultural. It is the path that twentieth-century social theory for the most part did not take. Perhaps the balance of explanatory burdens has now changed, and it is the path that should be taken.

Notes

This chapter was completed while the author was a Fellow at the Swedish Collegium for Advanced Study in the Social Sciences, whose support is gratefully acknowledged.

1. Cf. Turner 1994.
2. Smith 1996, pp. 353–354.
3. The model figures prominently in the philosophical literature as well; perhaps its simplest statement is to be found in John Searle's *Speech Acts,* in which it is claimed of language "that the speakers of a language are engaging in a rule governed form of intentional behavior" and the "rules account for the regularities in exactly the same way as the rules of football account for the regularities in a game of football" (Searle 1969, 53). Cf. Stephen Turner, "Searle's Social Reality," in press.
4. A. F. Goldman has already noted that Mead is a precursor to simulation in "Empathy, Mind, and Morals" (Goldman 1995b, p. 196).
5. In what follows, I will rely on two useful guides to these issues: Cook 1993; Kessler 1941. Kessler's dissertation was directed by Mead's student and follower A. E. Murphy.

6. Baldwin 1895.

7. The conceptual point is important, but in this case the empirical evidence supports the idea that some capacity for imitation is very basic. As one psychologist puts it, "By the second day of life, babies can reliably recognize their mothers; and also imitate facial gestures such as mouth opening and tongue poking" (Ellis 1998, p. 23). This is imitation preceding any sort of feedback that would enable the infant to learn how to "copy," and thus before having an "intention to copy." For this reason I would be skeptical about any attempt to salvage a pure form of Mead's account.

8. A simple account of the way such a process would work is available in Elgin 1996, pp. 205–211, esp. p. 210.

9. Weber is quite clear that these concepts cannot represent the shared theory of people: The "ideas which govern the behavior of a population of a certain epoch . . . empirically . . . exists in the minds of an indefinite and constantly changing mass of individuals and assumes in their minds the most multifarious nuances of form and content, clarity and meaning." If, for example, the "Christianity" of the individuals of the Middle Ages "could be completely portrayed," he adds, it would be a "chaos of infinitely differentiated and highly contradictory complexes of ideas and feelings" (Weber 1949, pp. 95–96).

10. Ekman 1993, pp. 384–392. The idea is also found in Darwin (1988), who attributes them to animals, and has a close affinity to Wittgenstein, who says that "the common behavior of mankind is the system of reference by means of which we interpret an unknown language" (Wittgenstein 1958, sec. 206).

11. Geertz 1973, p. 89.

12. Wierzbicka 1998, pp. 161–162.

13. Needham 1972.

14. As Chad Hansen explains, "The core Chinese concept is *xin* (the heart-mind). As the translation suggests, Chinese folk psychology lacked a contrast between cognitive and affective states [representative ideas, cognition, reason, beliefs] versus [desires, motives, emotions, feelings]. The *xin* guides action, but not via beliefs and desires" (Hansen 1998). At least one philosopher, Herbert Fingarette, has suggested that classical Chinese has no psychological theory (Fingarette 1972, pp. 37–56). This would be a quite literal example of a non-"theory of mind" community.

15. It seems that intentional language *is* more or less translatable but "belief" language is not. As Needham says, "Belief makes an extreme contrast. It is not a necessary concept, and it is not a distinct capacity of inner state; other languages make no recognition of a mode of consciousness of the kind, and other people order their lives without reference to any such capacity" Needham (1972, p. 146). "Belief," however, is a key concept in the "folk psychology" that theory theory purports to explain.

16. The culturalist account is not free of profound explanatory burdens either, for example, even a culturalist account is forced to posit some universal cognitive machinery. Recall the metaphors of "inheritance" that recur in Geertz's definition of "culture." What is the cognitive mechanism by which "systems of concepts" are passed from one person to another intact, that is, as a "system"? This question is the theme of Turner 1994 *(The Social Theory of Practices)*.

17. And, incidentally, to think intentionally about others, which Needham suggests is universal, in contrast to other elements of "folk psychology."

Chapter Four

Simulation and Epistemic Competence

DAVID HENDERSON
TERENCE HORGAN

1. Naturalized Epistemology

Increasingly, epistemology is taking the articulate form of an investigation into how we manage, and perhaps might better manage, the cognitive chores of producing, modifying, and generally maintaining belief sets with a view to having a true and systematic understanding of the world. Although this approach has continuities with earlier philosophy, it admittedly makes a departure from the tradition of epistemology as first philosophy. Such investigations are termed "naturalized epistemologies" insofar as they help themselves to scientific information regarding (1) human cognitive capacities and (2) the possibilities for social organization in the pursuit of the classical epistemic goal. Epistemology on this model has been on the rise at least since Quine's classic manifesto, "Epistemology Naturalized," declared our principled freedom from the obligation to provide a first philosophy.

So, epistemology (naturalized) is concerned with human capacities useful in the pursuit of that classical epistemic end—a true and systematic understanding of the world. When it yields a model of how we do commonly manage this pursuit with whatever success we now enjoy, it provides a descriptive account of our epistemic competence. Even such a descriptive account has a significant normative force, as it codifies what is acceptably effective in present practices, counseling us away from the residue of cognitive performances that do not so contribute. When the epistemological account employs information regarding the bases and plasticity of our present cognitive capacities in order to construct a model of how we might yet better manage the pursuit of our epistemic goal, we produce meliorative models of epistemic competence.[1]

Taken together, the capacities constituting our (descriptive or meliorative) epistemic competence will have certain characteristics making for their (joint) effectiveness in the pursuit of our epistemic goal. One very prominent general characteristic is the most familiar of externalist virtues: the reliability of processes implementing the capacities. Here, famously, reliability is a matter of the tendency of those processes to produce true beliefs in the environment that the epistemic agent inhabits as a matter of fact. However, this virtue cannot be the whole story. For one thing, it is a matter of the ratio of true beliefs to the total set of *individual* beliefs produced when capacities are set to work in the agent's environment—and thus a set of capacities could be reliable and yet not tend to the production of *sets* of beliefs that have the *systematicity* desired.[2] Our epistemic goal is systematic true understanding—not some loose assortment of individual true beliefs. So, truth-conducivity (reliability) is not the sole or decisive epistemic virtue.

However, truth-conducivity and systematicity-conducivity do not jointly exhaust the externalist virtues to be recognized. Suppose that, by dumb luck, some agents live an epistemically sheltered life—living in a narrow environment in which it is particularly easy to formulate systems of true beliefs. For example, in the possible world in which these hypothetical agents live, populations are so homogeneous that no sensitivity to sample representativeness is needed—the most hasty generalization from the most accidentally drawn sample will produce a true generalization in their world. Perhaps the agents are such damn-the-torpedoes generalizers, and thus employ processes that are reliable (and even conducive to systematicity) in their world of wimpy epistemic demands. Are their processes to be commended? It seems to us that the answer is not an unqualified yes. In view of the exigencies and uncertainties that are characteristic of epistemic life, it is desirable for agents to employ processes that are reliable (and conducive to systematicity) in a significant range of epistemically possible worlds—including those in which populations may be heterogeneous, for example. It is probable that an agent employing such processes is employing processes that are reliable and system-conducive, whatever the epistemically possible world that agent occupies (as long as it is not a perversely difficult one). Horgan and Henderson (forthcoming) call the indicated epistemic virtue *robustness*.

So, on the naturalized epistemological approach adopted here, cognitive capacities are epistemically valuable insofar as they take their place in a model of our descriptive or meliorative competence. For a capacity to have a place in such a model is a matter of the tendencies arising from its combination with select other capacities that we have or could have (given the base of capacities on which creatures like us build). For a capacity to have a place in our models of epistemic competence is for it to be a component of a set of capacities that is conducive to the truth and systematicity of our belief systems, and is so in a way that is not precarious.

In this chapter, we provide a rough characterization of the role of simulation in our epistemic competence for understanding others. Our characterization is intended to apply both to our descriptive competence and to our meliorative competence, as it reflects the limits and general promise of both theory-based and simulation-based understanding. We later suggest some implications for the social sciences. However, here at the beginning, we insist that nothing we say is intended to minimize the importance of the sort of sustained interpretive back-and-forth that is involved in constructing a body of information regarding someone's belief system. In keeping with the hermeneutic circle, the general understanding of someone's belief system results as a systematic accretion from increasingly successful treatments of particular cases, where these in turn depend upon an increasingly comprehensive general understanding of our subject(s). That is, a general understanding of our subjects' belief-and-desire system serves to inform our understanding of particular cases, whereas our faith in the general picture depends on apparent success in the particular cases. The focus in this chapter is on the capacities that are brought to the task of generating our understanding of particular cases. We believe that both the application of theory and simulation play roles in the treatment of particular cases and that this is compatible with an appropriate treatment of the extended task of developing an interpretive scheme for a people.[3]

Although we conceive of this chapter as a piece of naturalized epistemology, we do not draw explicitly on many particular empirical works. We work at one remove, drawing instead on a general understanding of human cognitive processing that is elsewhere developed at greater length, and with more direct comment on empirical work in cognitive science.[4] We sketch this background understanding in section 3.

2. Clarifying the Question, What Is the Epistemic Role of Simulation?

The simulation of another agent, in the sense of interest here, is a matter of taking certain cognitive processes "off-line" and setting them to work on input that is similar to those that the other (supposedly) had or will have; this is undertaken so that the resulting processing parallels what has or what will take place in the other. It is a matter of what Goldman (1995a) called "process-driven" simulation, in which the agent's own cognitive processes, acting on "pretend-input," generate ("pretend"-) beliefs, desires, or intentions as outputs. This is contrasted with "theory-driven" simulation, in which some representation of the interaction of parameterized variables within a system is put to work on some hypothetical values—as in computer simulations of a system. In process-driven simulation, the simulating agent need have no representation of the transitions to which the simulated agent is disposed. For, if the simulation is successful, the simulator's own capacities for dealing with inputs of the sort that the other had are themselves similar to the other's, and thus the transitions carried out in the simulator's own off-line capacities parallel those in the simulated.

In its rudiments, simulation may be thought of as a three-stage affair. First, there is the generation of a set of "pretend-beliefs," "pretend-desires," "pretend-perceptions," and perhaps other input. Here "pretend" is employed to signal a certain sort of discontinuity. These states are generated in ways that may be discontinuous with the common processes of belief and desire generation. They are generated so as to be highly similar to those that the subject of the simulation had in the relevant episode.[5] Further, the capacities into which these are to be fed will themselves be operating "off-line," that is, in a way that is discontinuous with their normal operation. After all, here, the system will generate as output "beliefs" and "desires" that are not themselves integrated into that agent's own belief- and desire-sets, and it will generate "intentions" that do not eventuate in actions. Second, there is the off-line processing itself, in which the simulating agent's own cognitive capacities are put to work on the input. Although these have been taken off-line, they supposedly work pretty much as they would otherwise. Third, there is the ascription to the other of the beliefs, desires, intentions, and reasoning instanced in the simulation.

It is important to note what is not entailed by the above rudimentary understanding of simulation. Centrally, there is no suggestion that simulation works alone when it is called into play. Both proponents and opponents of simulation theory have sometimes written as if simulation and discursive information were like oil and water—supposing that they do not mix. Accordingly, one would need to get by with simulation, untutored by discursive information, as some simulation theorists would seem to have it, or with discursive representations unsupplemented by simulation, as some theory theorists would have it. Perhaps these ways of seeing the matter are a hangover from the old debate between methodological separatists and naturalists. Proponents of simulation theory have sometimes sought to formulate their position so as to minimize opportunities for informing simulation by discursive information—perhaps fearing that such information (as rudimentary theory) would represent the nose of a camel that they seek to corral in a pen devoted to the natural and biological sciences. On the other hand, opponents have been happy with this framing of the matter. It would seem to make simulation "cognitively inpenetrable," that is, insensitive to discursive information that one might have. Since such inpenetrability is not observed, opponents happily conclude that simulation is not epistemically important. The above rudimentary understanding of simulation does not encourage such moves.

Our characterization allows simulation to be informed by discursive information both in the generation of input and in the ascription to another of the parallels (in contents as well as kind) to the off-line processes that are then spun out. What is required for simulation—what is at its core—is a set of cognitive capacities on which the simulator can draw in order to put into play off-line processes that are similar to the simulated agent's. It is this use of the simulator's own cognitive capacities that distinguishes simulation from those cognitive processes that turn on manipulation of representations of that agent's processes. So, the core of the simulation is free of theory representing the agent's cognitive capacities and the inputs on which they work.[6] But this leaves much scope for discursive information to play a role in determining what input to employ, what cognitive processes to call into play, and what confidence to place in the judgment that resulting process actually paralleled processes in the agent simulated.

The insistence on unsullied simulation or unsupplemented theory seems far-fetched from a general epistemological point of view. Our competence in dealing with a subject matter commonly comprises a mix of strategies, jointly providing multiple modes of epistemic access to matters of interest. The access provided by one method may complement that provided by another. One may compensate where the other encounters difficulty. And, where multiple strategies are applicable, they may check up on each other and provide opportunities for feedback and refinement. Henderson (1995) argues that simulation-employing and theory-employing approaches to understanding and explaining others complement each other in these ways. The present chapter continues this line of thought.

The place for simulation within our epistemic competence will then turn on how it works in yoke with other capacities that we have or might have. The issue that needs to be addressed is whether the capacity for simulation, in combination with other capacities, has the epistemic virtues of reliability, robustness, and systematicity—and, if so, just what roles are assigned to simulation in the package (or packages) of capacities with these virtues.

3. One Role for Simulation

We here begin to explore cooperative roles for our capacity for simulation. Some recent work by Jane Heal (1996b) provides one piece of the puzzle. Heal insists that we do have a good deal of discursive information regarding persons, their psychological states, and their cognitive tendencies. She allows that this information may itself be sufficiently extensive and interrelated to be called a "theory." However, she insists that our theory of mind, such as it is and is likely to be, is not sufficient to explain our ability to un-

derstand and explain others. She argues that, at the level detailing the interaction of contentful states, at just the level that theory would need to be applicable in order to yield the sort of concrete predictions and explanations
for which adult humans have a significant facility, our psychological theory
must be incomplete. It may help us along, but at some point we must turn
the particulars over to simulation. The theory may, presumably, have been
important in framing the simulation, but simulation is needed to really deal
with tracing out the particulars of the processing to be understood.

Heal, as we understand her, argues for two key claims. First, no theory of
intentional states and their interactions could be as successfully predictive
of people's actual psychological state transitions as we humans typically
are. Second, even if there were such a predictive theory, it still would be extremely unlikely that humans employ such a theory in understanding one
another. The first claim is more fundamental; for, if no suitably predictive
theory over intentional states exists at all, then people's predictive successes
in understanding one another could not possibly be based entirely upon
their use of such a theory.

Heal defends the first claim by appealing to four important facts about
thinking. First is the enormity of the information that any normal adult human agent has acquired. The amount and diversity of information contained in any normal human's belief system is impressive, even awe inspir-
ing. Second, the epistemic status of a thought is holistic. That is, it depends
on the rest of the agent's beliefs. (Or, in the case of thoughts that are desir-
ings, its appropriateness depends on the rest of the agent's beliefs and desires.) The holistic character of epistemic justification has at least two
prominent aspects. The first aspect is that the epistemic status of a given belief depends on the set of relevant beliefs that the agent has. But any one belief is potentially relevant to any other beliefs, with this being a function of
what further beliefs the agent possesses. So, the set of beliefs relevant to a
given belief, and thus that belief's epistemic status, depends on the agent's
global belief set. The second aspect is that the epistemic status of a given
belief is, in some measure, dependent on global characteristics of the containing set of beliefs—characteristics such as simplicity or overall explanatory power. The first aspect is particularly important for us here. It means
that the epistemic agent must somehow be sensitive to what other beliefs
within that agent's enormous set of beliefs are relevant to a given candidate
belief and that the agent should then bring these relevant beliefs together in
maintaining or rejecting the candidate belief.

The third fact that Heal emphasizes is that, remarkably, human cognitive
agents are fairly good at just this. They show remarkable sensitivity to what
are relevant beliefs, even in unusual cases in which normally unrelated beliefs become relevant. Her fourth point is that, to understand and account
for human cognition, we must be able to deal with people's sensitivity to se-

lective holistic relevance, and we must be able to track this capacity to cope with far-flung beliefs even in cases in which the constellation of relevant beliefs turns out to be unusual.

Heal designates a theory that could model human cognition with these characteristics, and with the nuanced twists and turns that result, a *theory of relevance*. In light of the four facts about human thinking lately mentioned, she maintains, it is very unlikely there can be a general and systematic theory of relevance. That is, there can be no psychological theory, stated in terms of intentional states and their interactions, that is as successfully predictive of people's psychological state transitions as humans actually are.

Heal also argues that even if there were such a theory of relevance, such a theory would be unlikely actually to be employed by humans as a means of predicting and understanding one another. She offers two considerations in defense of this claim. First, it is somewhat implausible that we have such a powerful implicit theory without this being reflected in an ability to make some significant start in its partial articulation—an ability that is strikingly lacking. Second, and more important, we should be wary of the suggestion that humans could implicitly deploy such a theory in understanding one another, given the very enormity of the task it is supposed to accomplish for us. It is supposed to provide the basis for theoretically modeling the ways in which information gets accommodated as human cognizers continuously update their sets of beliefs. It must describe how agents commonly hit upon the contents of their belief sets that need to be considered in accommodating a new piece of information—drawing a frame around those that are relevant and are to be put into the mix. It needs then to say how the resulting sets of beliefs will interact to produce a new ensemble. Given the size and complexity of human belief systems, given the nuanced and novel ways that pieces may come to fit together, actually applying such a theory would be a daunting task indeed. "As an information storage and processing task and given the range of our actual psychological competence," she says, "dealing with this imagined theory is orders of magnitude more formidable than dealing with any other tacit theory that has been proposed, e.g., for grammar or folk physics."[7]

Heal observes that the inability to uncover a theory of relevance is at the core of a problem that researchers in AI have persistently run into, the so-called frame problem, which Jerry Fodor has usefully characterized as "the problem of putting a 'frame' around the set of beliefs that may need to be revised in light of specified newly available information."[8] Heal's discussion suggests (although she does not quite say this explicitly) that the computational theory of mind, which construes mental processing as the rule-governed manipulation of syntactically structured mental representations on the basis of their syntactic structure, is itself mistaken in the absence of a theory of relevance.

We are very sympathetic to Heal's arguments. Concerning her principal claim that a general, systematic theory of relevance is not possible, similar pessimistic considerations about the likely nonexistence of a theory of relevance, and about how this makes the frame problem an apparently in-principle problem that seriously threatens the very possibility of accounting for cognitive processes like belief formation within the computational theory of mind are set forth by Fodor (1983). He stresses (1) the same holistic aspects of nondemonstrative inference emphasized by Heal, (2) the key role of these holistic aspects in the persistent failure of attempts to produce a rigorous theory of nondemonstrative inference, and (3) the parallel between the seemingly in-principle failure to systematize nondemonstrative inference and the apparently in-principle unsolvability of the frame problem within computational cognitive science. Such considerations are further elaborated by Horgan and Tienson (1996), who conclude both (1) that there cannot be a predictive psychological theory, couched in terms of intentional psychological states, of the kind that Heal designates a theory of relevance and (2) that the computational conception of human mental processing is very likely mistaken.[9]

Cognitive science evidently needs to replace the computational conception of mind with something more powerful. An alternative, more powerful picture of human cognition has indeed begun to emerge from within cognitive science. It draws upon connectionist modeling and also on a form of mathematics that is natural for describing connectionist models—dynamical systems theory. This nonclassical framework for cognitive science is described at length in Horgan and Tienson (1996). Here we offer a very brief summary, with emphasis on features that are especially germane to the debate about how humans understand one another.

Connectionism emerged as a large-scale research program in the 1980s, largely in response to the recurrent, recalcitrant difficulties that led Fodor to his bleak conclusions about the prospects for classical AI modeling central cognitive processes. A connectionist system, or neural network, is a structure of simple neuronlike processors called nodes or units. Each node has directed connections to other nodes, so that the nodes send and receive excitatory and inhibitory signals to and from one another. The total input to a node determines its state of activation. When a node is on, it sends out signals to the nodes to which it has output connections, with the intensity of a signal depending upon both (1) the activation level of the sending node and (2) the strength or "weight" of the connection between it and the receiving node. Typically at each moment during processing, many nodes are simultaneously sending signals to others.

When neural networks are employed for information processing, certain nodes are designated "input" units and "output" units, and potential patterns of activation across them are assigned interpretations. (The remaining nodes are called "hidden units.") Typically a "problem" is posed to a network by activating a pattern in the input nodes; then the various nodes in the system simultaneously send and receive signals repeatedly until the system settles into a stable configuration; the semantic interpretation of the resulting pattern in the output nodes is its "answer" to the problem.[10]

The most striking difference between such networks and conventional computers is the lack of an executive component. In a conventional computer the behavior of the whole system is controlled at the central processing unit (CPU) by a stored program. A connectionist system lacks both a CPU and a stored program. Nevertheless, in a connectionist system certain activation patterns over sets of hidden units can often be interpreted as internal representations with interesting content, and often the system can also be interpreted as embodying, in its weighted connections, information that gets automatically accommodated during processing without getting explicitly represented via activation patterns.

Connectionist models in cognitive science have yielded particularly encouraging results for cognitive processes like learning, pattern recognition, and so-called multiple soft-constraint satisfaction (i.e., solving a problem governed by several constraints, where an optimal solution may require violating some constraints in order to satisfy others—for example, successfully classifying a given three-legged animal as a dog, even though dogs have four legs).

In a connectionist system, information is actively represented as a pattern of activation. When the information is not in use, that pattern is nowhere present in the system; it is not stored as a data structure. The only representations ever present are the active ones. On the other hand, information can be said to be *tacitly* present in a connectionist system—or "in the weights," as connectionists like to say—if the weighted connections subserve *representation-level dispositions* that are appropriate to that information. In the terminology of Horgan and Tienson (1995, 1996), such information constitutes *morphological* content in the system (i.e., content that is present in virtue of the system's structure), rather than explicitly represented content. Among the apparent advantages of connectionist systems, by contrast with classical computational systems, is that morphological information "in the weights" gets accommodated automatically during processing, without any need for a central processing unit to find and fetch task-relevant information from some separate memory banks where it gets stored in explicit form while not in use.

Learning is conceived quite differently within connectionism than it is within classicism, since connectionist systems do not store representations. Because learning involves the system's undergoing weight changes that render its representation-forming dispositions appropriate to the content of what is learned, learning is the acquisition, "in the weights," of new morphological content.

The apparent moral of frame-type problems in computational cognitive science is that human cognitive transitions are evidently too subtle and too complex to conform to any general and systematic theory of relevance, and hence are too subtle and too complex to be subserved by computation over representations. Connectionism provides a promising alternative paradigm. Horgan and Tienson's (1994, 1996) proposed nonclassical foundational framework is inspired partly by the emergence of the connectionist movement, partly by some particularly suggestive connectionist work such as Berg (1992), Pollack (1990), and Smolensky (1990, 1995), partly by frame-type problems facing classicism, and partly by the natural links between neural networks and the branch of mathematics called dynamical systems theory. The mathematics of dynamical systems is more powerful than the discrete mathematics of algorithms; in effect, algorithmic systems are a limited special case of dynamical systems.[11]

Horgan and Tienson call this nonclassical approach the *dynamical cognition* framework (for short, the DC framework) because of the central role it assigns to dynamical systems theory. A key feature of the DC framework is that much of the information that gets accommodated in cognitive processing is morphological, not occurrent. Instead of being explicitly represented via occurrent states in the course of processing, such information is instead accommodated implicitly "in the weights."[12] Morphological content is especially important with respect to the holistic aspects of cognitive processing. According to the DC framework, these aspects are not subserved by processes that update beliefs (and other informational states) by computationally manipulating explicit representations of all epistemically relevant information (thereby implementing a general, systematic, and precise theory of relevance). The moral of frame-type problems in classical cognitive science is that this is just not possible. Rather, the holistic aspects of cognitive tasks like belief fixation are primarily subserved morphologically: Cognitive transitions are automatically appropriate to large amounts of implicit information and to holistic normative-justificatory relations involving that information. According to the picture of cognitive processing provided by the DC framework, holistic aspects of cognitive processing *must* be subserved morphologically; this is an essential aspect of nature's "design solution" to the problem of avoiding framelike breakdowns in human cognition, and to the closely related problem of managing significant inductive reasoning without intractability.

The DC framework does not deny the possibility of systematic psychological generalizations, or the claim that such generalizations have an important explanatory role in cognitive science. But the kinds of generalizations the framework envisions will not, in general, generate predictions of people's specific psychological state transitions; the generalizations will not be as predictively powerful as we are ourselves in our ability to anticipate and understand one another. There are at least two reasons why the generalizations will fall short of such predictiveness. First, normally they will be *soft* (in the terminology of Horgan and Tienson 1990, 1996). They will have ineliminable ceteris paribus clauses that advert to potential psychology-level exceptions—and not merely to nonpsychological exceptions like physical malfunction (e.g., having a stroke) or external interference (e.g., being hit by a bus).

A second reason why the kinds of generalizations allowed for by the DC framework normally will not be strongly predictive involves likely features of such generalizations that Heal herself emphasizes. (Her focus is on generalizations that are part of our commonsense knowledge of persons, but the point carries over to certain generalizations that cognitive science might produce within the DC framework.) Concerning the kinds of theoretical knowledge that we already possess, she says:

> We are capable of stating explicitly a fair amount about the sort of beings we take people to be, the factors which influence them and how they interrelate. For example they can perceive what is in spatial proximity to them through their various senses and can remember past events and can in these ways acquire beliefs. They have desires and, under the guidance of their beliefs, form projects on how to fulfil them. They feel emotions which are liable to influence their patterns of reasoning. And so on. . . . Such generalities say nothing directly on beliefs or projects about particular subject matters, e.g., under what circumstances a doctor will believe that a patient has measles or when a restaurant customer will order a meal.[13]

Since the kinds of generalizations Heal cites in this passage are about psychological state types *as broad classes,* in general they do not combine with specific facts about a person's total psychological state at a given moment to yield predictions about the psychological state transitions the person will undergo thereafter (not even hedged predictions with an attached ceteris paribus qualifier). This is because such generalizations do not have specific instantiations of the right form, namely, the form of a conditional statement whose antecedent describes a combination of specific beliefs, desires, projects, and so on, possessed by someone at a specific moment in time, and whose consequent describes such a combination of specific psychological states at a subsequent moment. As one might put it, they are not *plug-in* generalizations—it is not possible to take a description of a person's total psychological state at an initial moment and then plug it into an instantiation of the generalization in order to obtain a prediction of the person's total psychological state at a later moment.

Let us take stock. Heal is not doubting that theory and theoretical modeling may play some role in how we manage to understand others, and neither are we. In what follows, we attempt to say more about the complementary role of theory and simulation. For now, the point is just that the application of theory alone, either explicit or implicit, cannot plausibly be the sole component of our competence here. In general, the theoretical generalizations available to us will fail to be strongly predictive because normally they will be soft and/or they will not be plug-in generalizations. Even allowing that discursive information regarding cognitive tendencies can affect how we understand others, still, at some point, the task of tracing out how certain contentful states would interact with the agent's many others will commonly need to be turned over to simulation. Here, the one seeking to understand relies on his or her own processes to trace out just where a set of beliefs would lead. In Heal's terms, since we lack a theory of relevance in understanding others and in "grappling with content," we ultimately need to be able to simulate.

4. The Dynamic Duo

We have argued that simulation will need to play an important role in our understanding others. Although our understanding may be shaped by discursive information in ways yet to be sketched, commonly, at some point, we will need to rely on simulation to trace out the global interaction of content. To further appreciate the role for simulation in understanding others, we will need to get clear on the roles also played by processes driven by discursive information. How does our capacity for simulation hook up with other capacities to make for our full epistemic competence in understanding others?

Neither simulation nor theory application threatens to monopolize the capacity for understanding others; they should not be seen as competing models of our competence, for neither alone is up to satisfying the market for understanding. The reason is simple: Each, with a minimum of supplementation, has significant blind spots. Since their blind spots are not identical, we do well epistemically to employ simulation and theoretical modeling as complementary processes—and to employ hybrid processes. For the purposes of this discussion, we may do well to recast considerations found in Henderson (1995). To begin, let us think in terms of the two extremes within the possible mixes of theory and simulation. This will allow us to take some stock of the blind spots of each.

First, consider the extreme of reliance on theory: Discursive information (some sufficiently developed to be called "theory") carries the maximum load in understanding. To imagine a relatively pure case of theory reliance, suppose that we have a powerful psychological theory—implicit or explicit—that characterizes many of the sorts of transitions between contentful states to which humans are disposed. We may also suppose that we can draw upon an extensive discursive characterization of what certain folk be-

lieve and desire. Finally, we might add a characterization of how perceptual beliefs are likely to arise in folk against a background of beliefs.[14]

Even supposing this highly favorable theoretical situation, we should acknowledge that the strategic use of off-line processes plays a limited but crucial role in applying all this discursive information. Again, the theory characterizes the transitions to which agents are disposed in terms of relations between contentful states—typically not mentioning particular beliefs or desires. When the theory says that agents make certain sorts of transitions in their reasoning, we may need to rely on our ability to work with such contentful states themselves in order to trace out just where the particular initial beliefs and desires that the agent is characterized as having would lead her were she to make the sorts of generic transitions indicated.

To say that off-line processes have a crucial role in applying theory is not to say that simulation enters here. It is to note that closely related cognitive strategies enter. In simulation, off-line processes are employed with distinctive aspirations: to instantiate processes that in content and structure parallel those operative in the other. The simulator aspires to do this by turning his or her own processes to work on those distinctive beliefs and desires possessed by the other; the content at transitions of the resulting process is supposed to be the same. In contrast, the use of off-line processes to apply theory does not entail concern for strict parallels between the agent's and the investigator's processing. The off-line processes are put to a different use—identification of applications of a theory to the case at hand. In such cases, our own processes are employed off-line, but to trace out the implications of theory to the case at hand.

For concreteness, suppose our theory indicates that folk with certain training will be insensitive to sample bias. Our own processes may no longer run in such channels—due to different training. However, we can trace out the contentful results of such free generalization by adding into the pretend-belief mix a pretend-belief that the relevant sample is representative. But we should be under no illusion that the subject of our simulation has such a belief or that it plays a role in freeing the subject to make the generalizations that we trace out. It is not added in to our processing to parallel the agent's processes but to trace out where certain input would lead our subject, in keeping with our theory. In any case, the place for something closely related to simulation in the application of theory should give us further reason to question the commonly imagined tension between these strategies. Off-line cognition in the service of theory and theory-informed simulation are very close kin—the difference turning on how close a parallel in cognitive processing is aspired to.

In some cases, the off-line processes required to sustain the application of theory may themselves be plausibly viewed alternatively as small simulations. Suppose that our theory includes some descendant of Festinger's the-

ory of cognitive dissonance. It holds that a person who has a set of beliefs and desires that are "dissonant" will seek to revise his or her set in order to alleviate the dissonance. Perhaps we are told that dissonance is related to inconsistency but that a set of beliefs and desires can be dissonant without strictly being inconsistent. One also experiences dissonance when recognizing or sensing that one's set of beliefs and desires is inconsistent with the proposition that all is as it should be. We get the general idea, perhaps aided by some examples. Our own capacity for monitoring our own beliefs and desires for tension can then be put to work on beliefs and desires that we suppose someone to have. This allows us to register when the antecedent conditions for dissonance resolution obtain in a given case—when, that is, the subject of our investigation has cognitive dissonance. Then our own abilities to explore sets of intentional states may be put to work, identifying various ways in which the dissonance might be exorcised by emending beliefs or modifying the values assigned to outcomes, and so on. That is, our ability to work with such contentful states is put to work to identify some of the range of things that our subject might do in keeping with the theory. Suppose that an agent has just been induced to part with a very significant sum in purchasing a new Volvo, under the influence of a persuasive salesperson. Suppose also that the agent is widely recognized as a tightwad, with the associated values and beliefs. It is likely that we employ our cognitive capacities, off-line, to identify this as a likely case of dissonance—we see that such an agent would readily have misgivings regarding whether all is now as it should be in his or her financial life. We can project several ways in which the agent might then move to reassure him- or herself—alleviating the dissonance. We would not then be surprised to find our agent paying increased attention to safety data or to reliability data in *Consumer Reports*. These would allow the agent to reinforce his or her high evaluation of the new car.

In the application of the theory about cognitive dissonance and its effects, we have employed our own processes for identifying tension in our global belief sets, and for exploring ways of resolving tension. Strictly speaking, for the application of this theory, there need be no suggestion that such processes parallel those operative in the agent—all that is required is that these processes identify for us likely cases of dissonance, and prominent routes to its resolution. (Certainly there need be no suggestion that our new car buyer employs the notion of cognitive dissonance.) However, in the present example, it is highly plausible that the off-line processes we employ are similar to those operative in our subject. In such cases, we might conceive these processes interchangeably either as simply the off-line application of theory or as stretches of theory-informed simulation.

Whatever the details, what the two cases illustrate is that, even when maximally relying on theory, the off-line use of our own capacity for work-

ing with contentful states may be needed in the course of applying theory. If this is right, then theory with no help in its application from off-line processes will have very large blind spots due to the problems faced in its application. It is appropriate to think of the maximal reliance on theory in terms of what would be needed to apply the theory effectively. So, if our suggestions above are correct, the appropriate conception of the maximal reliance on theory in understanding, and minimal use of simulation, would allow for the use of off-line capacities for dealing with contentful states in tracing out the connections suggested by theory. In this case these processes are used less to parallel agents' cognitive processing and more to apply our theory. We think it fair to say that theory here can carry significant weight.

Let us now note the blind spots to which the maximal reliance on theory will be subject. Obviously, there are blind spots that result from the limitations of our psychological theory. It is uncontestable that our psychological theory remains less than we would like. Where it remains sketchy or silent, maximal reliance on theory without supplementation by simulation produces blind spots.

Some blind spots, arising from the limitations of our current theories, will disappear as theory is improved. Thus some of the blind spots of maximal theory reliance can be expected to disappear. However, we suspect that some blind spots will remain with us always. For, as suggested above, a fully developed theory of relevance is not to be had. Where theory touches on cognitive processes that turn on the individual's sensitivity to her global belief set, theory is and will remain sketchy. This systematic and principled limitation on what is to be expected of theory gives rise to a systematic blind spot for the maximal reliance on theory. As argued already, moving ahead epistemically with such cases requires handing them over to simulation.

What would constitute a maximal reliance on simulation? And what would be its blind spots? Again, simulation is a matter of using one's off-line cognitive processes to parallel the cognitive processes of the other, ascribing to the other parallel processes. To initiate such a simulation, we must take certain of our cognitive processes off-line and provide them with select input. The blind spots of maximal reliance on simulation are generally of two kinds: those that result from setting up the simulation in ill-informed ways and those that result from the inflexibility of our cognitive processes.

Theory (or discursive information generally) may condition in epistemically important ways how one sets up a simulation. Minimizing the role of theory can make for simulations that are less sensitive to the differences among persons. Such lack of sensitivity makes for blind spots. Theory may help one select which of one's processes to employ when simulating certain others. Theory, together with information about one's biography and the biography of one's subjects, may indicate that one has learned certain elaborations on rudimentary human cognitive tendencies that our subjects have not. Accordingly, in simulating the other, one needs to employ the less tutored processes—if possible. If one employs differently educated processes, errors will likely result. Of course, one's subjects may have been trained in ways that lead them to have processes diverging from both one's trained processes and one's (presumably largely shared) rudimentary processes on which one's earlier training worked. Perhaps theory can inform the simulator how to adjust processes accordingly for purposes of the simulation. Discursive information may also be important in determining the inputs to which subjects may be responding in a given context. One would want such information to inform one's pretend-belief and pretend-desire generator in setting up the simulation. Without information about systematic differences in processes and inputs, simulation would become a more bumbling affair, one insensitive to differences among people.

At any point in time, a person's cognitive processes are somewhat inflexible. Yet with training, over time, cognitive processes can be shaped somewhat. These simple points are the basis of an important limitation of simulation: My cognitive processes may not be such as can be made on demand to run on in ways parallel to those of various others.

Our cognitive processes are undergoing a slow metamorphosis day in and day out. Our teachers trained us; our colleagues continue to do the same. We, and our experiences of success and failure, contribute as well. While slow, the changes can be cumulative. We hope that, after four years of college, the students who have been our charges have acquired ways of reasoning that are significant refinements over those they possessed upon entering the academy. Similar shaping of cognitive processes is pervasive. Bird-watchers do it; beekeepers do it; even more educated and less educated clergy do it. And learning one way of reasoning is commonly unlearning others. To learn a sensitivity to sample bias, one both learns to determine that a sample is (likely) representative before generalizing to the population and learns not to generalize to a population from samples without such a determination. Since our rudimentary cognitive tendencies include tendencies to generalize from salient cases without attention to representativeness, this second process is unlearned while sensitivity to possible sample bias is learned. In other contexts, or other communities, cognitive capacities may be trimmed and trained differently.

Suppose that training results in a certain set of transitions being natural to me. For example, I may have learned to think of the probability of a given result in any one iteration of certain sorts of processes (like coin flips or roles of die) as independent of earlier results, and as a function of enduring structural characteristics of the process (like the shape of the coin or die, and the distribution of its weight). I am then unable to engage in the gambler's fallacy.[15] I may recognize how one committing that fallacy is reasoning, recognizing the contentful transitions in a person's reasoning as an instance of a way of reasoning to which some folk are disposed. (This is a significant applied theoretical understanding.) But if I take my cognitive processes off-line, they don't swing that way. When I feed them the information that a coin has come up heads on the first five flips and ask myself what to expect on the next flip, I get a question: Was there something "funny" about that coin? I feel compelled to answer this question before answering the question posed. When pretend-given that the coin was of an everyday sort pulled at random from someone's pocket, I conclude that the coin is "fair" and that there is no basis for expecting heads or tails on the next flip.

Our discussion of the DC framework gives us a useful way of conceiving the sort of cognitive inflexibility that concerns us here. Trained in one way, my cognitive system has come to take on a certain topology. Trained in another way, a different person's system has come to have a different topology. The sequence of activation states will take a certain trajectory in my system, given what is "downhill" from a given input point. The same input will take a different trajectory in the other, given that very different things may be "downhill" from the point in activation space that represents that input in that system. It may have taken a long time for each of us to acquire our respective cognitive topologies. Changing that topology would likely be a slow process. Changing my topology into the other's, so that my processing upon input would really parallel the other's, might be very difficult, if not impossible. Certainly, it would not be a low-cost route to understanding the other.

The picture that emerges from all this is of limited short-term flexibility in the cognitive processes that an individual can take off-line together with somewhat greater plasticity in the long term, as training shapes the cognitive processes within each of our repertoires. At any one time, there is some limited variation in the cognitive processes that I can call into play (either on-line or off-line). Thus the exact nature of my reasoning may vary as I find myself in various contexts at home with family, at professional presentations, in my office, in the gym, and so on. This variability is a psychological fact. Still, it is limited. Another person, with different life experiences, will have come to have a somewhat different set of processes that can be called into play. Presumably, there will be some overlap. However, it also seems that, in each of our cases, there may well be processes that the other cannot call into play. Successful simulation turns on the simulator's cognitive repertoire including processes of the same sort as those that the subject of the simulation calls into play in the slice of life that is to be simulated. Further, it turns on calling into play that process as opposed to others in the simulator's limited repertoire. As a result, maximal simulation faces two blind spots. First, when the simulator's repertoire includes processes of the sort that are in play in the simulated's processing, but when the simulator calls into play different processes, simulation leads to misunderstanding. Discursive information about individual biographies and about conditioned cognitive tendencies may play a role in setting up the simulation correctly. Maximal simulation thus increases the risks of misunderstanding—needlessly expanding the scope of the blind spots to which simulation is subject. Thus the first set of blind spots faced by maximal simulation arises from its selective blindness (or nearsightedness) with respect to differences in people and their cognitive processes. Second, even allowing for the use of discursive information to condition simulation, it is generally subject to blind spots owing to the limited flexibility of cognitive processes. When the processes in one's repertoire do not include those that the subject of simulation employs, simulation is blind.[16]

It is manifest that each of us can describe processes that we cannot readily employ. Again, the simple case of the gambler's fallacy provides a case in point. It is easy enough to describe the fallacy and it is easy enough to recognize instances. What is not easy, these days, is getting our own processes to freely run along those lines. Of course, after a fashion, we can trace out the agent's reasoning. But, as seen earlier, doing this seems rather more like the application of theory than simulation proper. Another example, one having more to do with desires, might be the compulsion that some reportedly experience with respect to certain forms of sadomasochism.

It is also plausible that one can simulate processes that one cannot describe. One can simulate being moved in certain ways by a movie or by a photograph while having very little discursive understanding of the processes that are responsible.

We can begin to appreciate the epistemic importance of these observations while thinking in terms of the epistemic virtue of reliability. To say that one has the capacity to simulate a range of human behavior and thought is to say that, as applied to that range of cases, simulation is reliable. It is to say that simulation is reliable in environments in which there is a preponderance of such cases. To say that one can successfully apply theory, thereby accounting for a range of behavior and thought, is to say that applying theory in this way to the relevant cases is reliable—or that one's application of that theory in an environment in which it covers the preponderance of cases is reliable. Regarding the epistemic benefits to be gotten from the joint application of simulation and theory, at least two conclusions now can be drawn.

First, insofar as both simulation and the application of theory can be reliable, each within its own somewhat varying range, applying them jointly, in a sensitive and coordinated manner, should be reliable in yet a greater range of cases than applying either of them in a maximally exclusive fashion. Although the application of theory by itself will be inadequate to deal with cases in which relevance within the cognizer's global belief and desire sets is crucial, simulation provides a natural supplement. Further, while theory will be limited in yet other ways at any one point in time, simulation allows us to reliably handle some of the cases in which theory is inadequate. On the other hand, simulation is intrinsically subject to limitations due to the inflexibility of any individual's cognitive processes at a time. Because theory will have applications to some of the resulting unsimulatable cases, it may extend the range of cases reliably handled. In any case, theory, and discursive information generally, informs simulation in important ways, contributing to the range of cases in which simulation is itself reliable. Thus the competence resulting from the coordinated application of theory and simulation would seem to be reliable in a set of cases that includes (roughly) the union of the sorts of cases in which the two are individually reliable.

The coordinated application of both theory and simulation expands the range of sorts of cases with which we can reliably deal. And, judging from the many true beliefs that we generate in our day-to-day dealings with folk, the partnership is sufficiently reliable that there need be no objection on that score to enshrining it in our epistemic competence.

The gains in range of reliability attendant upon a cooperative use of theory and simulation have some implications for other epistemic virtues. For example, cooperation seems a boon for systematicity. First, simply the generation of a greater range of true beliefs about the behavior and mental life of individuals enriches our set of beliefs. We come to understand a more diverse set of individuals. Second, because theory is here embraced as a useful component of our managing to understand others, it is natural to continue to develop theory so as to integrate this increasing diversity of cases into a systematic treatment that is even more encompassing.

We get a complementary picture when we recast our observations in terms of the reliability of the strategies as applied in differing environments. We find that the cooperative application of theory and simulation has the virtue of being more robust than simulation or theory application alone. For a striking comparison, begin by reflecting on maximal simulation with a minimum of help from discursive information (we will want to note the effects of then refining simulation using discursive information and ultimately of complementing simulation with theory application). Suppose that a person, call him Bob, has grown up in a highly homogeneous community, call it Russell, Kansas. In our first possible world, Bob and most all his contemporaries remain in Russell throughout their lives, happy to ignore the wider world. As a result, the great preponderance of cases to which Bob and other Russellians must turn their capacities for understanding are those involving people rather a lot like themselves in ethnic and family backgrounds, in formal and informal training, in beliefs, and in life expectations.

Suppose that Bob and friends, being little interested in psychological theory, rely largely on simulation and that their capacity for simulation constitutes the bulk of their competence in this area. Happily for them, simulation is fairly reliable in their environment. For such a set of agents, inhabiting a world in which their cognitive environment is limited and largely populated by folk much like themselves, simulation is fairly reliable all by itself. In fact, if the social environment is homogeneous enough, there seems little refinement for theory or discursive information to effect in setting up simulations. Even maximal reliance on simulation with minimal use of discursive information—even untutored simulation in which relatively little adjustment is made in processes to be taken off-line and in beliefs and desires supposed in the simulation—would seem acceptably reliable.

Now suppose that Bob lives in a somewhat different world. In this world, Bob leaves Russell as a young man to join the military and is exposed to a more diverse set of people. Perhaps he returns home and uses his veteran's benefits to pursue his education. Perhaps he becomes interested in anthropology or political science or law. In his subsequent years, he finds himself doing fieldwork in strange places. Or he enters political life and attains high office in Washington, D.C. In any case, Bob's environment is wider, and the occasions for putting his capacity for understanding to work are more varied. We may add that similar mobility characterizes many of Bob's old Russellian cohorts—they are scattered by vicissitudes of the contemporary job market, family life, corporate transfers, and so on. They also encounter a heterogeneous set of folk. In these contexts their capacities for simulation will be less reliable, perhaps unacceptably so. Until they bootstrap themselves into an understanding of the diversity they face and until they employ such information both to inform their simulations and to selectively curtail their reliance on simulation, they will often go wrong. There are two ways in which discursive information enhances the reliability of their practices, and thus two ways in which maximal simulation with minimal reliance on discursive information is epistemically compromising. First, simulation whose setup is minimally informed is less reliable than simulation need be. Second, when an epistemic agent cannot "fall back" on the application of theory where cognitive inflexibility becomes limiting, the resulting overextended simulation is systematically misleading. Until these agents realize that at certain points certain folk are difficult if not impossible to really simulate, their ready use of simulation will repeatedly lead them wrong.

Thus, as illustrated by the plight of the Russellians in differing worlds, the reliability of simulation will vary inversely with the heterogeneity in the cognitive processes to be encountered in a particular world or environment. There are presumably many worlds in which there is significant diversity in folk's social environment. Accordingly, the use of simulation alone may be reliable in some worlds, such as that in which Bob and his fellow Russellians stay at home, but simulation by itself fails to be robust.

We believe that this lack of robustness makes maximal simulation epistemically undesirable, even for the Russellians who happen to luck into a particular world in which it is reliable. Given that the epistemic situation is intrinsically one of uncertainty regarding what the world is like, it is desirable to employ processes that would be reliable in a wide range of possible worlds. To do otherwise is to court epistemic failure—it is to run an unnecessary risk of relying on unreliable processes. Even if an agent happens to inhabit a particularly undemanding world and thus lucks into employing processes with the virtue of reliability in that agent's world, still, that agent's cognitive processes nevertheless are unacceptably risky when lacking robustness. Epistemically, it is not enough to be lucky; one should also be good—and this is to employ processes with the epistemic virtues of robustness and systematicity, as well as reliability.

On the other hand, the cooperative use of theory and simulation could be fairly robust. In worlds in which a folk face a cognitively homogeneous environment, simulation will be reliable, as suggested above. If anything, this reliability will be augmented by refinements brought about as the setup of simulation comes to be better informed with respect to what diversity there might be. In worlds in which they face a heterogeneous social environment, the development and application of theory promises both to refine simulation, when it is feasible, and to cover for the limitations of simulation, when refinement is not to be had. Theory, joined with simulation, seems the way to salvage reliability in the face of cognitive diversity (if it is to be salvaged).

Our world seems to be characterized by a good deal of heterogeneity, and simulation alone fails to be either robust or reliable. On the other hand, the joint application of theory and application may well be both robust and reliable, and it is at least congenial to systematicity. We believe that such a joint application is reflected in the ways that we manage to understand others, and we conclude that this is central to our epistemic competence in understanding others.

5. On the Social Sciences

There has been a long debate over whether the social sciences are best understood as models of interpretation or models of explanation. This debate has been misguided. Its rotten fruit results from reliance on models of interpretation and explanation that are themselves deeply flawed. As more adequate understandings emerge, the putative contrasting and competing approaches to the social sciences—the explanatist and interpretivist model—cease to conflict. When explanation, for example, is no longer forced into the distorting

mold of the covering-law model, we come to recognize that interpretivist social science serves up explanations. Further, when we look at debates over the
merits of competing interpretations, we find much turning on evaluations of
the merits of the explanations that the competitors spawn. Thus successful
explanation turns out to be a desideratum for correctness of interpretation.
At the same time, explanations turn on interpretations—from which their
understanding of initial conditions, or their pretend-beliefs, are taken. Accordingly, our confidence that any given explanation is correct should itself
partially turn on the successes that can be claimed for the interpretive scheme
on which that explanation draws. Accordingly, an interpretivist model of the
social sciences must also be an explanationist model, and an explanation-
centered model should also be an interpretivist model.[17]

There has been some tendency to see the clash between simulation theorists and theory theorists against the background of the older debate, with
theory theorists viewed as partisans of the explanation-centered understanding and simulation theorists viewed as championing yet another interpretivist model. This is doubly mistaken. It compounds the mistakes of the
older debate by somehow forgetting that the simulation theorist seeks to
model our intentional explanations of folk. The mistake is understandable,
as the talk of applying theory suggests to some the sort of subsumption under covering laws that once provided the philosopher's model of explanation—but that time should be past. Both theory theory and simulation theory attempt to model our explanations of others in intentional terms. If we
are correct here, both manage to model some of our successful explanatory
practice. Both are partial models of our epistemic competence for intentional explanations. The full model requires a hybrid model—one providing for the coordinated application of these strategies. To emphasize, Henderson (1995) shows that these models should not be taken as competing
accounts of explanations—describing two very unlike sorts of putative explanation—but as characterizing different epistemic routes to a single sort
of explanation, one in which the causal antecedents of the action to be explained are identified (in response to a why question). In this chapter we
have elaborated these themes by showing how each strategy constitutes one
component of our epistemic competence for generating such explanations.
We have argued that the coordinated use of the two strategies has the full
range of epistemic virtues that we seek in our cognitive practices: It is acceptably reliable, is congenial to systematicity, and is robust.

Even so, we feel compelled to insist that even the account of our epistemic competence advocated here falls short of a full picture of the human
sciences (obviously). It is an account of our ability to generate explanations
or possible explanations, drawing on background theory and on background information about people. Sometimes we apply theory. Sometimes
we generate (in an informed way) pretend-beliefs and -desires. Sometimes

we do some of both. In any case, when what we are then led to matches, as far as we can tell, what is observed, then we have a possible explanatory success. When we are led in ways that do not match what seems to be observed, we know that either our theory was wrong (if we were applying significant theory) or that our information about our subject's beliefs and desires was wrong or that we did not manage to call into play cognitive capacities quite like those that our subject employed. (We noticed this range of pitfalls earlier.) In such cases, we must make informed choices of where to tinker. We may tinker with our theoretical understandings of human cognitive capacities, the forms they can take, and their plasticity with training and with situations. We may tinker with our putative information regarding the folk in question. In emending what we take our subjects to believe or desire, we commonly are also tinkering with our interpretive scheme for them. A full epistemic understanding of our practice in the social sciences would deal with our capacity for refining and developing theory, and with our capacity for building and refining interpretive schemes in the face of explanatory successes and failures.[18] Ultimately, then, a full understanding of the epistemic competence that underlies our social sciences will need to embed the capacity for coordinated use of theory and simulation as but one component, albeit an important one.

Notes

1. Henderson 1994a; Kitcher 1992.

2. Our point here is simply that certain sorts of interrelatedness of beliefs are important epistemically, presumably in addition to the simple number of true beliefs generated. The systematicity we have in mind includes the presence of general beliefs and models that allow one to subsume a range of particular beliefs—generating further cases, efficiently storing and recalling such cases, relating such cases to each other, and so on.

3. Henderson 1993; 1994b.

4. Horgan and Tienson 1996.

5. Although the pretend beliefs generated and then fed into our off-line capacities may be fairly numerous, this process always takes the form of marginal adjustments in the set of beliefs and desires that the simulator holds. Ordinary human belief sets are enormous, and even a relatively extensive set of adjustments will constitute only a limited subset of those beliefs on which any cognizer might draw. For example, Henderson (1994b) suggests that an anthropological monograph such as Evans-Pritchard's *Witchcraft, Oracles, and Magic Among the Azande* (1937) might well be conceived as a laboriously constructed handbook for making adjustments that would effect a limited purpose simulation of some traditional Azande. That monograph characterizes a hefty set of beliefs (and some value structures), but they are really only a sliver of any simulated Azande's beliefs. We might plug these in, to effect a similarity with an Azande subject, but any such set will be rounded out by background beliefs. The present point has striking parallels with Grandy 1973.

6. Unless, of course, what is simulated includes the subject's own reflections on his or her own cognitive processing.

7. Heal 1996b, p. 84. Heal herself does not distinguish clearly between the claim that a theory of relevance is not possible at all and the claim that even if it is possible humans do not employ it. But it appears to us that she is effectively arguing for both claims, in a way that our reconstruction of her reasoning makes explicit.

8. Fodor 1983, pp. 112–113.

9. See also Henderson and Horgan, forthcoming. In effect, the computational theory of mind posits two kinds of algorithmic rules over mental representations, isomorphic to one another. On the one hand, there are precise, exceptionless, rule-like generalizations over intentional mental states qua intentional. On the other hand, these "substantive" rules can be mapped onto purely *formal* rules for manipulating the representations qua syntactically structured objects. (See Horgan and Tienson 1996, sec. 2.1.) Rules of the former kind would amount to a general and predictive theory of relevance. So if there is no such theory, then there are no such substantive programmable rules over mental representations. Hence there is no set of purely formal–syntactic representation–manipulation rules that implement the (putative) substantive rules. For more on all this, see Horgan and Tienson 1996, chaps. 2–3.

10. Typically, the device employed is not an actual neural network but a simulation of one on a standard digital computer.

11. To describe some physical system (e.g., a planetary system or a connectionist network) mathematically as a dynamical system is to specify in a certain way its temporal evolution, both actual and hypothetical. The set of all possible states of the physical system—so characterized—is the mathematical system's abstract, high-dimensional *state space*. A useful geometrical metaphor for dynamical systems is the notion of a *landscape*. A dynamical system describing a physical system involving n distinct magnitudes can be thought of as a an n-dimensional analog of a two-dimensional, non-Euclidean, contoured surface, that is, a topological molding of the n-dimensional state space such that, were this surface oriented "horizontally" in an (n+1) dimensional space, a ball would "roll along the landscape" from any initial point p, in a way that corresponds to the way the physical system would evolve from the physical state corresponding to p. Connectionist systems are naturally describable, mathematically, as dynamical systems. The magnitudes determining the state space of a given connectionist system are the instantaneous activation levels of each of the nodes in the network. Thus the state space of a network is its "activation space" (which has as many dimensions as the network has nodes), and the dynamical system associated with the network is its "activation landscape." In connectionist models, cognitive processing is typically construed as evolution along the activation landscape from one point in activation space to another—where at least the beginning and ending points are interpreted as realizing intentional states.

12. In terms of the mathematics of dynamics, morphological content is embodied in the *topological contours* of the network's high-dimensional activation landscape.

13. Heal 1996b, pp. 77–78.

14. Ultimately, this last assumption is unrealistic for reasons reflected in our remarks on Heal's arguments. The generation of perceptual beliefs seems to us to be

another case in which cognitive processing is conditioned by one's global belief set in a way that renders it not susceptible to purely theoretically modeling.

15. The gambler's fallacy leads one to overestimate the probability of an event, when events of the relevant kind have been unexpectedly absent from the preceding course of events. For example, if the preceding five flips of a fair coin have produced only heads, one might insist that "tails is due" or "past due" and estimate that the probability of that result on the next flip is greater than one-half.

16. Earlier, following Heal, we argued that the persistent lack of a (descriptive) theory of relevance gives rise to an ineliminable role for simulation in dealing with the ways that contentful states interact globally. Since theory does not and (we suspect) cannot allow us to trace these interactions, at some point, theory must give over to simulation in these matters. However, it is worth noting that it seems plausible that simulation itself is in principle limited in taking up the slack for theory. The limitations here would seem to be remarkably like those plaguing simulation due to the short-term inflexibility of cognitive processes. If one is to simulate the nuanced global interaction of contentful states, it is presumably because one's own global set of beliefs is itself quite similar to that of the person simulated. The idea, it seems, is that one should be able to generate a fairly compact set of pretend beliefs to be fed into one's globally sensitive cognitive processes. These would prompt those processes to frame those beliefs that are relevant, given the new input, and to yield an output. All this—the globally sensitive processes, the global belief sets in which the new information mixes, the sets of belief that turn out to be relevant, and what then is made of the new information in that context—must be similar if the simulation is to work as simulation is advertised to work. In particular, if one's global belief set is significantly different, then the nuanced, globally sensitive processes will yield different results than those at work in the agent simulated. However, global belief sets, as opposed to relatively small substructures, are not the sort of thing that can be plugged in at will. Like cognitive capacities, they are presumably the sort of thing that is acquired over time, with training, and that has significant inflexibility. Thus, when global belief sets diverge markedly, simulation may not be up to the task it would need to perform, if it is to cover for the lack of a theory of relevance. What this indicates is that, when global belief sets diverge markedly, simulation and, along with it, understanding become awkward, increasingly approximate, halting, and problematic. Since theory is of limited use in these contexts and we were looking to simulation to bail us out, we seem to have come upon a real limit to what can be looked for in our cognitive capacities. Perhaps there is something to a limited doctrine of incommensurability. See also Henderson (1994b).

17. See Henderson 1993; Risjord forthcoming.

18. See, for example, Henderson 1993, chaps. 1–3, 7; Henderson 1994b; Risjord forthcoming.

Chapter Five

Understanding Other Minds and the Problem of Rationality

KARSTEN R. STUEBER

The nature and structure of interpretation is one of the most discussed topics in contemporary philosophy, in both the analytic and the continental traditions. Its central status in the philosophical debate is due to the linguistic turn that philosophy underwent at the beginning of this century, which resulted in the general consensus that linguistic meaning and mental content have to be regarded as phenomena that are in principle publicly accessible. Within this context, a comprehensive analysis of the way we interpret the linguistic and nonlinguistic actions of another person is philosophically important because it promises to be the only way through which we can gain deeper insights into age-old questions such as the nature of mental phenomena and the relation between language and thought.

One of the most prominent and influential positions within this framework, championed in different versions by Willard V. O. Quine, Donald Davidson, Daniel Dennett, and Martin Hollis, argues that a fundamental constraint for interpreting another person is to conceive of him as a rational agent, who agrees in some of his beliefs with us. Interpretation by necessity has to proceed in a charitable manner. According to this conception of interpretation, rationality is not merely an empirical trait of an agent but is constitutive for his agency.

The argument for such a strong assumption of rationality does not rest on an empirical investigation of the psychological mechanisms underlying either decisions of the interpreter or of the interpretee. Rather, it is based on an analysis of the manner according to which we would epistemically justify an interpretation to be empirically adequate in the situation of the field linguist. For that very reason, the argument for the strong rationality assumption has not gone unchallenged. It has been pointed out that the strong assumption of rationality cannot be maintained in light of empirical findings of cognitive psychology, which seem to show that human agents do behave irrationally in certain contexts without their actions being completely unintelligible and uninterpretable. The strong assumption of rationality and charity therefore cannot be regarded as a psychologically realistic assumption and as a constitutive principle of interpretation.

In this article, I will discuss the controversy regarding the status of the rationality assumption and I will evaluate it in light of the recent proposal of simulation theorists to develop a psychologically realistic account of the interpretation of another agent within the folk-psychological context. Interestingly enough, simulation theorists seem to conceive of their account of interpretation on the one hand as an alternative to the charitable approach to interpretation. On the other hand, they propose simulation as a central psychological mechanism that underlies the interpretive process within the framework of the rationality assumption. In the first section, I will briefly discuss the arguments for the simulation proposal. I will also argue that the above opposition between the various simulation proposals should best be understood as being based on an apparent disagreement. It rests on a certain vagueness in the definition of rationality. In the second section, I will maintain that the principle of charity should be understood as a global constraint for interpretation. As such, it is too weak to be a guide for deciding among different competing interpretations. Furthermore, such a conception of charity is fully compatible with the simulation proposal. Finally, in the third section, I will develop a conception of interpretation that cannot be regarded as a version of theory theory or of simulation theory, as it is commonly conceived. I will argue that simulation is only a necessary starting point for the interpretative process but that interpretation is not limited solely by our simulative capacities. Although I agree with the simulation theorists in rejecting a theory theory position, I will amend the simulation proposal by showing that in order to find behavior or thought processes intelligible, we do not necessarily have to simulate them. Rather, our conception of rationality is partially a reflective and theoretically informed one, which allows us to predict or understand the other person by cognitively extrapolating from our own case. Only in this manner can we also adequately explicate the interpretation of differently organized conceptual frameworks, as it is customary within the social sciences.

1. Simulation Theory and Rational Agency

In order to understand the interpretive position, which I will develop later and which I will contrast with the account of both theory theory and simulation theory, it is important to be clear about the main features of both positions. In the following, I will not pay too much attention to the differences among the various simulation theories, as they are not important for my argument. For the purposes of this chapter, a position should count as theory theory if it is maintained that the application of folk-psychological concepts to other persons is guided, at least tacitly, by knowledge about human psychology and certain belief/desire generalizations. It is also not significant whether such knowledge is organized in analogy to a scientific theory or whether it is organized alphabetically like the names in a telephone book. It is more crucial that the theory theory position maintains that our interpretive practices are necessarily guided by some claims about how human beings in general act or think. Simulation theorists deny this and maintain that on the most basic level we understand another person not by appealing to any general psychological knowledge but by putting ourselves in the shoes of the other person, imagining the world "as it would appear from his point of view" and "then deliberate, reason and see what decision emerges."[1] Such simulation requires sometimes that we feed our own decision system with pretend beliefs and desires and run it "off-line." It is quite consistent with simulation theory that we use information about differences between the interpreter and the interpretee in order to get into the right initial condition for the simulation by feeding our decision system with the right pretense beliefs and desires. But such information does not appeal to any general psychological principles. The prediction of the actions and thoughts of another person is based solely on the simulator's use of his own cognitive system.

One of the main defenses for the simulation theory, as outlined by Heal, proceeds under the assumption that a central point of our interpretative practices consists in making the actions and thoughts of an agent intelligible in light of some standards of rationality.[2] Heal draws her simulationist conclusions from the observation that the epistemic justification of contentful mental states is holistic and context dependent, that is, "no thought, whatever its subject matter, can be ruled out *a priori* as certainly irrelevant to a given question."[3] Hence the TT view could be right only if we have a general theory that would enable us to predict which other thoughts are epistemically relevant in a specific context. Yet empirically we are not very likely to tacitly possess such a complex theory of rationality. Moreover, even if we possessed such a theory, there would be no guarantee that we would apply it correctly in the relevant circumstances. We are threatened with a regress of theories, which can be avoided only by appealing to a specific nontheoretical capacity.[4]

To illustrate this line of thought, just imagine what would be the most plausible way of answering questions regarding how a person would behave or think in a restaurant after receiving a beer with a big spider in it. One is very unlikely to have stored a generalization about how people in general will behave in such a situation, since it is impossible that one has stored generalizations about every possible situation a human being can encounter. It is much more likely that one will imagine oneself in such a situation and process one's thoughts using one's own knowledge about restaurants in order to attempt to answer such questions. Even if one knew that people in general complain in such situations, one would not use such generalizations if one were told that this is part of a fraternity initiation ceremony and that the person wants desperately to be part of the beer-drinking camaraderie of such societies. Theories alone seem to be insufficient for finding the thinking of a person intelligible in a particular situation.

According to Heal, it is more plausible to conceive of thinking about thinking as thinking about a specific subject matter and not as a theoretical exercise of using an abstract psychological theory, which describes what is rational to think about an arbitrary subject matter. Only because we are able to actually think about the same subject matter as another person are we able to understand his thought processes. Lacking a general theory of rationality, our only option to grasp the rationality of thought processes of another person is to simulate or, as she now prefers to say, to co-cognize these thought processes in us since our own thought processes are rationally organized in the same manner.[5]

Simulation theorists, however, are divided over whether the simulation position should be seen as part of the rationality approach to interpretation or as a rival to such an approach. Goldman, in his exposition of simulation theory, stresses that we have no problems in predicting the behavior of people even if they behave irrationally according to the principles that we regard to be the best normative standards of rational inference and decision procedures. Furthermore, since we feel no need to attempt to attribute rationality to the agent in these circumstances, Goldman rejects the rationality approach to interpretation and claims superiority for the simulation approach. The simulation position can account for our interpretative intuitions without any problems, since it postulates that interpretation requires only similarity between the cognitive structures of the interpretee and the interpreter. We are able to correctly predict the behavior or thought processes of the target in these situations because our mind behaves as irrationally as the mind of the person to be interpreted.

To use one of the well-known examples from the relevant literature in cognitive psychology, we generally find it quite intelligible that a subject judges the fact that Linda is a bank teller and active in the feminist movement to be more probable than the fact that she is merely a bank teller, if Linda is described to him as being thirty-one years old, single, outspoken, very bright, a former philosophy major who is deeply concerned with issues of discrimination and social justice.[6] Even though such a judgment flagrantly violates our probability calculus, we all seem to be prone to making such irrational inferences. We therefore do not have any problems in predicting such irrational behavior.

Nevertheless, it should be pointed out that our ability to predict such irrational behavior does not alone constitute a knockdown argument for simulation theory. Cognitive scientists speculate whether these experimental findings show that we follow other inference mechanisms than the procedures recommended by the probability calculus. They suggest that we derive the wrong conclusion by following a representative heuristic, according to which Linda's profile corresponds to our conception of somebody who is active in the feminist movement. If this is the case, it is not clear why our predictive success could not be accounted for within the context of a theory theory position. A theory theory position would only have to maintain that our tacit theory of mind contains an appropriate generalization like the rule of thumb that people find an occurrence of an event more probable if it fits a particular representative stereotype.

More important is the question of whether or not Heal subsumes the simulation theory under the rationality approach to interpretation in the same sense that Goldman rejects such subsumption. The answer to this question is probably no, even though Heal's vague usage of the term "rationality" and her insistence on distinguishing her position from Goldman's does not make things any easier. In contrast to Goldman, Heal does not conceive of rationality in terms of a formalizable concept of ideal rationality, which is analyzed by our best theories of inductive or deductive inference and decision theory. Rationality should not be interpreted "in a narrow and demanding sense" and hence not "everything 'irrational' in the strict sense falls outside the domain of simulation."[7] One therefore has a right to wonder whether the cases of irrationality mentioned above are cases of rationality in the nondemanding sense. But if this were the case, there would be a merely nominal difference between Goldman and Heal. With Stich and Nichols, one would be right to wonder whether the term "rationality" has any precise empirical application or whether Heal defines rationality merely vacuously in terms of inferences that we can predict.[8]

In the next section I will address the issue of the extent to which we have to assume that agents are rational directly by evaluating Davidson's argument for the principle of charity. For the rest of the chapter, however, I will talk about rationality in the ideal sense as articulated by our accepted formal theories of reasoning, unless otherwise indicated by quotation marks. As far as the argument for simulation theory is concerned, I would suggest that nothing important hinges on the issue of whether or not we have to interpret according to any formalizable standards of rationality and on the question of how exactly we should define such standards. For a successful argument in favor of simulation theory, one only needs the premise that we interpret other persons in light of some standards of appropriateness, or more neutrally described, in light of some principles about what can be expected from a person in a specific situation, independent of whether these principles conform to our ideal and formally analyzable conception of rationality. As examples, one might think of principles of taste, principles of politeness or good manners, and principles of honesty.[9] That we approach interpretation from such a perspective can hardly be denied because a denial of such a premise would imply that we do not have any criteria to select justifiably among an infinite number of interpretive hypotheses. Moreover, we do not only interpret another person's behavior by these standards but are also able to judge our own behavior implicitly by them.

If one accepts this premise, the thesis that simulation plays an essential role in the interpretive process is just the other side of the coin engraved by Aristotle's and Wittgenstein's considerations on rule following. Even if we assume for a moment contrafactually that we have general standards or expectations that govern our behavior in every situation, these standards—whether tacit or explicit—can only be formulated on a very general level. These general standards are therefore to a certain extent open-ended. Each application requires a practical capacity to apply these rules in a particular situation. As Aristotle in his *Nicomachean Ethics* and Wittgenstein's rule following considerations in the *Philosophical Investigations*[10] show, such a capacity cannot be conceived of as being regulated by general rules, since it would lead to an infinite regress. Aristotle defines the capacity of the ethical person to apply general ethical rules in particular situations and to act appropriately as *phronesis,* or as a special sort of *know-how.* For that very reason, he claims that only the ethical person will be able to judge how to act ethically in a specific situation. Extending this argument, Aristotle would also have to say that only the ethical person will be able to predict how another ethical person will act, since he alone is able to simulate the decision of an ethical person in a specific situation. No purely theoretical knowledge can help him with this task.

These considerations gain even more weight if one recognizes that in normal situations agents are not only applying one rule to a particular situation but that they have to consider and weigh a variety of sometimes conflicting rules. The rule of politeness, for example, might advise one against telling one's neighbor that painting his house blue is a bad idea, whereas the rule of honesty, considerations of self-interest, and convictions of good taste strongly advise letting one's neighbor know how one feels. It is rather implausible to assume that we tacitly have a theory, which tells us what weight agents in general attach to these different norms in various situations and how they then decide to act. Consequently, predicting how somebody might act in such a situation would require using one's own decision procedure and practical know-how. Contrary to the claims of theory theorists, simulation would have to be regarded as a necessary ingredient for any interpretive process, whether or not one regards our behavior as actually being guided by what we regard as the ideal and formal standards of rationality.

2. Charity, Simulation, and Rationality

The argument for simulation theory should be understood to be independent from the question of whether or not interpretation is in general bound by the constraint of charity and a formalizable concept of rationality. In the following section, I will, however, attempt to derive a version of the rationality assumption from an analysis of radical interpretation, which is compatible with both the simulation proposal and Goldman's critique. Although I do think that the outlined argument is true to Davidson's own writing, my primary purpose is not a Davidson exegesis.[11]

For Davidson, the principle of charity advises the interpreter to optimize agreement between him and the interpretee. As such, it advises the interpreter to ascribe an unspecified body of true beliefs, which are in some way "rationally" organized. Davidson derives the principle of charity, as a constitutive principle of interpretation, by paying close attention to the underlying assumptions implicit in our practice of justifying an interpretation of the linguistic and nonlinguistic actions of another person. That is why Davidson focuses so much attention on the analysis of the thought experiment of radical interpretation, that is, an interpretation of a person from a culturally unknown environment. That thought experiment is not designed necessarily to give a realistic account of the actual work of the field linguist but is designed to force us to explicate the implicit assumptions underlying all our interpretative procedures.[12]

In the situation of radical interpretation, our only hope to justify interpretative hypotheses about the meaning of the speaker's utterances proceeds by assuming that the interpretee asserts something about his immediate environment, that is, we assume that the speaker expresses something that he believes to be true. Since his behavior is our only evidence for such an interpretive hypothesis, especially at the beginning of radical interpretation, we do not have any choice but to make such an assumption. Otherwise we could not conceive of his behavior in that situation as evidence for our interpretation because under the assumption that the speaker expresses a belief he thinks to be false, we would not be justified to assume that the environment provides any hint for the attribution of content and linguistic meaning. For similar reasons, we also have to assume from our perspective that a speaker's utterances are true in that particular environment. So in order to take his utterance "da ist ein Baum" as saying that there is a tree, we have to assume that he is saying something that he believes to be true and that is true by our standards.

However, as Quine's arguments have shown,[13] that the speaker really means that there is a tree cannot be conclusively justified by the above evidence alone. On the basis of it, we cannot determine whether he means to say that there is a tree or that there is an incarnation of a tree god, and so on. We can decide between these various hypotheses only in the context of interpreting his other beliefs and utterances. For his utterance to mean that there is a tree we also have to assume that he holds true sentences like "trees have branches" and "trees are plants" or that he has other beliefs about trees that he shares with us. Since the interpretation of a particular sentence is justified only in regard to the interpretation of other sentences, we have to assume that the speaker generally has opinions about the objects of the world that are similar to the ones we have and that he lives up to our standards of appropriate behavior and reasoning. It is not possible to assume that the speaker might follow utterly different standards of thought and reasoning because that would undermine the very notion of being able to justify any interpretation of his or her behavior. Under the assumption, for instance, that a speaker might have a system of beliefs in which every two beliefs contradict each other, no interpretative assumption could be justified. In such a case, his future behavior would always falsify our chosen interpretive hypothesis for a particular utterance. We thus would also have no reason to assume that his behavior constitutes linguistic behavior.

The interpretation of a particular sentence or action is justified only if it fits into an empirically supported interpretation of the agent's whole behavior. Since the justification of any interpretation proceeds holistically, insofar as the question of truth is concerned, it is more appropriate to understand charity as a principle constraining the interpretive process *globally* and *not locally*. It is a mistake to think of charity as an algorithmic procedure advising us always to interpret an utterance as being true or to prefer an interpretation merely because it would attribute quantitatively more true beliefs to an interpretee. Even though Davidson might sometimes have encouraged such an interpretation of charity, this view does not fit a holistic conception of the interpretive process. From the perspective of a holistic conception, attribution of a false belief might even be required if such attribution would make the overall behavior of the interpretee more intelligible. Charity, however, implies that such attribution is intelligible only if a certain background of agreement has been established.

Compared to the presupposition of truth, the issue of rationality is a bit more complicated.[14] Davidson seems to suggest on the one hand that the basic principles of our best theories in deductive and inductive logic and decision theory are constitutive for the attribution of propositional attitudes and for that reason are normatively valid for all agents. On the other hand, he allows for the occurrence of irrational yet interpretable behavior and maintains that there is no definite "list of 'basic principles of rationality'" and that the "kinds and degrees of deviation from the norms of rationality that we can understand or explain are not settled in advance."[15] As Cherniak has persuasively argued, given the processing capacity of the human brain, the organization of its cognitive architecture, and the structure of human memory, it is psychologically not realistic to expect human beings to meet the demands of our conception of ideal rationality. It can, for instance, hardly be assumed that human beings have no contradictory beliefs in their belief set, since they do not have the capacity to check their whole belief system for logical consistency in a reasonable time span.[16]

Given these considerations, ideal rationality cannot be expected from any human agent and it cannot be constitutive for the attribution of propositional attitudes as a whole. However, if the above analysis of radical interpretation is right, then a person is interpretable only if one can subdivide his total belief set into at least some subsets, which are not obviously inconsistent by the interpreter's standards and *are large enough to have a certain amount of complexity and structure.*[17] This position is, in my opinion, compatible with Davidson's own account of irrationality in terms of a certain partition or compartmentalization of the mind. But Davidson, given his use of Tarski's theory of truth as a theory of meaning, tends to stress that the interpreter's standards of rationality are the standards of our best theories of rationality. I require merely that the actual interpreter finds some structured subsets of beliefs that he judges to be consistent whether or not the interpreter is ideally rational in a formal sense. In their evaluation of the consistency of a certain set of beliefs the interpreter and interpretee are normally also bound by the same finitary predicaments Cherniak mentions and by the same shortfalls in rationality that cognitive science explicates. The normal interpreter is thus not necessarily bound by our best theories of rationality unless he has undergone rigorous logical and statistical training. Such lapses of irrationality do not constitute any impediment to interpretation, since they are normally shared by both interpreter and interpretee and are only recognizable on reflection.

Nevertheless, I would argue that there have to be some subsets of beliefs *with a certain amount of structure* that are judged to be consistent by the standards of ideal rationality. Assume for a moment that we are interpreted by an ideally rational interpreter. He will still have to find at least some subsets of our beliefs that he judges to be consistent, even though he might not agree with an ordinary human interpreter about which subsets are consistent. He would also disagree with the human interpreter about what would count as obviously irrational behavior in some cases. But the ideally rational interpreter would have to find such subsets or he could not regard our behavior to be linguistic behavior. More importantly, there has to be some agreement between the judgment of the normal interpreter and the ideally rational interpreter regarding the consistency of some subsets of beliefs. Or we could not conceive of the ideally rational interpreter from our perspective as somebody who has a language, if one follows the argument from radical interpretation. If we cannot conceive of the radical interpreter as somebody who is interpretable from our perspective, we could not conceive of him as an ideally rational interpreter. Since every subset of beliefs of the ideally rational interpreter is consistent by the standards of ideal rationality, it follows that some of our subset of beliefs must be judged consistent according to the same standards.

We might be inclined to challenge the above thought experiment in two ways. We could maintain that it begs the question, since it presupposes that the ideally rational interpreter is able to interpret us. Moreover, it seems that the exact opposite conclusion would follow if one would consider the "utterly irrational interpreter."[18] Both objections, however, rest on a misunderstanding of what is presupposed in our conception of an ideally rational interpreter. In light of the above considerations, an "utterly irrational interpreter" is not conceivable from our perspective as a linguistic being and thus as an interpreter. There is a certain asymmetry in the conceivability of an ideally rational agent and its complete opposite. Although we are able to recognize our own rational limitations vis-à-vis some ideal and formal conception of rationality, we cannot conceive of a linguistic being who does not abide by any norms of rationality. Yet our conception of an ideally rational interpreter implies that we conceive of him as a linguistic being who is in principle interpretable from our perspective. Interpretability, however, can only be conceived of as a reciprocal relation.

It has to be pointed out that the above conclusion regarding the ideal rationality of some of our subsets of beliefs is not contradicted by the empirical findings in cognitive science. They show that our belief set on the whole is probably not organized in the most rational fashion, but they do not imply that no subset of our belief system is consistent by the ideal standards of rationality. I would also assert that such a claim can, in principle, not be justified empirically because the interpretation of the relevant experiments always presupposes the attribution of definite beliefs and desires to a particular agent and thus presupposes subsets of beliefs that are rationally organized.

My interpretation of the principle of charity, as a principle that guides interpretation globally, implies the following three claims. First, it is constitutive for the interpretation of another agent that not only false beliefs can be attributed from the interpreter's perspective. Second, it is inconceivable that a system of beliefs is attributed, in which all its subsets with a certain amount of structure are inconsistent as judged by the interpreter's standards. Third, if I am right, the ideally rational agent and the human agent will have to agree in some of their judgments regarding the consistency of certain subsets of beliefs. My conception of the principle of charity thus implies the minimal conception of rationality, favored by Cherniak, according to which an agent fulfills some but not all of the requirements of our ideal and formalizable conception of rationality.

Goldman, in his critique of the charity approach to interpretation and in his argument for the simulation proposal, laments that such a conception of the rationality principle is too vague to be of any help for guiding the interpreter's "predictive and explanatory inferences" about an agent's beliefs.[19] Yet Goldman's critique of charity rests on a misconception. Charity, correctly (i.e., globally and holistically) understood, is a constitutive principle of interpretation without defining an algorithmic procedure of how to construct an interpretation for a particular person. Moreover, if charity is merely globally constraining the interpretive process, the interpreter is in need of a mechanism that allows him to fill out the details of his interpretation. Putting oneself into the shoes of the interpretee, in the way the simulation theorist proposes, is indeed one of the methods that would guide the interpreter in his interpretive attempt. If the considerations of the last sections are correct, it is not only a plausible method but it is necessary, since it is only in this manner that an interpreter can guess what the interpretee finds relevant in a particular situation. Contrary to Goldman, simulation then is not an alternative to the rationality approach; correctly understood, both approaches are fully compatible. The rationality approach focuses on the general principles constitutive for the interpretive process, whereas the simulation proposal focuses more on the mechanism that allows us to come up with a specific interpretive hypothesis within this larger context. Both charity and simulation are not options but are forced on us, albeit for different reasons.

3. Cognitive Extrapolation and the Limits of Simulation

Following the line of reasoning in the last section, simulation has to be regarded as a mechanism through which charity gets implemented in the interpretive process, at least to a certain degree. Interpretation can proceed only if the interpreter is able to think about particular areas—particularly such mundane objects as grass, trees, spiders—in the same way as the interpretee. I will, nevertheless, argue that the simulation proposal cannot account for the way in which we explicate the "rationality" or intelligibility of a person's thoughts from a very different cultural environment. I regard simulation even here as a necessary ingredient in the interpretive process that provides us with a starting point and allows us to identify interpretive puzzles. But the solution of these interpretive puzzles does not solely depend on our simulative capacities.

I will suggest that the simulation position fails to describe the full range of interpretive strategies accessible to human interpreters. In my opinion, it is fully compatible with the rejection of a theory theory position to conceive of the understanding of another person as being essentially "theoretically" guided without denying that my own thought processes about a particular subject matter are involved and without committing myself to a general theory of rationality. But I will deny that my thought processes have to be involved in the way the simulationist model conceives them to be engaged.

My argument can be understood both as a critique of Heal's earlier articles on the subject and as a friendly amendment to the position she develops in more recent writings. In her earlier articles, Heal seemed to argue that in order to find another person's thoughts intelligible we have to instantiate the same thoughts because we lack a general theory of rationality or relevance. I regard that argument as a non sequitur, since it assumes that our only choice is between a theory theory view with its commitment to the existence of a general theory of rationality and the simulation view, according to which we have to feed our own cognitive system with pretend beliefs and desires.

In her recent writings Heal has clarified her view. Instead of speaking of simulation, she now prefers to speak of co-cognition or the ability to think about the same subject matter. Heal regards the co-cognition thesis as an a priori thesis about how we predict another person's thoughts on the personal level. Simulation for her is an a posteriori thesis about the psychological processes on the subpersonal level. Although the co-cognition thesis supports arguments against the theory theory position at all levels, it is not required that co-cognition is realized by a mechanism of off-line simulation in which we feed our own cognitive system with pretend beliefs and desires. Other forms of simulations are also conceivable, depending on how our cognitive system is in fact organized. Heal also seems to be aware of the fact that the thesis of co-cognition is less plausible when we encounter very different worldviews, or "Weltanschauungen."[20]

Given these recognized limitations of the co-cognition view, I would regard my proposal as a friendly amendment. Furthermore, while Heal might be right that pretense–off-line simulation is only one possible way of realizing co-cognition, such a conception of simulation is a rather plausible account. It is also the only proposal on the table that deals with cultural differences within the context of simulation. According to this view, especially favored by Gordon,[21] we simulate another person by making room for relevant differences and by feeding our own cognitive system with certain pretend beliefs, desires and preferences, and so on. If the argument in the following is plausible, both Heal's co-cognition thesis and off-line simulation as conceived by Gordon have to be regarded as being of rather limited use for understanding central cases of cultural differences.

Take the following example, which will bring out the basic model for my improved conception of the interpretive strategy overcoming both the shortcomings of theory theory and simulation theory. Assume that you (having grown up in an environment in which the temperature is measured in degrees Fahrenheit rather than in degrees Celsius, as in most other countries) have to interpret and predict another agent's thoughts and behavior. To be more concrete, assume that the agent hears on the radio that it will be freezing in the night and that he is then asked to specify what temperature measurement would falsify such a statement. Obviously you would be wrong to predict that the agent will answer that a measurement of more than thirty-two degrees is required. But it would be easy for you to predict that the other person would say that it has to be higher than zero degrees, given that you know what you would predict in such a situation and your knowledge about the systematic relationship between the temperature scale in Celsius and in Fahrenheit.

The above ability to predict the other person's thought is structurally very different from either the proposal of off-line simulation or Heal's co-cognition thesis. According to that proposal, we would have to use the information about the difference between Fahrenheit and Celsius only at the beginning of the simulative process in order to feed our system with the right input and then co-instantiate thoughts of the interpretee, that is, we would have to think thoughts using the Celsius scale. The correct prediction would then be derived merely from the result of letting our own cognitive system run off-line.

I suggest that prediction actually succeeds as long as we recognize how we would think in a specific situation and then use this knowledge in conjunction with information about the cognitive and cultural differences between us and the interpretee in order to predict the different reaction of the interpretee. Even if we lack a general theory of "rationality" or relevance, as Heal persuasively argues, thinking about thinking is not only possible as first-order thinking about a specific domain in the world. Simulation theorists overlook that we have the second-order capacity to recognize the differences between our and the interpretee's basic cognitive or pragmatic presuppositions. These are the presuppositions that make a specific line of thought more acceptable than another alternative in a certain context. In light of such reflective second-order capacities, we are able to find an action intelligible without actually co-instantiating the same or similar first-order thoughts. We can predict our own reaction and have the ability to extrapolate the reaction of the other person based on our recognition of the different cognitive parameters or different background assumptions.

This characterization of the interpretive process is more realistic than either the co-instantiation or the off-line simulation proposal and it better describes the interpretive strategies that are central to our understanding of agents from very different cultural backgrounds, since it does not require that we actually have to start thinking in Celsius or to start seeing the world in terms of witches or demons in order to find such thoughts intelligible. Not only would we have to feed our cognitive mechanism with a few pretend beliefs; we would also have to "reorganize" our whole cognitive paradigm with its presuppositions, on which our normal contemporary thought processes rely. The co-instantiation and off-line simulation proposal underestimate the difficulties of simulating another person's thought processes, especially when culturally well-entrenched habits of thoughts and well-entrenched sets of beliefs are concerned. Although I am not denying that it is possible to start thinking about temperature in Celsius instead of Fahrenheit, especially after one has lived long enough in a culture, it certainly is not necessary. And since our ability for such reorganization is rather limited, to require such reorganization would imply serious limitations of our interpretive capacities and our ability to recognize the intelligibility of another person's actions.[22]

My argument should not be taken as denying simulation an important role in the interpretive process, but I do deny that the success of an interpretation always depends on our ability to simulate the other person. Interpretation is better conceived of as the ability to gather information about the central differences in cognitive and cultural frameworks, which would make the other person intelligible and "predictable" because of our ability to extrapolate the interpretee's reaction in the above manner. Evans-Pritchard's work on the witchcraft among the Azande is a good exemplification of my description of the interpretive strategy. His *Witchcraft, Oracles, and Magic Among the Azande* should be understood as a book that provides exactly the information needed to extrapolate the Azande's thoughts from my own thoughts in particular situations. His book also illustrates that the interpreter's own reaction and simulative capacities provide the puzzles that he has to solve in order to explicate the Azande's magical belief system. When we encounter a different line of thought that is prima facie implausible from our perspective, we do not necessarily adjust our cognitive system and then pretend to think those same thoughts ourselves. Rather, we ask a second-order question about the differences in the organization of our respective first-order thought processes. We have understood the other person when we are able to come up with a theoretical diagnosis that explains the prima facie implausibility of the first-order thought process by pointing to a difference in certain cultural background assumptions. In order to understand the Azande, for example, one has to recognize that "witchcraft explains why events are harmful to man and not how they happen."[23] Belief in witchcraft is for the Azande also compatible with the idea that human beings are responsible for their actions to a certain degree. For that very reason, the Azande do not blame witchcraft if an unskilled house builder builds a house that collapses. But they will blame witchcraft if a house that was built by a skilled person who followed all the appropriate standards of his trade collapses. Such information allows us to predict how the Azande would react in a situation in which we would blame human error without having to think the same thoughts that the Azande think.

In the end, I wish to introduce three caveats for my description of the interpretive strategy. First, I want to emphasize that the model of interpretation that I intend to propose is valid only as far as the behavior of the person can be accounted for within a folk-psychological belief–desire framework. I am not denying that certain cases of irrationality might not be solvable on that model but are only explainable in light of certain specific psychological theories about abnormal behavior. Certain behavior, for instance, might only be explicable as behavior under the influence of specific drugs or as the manifestation of a mental illness. In such cases, interpretation as conceived above breaks down and a more objectifying attitude toward the observed phenomena is needed.

Second, the above discussion of simulation theory has focused on the question of the scope of simulation insofar as rational thought processes were concerned. By doing that, I do not want to be understood as denying that our grasp of another person's emotional state is important for predicting and understanding his future actions or his state of mind. Rather, I agree with Gordon that simulation probably plays a central role in this context. I would, however, be inclined to argue that even here the role of simulation may be limited and has to be supplemented by cognitive extrapolation. Such second-order capacities are required in order to take full account of the social and cultural context, which at least influences the way our emotions get expressed, if it does not color our emotions themselves. As an example, one could point to the very different social conventions that guided the medieval phenomenon of courtly love. In order to understand such a phenomenon, one must implicitly appeal to one's own experiences of romantic love, but such "simulation" falls short of being able to grasp the medieval phenomenon. Short of becoming a medieval knight, cognitive extrapolation seems to be the more realistic option.

Third, nothing I have asserted contradicts Gadamer's insights about the prejudicial nature of all interpretation. Rather, I would argue that "prejudices" and preconceptions about the person to be interpreted determine exactly how the interplay between projection and cognitive extrapolation gets enacted in a particular interpretive enterprise. The anthropological debate about different forms of rationality as evidenced in the discussion about the correct interpretation of the Azande, the Tully River blacks, or more recently about "how the natives think about Captain Cook for example,"[24] can best be interpreted as being driven by concerns about the appropriateness of a certain preconception of the otherness of the interpretee. It is in light of these prejudices that we evaluate the appropriateness of the information for extrapolation. One would require different information for the task of cognitive extrapolation if one regards, for example, "natives" as primarily driven by a mytho-practical conception of the world, instead of regarding such a conception of the "native" as merely a myth of European origin, which forgets that "natives" are primarily driven by the same instrumental concerns that we have.

In this context, it has to be pointed out that Evans-Pritchard provides a perfectly good account of why the Azande are not interested in drawing the obvious conclusion that all men of a clan are witches if it is proven by postmortem investigation that one man is and it is further assumed that witchcraft is inherited by the son from his father and by the daughter from her mother. Evans-Pritchard seems to suggest that such inference would involve the "whole notion of witchcraft" in contradiction. He also insinuates that the Azande are less theoretically apt, at least compared to our own scientific standards. His own explication of this behavior belies such judgment, however. As Pritchard stresses, the Azande are not interested in witchcraft as such. A person's being a witch does not automatically prove that he is harming you. The Azande are only trying to find out with the help of the oracle whether somebody is bewitching them at a particular time and place.[25] They are not interested whether somebody has powers of witchcraft that he never uses. But if the Azande are not interested in witchcraft as such, then their reaction to the above logical conclusion is intelligible even from the perspective of a scientific worldview, given this information.

Winch has objected to this explication mainly on the basis that the Azande's system of witchcraft does not constitute a "theoretical system" and that Evans-Pritchard is committing a "category-mistake."[26] Even though I do not agree with Winch's claim that radically different forms of rationality are possible, his objections against Evans-Pritchard can be given a different reading. I understand him to be arguing that Evans-Pritchard provides merely information that would allow us to extrapolate the Azande from a scientific perspective, while it is more appropriate to see the Azande as being engaged in practicing a certain social ritual. To interpret the Azande appropriately, therefore, we should not extrapolate them from the perspective of a modern scientist but from the perspective of a religious believer who is familiar with his own religious rituals. Needless to say, we would need different information in order to accomplish such a task.[27]

These debates do not challenge the model of interpretation I have outlined above. Rather, they concern the question of what one should regard as the basis for the task of cognitive extrapolation. Such debates are never merely resolvable through evidence. They also require a reflection on the prejudices that the interpreter brings with him in accounting for the evidence. Even if one conceives of interpretation as an interplay between simulation and cognitive extrapolation, it still has to be seen as an open-ended process.

4. Conclusion

As I have tried to argue, the defense of a simulation position is most plausible if one understands it as following from the recognition that we do not possess a general theory of relevance and that our judgment about what is appropriate in a particular situation is based on an irreducibly practical capacity. I also argued that the simulation position is fully compatible with the principle of charity, conceived of as a *global* and *not a local* constraint of interpretation. Although I am not denying that simulation is required in order to get interpretation off the ground, I regard co-cognition, or off-line simulation, to be of limited use for the recognition of the appropriateness of certain behavior or thought process in a culture different from our own. If my contribution to the debate on interpretation is correct, simulation theorists overlook our ability to extrapolate cognitively the reaction of the other person based on information regarding differences between our and the interpretee's cognitive frameworks. Yet the above view should not be understood as a version of theory theory, since it does not conceive of the interpretive process as the application of one general psychological theory, which is valid for all cultures and which we possess either tacitly or explicitly. Differences between the central assumptions of different cultural backgrounds are specific to the compared cultures themselves. Interpretation has therefore to proceed through the interplay of projection and cognitive extrapolation. Only in the limiting case when the interpreter and interpretee share most of the central cultural assumptions is the thesis of co-cognition and off-line simulation plausible. But it is not the case that the limits of simulation can generally be understood as the bounds of interpretation.[28]

Notes

1. Heal 1995a, p. 47; Goldman 1995a, p. 85.
2. For a short description of the differences among the various simulation positions, see the introduction in this anthology. For Heal, simulation is essential mainly for the prediction of another person's thoughts on the basis of knowledge of his or her prior thoughts.
3. Heal 1996b, p. 79.
4. Heal 1996b, p. 83f.
5. Heal 1995a, p. 52.
6. For a good survey of the literature on irrationality, see Nisbett and Ross 1980. For a discussion of its philosophical implications, consult Stich 1990; Stein 1996.

7. Heal 1996a, pp. 57–58.

8. See Stich and Nichols 1997, p. 321.

9. In phrasing the issue in this manner, I am quite aware of the fact that one might justifiably wonder whether the concept of formalizable rationality appealed to by Goldman is too narrow. Shouldn't principles of taste, etc., be counted as part of a "thicker" concept of rationality, which would also break the boundaries of the concept of belief–desire rationality? This question certainly deserves further attention. In this article I can stay neutral on this topic. However, I would like to point out that the case for simulation theory is even more persuasive if one conceives of rationality in a "thicker" and less formalizable manner. See also McIntyre 1986; Heil 1992.

10. See also Stueber 1993, chap. 4; 1994b.

11. See especially essays 10, 11, and 13 in Davidson 1984. For an elaborated articulation of my view on Davidson, see Stueber 1993.

12. For a defense of this claim against criticism by Fodor and Lepore 1992, see Stueber 1997b.

13. See the first two chapters in Quine 1960.

14. The following paragraph benefited from Thargard and Nisbett 1983; Cherniak 1986; Stich 1990.

15. Davidson 1985, p. 352.

16. Cherniak 1986, pp. 92ff.

17. The second requirement is implied by my rejection of an atomistic position, that is, the idea that a belief set could contain only one belief. The belief sets I have in mind must be large enough to count as a system of beliefs. My requirement cannot be trivially fulfilled by the consistency of the unit set of a noncontradictory belief or a set that contains only logically equivalent beliefs.

18. This paragraph was written in response to questions that Peter Baumann has raised.

19. Goldman 1995a, p. 78.

20. See Heal 1998; 1996a, p. 58.

21. See Gordon 1995c.

22. I would also deny that a person who does not have the very same experiences or thoughts that another person has cannot in principle understand him or her. Instead, I would suggest that we should distinguish between "immediate understanding," which requires a lived familiarity with a certain culture and social context, and "reflective understanding," which involves what I call cognitive extrapolation and the use of our second-order capacities.

23. Evans-Pritchard 1937, p. 72.

24. For the debate about the correct account of the observed ignorance of the Tully River blacks regarding the issue of biological paternity, see Spiro 1968; Leach 1967. For the debate about Captain Cook and the Hawaiians, see Sahlins 1995; Obeyesekere 1992; Geertz 1995.

25. Evans-Pritchard 1937, pp. 24–26.

26. Winch 1964, p. 93.

27. For my view about how this might affect the question of interpretive relativism, see Stueber 1994a.

28. I would like to thank Peter Baumann, Bob Gordon, Thomas Grundmann, Bert Kögler, Manisha Sinha, Paul Roth, and Georg Vielmetter for helpful comments on an earlier draft of this chapter. It also benefited from a discussion at the University of North Florida. I am grateful to the College of the Holy Cross for supporting my work on this chapter through a faculty fellowship.

Chapter Six

Simulation Theory and the Verstehen *School: A Wittgensteinian Approach*

THEODORE R. SCHATZKI

Eager to set the social sciences, especially history, apart from their natural brethren, early representatives of the *Verstehen* School argued that these fields are wholly consumed by the pursuit of understanding. The idea that social science is primarily a search for understanding has lived on in the twentieth century, its most impressive reincarnations being Peter Winch's rule Wittgensteinism and Hans-Georg Gadamer's hermeneutics. At the same time, many sympathetic to the *Verstehen* cause have seen fit to defend a more limited claim, namely, that although the pursuit of understanding is not the only social-scientific task, all social inquiry rests on understanding. Two theses, characteristic of the *Verstehen* School throughout its history, are above all defended in this regard (though not all *Verstehen* theorists advocate both).

The first thesis is that understanding is the avenue of access to the object domain of social science (people, artifacts, and organizations thereof). The second is that explaining action is understanding it, that is, grasping its intelligibility and not accounting for it causally via laws. Together with further features, the *Verstehen* tradition has argued, these theses make the social sciences fundamentally different in nature from the natural ones. Notice that these theses leave untouched many central issues in social ontology and epistemology, for example, the compositional and causal role of action in social life and the explanation of such large-scale social phenomena as oppression, telecommunication systems, and gender arrangements. The theses are thus compatible with the claim that social science cognition and endeavor encompass much more than understanding and its pursuit.

A prominent position in contemporary philosophy of mind is the so-called simulation account of the use of mental predicates. According to this account, what underlies the predictive and explanatory use of these predicates is the act, or operation, of imagining being in other people's shoes. To many advocates and observers, this analysis resembles *Verstehen* accounts of understanding others, in particular those accounts that took empathy to be central to this understanding. This resemblance raises the question of whether simulation theory furthers the *Verstehen* conception of social investigation.

This chapter examines the issue by asking whether the simulation approach abets the two aforementioned claims central to this conception: (1) that understanding is the mode of access to social affairs (section 1) and (2) that explaining action is understanding it (section 2). For reasons to be explained, section 1 construes the question of access as an issue about the identification of action while section 2 focuses on a prominent class of action explanations, namely, mental explanations thereof. My overall thesis is that simulation theory lends at best limited support to the *Verstehen* conception of social inquiry, since, first, simulation, or imagining being in others' shoes, plays no role in the identification of what philosophers call "basic actions" and only an occasional and non-self-sufficient role in the identification of other actions. As a result, it does not significantly advance the claim that social affairs are accessed through understanding. Second, the imaginative act that simulation theory places at the core of the explanatory grasp of activity, and that resembles certain acts of understanding that the *Verstehen* tradition deemed central to social investigation, is only one of three operations that yield mental explanations. As a result, simulation theory can in principle only modestly advance the proposition that explaining action is understanding it.

The arguments in this chapter are based on ideas developed from the work of Ludwig Wittgenstein.[1] Wittgenstein averred that understanding human existence does not require delving behind the surface of human life via postulated structures and mechanisms (the surface of human life is the lived through human world). Rather, understanding is achieved through careful description of surface phenomena. Moreover, although these phenomena are exceedingly diverse and exhibit little system or unity, human activity, organized as social practices, is central to them. As a result, the description of practices is essential to understanding human life. A grasp of language is also crucial to this understanding, for linguistic acts are central to human practices. In addition, a Wittgensteinian perspective treats a wide variety of human phenomena, including meaning, mind, and action, as "constituted" (formed, determined, and instituted) within social practices. Such phenomena, consequently, are inherently social in character. A final feature of a Wittgensteinian account of human life would be the twin claims that mental conditions are bodily expressed in human activity and that such conditions are expressed in given actions rests on the situational, biographical, and practice contexts in which the activity transpires. Conjoined, these ideas support the two aforementioned *Verstehen* theses concerning the centrality of understanding, as well as the accompanying contention that the social sciences differ both epistemologically and methodologically from the natural disciplines. At the same time, I claim, these ideas imply that simulation theory provides limited succor for these propositions.

It will prove useful to fill in a bit more of the historical background of these two theses about understanding. Both understanding as access and understanding as explanation have been interpreted in two major ways: as a grasp of mind and as a grasp of matrices of significance. For thinkers such as Wilhelm Dilthey and R. G. Collingwood, the understanding that accesses social reality is a grasp of mental contents: purposes, values, and representations, for example, in the case of Dilthey and thoughts in that of Collingwood.[2] It is because these contents imbue human activity and, in addition, on Dilthey's account what he called "objective spirit" (e.g., tools, buildings) that activities and artifacts are elements of social, as opposed to physical, reality. According to these thinkers, moreover, the grasp of mentality through which human/historical phenomena are accessed also ipso facto provides an explanation of the actions (and artifacts) involved. For Dilthey and Collingwood, as for most other thinkers in the modern Western philosophical tradition, what people do depends on the state of their mind. A grasp of people's mental conditions explicates, therefore, why people act however they do. For these paragon thinkers, consequently, social science is *Verstehen*, centrally, because social affairs are accessed and actions are explained by one and the same grasp of mind.

By contrast, for such post-Wittgensteinian and Heideggerian representatives of the *Verstehen* tradition as Peter Winch, Charles Taylor, and Clifford Geertz, the understanding, or rather interpretation, inherent to the investigation of human beings is not, at least in the first place, a grasp of mind. Two principle alternatives are offered. According to one, understanding is primarily a grasp of the rules that govern activity.[3] According to the second, it is a reading of actions, artifacts, and organizations thereof within social matrices of significance. Taylor, for instance, claims that social-scientific interpretation involves a grasp of the "interpersonal" and "common" meanings, marked in people's language and carried in their practices, through which they carry on their lives.[4] Similarly, Geertz argues that interpretation is a grasp of the interpretations and formulas, embedded in "piled-up structure[s] of inference and implication," through which actors act, perceive, and interpret themselves and one another.[5] Although neither meanings nor inferential structures are mental phenomena (e.g., beliefs, ideas, or attitudes), interpretation still fulfills the twin tasks of access and explanation. It achieves access because social reality, for Taylor, and culture, for Geertz, are constituted by matrices of signification. It achieves explanation because action proceeds in terms of the significations involved (the story is more complicated in Taylor). Hence, a grasp of public meaning, not of mind, realizes the two central tasks assigned to understanding.

Proponents of simulation theory agree that it accounts for the explanations (and predictions) that people offer of others' activity that cite mental states. Whether or not it is also an account of the attribution of mental states and of the use of mental state language and concepts more generally are issues that divide its advocates. Of significance here is the very fact that the explanations of activity on which it focuses cite mental states. For this indicates that if simulation theory supports the *Verstehen* tradition, it likely promotes its older, mind-oriented form. In contrast, a Wittgensteinian position recognizes that each phase of the *Verstehen* tradition captured part of the truth. Since people regularly explain one another with mental state locutions, the older form correctly maintained that action is explained psychologically. At the same time, the younger form correctly espies that such explanations presuppose social matrices of some sort. More precisely, mental explanations of people are only possible and intelligible given familiarity with the social practices within which their minds and actions are constituted. In other words, understanding human activity fully requires a grasp of both mind and social context.

1. Access and Action

Simulation theory focuses on certain uses of mental state locutions. Hitherto it has not explicitly considered the use of expressions for action, instead effectively treating action ascription as a given. Clearly, however, the ascription of action is intimately bound to its chosen topic. Indeed, actions and mental states are best thought of as composing not two distinct realms but a single domain of mind/action, or as I would prefer less "Cartesianly" to describe it, the single domain of life conditions.[6] It is worth adding that there are four categories of life condition: states of consciousness such as being in pain, imagining, and seeing; emotions such as being joyful, being fearful, and being happy; cognitive conditions such as intending, believing, wanting, and expecting; and actions of all sorts.

I focus section 1 on a topic that simulation theory has not expressly examined because most social investigators and theorists consider action to be the chief compositional and causal ingredient in social life. As a result, they typically believe that investigators access social phenomena, first, by identifying what people do. As indicated, moreover, the *Verstehen* tradition contends that social phenomena are accessed through the understanding of action. The question, then, is whether simulation theory can help promote this thesis.

Philosophers often distinguish between basic and nonbasic actions. A basic action is an action, usually a bodily one, that a person performs directly, that is, not by way of doing something else. Examples are hammering, handing over money, uttering words, and typing on a computer keyboard. A nonbasic action is one a person performs by way of performing a basic one. Examples are repairing a house, paying for groceries, and writing an essay. Identifying basic actions is typically a direct and automatic perceptual affair. Uncertainty about what basic actions people are performing does occur, but only infrequently, for example, Is that tribal priest singing or emitting a sound? Is he touching her or is she touching him? Explicating the skills, furthermore, that are exercised in perceiving basic actions rests on what can be called a "body semantics." A body semantics is an account of the constitution of intentional bodily movements as particular basic actions. Although this topic cannot be explored at present, let me very briefly sketch what such a Wittgensteinian body semantics might look like.

Very few bodily movements are determined biologically to be particular basic actions. Not only are most such movements learned behavior in a broad sense of "learned," but what basic actions they constitute depends on the concepts of basic actions that are woven into the practices in which the movements are learned and carried out. (These concepts, be it noted, are often shared across cultures.) What meaning qua basic action a given movement possesses, in other words, is a practico-conceptual and, thus, social matter. It follows that the ability to perceive such actions is likewise a social affair, and for two reasons. First, it rests on familiarities with concepts and practices and, second, people acquire this ability as they are integrated into the social practices around them.

The point I want to make about basic actions is that simulation contributes virtually nothing to their identification. To begin with, only on the few occasions when it is not perceptually evident what basic actions people are performing does a further operation such as simulation even in principle need to come into play. It is not obvious, moreover, how imagining being in someone else's shoes can reveal what basic actions he performs when this is not already evident. One might think that, parallel to the manner simulation subtends the identification of intentional actions (see below), it aids the identification of basic actions by ascertaining mental conditions (e.g., intentions, wants) and situational elements (e.g., the nature of the tribal ceremony or game) that disclose their identity. Not only, however, can these matters be grasped otherwise than through simulation; in a situation in which it is not evident what basic actions a person performs, it is anything but obvious that simulation can manage to uncover the relevant conditions and elements.

Nonbasic actions are ones people perform by way of performing basic ones. What does a person need to know to be able to ascribe nonbasic actions to another person—possibly, though not necessarily, on the basis of cognized basic ones? Considerable disagreement reigns even among advocates of *Verstehen* with regard to social investigation on this point. Rule theorists such as Winch and Apel argue that knowledge of the rules that govern activity is the needed ingredient. Taylor contends, by contrast, that a grasp of the practices in the carrying on of which basic actions are performed is required. For practices carry fields of meanings for behaviors and situations, and what someone is doing depends on how her action fits into this field and is understood by participants in terms of the meanings it carries (at a further level it also depends on the implicit norms and ideals imbuing practices). That, for instance, scratching marks on a piece of paper constitutes voting depends on the scratching being a moment of voting practices and being understood by participants in terms of that practice's field of meanings. For Geertz, meanwhile, identifying the actions people perform—in his language, giving "thick descriptions" of what they do—is a matter of ascertaining the constructions actors place on what is going on. These constructions are elements of the inferential structures that constitute culture and are located in a public "conceptual world" in which people act, perceive, and interpret one another.

According to these *Verstehen* accounts, grasping "what people are doing" and "what is going on" rests on comprehension of some sort of social matrix: of rules, interpretations and fields of meaning, or public inferential structures. It does not rest on apprehending mind. Indeed, Winch, Taylor, and Geertz stress that rules, meanings, and constructions are not mental phenomena. For them, consequently, the understanding through which investigators access social reality is a grasp of a social matrix of signification.

The Wittgensteinian position promoted in the current chapter agrees that, since what someone is doing when acting reflects a social matrix, namely, the social practices in which the actor participates, identifying what someone does rests on familiarity with these practices. This position also maintains, and here it would be joined by the above contemporary *Verstehen* theorists, that what someone is doing also depends on the situation of action and the actor's biography (e.g., past and future activity). Identifying action also rests, as a result, on a grasp of these phenomena.

When a person possesses familiarity with these three matters, he or she is usually able to recognize (i.e., perceive or ascertain) nonbasic actions automatically. When the interpreter lacks or scarcely possesses one or more of these familiarities, identifying actions requires thought, deliberation, and discussion; it also rests on diverse generalizations, for example, about specific people, persons in general, or people of particular classes, ethnicities, tribes, religions, and so on. It is not obvious what role simulation plays in either the automatic or the worked-out comprehension. For understanding is achieved through familiarity with practices, situations, biographies, and generalizations about people. And it is not immediately clear that these familiarities can be acquired via simulation or that identifying action on their basis involves this operation.

It turns out, however, that practices, situation, biography, and generalization are not the only phenomena, a grasp of which is relevant to ascertaining what nonbasic actions someone performs when carrying out basic ones. As many philosophers have pointed out, one way of discerning what someone *intentionally* does is to unearth the person's intentions along with the beliefs and desires (etc.) informing this. Suppose, for example, one sees a neighbor barking at the moon. Uncovering the person's intention, for example, to play with her dog or to practice her part in a theatrical play, along with the beliefs and desires given that she has this intention, for example, the belief that her pet likes company or that she hasn't got the barking down yet, reveals that she is playing with her dog and trying to please it or practicing her part and attempting to overcome her weaknesses.

This example shows that a grasp of mind, and not just of practice, situation, biography, and generality, can help identify what people do. So too does ascertaining the causal chains bound up with activity. Only if, for example, the barker in fact pleases her mate or hones her skills is she pleasing her dog or overcoming her weakness and not just attempting to do so. It is important to stress, however, that a grasp of mind is never sufficient in this regard. Familiarity with the practices amid which the activity occurs is always required. (Knowledge of causal chains is also crucial.) For instance, uncovering the intention to overcome weakness can reveal that the neighbor is practicing her role only to someone familiar with theater and the practices of rehearsal and preparation bound up with it. Still, as the earlier form of the *Verstehen* school claimed, a grasp of mind can contribute to the identification of actions. What role, then, might simulation play in achieving this?

A natural suggestion is the following: One identifies intentional actions by (1) identifying, through simulation, the cognitive conditions that could have given rise to the basic actions someone performs and (2) determining what intentional actions are constituted by the conditions involved.[7] It turns out, however, that simulation is misconceived if it is construed as focusing on mentality alone. According to Jane Heal and Robert Gordon, simulating is imagining being in other people's *situations*: When a simulator imagines being in another's shoes, she looks at the actor's situation and not just his mind.[8] For example, the act of imagination that underlies identifying someone who turns and runs as fleeing a bear is an act of imagining being in the situation of, say, turning a corner and being confronted with a bear in the middle of the trail. Now, in a case such as this, one actually, I believe, imagines mentality. To simulate another's situation in this way is to imagine seeing what the other person sees, feeling what he feels, expecting what he expects, believing what he believes, and so on. The present significance of Heal's and Gordon's emphasis on situation versus mind, however, is that much of what is typically conceived of as situation or biography—two of the phenomena with which a person must be familiar to be able to grasp what someone does—can be worked into simulations. What's more, features of situation and biography that cannot be brought into the simulation in the form of imagined mental conditions (e.g., the fact that the hiker's brother died in a hiking accident the previous year) can nonetheless be incorporated as follows: A person imagines being *someone of whom these situational and biographical features hold*—seeing this, feeling that, expecting this, and believing that.

I do not know how much of situation, biography, and even generality can thus be brought into simulation in this way. The more that can be incorporated, the more it is possible in principle to proclaim simulation the primary operation through which action is identified. But even if all of these matters can be so incorporated (causal chains seem more recalcitrant), two points must be stressed. First, incorporation would only show that simulation is *one* way to identify what others intentionally do. It would neither exclude nor demonstrate the priority of simulation over such alternative ways as perceiving, inferring, and asking people what they are doing. (Section 2 explores further the idea that perception, inference, and simulation are three ways of achieving the same sort of cognitive grasp.) Second, the contribution of simulation to the identification of action, like those of perception and inference, requires familiarity with fields of practice. A grasp of sociality, in other words, is essential to identifying human activity.

In addition, what people do is almost inevitably subject to a range of descriptions under which it is nonintentional. These descriptions largely rest on wider social contexts or on causal chains that arise from basic actions, either of which the actor is often unaware or only dimly aware. Examples are "wearing out her vocal cords," "spending the evening with her companion," "making a fool of herself," "carrying on human–pet practices," "annoying the neighbors," and "marking a turning point in her life." It is critical to call attention to the phenomenon of nonintentional action because social life is composed of nonintentional as well as intentional actions, and social inquiry considers and writes about actions of both sorts. (Imagine trying to write a history or sociological analysis of employment that forsook all reference to nonintentional actions.) It is patent, however, that simulation does not underlie the specification of nonintentional actions.

In sum, although imagining being in other's shoes can subtend the identification of what people intentionally do, it is not the sole operation that does so, its capacity in this regard presupposes social understanding, and it is irrelevant to the identification of nonintentional actions. Hence, simulation theory lends only modest support to the thesis that social life is accessed through understanding, in particular, through understanding what people do.

2. Explaining Action via Mentality

A second prominent thesis of the *Verstehen* tradition is that explaining activity is understanding it and not accounting for it causally by reference to laws. Section 2 explores whether simulation theory furthers this thesis. My discussion, moreover, focuses on those explanations of activity that employ common mental locutions, for example, "being in pain," "imagining," "seeing," "being happy," "fearing," "expecting," "understanding," "believing," "wanting," and "thinking." Unlike the identification of action, its mental explanation lies squarely within the terrain simulation theory claims: According to simulationists who examine the topic, mental explanations rest on simulations of others' minds/situations.

Two preliminary points are in order. The first is that focusing on explanations that employ common mental locutions is no grievous restriction. For explaining activity in this way is the primary means by which people commonly account for one another. That is to say, life condition vocabularies, including terms for actions, are the principle medium of the articulated comprehension that people have of one another. Of course, people sometimes explain actions without using mental locutions. "Why did she bow?" "You're supposed to bow before the queen, dummy." People explain one another also by invoking norms and rules, citing ends and purposes, or describing situational elements. Ends and purposes, however, are the contents of wants and desires. What is more, in explaining an action no one would cite a rule, norm, or situational element of which she did not think the actor was aware. These facts imply that explanations of activity that do not cite mental conditions are intrinsically interwoven with that grasp of others that is formulated with mental locutions—and maybe also that their explanatory power derives from this grasp. Nonmental explanations of activity do not, therefore, challenge the centrality of mental locutions in the understanding of self and other.

Second, simulation theorists disagree among themselves not only about whether mental explanations of action are causal explanations but also about whether simulation theory is neutral on the issue. In itself, this discord suggests that simulation theory per se cannot promote the *Verstehen* tradition. In the following, however, I want to abstract from this issue and to concentrate on the alleged role simulation plays in proffering mental explanations. As noted in the introduction, imagining being in another's shoes bears strong prima facie resemblance to certain types of understanding (especially empathy) that the *Verstehen* tradition has claimed yield noncausal, nonnomological explanations of action. Simulation theorists, moreover, avow this resemblance. Consequently, I want to take this resemblance and these avowals at face value and ask, Even if one assumes that simulation yields noncausal explanations, does simulation theory significantly further the cause of *Verstehen?*

What is going on when people explain activities with the vocabulary of mentality? According to a host of thinkers, including some simulation theorists explicitly, it is to articulate intelligibility. Disagreement, however, reigns among proponents of this thesis (including advocates of interpretive social science) over the proper interpretation of intelligibility. For many, intelligibility means normativity: appropriateness, acceptability, or rightness.[9] For others, it connotes rationality. Heal, for instance, writes that "in giving a psychological explanation we render the thought or behavior of the other intelligible. Another way of putting this truism is to say that we see them as exercises of cognitive competence or rationality."[10] Still other thinkers combine normativity and rationality and equate intelligibility with rational oughtness. According to them, to explain action psychologically is to exhibit it as what a rational person ought to have done.[11]

I agree that mental explanations articulate intelligibility. Interpreting intelligibility as rationality or normativity, however, reflects philosophical wishfulness more than mental reality. The rationality interpretation either entails that the explanatory use of any mental locution depicts human activity as rational or implicitly proposes to ignore those locutions whose use often construes activity as something other than rational (e.g., locutions for emotions and many states of consciousness). People, however, are often something other than rational. Consequently, the first option implies that the common explanatory use of mental locutions is frequently illegitimate. The second option, meanwhile, simply closes its eyes to reality. Both options, therefore, refuse to accept the common practice of mental explanation *as it is*—for example, the fact that the use of mental locutions tracks how humans are often less than rational. (When, for instance, a person is said to have struck another out of jealousy, chances are that the intelligibility therewith articulated is not a matter of rationality.) So the intelligibility that the use of such locutions articulates cannot be equated with rationality *tout court*.

Nor can it be equated with normativity straight off. Normative interpretations underplay the mind's powers of determination, whereby "determination" I mean what Aristotle called formal and final, as opposed to efficient causal (bringing about, making happen) determination.[12] Careful description of common practices of explaining others mentally reveals that such explanations document the formal and final determination of activity.

As a result, normative glosses of these explanations, in transforming them into specifications of appropriateness and oughtness, can in principle hope to capture only those lines of mental determination that bear upon activity qua something appropriate. They thereby leave action unexplained to the extent that it is inappropriate and obfuscate that mental explanations can and regularly do explicate inappropriate activity.

Without abandoning the idea that mental explanations articulate intelligibility, an analysis of them must acknowledge that (1) they do not always render behavior rational (this also holds for "reason explanations") and that (2) they document the determinative powers of mentality. One way of meeting these *desiderata* is to treat intelligibility as what makes sense to people to do: as a *practical* intelligibility that governs their activity. What makes sense to someone to do governs her activity by specifying that she next do such and such. A person, moreover, almost always does what makes sense to her to do, performing one particular basic action after another because of the continual specification of what makes sense. What makes sense to someone to do is not, however, the same as either (1) what is or seems to her rational to do or (2) what is appropriate or correct (though the actions specified as making sense often happen to be ones that the counsels of rationality single out or ones that are appropriate or correct). One reason for these differences is that what makes sense is determined not just by an orientation toward ends but also by how things matter, that is, by emotions and moods. In sum, the intelligibility laid out in mental explanations is neither rationality, normativity, nor a rational normativity. Rather, it is a teleoaffectively determined making sense to someone to do X that "in-forms" and "finalizes" activity.

The issue in section 2 is, What operation yields explanations of others' activity with mental locutions (i.e., how do people do it)? The issue now becomes, What operation yields explications with these locutions of the intelligibility that governs activity? Contrary to most philosophical positions on such issues, I believe that there is no one thing realizing this feat—no one way people do it. A careful examination of what goes on ("the surface") when people carry on the practice of explaining one another mentally reveals that psychological explanations result from at least three major sorts of operation: reading, inferring, and imagining. The evidence for this claim is the fact that people are aware of carrying out these different operations on different occasions.

By "reading" I mean a perceptual grasp of others' mental conditions, through which one understands why they are acting as they are. This cognitive achievement pertains primarily to emotions, moods, and certain states of consciousness like being in pain and only occasionally to cognitive conditions such as beliefs, desires, and intentions. What's more, one comes to be able to read others perceptually and to appreciate that what they do reflects perceived mental conditions by participating in social practices. For through such participation one acquires a familiarity with what Wittgenstein called the "characteristic behaviors" and "life patterns" *(Lebensmuster)* of behaviors-in-circumstances that are associated with emotions and states of consciousness; this familiarity is central to understanding the concepts of the conditions involved; and the ability to read, directly in others' behavior, the condition they are in and the fact that their behavior reflects these conditions rests on this conceptual understanding together with familiarity with people's situations, biographies, and other extant conditions. This last point holds, incidentally, because perceiving others' conditions centrally consists in seeing what they do as characteristic of or as part of the pattern associated with the condition. (The neologism "behaviors-in-circumstances" indicates that the patterns associated with these mental conditions are never simply repetitions of behavior or behavioral style but sets of basic actions in the circumstances in which they occur that are related by family resemblances.)

The second operation that underlies articulating intelligibility with mental locutions is "inference." Inference, in contrast to the direct recognitional uptake of perceptual reading, involves moving in thought from facts or suppositions about others to conclusions about them. In the present context, this act applies primarily to cognitive conditions and only secondarily to emotions and states of consciousness. Like perceiving conditions, inferring them rests on information and concept understanding. The information involved can take many forms, for instance, facts about particular people (their biography, occupation, education, and taste in food, sports, and entertainment); ideas about the typical beliefs and wants of particular ethnic, religious, gender, scientific, or national groups; familiarity with these groups' traditions and styles of reasoning; and generalizations both about how people who possess particular cognitive conditions act and about the conditions under which they acquire such conditions. Concept understanding is involved because (1) such understanding centrally consists of a grasp of configurations of relevancy (the myriad ways social, situational, biographical, and mental matters can be such that someone is in specific cognitive conditions) and of lines of intelligibility (that link these different combinations of matters into abstract patterns) and (2) such grasps are essential to figuring out whether specific cognitive conditions determined that it made sense to someone to perform given actions. Inference, consequently, resembles perceptual reading in resting on a action-context-concept triad. It differs in requiring considerably more information or suppositions about context and because the patterns associated with cognitive conditions are much more abstract and not nearly as phenomenally palpable and insistent as those associated with emotions and many states of consciousness. Indeed, these are two reasons why interpreters can infrequently read cognitive conditions in behavior and must instead think about which ones are at work.

The main alternative to simulation theory in the literature is the so-called theory theory. I might point out, consequently, that because the information on which inferences rest rarely amounts to or is part of a theory, inferring is not a theoretical operation. I offer three warrants for this claim. First, this information does not encompass laws. Laws of the form, If X has mental conditions a, b, c, then (typically, normally, ceteris paribus, absent countervailing factors, etc.) X y z's are philosophers' creations that do not underpin the psychological explanations people routinely offer of one another. These explanations, therefore, do not rest on laws. To the extent, then, that theoretical explanation requires laws, these explanations are nontheoretical. Second, what words for life conditions mean does not derive from the generalizations in which they appear (which is not to say that meaning is independent of these generalizations). Not only is the explanatory use of these words not limited to inferences based on generalizations, but these locutions are used in multiple *nonexplanatory* ways in other sorts of speech act.[13] Third, the information involved is not systematic, and systemicity is one mark of anything deserving the name "theory." In sum, there is little parallel between this information and scientific theories. Indeed, this knowledge, to use Heal's example, more closely resembles what a wise medicine woman knows than what her scientific, university-trained Western counterpart does.[14]

The third operation that can underlie explaining others with common mental locutions is imagination. By "imagination" I mean two of the phenomena that simulation theorists call "simulation." The first, isolated by Gordon, is imagining another's situation from his or her point of view and then, say, deciding, given that situation, what to do. In imaginings of this type, one simulates another in his or her situation: One imagines being another in his or her situation and deciding *as that person* what to do.[15] A mark of such acts is thus the endeavored neutralization of one's own peculiarities. Working one's way "into" another, one attempts to grasp the other's experiences, thoughts, and feelings and to imagine being that person.

"Imagination" designates, second, an operation associated with Alvin Goldman: imagining what one would do if one were in another's shoes. This differs from Gordon's simulation because the simulator does not attempt to neutralize herself. She does not imagine being another, but instead herself being another. As Gordon puts it, one "simulat[es] *oneself* in O's situation" instead of "simulating O in O's situation."[16] One then transfers to the other the results of the simulation, for example, a decision to do such and such, by supposing that the other is psychologically similar to oneself. What, consequently, one imagines being thought or done depends on one's own psyche. In Goldman's words, "the point [is] that interpretation primarily starts from the home base of one's own experience."[17]

My use of the term "imagination" does not, however, encompass the operation that Heal calls "simulation": thinking through what actions would be reasonable if things stood and were going certain ways. This operation is not an act of imagination. Heal's simulator does not attempt to imagine what a specific other would do or think in some situation or—on the assumption that others are like me—what I would do or think in that situation. Rather, the simulator, using her own cognitive apparatus, excogitates what thoughts and actions follow from (and entail) specific contents she attributes to others. Since, moreover, the faculties of reasoning therewith employed are (supposedly) shared with others, her thought processes simulate those occurring in others.

> So if I take on merely as a hypothesis what someone else actually believes then what I do in further thought simulates what he or she does, inasmuch as we both exercise the same intellectual and conceptual capacities on the same subject matter and so may move through the same sequence of related contents to the same conclusion.[18]

What, consequently, Heal's simulator is in effect doing is working out what a person, who possesses certain intellectual capacities and such and such thoughts, beliefs, and desires, will do. This operation is a subclass of what I call "inference," one in which conclusions about others' mentality are drawn nontheoretically by thinking for oneself what follows from given thoughts.

This chapter has emphasized the centrality of practices in human life. Consequently, I should stress that reading, inferring, and imagining require familiarity with social practices. One reason for this is that these operations presuppose a grasp of mental concepts, and the relevant concepts are those woven into the practices that the actors to be understood carry on. (Providing mental explanations of a group of people thus requires a grasp of the mental condition concepts carried in that group's practices.) Perceiving, reasoning, and imagining, one might say, are the ways in which people who have become participants in and connoisseurs of social practices understand one another.

Mental explanations of others are thus marked by at least two sorts of multiplicity. A variety of operations can underlie their provision, and these operations (e.g., simulation) can take different forms. These multiplicities indicate that what people do in explaining one another psychologically likely varies across occasion. If a waiter in a fashionable New York restaurant approaches the table and addresses one in a Slavic-sounding language,[19] one will likely think inferentially in attempting to understand why. It is highly unlikely, pace Gordon, that one will try to imagine from a first-person point of view being the waiter. By contrast, the fact that someone is crying out of grief can be seen directly in behavior, given certain information and concept understanding.[20] Pace Goldman, it does not require, though on occasions it might involve, imagining oneself being in the other's situation and appreciating that crying is an understandable response. People certainly do simulate others now and again. But not only do they perform simulations of different sorts on different occasions; they do something other than simulate on still many further occasions. Hence, even if simulation yields noncausal, nonnomological explanations, recognizing its existence is only one prop for the *Verstehen* thesis that people explain activity by understanding it. Perception and inference also, I believe, yield noncausal explanations and are further props for this thesis. This, however, is a topic for a different book.

Of course, simulation theorists claim that their preferred operation is what primarily occurs when people explain others mentally.[21] Since people are not consciously aware of simulating on most occasions when they use mental locutions to explain others, these theorists argue that it occurs *tacitly*. Goldman writes, for instance, that simulation has little "phenomenological salience" and is an acquired, automatic skill exercised with no conscious awareness of doing so.[22] Gordon contends that simulation (once acquired) is a subverbal operation whose occurrence, conclusions, and considerations are completely unknown to people.[23]

I do not intend to file a brief against the notion of tacit mental conditions and processes. People clearly can perceive, infer, and imagine without their being thematically (i.e., consciously) aware of doing so and without there being some conscious going-on in which the execution of the act consists. The question I want to raise is the following: Why think that operations of just one of these three types yield all (or most) mental explanations of activity?

Suppose simulation is the primary type. People are just usually not thematically aware of simulating. It is also highly unlikely that on most occasions when they explain others mentally they are even "nonthematically aware," that is, know in any way that they are simulating. If, consequently, simulation underlies psychological explanation, Gordon must be right that it is (usually) subverbal and utterly unknown. Of course, people sometimes simulate consciously and deliberately, for instance, when they *try* to imagine being in another's shoes. This raises the question of whether the ungrasped, preverbal and conscious, deliberate operations are processes of the same or of different types. If the same, simulation theorists need to explain how people can at times consciously perform or know that they are performing an operation that routinely occurs without their having—or even, more crucially, being able to have—the slightest cognizance of it. If the operations are of different types, the preverbal one probably should be described in the technical vocabulary of some cognitive neuroscience and not with common mental locutions such as "imagining." After all, the latter locutions are commonly used (and are thus meaningful) in comprehending lived-through activity and the intelligibility informing it. Unless transformed into technical expressions, they are not obviously suited for specifying postulated nonconscious processes. Either option thus makes problematic the claim that simulation underlies all mental explanations.

More decisively, people are also sometimes aware (thematically or non-thematically) of doing something *other* than simulating when explaining. Examples are perceiving that people are gripped by certain emotions and figuring out, through knowledge-based inferential reasoning, what's going on with them. There is little point to saying that what primarily occurs when any of these processes takes place is a tacit version of *one* of them. Indeed, claiming this entails that conscious awareness of performing an operation of a type other than the primary one is usually delusory. If one primary thing is going on whenever any of these processes occur, it is bound to be something different from these processes and properly described in the theoretical vocabulary of some cognitive neuroscience—not in language that designates what people can consciously or knowingly do. Simulation theory cannot be right that simulation is the primary operation that occurs when others' actions are explained mentally.

Finally, the same move, that of rendering an operation nonconscious or subverbal, can be made to bolster the theses that people understand one another primarily through inference and that they understand one another perceptually far more often than they realize. So this strategy does not strengthen the proposition that people primarily understand one another through simulation. It is more propitious to claim that there are different operations through which people understand one another and that any of these can occur thematically or nonthematically. Sometimes we deliberately and consciously try to understand others perceptually, through inferential reasoning, or by imagining being in their shoes. On other occasions we do this automatically and without thinking about it. There even may be occasions when we do this without having the slightest inkling that it is occurring. But there is no one thing that we always do to understand.

3. Simulation and Technical Vocabulary

The issue of whether simulation theory promotes the *Verstehen* conception of social inquiry centers on whether it abets the theses that understanding affords access to social life and that explaining action is a matter of understanding it and not accounting for it causally via laws. In this chapter I have suggested a weakly positive judgment on the issue. Treating the question of access as an issue about the identification of action, section 1 claimed that simulation can make a limited contribution to this achievement. Focusing on the provision of action explanations, section 2 claimed that simulation cum imagination is one of at least three types of operation that yield such explanations. All in all, simulation theory can at best be one of several pillars of a defense of the *Verstehen* tradition.

My discussion has focused on the use of common locutions for activity and mentality. I have eschewed the pervasive philosophical characterization of this language as "ordinary language" because these locutions are also widely employed in social science. It must be stressed, however, that the considerations advanced in this essay hold of social science *only* to the extent that it utilizes this terminology. Today, consequently, they hold of above all the disciplines of history and political science and the qualitative nooks in sociology, anthropology, and social geography. To describe and explain human behavior, much contemporary social inquiry instead utilizes invented technical vocabulary or common locutions of mentality and action transformed into technical terms.

It is worth hazarding the guess that simulation cum imagination has little role to play in the descriptive or explanatory use of technical terminology. Simulation theory finds application to the descriptive and explanatory use of common locutions because (1) this vocabulary is a key medium of people's mature articulated understanding of themselves and others and (2) people are able to imagine being in another's shoes only in, for example, a vocabulary that—because it is used as people mature, in their interactions and in the texts they read (thereby becoming a medium through which they carry on their lives amid one another)—opens up the conceptual space in which imagination can fill out how things stand and are going for others. In contrast, comprehending others with a technical vocabulary requires a cognitive-intellectual extension beyond one's understanding as it is formulated in common locutions. The use of technical vocabulary is thus mostly an inferential affair based on information, theory, and explicit definitions. And simulation and perception have relatively minor roles to play, simulation perhaps none whatsoever. Similar remarks apply to the use cognitive neuroscience makes of technical vocabulary to specify the cognitive-neurological processes that underlie these three operations.

None of this entails that technical social science is non-*Verstehen,* however anti-*Verstehen* most of its schemas and self-understandings might be. But it does imply that simulation is irrelevant to the issue. Simulation qua imagination enters explanatory social science only insofar as explanations of action utilize common locutions.[24]

Notes

1. For detailed discussion of these ideas, see Schatzki 1996.
2. See Dilthey 1982b, "Plan der Fortsetzung zum Aufbau der geschichtlichen Welt in den Geisteswissenschaften. Entwürfe zur Kritik der historischen Vernunft,"

7:191–220; Dilthey 1982a, *Ideen über eine beschreibende und zergliederende Psychologie*, "Struktur des Seelenlebens," 5:192–204; Collingwood 1946, pt. 5, sec. 4.

3. See, for example, Winch 1958; Apel 1967; Habermas 1988.

4. Taylor 1985.

5. Geertz 1973, p. 7.

6. For discussion, see Schatzki 1996, chap. 2.

7. This strategy is implicit in Gordon 1995a.

8. See Heal 1995a, p. 48; Gordon 1995c, p. 102.

9. See, for example, Winch 1958, chap. 3; Louch 1966.

10. Heal 1995a, p. 52.

11. For a recent example, see Brandom 1994, chap. 4.

12. This assertion is well illustrated in Heal's essay quoted two paragraphs above. After criticizing functionalism for its attempt to separate semantics from causality and explanation, she offers an account of psychological explanation that renders semantics normative and explanatory and simply dispenses with causality or determination. See 1995a, pp. 54–58.

13. This is a running theme in the work of Wittgenstein. See, for instance, his discussion of "belief" and "know" (1977).

14. Heal 1996b, pp. 77, 84.

15. See Gordon 1995b, pp. 53–67.

16. Gordon 1995b, p. 55.

17. Goldman 1995a, p. 88.

18. Heal 1996b, p. 78. Compare her more simulator-referential description of simulation at 1995a, p. 47.

19. See Gordon 1995a, pp. 64–66.

20. See Goldman 1995a, p. 88.

21. I write "primarily" because Goldman and Heal (though not Gordon) acknowledge significant roles for some sort of knowledge-based inference alongside simulation. Vis-à-vis explaining and predicting action, see Goldman 1995a, pp. 83, 88. I add that there is no space to address the empirical claim that simulation is not the primary operation, but instead the most basic one from which the others derive. See Goldman 1995a, p. 88.

22. Goldman 1995a, pp. 87–88; cf. pp. 78, 80, 93.

23. See Gordon 1995a, p. 70.

24. I would like to thank the editors, Hans Herbert Kögler and Karsten Stueber, for extensive, thoughtful, and illuminating comments on an earlier version of this chapter.

Chapter Seven

From Simulation to Structural Transposition: A Diltheyan Critique of Empathy and Defense of Verstehen

RUDOLF A. MAKKREEL

Empathy, once reviled as an intuitive mode of understanding, is now being hailed as an imaginative form of simulation. The idea of simulation is currently being used in philosophical psychology to undercut the implausible thesis that we tend to predict the behavior of others on the basis of generalizations (about human motivation, etc.) that constitute a kind of "folk-psychological theory."[1] Alvin Goldman (among others) claims that we can account for the behavior of others more directly through a simulative projection on the basis of our own experience. Simulation allows me to identify with others by pretending to be in their situation. Not only do I identify with others by feeling at one with them (empathy), but I also predict their behavior by imagining (simulating) what I would do if I were in their shoes. Empathy is thus being repackaged in a more experimental form. Not just a feeling or mysterious intuition, simulation allows me to project myself into a series of hypothetical situations to test the most likely course of behavior. Whereas empathy is thought to be something that you are born with or not, simulation is more like a technique that can be learned and refined.

The thinkers who have revived empathy in the more active mode of simulation do not, however, all agree with Goldman's model. Robert M. Gordon points to an important "difference between simulating oneself in O's situation and simulating O in O's situation."[2] Whereas Goldman seems to regard the understanding of others as an extension of self-understanding, Gordon's second alternative requires a "recentering" and "transformation" of the self.[3] There is one assumption, however, that all the proponents of simulation seem to share, namely, that it is a new manifestation of what historical thinkers like Dilthey and Collingwood called *Verstehen,* or empathetic understanding or reenactment. This would make simulation the heuristic method of the human sciences.

In this chapter I will compare the present-day theory of simulation with Dilthey's views on empathy, *Verstehen,* and the methodology of the human sciences and argue for some important divergences. We will see that Dilthey's theory of the human sciences bridges the gap between a prescientific folk psychology and a law-governed science of psychology by means of a structural psychology that at the same time makes it possible to frame understanding in historical and cultural terms. Subsequently, for one person to understand another a structural transposition is necessary—something not adequately accounted for by the simulation model.

1. Dilthey's Structural
Psychology of Understanding

The first thing to note about Dilthey's approach to understanding *(Verstehen)* is that it is never equated with empathy *(Einfühlung).* Indeed, the term *Einfühlung* occurs only seldom in his writings. One possible reason for this is that the term was being defined psychologically by his contemporary, Theodor Lipps, in ways that Dilthey found too restrictive. Lipps characterized empathy as a process of inner imitation whereby a subject projects its own kinesthetic feelings into some object being attended to. This means surrendering one's own feelings of motion and transferring them into some perceived object to give it the appearance of motion. As Lipps wrote in 1903, "In aesthetic imitation I become progressively less aware of muscular tensions or of sense-feelings in general, the more I surrender in contemplation to the aesthetic object."[4]

If empathy involves a kind of projection through which the subject loses itself, then it is not conducive to understanding. It is not surprising then that Dilthey prefers the term *Mitfühlen.* To feel with or sympathize with does not demand a loss of self and is therefore more compatible with understanding. But even sympathy cannot guarantee understanding. Empathy and sympathy are feelings that directly relate one subject to other subjects. But for me to understand other subjects is to come to see them as standing independently of me. Understanding is never direct but is always mediated. What I see in the other is not taken simply at face value but as the expression of something. When I see tears in a woman's eyes I should not just assume that she is sad. Only by understanding the tears in relation to a contextual situation can I hope to determine whether they are tears of sorrow or tears of joyful relief. Understanding in the human sciences always takes what is objectively given as the objectification of something. Empathy may be heuristic in suggesting possible states of mind as the source of human expressions. But it is also dangerous in that I may prematurely project my own concerns onto the other. A husband who suspects his own wife of infidelity may have an intense response to Shakespeare's *Othello,* but he is hardly the ideal person to appreciate the subtleties of the play. His empathy for Othello will probably get in the way of a proper understanding of its meanings as the plot unfolds. Empathy is likely to reduce the meaning of Shakespeare's play to a psychological condition, but Dilthey's concern was to understand meaning in a broader cultural sense. As a historian, Dilthey relates the method of understanding less to feelings such as empathy and sympathy than to a process of reexperiencing *(Nacherleben)* that can structurally exposit what has been understood in temporal terms.

What is reexperienced through understanding is not a mental reenactment of the state of mind of some past subject. Thus when we read a poem, we do not reproduce the psychological state of mind of the poet in composing it, but rather reexperience the state of the imagined figures in the poem itself. There was a brief period when Dilthey held the reenactment view, namely, in his *Poetics* of 1887. But Dilthey's last writings reject it as too psychological. Thus we can be reasonably sure that even if empathy were taken in the more inclusive sense of present-day simulation theorists, it still would not be endorsed by Dilthey as a mode of understanding.

Dilthey's thought does, however, come to mind in the empathy-simulation debate because he explored the relation between psychology and the general task of understanding in the human sciences. Seven years after the publication of his *Poetics,* he came out with a programmatic essay, "Ideas Concerning a Descriptive and Analytic Psychology," that lays out the basic psychic nexus that frames human understanding. Normally, psychic life is a sequence of lived experiences or a continuum in which things follow one another in ways that tend to make sense. This connectedness of much of our psychic life allows us to understand many of our experiences. These observations about the nexus of psychic life lead Dilthey to also posit a basic difference between the human sciences and the natural sciences. The latter are primarily concerned with external experience where things tend to be presented in a discrete and piecemeal fashion. To make sense of what happens here natural scientists appeal to lawful regularities to connect natural events. A natural event is explained when it is properly subsumed under a general law. When Dilthey goes on to claim that the human sciences aim at an understanding of human behavior whereas the natural sciences seek explanations for natural events, he is not ruling out explanations for human behavior as well. There are often gaps in the narrative continuum of human life, and these gaps demand explanations. But to the extent that we find the basic structural outlines of human experience to be intelligible we have at least an implicit understanding of human life.

The human sciences have as their task to describe the general structures of our lived experience and to analyze them into more specific substructures. On that basis the human sciences have as their further task a kind of rearticulation of all these structural relations in order to explicate what is distinctive about individual experience and specific modes of human interaction. We see from this that the initial narrative understanding of human life may need to be revised. The human sciences allow us to move from an indeterminate understanding of the meaning of human life to a more determinate understanding whereby truth claims can be tested. Such a determinate understanding will often incorporate causal explanations of details.

In "Ideas Concerning a Descriptive and Analytic Psychology" Dilthey claims that the most basic structures of human experience are psychological. At the same time he rejects the more traditional associationist psychology of Hume and Mill because they assumed that the basic elements of psychic life are cognitive representations that may or may not evoke feelings and desires. Descriptions of actual experience make it apparent that we possess a more immediate, prerepresentational access to reality. As living beings, we feel ourselves to be part of a reality of which we are directly aware. The idea of an independent world arises as a consequence of resistance to our will. When expectations based on certain habitual experiences are frustrated, we are forced to accept them as merely our own representations and only then does it begin to make sense to speak of representational consciousness. Moreover, Dilthey points out that our lived experience of the world does not merely represent it cognitively. What we perceive is already influenced by the interests of our feelings. Any perception is always selective in accordance with what is felt to be worth noting. Nor can we properly know anything without carefully attending to it, which is a function of the will. Thus after a brief glance into a room we are more likely to remember details about the people in it than about the furniture—assuming that the former are more germane to our values and purposes. All these aspects of experience are always operative. Thus at every moment our lived experience of the world is a nexus of cognitive, evaluative, and volitional responses.

The basic structure of psychological life is this nexus of lived experiences that traces these modes of response to reality. Analysis can then account for the fact that we do often distinguish states of mind as being representational, evaluative, or volitional. Partly this is determined by which mode of consciousness predominates, but it is more complicated than that. As Dilthey writes: "The inner relation of these diverse aspects . . . the structure in which these threads are bound up with one another, is not the same in the affective state as in the volitional, which is again not the same as in the representational state."[5] These three aspects of our experience do not come separately, but on the basis of a functional distinction it makes sense to relate representational states of mind into a structural cognitive system whose function is to know what the world is like. Within this cognitive system it is possible to relate the perceptual and conceptual aspects of experience and to examine how memory and imagination allow us to represent things. The felt and evaluative aspects of experience can similarly be related to form a second structural system, which allows us to coordinate the value of things. Finally, Dilthey speaks of a volitional system that generates the overriding purposes in life. Here it becomes necessary not only to rank values but also to provide the basis for estimating which ones might be worth acting on through an analysis of means-ends relations.

It is thus only in functional terms that we can distinguish the three main divisions of psychic life that have commonly been accepted since Kant. But there are no separate faculties of knowing, feeling, and willing that operate independently. More than anything else Dilthey stresses the interdependence of what goes on in human consciousness. Developmentally, this means that it is impossible for the same representation to recur. The second time I look at a painting will make for a different experience because I will be in a different state of mind. Also, I will probably remember having seen it before, which imparts a resonance to the new experience. Indeed, there is a fundedness to our experience that Dilthey attempts to understand in terms of a more complex structure to which we will now turn.

The three general structural systems of psychic life are a product of a functional analysis that is common to all human psychic life and relatively abstract. However, with time each individual develops what Dilthey calls an "acquired psychic nexus" that structurally recapitulates the results of his or her historical past.[6] This acquired nexus is a concrete structure that reflects not only the overall cognitive sense of reality but also the most cherished values and goals of that individual. In his late writings Dilthey would characterize this complex structure as the individual's worldview. This idea of a worldview serves to underscore that the acquired psychic nexus is not merely retrospective but comes to guide future experience.

Whereas the three general structural systems analyzed earlier were relatively constant—but not static—in that they distinguish the results of our experience according to their main functions, the acquired psychic nexus expresses a new dynamical sense of structure. This is an important advance in the conceptualization of structure that would influence Dilthey's theory of all the human sciences. Their first task is to describe the basic coherence of human experiences, interactions, and relations. This coherence, which we now tend to call the narrative that gives our life its initial intelligibility, manifests a minimal sense of structure, that is, the loose *connectedness* or continuity of a nexus. In his psychology Dilthey regarded the nexus of lived experiences as such a basic structure. Second, the human sciences analyze or discriminate formally distinct features within any such nexus. Here connectedness is specified in terms of specific possible *connections*. Accordingly, we saw Dilthey specify three functional structural systems in his psychology. Analogously, the human science of economics can analyze the productive wealth of any society in terms of banking systems, trading systems, property systems, and so on. The third task of the human sciences is integrative and produces concrete understanding. In his psychology Dilthey achieved this task through his conception of the acquired psychic nexus in which general systems interact to become an organizing system. Whereas structural systems can be called functional, I shall call a concrete structural system such as the acquired psychic nexus a "dynamical system" *(Wirkungszusammenhang)*[7] to anticipate a term from Dilthey's last writings. Dynamical structural systems articulate the ways that various strands of influence *interconnect* or intersect. When the human sciences examine such intersections of psychological, political, social, cultural, and legal systems, they become historically integrative.

Returning to the acquired psychic nexus as Dilthey's first example of a dynamic structural system, we note that he compares it to an apperceptive mass that influences subsequent perceptions by selecting from what is given that which reinforces my expectations, speaks to my values, and favors my purposes. Sometimes my expectations are contradicted, and this may require that my acquired psychic nexus be revised. The inability to revise this acquired psychic nexus is a mark of an abnormal individual. Healthy people are able to accept a modicum of change and may even form an acquired psychic nexus that also incorporates the views and norms of others. The acceptance of too much random change would, however, indicate a lack of character. Through the acquired psychic nexus I simultaneously manifest my character and become a kind of structural microcosm of the world at large. In this way I reflect otherness without obliterating my own perspective. A self can appropriate aspects of otherness into itself, but there is no way in which the acquired identity of two selves can be identical. Each individual must be understood in terms of his or her context. The acquired psychic nexus turns out to be not merely a psychological concept but one that is fundamentally historical.

2. The Understanding of Individuality and Transposition

I have gone into some detail about Dilthey's descriptive psychology because it raises further questions about the adequacy of empathy or simulation theories. The idea that a state of mind of one person can be projected onto another person becomes questionable once we acknowledge the

structural and developmental character of psychic life. If as suggested earlier, I cannot predict what my reaction to a painting will be the second
time I observe it, then it is all the more difficult to predict how someone
else will respond to it. Since psychic states need to be understood as part of
larger structures, and self-understanding is always contextual, generalization on the basis of one's own experience is a risky business and subject to
qualification. Gordon seemed to be more aware of this than Goldman
when he warned that imagining oneself in the other's shoes is not sufficient
to properly understand the other. We saw Gordon speak of a necessary recentering or transformation of oneself. Dilthey adds the term "transposition" to the mix. He uses both the terms *Transposition* and *Sichhineinver-
setzen,* which means to transport oneself into something. These acts of
relocating *(versetzen)* involved in understanding *(verstehen)* can be directed either at a human being or at a human product. We will examine
the latter option later, but when it comes to the possibility of transposing
oneself into another self this must be understood on the basis of Dilthey's
structural psychology. Whereas simulation may project a simple emotion,
state of mind, or desire onto another person, transposition is the more
complex process of relating the structural nexus of my own experience to
the structural nexus of the other.

Dilthey's "Ideas" ends with a chapter that takes stock of the ways in
which psychological life is articulated in individuals in order to define individuality. He refuses to define individuality by means of special qualities
possessed by some and not others. Even if we posit the same qualities in all
human beings, we can differentiate them quantitatively in terms of their intensity. We first characterize people by the qualities that manifest themselves most strongly. An irritable person discloses anger, impatience, and so
on. But even the most sanguine can have their patience tried and become
angry, which indicates that they too have a threshold of irritability.

But Dilthey does not define individuality merely on the basis of quantitative difference, that is, degrees of intensity. Because our attributes are part of
a structural nexus we can point to a certain amount of interdependence
among them. The development of the prominence of one attribute such as
ambition will require a person to also develop other attributes such as as-
sertiveness and courage, and to downgrade others such as kindness and concern for others. There seem to be no rules governing compatibility and incompatibility among attributes. Dilthey points out that we tend to think of
pious people as also being honest, but this is not always the case. This makes
the understanding of individuality a problem of structural articulation, that
is, of discerning "what proportional relationships exist in the structure of
psychic life among the different constituent parts."[8] Since each person develops a distinct structural articulation or proportion, for one to understand
another requires an internal transformation of self-understanding. That is

why Dilthey made the equation that "transposition is transformation"[9] an important part of his hermeneutics.

Because understanding is a structural or contextualizing process, there cannot be a direct and reliable transference between individuals. Instead, we must rely on the mediation of expressions. When we express ourselves, whether in speech or writing, in action or gesture, we objectify certain intentions or needs. What is ephemeral in a state of mind can be laid out in a more durable mode in a letter or in a poem. But more than that, expressions often disclose more than is present in the consciousness of the subject that is expressing itself. Several attributes that may be relatively submerged in the structural psychic nexus of a given individual may slip out nevertheless. Dilthey points out that writers may create fictional characters that unexpectedly disclose hidden aspects of themselves. This entails that introspection can never exhaust the significance of our own lived experience. From the 1900 essay "The Rise of Hermeneutics" up to the 1911 essay "The Understanding of Other Persons and Their Life-Expressions" Dilthey begins to increasingly question whether we can understand ourselves from within. Understanding proper starts from the outside of things to seek their inner meaning. As illuminating as my own lived experience may be about the significance of my states of mind, I do not fully understand myself until I can look at myself as others see me. This realization that psychology may not be as fundamental to the understanding of human agency as Dilthey had initially thought represents his Hegelian turn. Our consciousness is only partially self-generated; from infancy it is infused with and guided by familial, social, cultural, and linguistic meanings. *Elementary understanding* is no longer what is available through psychological description but indicates what things mean on the basis of the norms and conventions of a community.

Here Dilthey appropriates Hegel's concept of objective spirit, which we may regard as the public medium in which we grow up. He writes that a child "learns to understand gestures and facial expressions, motions and exclamations, words and sentences only because they confront him as being always the same, and as always having the same relation to that which they signify and express."[10] Through objective spirit we inherit the meanings that our tradition has assigned to things. We are so immersed in these meanings that they can be taken for granted. And they are so obvious that no explicit or "conscious inferential process based on the relation of expression and what is expressed"[11] is necessary. Linguistically, elementary understanding provides a simple but communal reading of a text—something that a native member of a community has appropriated in terms of a kind of mental dictionary, but for which a stranger would consult a real dictionary. Because dictionaries often provide a plurality of meanings for a single word, elementary understanding may leave us with ambiguities. We must then turn to *higher understanding* to arrive at a more determinate interpretation.

If the communal context is inadequate to define the meaning of a textual passage, we must concentrate our attention on a more specific context. We can consider other occurrences of the same passage in the same work, or in the corpus of the same author. If this does not suffice to determine the meaning, we may want to consult other works of its genre and of its specific period. Note that all these more specific contexts are public in nature. Only after exhausting these contextual modes of possible clarification does Dilthey shift to a different structural mode. Here higher understanding moves from considering the relation between an expression and what is expressed to the relation between an expression and the expressor. When it comes to the latter, that is, those expressing themselves, Dilthey observes that they need not be the author of the words used but may be the fictional character who utters them if the work is a drama or a novel. This structural mode of higher understanding produces a living nexus that makes it possible to imagine the full meaning of a work. Here psychological understanding becomes a creative reexperiencing.

When we complete the various modes of contextual higher understanding with psychological understanding, we move backward toward the moment of creation. Dilthey allows for this possibility but only as a kind of last resort. Psychological understanding has now been downgraded from the first to the last mode of understanding. Its regressive nature confirms that understanding is generally retrospective. The ultimate aim of hermeneutics for Dilthey is to reverse the retrospective direction of understanding into the forward direction of reexperiencing. At this point of reversal the transposition involved in understanding is broadened. When "the totality of psychic life is fully active in understanding," it becomes possible for transposition to reexperience "a complex *(Inbegriff)* of life-manifestations."[12] The interpreter becomes able to imagine what it means for someone to live through a specific situation. It is as if the interpreter were creating the structural life-nexus anew, but it is neither that of the original author nor that of the interpreter. It is after all the task of the human sciences to make possible a general mode of understanding—raising the question of whether genuine universality can be attained. We can never fully disengage ourselves from the facticity of the various traditions we derive from and can therefore expect typical results at best.

3. The Cultural Embeddedness of Understanding

I indicated earlier that elementary understanding was not based on any explicit or conscious inference. It is, however, characterized as "an inference by analogy,"[13] which Dilthey regards as an implicit inference. It is differentiated from an inductive inference as follows: An inference by analogy proceeds from particular to particular, whereas an inductive inference proceeds from particulars to a universal. Whereas the processes of higher understanding are all inductive and aimed at a theoretical comprehension, elementary understanding is analogical and pretheoretical. The specific arrangement of the furniture around us is meaningful in an elementary way if we have grown used to it. As we remember for what purpose some cabinet has been used over the years, it comes to embody a certain value. There is nothing universal about these associations, but to the extent that we grow up in a certain community some of these meanings may reflect common cultural practices such as the preservation of sacred objects or rare treasures. This common or public sphere amidst which we grow up is what Dilthey called objective spirit. Let me cite another passage from Dilthey about it: "Everything in which the human spirit has been objectified contains in itself something which is common to the I and the thou. Each square planted with trees, each room in which chairs are arranged is understandable to us from our childhood, because human goal-setting, ordering, and value-determination as something common to us has assigned to each square and to each object in a room its place."[14] Here particular things in their familiar arrangements are a source of common meanings. These common meanings cannot be conceived of as universal in scope—at best they are typical for certain groups of people.

This cultural embeddedness of elementary understanding challenges the view that there are pure psychic operations that we can appeal to in the attempt to understand other human beings. Already in his descriptive psychology Dilthey focused on the acquired psychic nexus that incorporates a public-historical dimension into psychic life. The last writings strengthen this insistence on the intersection of the psychological and the historical by reinterpreting the incorporation process as proceeding inversely. We no longer merely mentally represent the historical world as something outside us, but we experience the historical world as participants in it. However, we can only be participants in a limited context. We may initially assume that what is typical for our community is universally accepted. But eventually we will confront phenomena from other contexts that do not conform to our expectations. Then we must recognize that the common is not the same as the universal. Dilthey's theory of the human sciences works at the interface of the common or everyday, and the more traditional demand that science must provide a universally valid mode of explicating its subject matter. This reinforces his move away from the natural science paradigm of his contemporaries and their assumption that theoretical clarification must always be based on finding lawful regularities. The most important uniformities in the human sciences are structural. Structural analysis serves more to coordinate the complexities of human life than to subordinate it to general rules. If there are laws to be found in the human world, their efficacy must be limited to specific contexts. It is an illusion to hope for laws of historical progress in general, but there may be lawful ways in which specific human domains such as economic activity and scientific inquiry unfold or develop.[15]

The main task of the human sciences as conceived by Dilthey is to structurally articulate the indeterminate continuities of our everyday experience. The commonalities that link us to our surroundings allow us to have an elementary understanding of those around us. But if we are successful here it is not because we project our own mental states into the other but rather because we start with common bearings. Empathetic projection when it does occur functions only in very limited contexts. Once we move outside the realm of the familiar and confront more puzzling matters, we must revise our initial bearings based on participatory involvement and refine it into a more inclusive structural orientation. Understanding is thus always contextual and requires finding one's location. One could say that elementary understanding is rooted in a felt sense of *place,* whether historical or social. Higher understanding refines this mode of placement structurally. With more general orientational concepts of space and time at its disposal, higher understanding aims at a more determinate sense of *locus.* It may either contract the scope of inquiry to specific relevant contexts or expand it to the universe of discursive thought as such. Thus if there is an ambiguous passage in a philosophical text by Kant, we can either compare it to analogous claims in the specific debates in which he participated at his time and place or we can judge it on the basis of logical and syntactical rules in general. That is, we can study the periodicals and correspondence of Kant's circle to determine more exactly to whom he is responding in a particularly puzzling passage. Knowing that he is arguing against another thinker's position may help clarify Kant's meaning. But we may also relate the passage to the universal framework of thought and choose to disregard his specific intentions, claiming that linguistically it must mean such and such and betrays a tendency in Kant's thought that he may have been unconscious of and that may even be in conflict with the main thrust of his philosophy.

One could argue that Dilthey's elementary understanding rooted in a group's common bearings to a set of inherited customs and practices allows for the shared sense of meaning that is assumed to be felt in empathy. But what proponents of empathy conceive of as a kind of mental projection is in fact accounted for by a prior historical and cultural embeddedness. *Einfühlung* is not one individual's projection into the other but the feeling of their common embeddedness in a specific context.

Similarly, the more active technique of simulation could be said to have its counterpart in the inductive processes that Dilthey claims to be part of higher understanding. However, these inductive processes are not context neutral. Gordon speaks of "using simulated practical reasoning as a *predic-*

tive device."[16] As a way of predicting what he will do in a situation different from his own, Gordon would pretend to be in that situation. He gives
the example of imagining what he would do if he heard the sound of footsteps in his basement. Assuming that there was an intruder, Gordon says he
would probably reach for the phone to call an emergency number.[17] He
goes on to say that predicting the behavior of others in that situation requires him to "make *adjustments for relevant differences.*"[18] Simulating O
in O's situation requires Gordon to also pretend that some facts about himself would be different. Indeed, he suggests that such things as his profession, nationality, and intelligence level might need to be modified. Explicating the effect of the last factor, we could assume that if the other had a
rather low level of intelligence we are entitled to imagine that on hearing
footsteps in his basement he would not know what the emergency number
is and simply scream for help instead of picking up the phone to dial 911.
These two reactions may seem natural in today's crime-ridden America,
where most people live in privately owned homes. But these responses
would not be so likely if we lived in communal homes with many people
around and if guns were not so readily available.

In another historical context other suspicions and reactions might be
aroused. One can of course try to eliminate obviously contemporary aspects of any response such as the reference to telephones. But given the cultural embeddedness of even elementary understanding, it is unclear how
simulation by itself can produce what it takes to transpose oneself from one
context to another. Merely to change some facts about myself and my situation may suffice to predict certain general patterns of behavior in people
from other cultures. But to understand what that behavior means, I need to
recognize the more pervasive structural ways in which experience is framed
by a historical and cultural context. The simulation theory does not seem to
provide the basis for effecting the transitions from the structures of one
context to another. To imagine a few of my attributes as changed could in
principle lead me to reconceive others as well. But how other attributes are
affected cannot be imagined without knowing more about the specific contextual differences. It is the task of higher understanding to bring theory to
bear to refine the appropriate contexts. We might agree that any unknown
sound has the potential to worry us and can put us in a defensive mode. But
if there is such a structural uniformity in the ways human beings respond to
stimuli, the task of higher understanding is to articulate the typical ways in
which this response can manifest itself in historically specified contexts. Instead of looking for a general law to which all behavior must be subsumed,
we must structurally differentiate a general premise to define what is relevant in a particular situation.

To the extent that empathy and simulation seem to operate in a historical
vacuum they cannot be models for *Verstehen*. Dilthey's procedures of un-

derstanding are not only more historically rooted, but they also allow for more of a theoretical contribution to the process. This is because his conception of theory is not law based but structure based. Laws are not excluded from the human sciences, but their validity is restricted to abstract or artificially defined contexts. Determinate lawlike explanations of change can only be expected when the variables at stake are clearly delimited. The main task of the human sciences is to articulate the complex structural relations in which we find ourselves as we live our lives. The elementary understanding of commonalities shared with others in our immediate surroundings needs to be refined by an analysis of the structural systems that regulate the more important functions of our lives, whether they be the political structures that define our mode of being governed, the economic structures that influence our livelihood, or the educational and cultural systems that structure our patterns of thinking about things and valuing them. Because these are the structures that need to be negotiated as we attempt to understand each other, the most appropriate way to conceive this process is not through empathy or simulation but through transposition.

Notes

1. Goldman 1995a, p. 75.
2. Gordon 1995b, p. 55.
3. Gordon 1995b, p. 55.
4. Lipps 1979, p. 376.
5. Dilthey 1977a, p. 85.
6. Dilthey 1977a, pp. 59–60.
7. See Makkreel 1992, pp. 314–318.
8. Dilthey 1977a, p. 113.
9. Dilthey 1996, p. 253.
10. Dilthey 1977b, p. 127.
11. Dilthey 1977b, p. 128.
12. Dilthey 1977b, p. 132, translation revised.
13. Dilthey 1977b, p. 128.
14. Dilthey 1977b, p. 127, translation revised.
15. Dilthey 1989, pp. 136–165.
16. Gordon 1995a, p. 62.
17. See Gordon 1995a, p. 62.
18. Gordon 1995a, p. 63.

Chapter Eight

Empathy, Dialogical Self, and Reflexive Interpretation: The Symbolic Source of Simulation

1. Introduction: Simulation Theory Versus Hermeneutic Theory

This chapter begins by distinguishing two models of a nontheoretical approach to interpretation. According to the first model, I can understand others on a precognitive and thus pretheoretical level by simulating how I would feel and act in their shoes. The idea is that the psychic similarity of human subjects allows for the empathetic grasp of emotional states, the transformation of myself into the other and her situation, and the analogical inference from myself to someone else, without invoking any explicit theory or discursive mediation. I can thus simulate being in the other's situation and, given that I and the other are basically similar, understand and predict the other's behavior by observing my own responses. Any discrepancy between myself and the other's perspective or situation has somehow to be integrated, or "added on," to what is basically an intuitive and psychological process of understanding. According to the second model, understanding someone else requires in principle an interpretive reconstruction of their basic beliefs, assumptions, and practices. Since the meaning of a situation is taken to be disclosed through a holistic framework including individual, symbolic, and practical dimensions, any adequate understanding of another agent demands a thorough grasp of the respective cultural, social, and historical background. In addition, since the interpreter can only make sense by drawing on a symbolically mediated perspective, and since the existence of a similarly structured background has itself to be established in interpretation (and cannot be taken for granted), the explicit and discursive reconstruction of the other's (and in turn of one's own) situation alone yields a reliable understanding of the other. Although implicit assumptions and practices are necessarily invoked in such a process, the intuitive background is *not* taken to provide a pretheoretical and universal ground allowing for the prediscursive prediction of the other's behavior.

It should be emphasized from the start that both models are opposed to the nomological explanation of human agency as well as to the use of models of formalized rationality. Indeed, both simulation theory (our first model) and hermeneutic theory (our second model) do well understand that the first-person relatedness of understanding is not an impediment or hindrance to social cognition but rather provides a condition of possibility for the interpretation of others. Yet the nature of the intersubjective similarity that allows for a nonobjectifying and nonformal understanding is seen quite differently. For simulation theory assumes, in all its different versions, a psychic core on the basis of which one agent, the interpreter, can reliably process hypothetically, or "off-line," the constituents of the other's situation and mental states. The constitution of meaning and the respective behavior are seen as a subject-based psychological process that provides, prior to explicit cognitive reasoning and theory, a reliable basis for social cognition and prediction. In the alternative hermeneutic model of dialogical interpretation, the so-called basis of the interpreter's self-understanding is itself taken to be a product of interpretive and symbolically mediated processes. Since the "psychic" self-understanding is ultimately "grounded" in a culturally situated preunderstanding, there simply is no recourse to a psychically pure and reliable sphere. Although the psychological similarity is rejected as a methodological fiction, the fact that all humans are formally situated in interpretive social practices and are all essentially interpretive beings in intersubjective settings provides itself for a distinctive approach to social cognition and interpretation. Instead of conceiving of the disclosure of another's meaning in terms of psychological simulation, it is now seen as an interpretive and reconstructive perspective taking in which the other's and one's own symbolic and cultural attitudes are explicated in an ongoing interpretive process.

In what follows I argue that the hermeneutic model of dialogical perspective taking provides us ultimately with a richer and more promising replacement of the theoretical and formal-rational models than simulation theory. This is not only, as I will try to show, because the hermeneutic model takes more adequately into account that meaning is not constituted on a purely psychological level but rather consists in its core of symbolic and interpretive processes. It is also and especially because the richer grounding in a symbolically mediated self-understanding alone seems to be able to bridge the gap between everyday social cognition and the more refined and methodically controlled processes in the human sciences. My general thesis in this chapter is that simulation theory, due to its psychologism, fails to give an adequate account for how interpretation in the human and social sciences is grounded in the everyday cognitive and interpretive capabilities of human agents. Only such a grounding in everyday cognition can secure (and here both models agree) a nonobjectifying and adequate approach to understanding others. The explication and reflexive refinement of interpretive processes in the human sciences requires that everyday interpretations can be made explicit and articulated on the level of discursive representation, and they equally require that the specific differences that inform the interpreter's and the interpretee's background understanding are reflexively taken into account. Since simulation theory conceives of the "background" of the interpreter as a psychically pure dimension that can serve as a reliable generator of interpretive output, it fails to explain how such implicit mechanisms can be articulated in discursive forms and how they might be implicated in implicit cultural and symbolic assumptions. In contrast, the hermeneutic model that I will sketch in the following pages takes both those requirements into account.

First, I will attempt to show that the processes that supposedly allow for a psychological simulation of the other's mental state are insufficient or inadequate for grounding intersubjective understanding. Second, I will nonetheless follow simulation theory in its well-taken aim to avoid recourse to third-person or formal-rational models of understanding. By taking up issues of cognitive development and social cognition that emerge in the simulation theory debate, we will come to understand the extent to which the first-person perspective is wedded to linguistic socialization and communicative participation. Finally, I will use the stance of a socially situated first-person perspective as a starting point to understand interpretation in the social sciences. By analyzing the interpretive self as a product of dialogical processes of understanding, we can ground the epistemic claim of taking another's background into account. Interpreting human agency can thus be seen as requiring a dialogical perspective that methodologically recognizes the other's self-understanding. Yet such a situated approach can also avoid the abstract hermeneutic idealism that conceives of interpretation as a pure sharing of meaning perspectives in a power-free discursive universe. I will show how interpretive perspective taking can lead to a theoretical thematization of implicit and taken-for-granted social arrangements involving power and subordination.

2. Simulation and the Idea of Interpretive Immediacy

In this section I want to show that the misplaced psychologism of simulation theory leads to a conflation of the immediate and noninterpretive understanding of meaning with the idea that meaning is unmediated and unstructured by discursive, cultural, and social factors. Simulation theorists rightly oppose the exaggerated and artificial claims of mainstream philosophy of mind, which assumes that "folk psychological" theories or formal rationality assumptions implicitly guide social understanding.[1] Yet the rejection of misplaced cognitivism should not lead to an equally misplaced psychologism that overlooks the pervasive and constitutive influence of symbolic mediations of meaning altogether. If simulation theory wants to make good on the claim that understanding others is indeed a prediscursive and purely psychological process, it has to show on the basis of which phenomena or processes interpreters are able to gain *immediate access* to another agent's self-understanding. In addition to the rather dogmatic claim that we can understand one another pretheoretically through simulation because we are all psychically similar, we need more concrete and detailed explanations of how to access the other's mind and meaning. As far as I can see, simulation theorists have presented three basic phenomena or procedures that are supposed to cash in on the thesis concerning intuitive and immediate understanding. In the current discourse, reference is made to the immediate understanding of emotional expressions, to the prediscursive and imaginative identification with being in another's situation, and to the analogical inference from my (immediately given) mental states to those of another. In all cases, modes of immediate understanding (i.e., of emotional expressions, situational constellations, or conscious states) are presented as evidence for a preinterpretive mode of understanding. Yet the fact that such phenomena are understood without engaging in explicit and reflexive interpretations (or so I shall show) in no way establishes the prediscursive and psychological nature of the disclosed meaning and thus cannot establish the claim for immediate and noninterpretive access to another's meaning.[2]

1. In the current discussion, the immediate grasp of emotional expressions is often taken as evidence for a nontheoretical mode of understanding others.[3] Presumably, there is a host of research establishing the "hard facts" that young children "understand" the expressions of others by imitating them pretheoretically. Forms of bodily imitation, mimicry, are taken to point to a preconceptual yet universal dimension of intersubjective understanding that can be productively employed for making sense of others. The idea that there is a presymbolic, discursively and culturally uncontaminated dimension of making sense of the emotional and motivational states of others has previously been defended by philosophers in the (roughly) phenomenological tradition. Thinkers like Max Scheler, Ernst Cassirer, and Helmut Plessner argued early on that bodily states such as facial expressions can be taken as immediate and yet universal expressions of inner mental states.[4] Accordingly, prior to the symbolic form of language or discursive thought, there is a prediscursive and pretheoretical body language that immediately *signifies* what it means, thus exemplifying a function that

is both symbolic (because expressive of a mental state) and universal (because grasped without any conventional and thus culturally relative language). Cassirer labels this dimension the "expressive function," and Scheler is convinced that the evidence of such an immediate, nontheoretical comprehension of emotions points to a "universal grammar" of feelings in which experience (meaning) and expression (form) are necessarily correlated.[5]

Yet a closer look into the classic defenders of the phenomenological claim regarding the empathic understanding of emotional states will make clear that the fact of *immediate* understanding—as the absence of any *conscious or discursive* conceptualization—does in no way establish a pure or culturally *universal* form of meaning. By attempting to make his point for a nondiscursive (and thus noninterpretive) grasp of emotions, Scheler compels us to understand that emotional expressions and their meaning are just as immediately experienced as physical objects of our environment: "We perceive the shame in the blushing, the happiness in laughter . . . in the visual appearance of folded hands, for example, the pious request is just as present as the bodily object in visual perception."[6] The point that such understanding is exercised without any conscious or reflexive thematization is well taken, but it is a far cry from establishing the fact that such interpretive immediacy points to a universal and nonconventional core of meaning. In a sense, we can even argue that Scheler has shown the opposite, since in his example the experience of "happiness" in laughter, "shame" in blushing, and "piety" in folded hands are equally taken to be immediately understood. While recent psychological research claims to have indeed established certain facial expressions as immediate and universal signs of a state named happiness, no such universal expression has been found for shame, and folded hands as an expression of piety are even more clearly a conventional cultural gesture. Accordingly, the assumption that the immediacy of understanding emotional body signs points in itself to a preconceptual and culturally pure dimension of meaning seems unfounded in the phenomena.[7]

To be sure, defenders of immediate emotional understanding might put forth the more recent psychological theory that claims to have identified a set of what are called "basic emotions." According to an influential paradigm, basic emotions can be identified by similar facial expressions in all human cultures, which are thus taken to identify and exemplify similar emotional states in the respective human agents.[8] Yet the idea of basic emotions is plagued by the very same problems that already haunted the earlier phenomenological paradigm. To begin with, even though a certain number of so-called basic emotions correlated to basic expressions are taken to be identifiable (such as happiness, sadness, anger, fear, and disgust), a high number of emotions lack any correlation to a cross-cultural and fixed expressive form (including guilt, shame, remorse, hope, depression, etc.). It seems ludicrous to assume that emotions that are not universally fixed through a facial expression and/or have no cross-culturally valid sign are less real or crucial to the self-understanding of situated agents. Accordingly, the reference to universal basic emotions would only open a small slice of the emotional experience to an intercultural interpreter, who would always have to draw on additional symbolic, practical, and individual information to reconstruct what kind of emotional states might really be involved. Furthermore, it is unclear with regard to which reference system one should attempt to classify and organize so-called basic versus derivative emotions. Some researchers with Darwinist leanings prefer biological criteria that classify emotions according to their biological functions, but it seems equally plausible to see emotions as culturally and socially embedded expressions of situated agents. As such, an emotion like "crazy like a pig" might well be a basic experience for one culture, whereas "manic depression" might indicate a socially shared state in another. The true phenomenon of the emotional experience seems indeed truncated if reduced to a supposedly more immediate and basic biological state. Moreover, since the emotional experience takes place in the individual agent, we could also see psychological criteria relating to the agent's sense of self as most fundamental, which would require specific biographical and psychological knowledge in order to understand. Accordingly, the social dimension could in turn be questioned as providing valid criteria for basicness.[9]

What these skeptical reflections on hard-and-fast criteria for basic emotions point to is the culturally mediated character of most emotional experiences. Just as much as the modes of expression are infused with symbolic and conventional forms, so are the multiple and complex forms of emotional experience that are related to them. Seen in this light, the attempt to distill basic emotions from a set of pictorial prototypes must be seen as a highly reductive process possessing little value for the culturally situated interpreter.[10] The streamlining and reductionist process that abstracts basic emotional terms such as "happiness" or "anger" from their complex practical and symbolic context and then correlates them to equally decontextualized facial images does not tell us much about the actual emotional states of situated subjects. The abstraction of linguistic terms precedes and makes possible the very identification of basic emotions through enabling a correlation between terms and pictorial types. Yet the abstractive labeling, itself suitable for the task because of the already abstracted facial types, correlates to such images a generalized meaning that it rather *constructs* through the abstractive procedure, in spite of its claim to merely find these emotions underneath the bodily expressions.[11]

For a situated interpreter who has to understand how the agents make sense of themselves in the context of their social and cultural practices, the set of a few basic emotions can hardly provide a promising path into the other's experiential and cultural world. On the one hand, the reconstruction of basic emotions, even if valid and successful in a few compelling cases, seems to reduce the complex cultural and contextual connotations that concrete emotional states imply. Even defenders of basic emotions contend that the actual mental state might only last a few seconds while many such states might follow each other. To identify oneself as being in love, being depressed, or being happy rather involves a synthetic interpretive process that is made possible by interpretive schemes available in the respective cultural context. As Richard Shweder put it: "'Emotion' terms are names for particular interpretive schemes (e.g., 'remorse,' 'guilt,' 'anger,' 'shame,') of a particular story-like, script-like, or narrative kind that many people in the world might (or might not) make use of to give meaning and shape their somatic and affective 'feelings.'. . . The emotion is the whole story, the whole package deal—a kind of somatic event (fatigue, chest pain, goose flesh) experienced as a kind of perception (of loss, gain, threat, possibility) linked to a kind of plan (attack, withdraw, confess, hide, explore)."[12] On the other hand, the intertwinement of linguistic and symbolic concepts with somatic and affective feelings also undermines the clear-cut distinction between universally correlated natural expressions and conventionally constructed bodily gestures. For example, the understanding of happiness cannot proceed from the assumption that a certain facial expression unmistakingly expresses such a state, since another cultural context might have employed the same facial expression in order to convey very different experiences and attitudes. Accordingly, the understanding of emotional states, just as much as the understanding of more conceptual and articulated mental states, requires a reconstruction of the respective beliefs, assumptions, and practices that prevail in a given context.

2. There is a second strategy for arguing in favor of an immediate understanding of others. It avoids placing major emphasis on immediately grasped bodily signs and instead focuses on the more complex imaginative mechanism of putting yourself in the position of the other. Bodily expressions or behaviors perhaps indicate certain mental states, yet the gestures or behaviors as such are not taken to reveal the meaning; instead, only by putting yourself imaginatively into the other's situation can you fully grasp what triggered the agent's situational response. To be sure, the mechanism or procedure of imaginative identification places, as we will see, just as much emphasis on the experience of precognitive mental states such as emotional and practical responses to the environment. As Robert Gordon put it, transposing myself into the other's situation "is not a matter of looking dispassionately for features believed to produce certain characteristic actions or emotions" but rather of actively engaging "your own practical and emotional responses."[13] Accordingly, what now gets invoked are first-personal experiences that all humans share with regard to the objective (so-

cial and natural) environment. Without any reference to a generalized and implicit theory concerning belief-desire relations in the other, I am taken to simply reproduce the other's situation imaginatively, and then, based on my own intuitive reactions, predict what the other would do.[14]

To be sure, the assumption that I can imagine myself in the other's shoes without any additional cultural, historical, or social understanding seems quite implausible. Indeed, the actual prediction of another's reactions usually implies (this constitutes the classic hermeneutic challenge) not just imagining *yourself* in the other's situation but actually imagining *yourself as the other* in that situation.[15] The theoretical challenge for an anticognitivist position like Gordon's transpositional simulation lies in accounting for the fact that we have to make adjustments for the other's perspective (adjustments that usually imply discursive or theoretical elements), and still be able to hold on to the claim that the *primary* mechanism of understanding others is a noncognitive grasp of emotional and motivational attitudes. Gordon's proposal to deal with this dilemma is to distinguish between "total projection"—in which I assume the complete similarity of my own and the other's responses to the environment—and "partial projection"—in which I dynamically transform myself into the other by "working into" my simulation as much information as necessary regarding the other's disclosure of the situation. Yet if the understanding and prediction of the other now depends equally on the grasp of her (however tacitly exercised) assessment of the situation, and if that assessment requires us to take, for example, discursive, cultural, and social structures into account, then don't we have to acknowledge that the understanding of social situations is essentially an interpretive process involving discursive and symbolic dimensions? How are we to distinguish the basic moment of emotional and motivational affectedness from the (supposedly) secondary and supplemental aspects of the discursive and cultural mediation, thus justifying the grounding of social cognition in the immediacy of "total simulation"?[16]

Imagine that I am hiking with a friend who suddenly stops in front of me, turns around, and cautiously walks downhill.[17] Surprised at first, I move on to his position and spot a bear. Obviously, without reflection I immediately understand, since the bear is a dangerous animal, that my friend is afraid and flees.[18] Consider, however, that I discover instead of a grizzly a Newfoundland dog: I probably assume that the dog was wrongly identified by my friend as a bear. Or imagine that my friend and I indeed encounter a grizzly, yet my friend shows no signs of fear nor any intention to flee. Since I know my friend to be a committed biologist well attuned to animal behavior, I immediately understand that there is no impending danger. Similar variations of the initial example of immediate identification are interpreted by Gordon and his followers as exemplifying the switch from total to partial simulation. The idea is that there are basic situations that allow for total identification with the other, but that in many cases additional information is needed to adjust one's own perspective to the other's viewpoint in order to make sense of his or her behavior. Although there is nothing to object to in the description of the process, what is problematic is the general philosophical claim that we have a pure and immediate basic situation in which no symbolically mediated disclosure is involved at all, and in addition more complex constellations that require such information. What is peculiar is that simulation theorists do not see that even the initial situation itself requires some perspective and experiential attitude in light of which the situation is disclosed. What the imaginative variations of the example in fact reveal is that even in case of the original situation of experiencing fear, the bear *is disclosed as* a dangerous animal. In order to identify the bear as something that can cause me harm, I first have to understand it as a dangerous being. Instead of having any direct or immediate understanding of the bear as such, all the variations of the situation of encountering "the bear" involve a perspective of that being as such and such and thus a disclosure that reads the situation *in a certain way*.

Yet even if this is granted, the question remains whether there aren't some basic features of agents that prestructure, or better predispose, a psychically similar subject to respond similarly to the same environmental challenges; or, differently put, we might ask whether the 'as-structure' has necessarily to be propositional.[19] It is at this crucial step in the debate over prepropositional understanding, pushed to the fore by our inquiry into the fundamental status of emotional states for simulation, that Gordon's causal theory of emotions comes into play.[20] By arguing that emotional states are universally caused by the environment and thus do not require the mediation of propositional belief states, Gordon's causal conception of emotions functions as something like a hidden warrant for his antitheoretical conception of understanding. The crucial point that distinguishes this model from standard belief-desire psychology—and this has motivated the antitheoretical stance of Gordon's version of simulation from the very start—is that emotional states are caused and experienced *without any significant intervention or mediation by propositional attitudes*. As far as I can see, there are two basic and highly important rational motivations to adopt such a theory. First, Gordon rightly emphasizes that emotional states entail the structure of aboutness, without as such implying that they are mediated by a belief that such and such be the case. When it comes to emotions, the knowledge (and not "just" the belief) that something is the case is crucial, conjoined with our subjective evaluative attitude toward that fact.[21] For example, when I am angry at something, I am not angry *at the belief* that something is the case, but angry at the object itself.[22] Second, Gordon maintains plausibly that we can be in a mental state without believing to be in a mental state. This makes the important point that the

disclosure of states of affairs with mental effects or responses need not entail an *explicit* account or reflexive thematization of such states. As the
hermeneutic theorist would say, in such an experience I am fully absorbed
and thus unreflectively oriented at the intentional object, which I disclose
to be such and such.

However, the real question is whether the nonreflexive quality of mental
states such as emotions is by itself sufficient to convince us that emotional
states are causally dependent on the environment, and do not imply a relevant discursive or symbolic mediation of some form. It is with regard to the
strong claim that moves from the nonreflexive nature of emotional experiences to the assumption that emotional states are symbolically unmediated
and culturally neutral that we have to object.[23] Take the (counterfactual)
example of my being depressed about Clinton's election defeat.[24] To begin
with, suppose I find out later that Clinton was in fact elected. In turn, I
must come to understand that I was sad because I *believed* that he had not
been elected. In retrospect, the aboutness assumption, which presents itself
as immediate knowledge in the present experience, turns out on reflection
to be housed in the realm of a mental disclosure. Moreover, on further reflection I might realize that although it is true that my disappointment concerning the election is directed at the election (and not at my belief about
the election), it is nonetheless equally true that the very emotion is embedded, and deeply shaped, by a whole host of assumptions regarding Clinton.
In other words, the sadness exists due to, and is defined by, beliefs such that
Clinton is best for the continuous growth of the economy, that he would
have been better for issues like health care, gun control, social security, tax
reform, and so on. A seemingly singular and intentional emotion thus reveals itself to be situated in an underlying interpretive scheme, in what
Mannheim called a "political weltanschauung," in light of which I disclose
the situation both cognitively and emotionally. Finally, imagine that Clinton actually loses the election but a friend convinces me about the worthi-
ness of this defeat. Since this most likely happened by changing my beliefs
regarding the value of Clinton's presidency, it equally points to the deep interconnectedness between symbolic assumptions and emotional states.[25]
What this actually shows is a fact that the Stoics have long been aware of:
The emotions are not simply caused by the environment but rather depend
to a significant degree on our symbolically mediated attitude toward it.

All of this, I believe, points to the fact that the assumption of discursively
uncontaminated emotional states—mental states that exist prior to and independently from our general discursive and conceptual frameworks—is a
highly implausible construction with regard to the real emotional states of
culturally situated agents. It so seems that the very experience of emotions is
intertwined with, and in fact might well be intrinsically structured by, our
cultural and symbolical contexts of life. In order to grasp that interconnect-

edness between emotional states and symbolic assumptions, we would need an interpretive starting point that does not reduce but actually takes into account the conceptual and symbolic mediation of our mental experiences.[26]

3. At this stage of the analysis, the alternative proposal by Alvin Goldman becomes relevant, since it does not ground simulation in prepropositional empathy but rather starts with the assumption of a cognitively fully equipped, propositionally structured mind. It might thus be able to account for the previously encountered symbolic mediation of emotional and practical attitudes, without attempting to reduce the interpretive experience to some precognitive and prediscursive dimension. Indeed, instead of arguing for an antitheoretical stance toward understanding by reducing cognitions to prepropositional factors, the idea now is that agents (who possess a holistic, complex, and discursively structured self-understanding) use *their own beliefs and assumptions* as a "heuristic device" to make sense of other agents' actions and expressions. Accordingly, in Goldman's influential formulation, simulation is conceived as the "off-line" processing of the other's cognitive states by using myself as a model. The model of *generative simulation* (generative because my psychic system is supposed to generate the relevant output based on similar input) is different from the transpositional and dynamic simulation, since it does not require a transformation of myself into the other self. The basic similarity between our underlying psychic systems is deemed sufficient to allow for the use of myself as a heuristic simulator. Moreover, since I am aware of hypothetically "feeding" beliefs and assumptions of the other into my system, I am equally aware that I am 'playing' with pretend beliefs. Instead of attempting a complete and full "imaginative identification" (Gordon) with the other's experiential viewpoint, I merely rethink or "refeel" the newly incorporated psychic states in the make-belief mode. In this generative conception of simulation, I become a simulating engine into which I feed all the relevant information regarding the other's perspective and situation, and then "run" those beliefs "off-line" to see what *I* would do and how *I* would react in the other's shoes.

We might thus have found a model of simulation that reconciles the antitheoretical stance with the requirement of the intentional 'as-structure' that underlies an agent's experience of something as something. Yet even though Goldman defines simulation as a heuristic device that takes conceptually structured belief states into account, the states themselves are equally considered to be immediately given to consciousness, and as such considered to be unmediated by cultural, historical, or social factors. The qualitative states that the interpreter experiences are taken to be *ultimate experiences* that allow the inference from the interpreter to the interpretee. According to the generative model, I use my psychic self as a simulating engine, to be fed with all the relevant input, in order to produce relevant and reliable (though simulated) output. Since the other and I are psychically similar, I can, by analogy, infer that he or she will do what I simulated myself doing or intending in the same situation. The attribution of mental states is here based on analogical inference from my own self-knowledge to another. Yet, as our previous discussion of basic emotions with regard to the mediation of beliefs and emotions has shown, the *immediacy of experiencing* an emotional state does not imply its *symbolically unmediated nature*. If, on the contrary, the qualitative states regarding emotions and motivations are intertwined with beliefs, assumptions, and practices, then the understanding of differently situated agents cannot proceed by taking one's own mental states as its cue, since we cannot assume that the holistic and linguistic frameworks are sufficiently similar to allow direct correlation of our and their beliefs. Understanding them would require instead a reconstruction of the symbolic and practical contexts that mediate and permeate the qualitative experiences of the first-person perspective. The generative model suggests that we can nicely demarcate (1) a level of contextual, cultural, or linguistically mediated belief states, which we identify as relevant for the other's situation and which we have to feed into our system so as to run the off-line, and (2) an underlying, pure, self-contained psychological system that will process those cultural info bytes just as every other human agent— all of them being essentially similar—would do.

If, however, we have to give up the idea of first-person immediacy as evidence for symbolically unmediated qualities, we also lose our foothold in a neatly separated psychological sphere.[27] That the experience of conscious mental states will indeed have to be conceived as deriving from the concrete symbolic, linguistic, and cultural practices in which the conscious self is embedded will be developed in the next section. By recourse to a developmental account of the interpretive first-person perspective, we will show that the meaning of the experiential states has to be seen as intertwined with the conceptual and linguistic practices of taking the symbolically mediated perspective of another agent. If the "introspective" self emerges from the participation in dialogical practices, the very existence of an uncontaminated psychic self is rendered implausible, as is consequently its methodological function.

3. The Dialogical Constitution of the Interpretive Self

It seems that if we were to find a way to reformulate the self-givenness of our mental states in terms of symbolically mediated beliefs, we might find a position that could save the first-person perspective as an interpretive starting point without committing the fallacy of interpretive immediacy. To fill in this claim, we would need an account of representational or symbolic mental states without invoking the *solipsistic* psychology of pure introspec-

tive mental states. In this respect, an account of the development of reflective mental states can show how a hermeneutic mode of self-understanding,
that is, an interpretive self, emerges from the social practices of language
learning by participating in interpersonal communication. Such an account
is necessary because it alone explains how the psychological mechanism of
role taking is absorbed and involved in the symbolically mediated understanding of others, and thus can provide an argument against the psychologistic position on its own ground.

If we want to employ a developmental reconstruction for an argument
in the logic of interpretation, we have to be careful not to confuse the different requirements of both areas. If we want to show how the development of the hermeneutic competence can avoid the Cartesian dilemma of
grounding intersubjective understanding in private and immediate self-
consciousness, we have to analytically distinguish between the two
different functions of a developmental and a hermeneutic logic. Both aspects require an opposed, and seemingly contradictory, approach. Developmentally, we have to avoid presupposing a reconstruction that would
read reflective mental states into prereflective stages, thus smuggling into
the description the very consciousness that it claims to show as only later
emerging.[28] Hermeneutically, however, we have to conceptualize a background structure of understanding that is rich enough to allow for conscious interpretive performances, thus avoiding the reduction of higher-
order interpretations to basic, nonreflective mechanisms. If we do not
confuse these separate requirements, then the developmental reconstruction of how agents acquire their complex interpretive capabilities can
function as a quasi-transcendental grounding of the hermeneutic procedures in the human sciences.

The task is indeed to show that the empirical evidence with regard to the
development of cognitive structures, in particular the attribution of belief
states to other agents and in turn reflexively to oneself, is best accounted
for in a model that draws on our participation in dialogical practices and
on linguistic world disclosure.[29] In order to understand at what age children understand that agents mediate the experienced reality by means of a
cognitive perspective (which in turn allows the self-attribution of reflexive
beliefs to a conscious self), cognitive psychologists construed the so-called
false-belief task.[30] The ingenious idea behind that experiment, in the course
of which children are asked to predict the behavior of someone who has
different and false information regarding a certain situation, is that the successful solution implies that children manage to picture or reconstruct how
the other would act *based on her false beliefs*. In a famous version of this
experiment, children observe a puppet scene in which Maxi puts a piece of
chocolate in a box, mother enters and replaces the chocolate in the cupboard, and Maxi returns in order to look for his chocolate. The questioned

children, in order to predict Maxi's behavior correctly, have "to take into account" that Maxi "assumes" or "believes" the chocolate to be in the box (instead of the cupboard, where mother put it). As it turns out, children aged two to four fail, whereas children aged four to six usually succeed. The actual question, to be sure, is how to account for that developmental leap in terms of a plausible psychological theory.

For the simulation theorists, the fact that very young children fail and slightly older children succeed has to be seen as an advancement in their intuitive role-taking capacity.[31] Based on the plausible rejection of the sudden emergence of a full-fledged nomological theory that attributes belief-desire states to other agents around age four, simulationists argue that the increase in hypothetical reasoning or imaginative identification explains that children can now put themselves *intuitively* in Maxi's shoes and thus predict correctly that he would act based on information that he, not they themselves, deem correct. We should note, however, that in terms of Gordon's account of simulation as total projection, the false-belief task is already one step more complex, since the interpreting child has precisely to make an adjustment to the specific *perspective* in light of which Maxi discloses the situation. Based on this crucial difference, cognitive psychologists like Josef Perner or Alan Leslie suggest that only a developmental theory assuming that a new, qualitatively different way of understanding others has been reached can account for the consistently higher success rate of older children.[32] According to a scheme that defines an agent's experience of her environment as in principle mediated by cognitive representations, the two- to four-year-olds are captured in just one model of reality and are, just like naive realists, incapable of switching their cognitive framework so as to account for Maxi's false perspective or to understand the disclosure of reality in terms of representational media at all. The four- to six-year-olds, however, have grown to become "situation theorists" who are able to move between different models of reality. Accordingly, while they do not as yet reflexively relate to representational media as such, they are now able to model, however implicitly, reality *as it appears* to Maxi, thus seeing the situation from Maxi's perspective, which in turn allows for the correct prediction of his behavior. At an even higher stage, children or agents will become able to not only model reality according to a pluralistic interpretive universe but actually take a reflexive stance toward the representational medium as such and become capable of reconstructing the basic mechanisms and assumptions that go into the various disclosures of reality. Children at that stage would have become "representation theorists," since they can now represent the medium of representation itself.[33]

However skeptical we might be with regard to the idea of implicit, or tacit, models of reality, Perner's suggestion is crucial for our discussion because it captures (albeit in a form we will ultimately not endorse) two essential dimensions of the understanding of others. On the one hand, it is decisive that reality is experienced *as it appears to the other*, which requires that we account, in whatever form, for some grasp of the symbolic, or "representational," as-structure of the particular "world disclosure" of the other. On the other hand, Perner is aware of the fact highlighted by the simulation theorists that to take such a perspective of "experiencing-as" must not already imply the metarepresentational capacity to explicitly represent the different interpretive perspectives in one shared symbolic medium (even though it must involve a certain grasp of the symbolic mediation of representing something as something).[34] Empirically, children who can predict Maxi's behavior correctly are often not yet capable of representing their representations explicitly or of taking conscious account of their own and the other's interpretive perspective. Conceptually—and here is where the simulationists find their evidence—the capacity to take someone's perspective is independent from the higher-order capacity to represent someone's perspective on a discursive level, since children lack at this age the concept of belief.[35] Yet if we want to do justice to the empirical evidence, which demands that (1) we account for the taking of the *particular* perspective of the other and (2) we account for the nonrepresentational nature of such perspective taking at a certain developmental stage, we have to name a mechanism that can explain both. Moreover, we have to identify a structure that can also explain how such an implicit and nonetheless perspectival understanding of the other can ultimately be made explicit in a reflexive medium. This last requirement is important because only then can we bridge the gap between implicit role taking and discursively explicated perspective taking, and it holds particular relevance for an approach that attempts to connect the development of a hermeneutic competence, which passes through the stages of implicit role taking toward discursive self-understanding, to the practice of reflexive interpretation in the human sciences.[36]

The previously indicated solution to this requirement can, based on recent empirical evidence, be seen in the acquisition of linguistic or, more precisely, conversational competence. Following Paul Harris, it is a remarkable and significant fact that the decisive turn in solving the false-belief task (and similar cognitive problems) occurs just about when children begin to be fully socialized into communicative practices.[37] The co-occurrence of this fact is itself already an indication that learning to use linguistic symbols is an enforcing, if not necessary, precondition for learning to attribute "epistemic" perspectives to others. This suggestion, however, develops its force fully once we take a closer look at the structural implications of conversational practices. What is telling in this regard is that in order to be able to follow and participate in a conversation, some sort of conceptual or experiential perspective taking necessarily has to take place. The supposedly simple mechanisms of responding, listening, replying, emphasizing, explaining, asking, and so on in response to another's speech acts all imply, however unreflectively, a *Mitgehen,* a "following track" of what the other is getting at. It thus implies the capacity to look at things from the other's perspective so as to "simply" understand her or him in order to avoid talking past each other or falling into monologue instead of having a dialogue.

However, if we take an even closer look into the structure of linguistic world disclosure, it becomes clear that language, by providing the basic symbolic medium of self-understanding, can account for the specific features of mental attitudes in the false-belief task. Due to what we could call the "symbolic intentionality" of linguistic meaning, linguistic schemes preorganize and orient our conscious experience without being itself a conscious factor in our understanding.[38] Linguistic meaning in its original mode is never oriented at itself but always discloses something, which is nonetheless thus experienced in a certain manner. Accordingly, that fact that four- to six-year-olds can take the perspective of the other without reflexive perspective taking can be accounted for by the communicatively acquired capacity to move between different, linguistically disclosed perspectives. Those perspectives, or their underlying representational medium language, must not as such be thematic, since the linguistic practices are rather learned as a skill, through participation, and not through distanced or theoretical reflection. Yet the nontheoretical, dialogical socialization into the linguistic dimension of experience can also account for the subsequently emerging capacity of reflexive thematization. Although linguistic disclosure remains usually unthematic, language as such is nevertheless, in a word by Apel, its own metalanguage and thus provides the agent with a conceptual medium that allows for its own reflexive thematization. It thus allows for what Perner called "meta-representation," that is, the representation of the representational relation itself.[39] Agents are thus practically, unreflectively, and dialogically socialized into the linguistic medium that entails the objective potential for reflexive self-understanding (which only emerges at a subsequent stage in the cognitive development). Although the socialization into dialogical practices first takes the step of implicit perspective taking, the acquisition of the symbolic medium equips the agent with a mechanism to relate reflexively to her own as well as to the other's experiential perspectives.[40]

We are now in a position to tie these reflections back to our interest in a methodological grounding that can do justice to the developmental and the hermeneutic requirement of the interpretive stance. According to this proposal, a reflexive self-consciousness (which is both a presupposition and an objective of the human sciences) is made possible through a basic, preconceptual role-taking competence that allows the developing self to participate in dialogical practices. Those dialogical practices imply a symbolically mediated perspective taking that allows agents to understand the particular viewpoints of differently situated agents. Due to the inherently reflexive structure of language, this process finally allows for a representational self-relation. In the developmental logic, we can assume with Mead a basic capacity to take the role of the other.[41] As recent empirical evidence suggests, we can moreover show that the conception of belief—in the sense of a reflective or conscious belief or as the introduction of belief states as mediating experience and reality—is learned by participating in linguistic dialogue. This suggests that the basic role-taking device is moved to a higher (and qualitatively different) stage by entering conversational practices that force agents to take, more or less reflectively, the epistemic stance of other agents into account. This nicely dovetails with the hermeneutic account of self-consciousness, which takes it to have the structure of a *dialogue with oneself*. Accordingly, the supposedly primordial stance of introspective consciousness, or the much emphasized first-person attitude of simulation, is itself grounded in a dialogical mode of perspective taking that unfolds once the self participates in intersubjective communication. Self-understanding now becomes, in terms of Mead, the symbolically mediated conversation in which "I" as the thinking self relate to "me" as the "object" of my reflection. The developmental reconstruction of the reflective, assumedly pure, and introspectively given self shows the very possibility of self-knowledge to be derived from a socially shared and intersubjective source.

4. Perspective Taking, Social Power, and Critical Reflexivity

What follows if we replace the psychological grounding of simulation theory with the conception of a dialogically constituted interpretive self? How do we have to reformulate the basic tenets and tensions of the hermeneutic process, and how precisely does this bear on the methodology of the human and social sciences?

To begin with, we should realize that the specificity of the interpretive first-person perspective (which in turn gets attributed to the other in interpretation) can only be captured if we take the symbolic mediation of our sense of self into account. Simulation theory has based its claim to a superior mode of "explaining" others on the first-person attitude. Yet it is hard to see how the immediate identification of emotional expressions, the prediscursive transposition into another's situation, or the introspective access of one's qualitatively distinct mental states can account for the unique and experientially rich self-understanding of culturally situated agents. Immediate, biologically anchored "meanings," causally triggered emotional states, or introspective "first-person" access do not grasp the full scope of self-understanding that underlies our intuition regarding first-personal experiences. As Mead has aptly argued, mere states of consciousness, however immediate, lack any relevant and rich sense of self. In turn, only after a (symbolically mediated, since dialogically constituted) self as a reflexive self has emerged can such states be (self-) attributed and thus be experienced, by a self or as part of a self.[42]

With the conception of a symbolically mediated self, we can connect everyday understandings of agents to the reflexive interpretations in the human and social sciences. In this perspective, we see agents *as* understanding themselves in light of some culturally situated conceptions, assumptions, and practices, which thus accounts for the (usually to a large extent implicit and taken for granted) as-structure of meaning mentioned before. (The fact, however, that the self "constructs" its self as being this or that person in the context of intersubjective practices means also that she or he never has an absolutely privileged position vis-à-vis the meanings that make up her sense of self.) Early on, the self emerges in the contexts of dialogical practices and continuously builds up a more or less fixed self-scheme, according to which she or he understands her- or himself. That scheme, to be understood as a cultural habitus, a kind of symbolically mediated and practically situated worldview, has to be flexible enough to allow for participation in the differing social contexts, thus taking over diverse perspectives or roles and enabling the participation in ever new ones while yet defining in some underlying sense the deeper and more enduring identity of that self.[43] Insofar as the construction of selfhood is only possible by establishing a reflexive self-relation, which has to be mediated by the use of language, the self comes to develop over time a deeply engrained, culturally mediated self-conception. Since the self is thus structured (literally) in terms of basic conceptions and assumptions, the very symbolic forms or self-schemes in light of which it makes sense of itself can be articulated. The articulation of such "prearticulated" schemes of self-understanding, insofar as it makes sense of another's expressions and actions, can be seen as a core task of the human and social sciences.

Perhaps the most important methodological consequence of the difference between simulation theory and hermeneutic theory in conceiving selfhood pertains, paradoxically, to a basic agreement of both approaches. Both simulation theory and hermeneutic theory proceed from the assumption that interpreter and interpretee are in crucial aspects "ontologically" similar. Both address the well-known epistemological and antirealist objections to this charge by referring to the experiential dimensions and implications of the interpretive process itself. Psychological access here, dialogical experience there are taken to sustain sufficiently the similarity assumption vis-à-vis the other. Yet simulation theory and hermeneutic theory conceive of this "human similarity" in radically different ways. For simulation theorists, the psychic similarity implies that we can rely on some immediately given meaning in order to gain access to the other's mental states. Since the hermeneutic conception conceives of the self and its mental states as intrinsically shaped by the cultural and social environment, no such access via immediate meaning is possible. Indeed, just as much as the other is seen as being shaped by individual perspectives, symbolic assumptions, and implicitly pervasive practices, so the interpreter her or himself is "caught" in a formally similar and yet concretely diverging context. In other words, after the switch to the hermeneutic perspective, the similarity thesis forces us to take into account from the very start the differences in cultural, social, and historical background.

If our previous analysis of the interconnectedness between emotions, symbolic assumptions, and cultural practices is correct, we cannot assume that the cultural background knowledge is the same for all agents. Instead of replacing the abstract theory or rationality models thus with a pseudo-concrete yet equally generalized model of "hypothetical reasoning" (which draws on *psychological* background capacities supposedly shared by everyone), we now face the hermeneutic task of coming to grips with the force of implicit preconceptions and practical assumptions, without simply suggesting that those "knowledges" allow us to transpose ourselves into their shoes.[44] Rather, at our level of discussion, we have to conceive of the disclosure of the other's perspective as an interpretive process that requires, from the very beginning, a reflexive acknowledgment of one's own cultural position vis-à-vis the other. Interpretation, which unavoidably needs to invest one's own symbolic resources in order to make sense of others, must be equally on guard of not infusing or imposing one's own taken-for-granted categories and assumptions onto the other's perspective. Once we move from the psychologistic to a hermeneutic grounding of the interpretive process, the similarity between interpreter and interpretee provides nothing but the open-ended challenge to determine identity and difference in the interpretive encounter itself.[45]

The task is to make sense of another human agent, to understand his or her expressions, actions, gestures, or beliefs. We are aiming at the other, whom we conceive as being structurally similar to ourselves. We are thus oriented to the other's understanding of a situation, since the similarity thesis forces us to attribute self-understanding, an interpretive self-relation, to the other agent. We are, due to the intentional orientation of the project of interpretation, forced to take the self-understanding of the other agent into account.[46] Although we are not oriented at our understanding of the other's expressions and actions, and thus are aiming at the other's meaning itself, we are nonetheless caught in an interpretive perspective that discloses the other's self-understanding in a specific manner *for us*. Interpreting another, precisely if we stick to the similarity thesis, now has to be seen as a process determining and profiling the other's vision with regard to our own. Yet how exactly can we "enter," or take on, the symbolic-practical perspective of the other? What allows us, or which kind of interpretive strategies and attitudes, assure best that we reconstruct most truthfully how the other experiences and assesses a situation? I will answer this question by distinguishing five essential points that define the methodological profile of interpretation as dialogical perspective taking.

1. On the most basic level of methodology, we have to understand that the holistic and culturally, socially, and historically impregnated nature of the background rules out any class or phenomena that could provide genuine and "direct" access to the other's meaning. We have carefully analyzed—and rejected—the most plausible proposals for such immediate understanding in the first part of this chapter. We have now to realize that there simply is no genuine access to the other's perspective. In order to begin the interpretive process, we have to project, of course, some understanding (naturally our own) onto the other's expression and behavior. Yet such an interpretive projection can be nothing but a bridgehead into the other's perspective, which needs to be continuously checked, revised, reassessed, and replaced as the interpretive process unfolds. Phenomena that seem self-evident are taken not to point to a universal or immediate core meaning but rather represent a mediated familiarity, a habitualized background scheme of meaning that gets unconsciously applied to the other— and must await confirmation—or rejection or transformation—as the understanding progresses.[47]

2. The rejection of interpretive immediacy, however, does not mean that we now have to accept "the principle of charity" when it comes to truthfully understanding the other. Such a perspective, which assumes that we extend our own rationality to the expressions and behaviors of the other and then build up the most plausible and rational interpretation of his or her behavior according to our standards, confuses the necessary starting point of interpretation (our own taken-to-be-true preconceptions) with a consensus-based model of the interpretive process itself. The principle of a rational projection from our perspective onto the other, if combined with the belief that we have to "maximize agreement" if we really want to understand, seems flawed on two accounts. First, it does not convince on a phenomenological level, since it conceives interpretation as a symbolic one-way street on which we extend true beliefs and assumptions to the other and continue to do so until we have either reached a consensus or have to switch to an "explanatory" mode.[48] Yet the experience of historical and intercultural experiences can teach us that in the process of the hermeneutic encounter, both interpreter and interpretee often have to undergo deep transformations. It is not the case that one set of rigid standards gets employed and "projected" onto the other (such a projection would rather fit the psychoanalytic definition of paranoia!); rather, both partners in the interpretive dialogue learn to see the other's perspective and learn to see one another in turn from the perspective of the other. That process usually

changes both perspectives involved. Second, and touched upon before, the rationality models tend to make a problematic division between a rationality- or plausibility-based assessment of the other's meaning, and a switch toward explanatory and third-person models once a rational assessment seems impossible. Accordingly, while one interprets oneself purely in first-person rational terms, one uses both a first-person and a third-person approach to make sense of the other. Yet such a disparity between the interpretive models cannot be justified based on the very similarity thesis that the principle of charity claims to endorse, and it surely undercuts the spirit of true interpretive dialogue in which we both understand each other *on an equal footing*.

3. Accordingly, interpretation cannot be based on immediate understanding and must not be oriented at rational agreement. The true and unique function of the interpretive encounter consists rather of producing a heightened sense of reflexivity both in the interpreter and in the interpretee. We can compare the interpretive taking the perspective of another to learning a new vocabulary, to mastering a different symbolic disclosure. Although the analogy to language learning carries us some way, the differences between learning your first language and interpreting a symbolic perspective are crucial. The difference consists of the way in which entering a symbolic world relates to your conscious sense of self. As Mead and our previous analysis have shown, I become a conscious and interpreting self only by entering into dialogical practices. Those practices immerse me in a symbolic identity by taking the attitude of others toward me. The symbolic representation allows me to fix such meaning and represent it to myself *as* my meaning. Accordingly, in this primary process of symbolic self-constitution, I come to identify with symbolic acts as my own acts, and I thus develop a personal narrative, a symbolically and culturally rich self-understanding.

Now, when such a symbolically mediated self as interpreter encounters another agent's symbolic perspective, the task is not to build up a sense of self but to mediate and reconstruct how the other discloses the situation. This in turn requires a reflexive reconstruction of the underlying beliefs, assumptions, and practices, which forces the interpreter to take a reflexive attitude toward his or her own taken-for-granted premises. By being forced to explicate the other's implicit assumptions, the interpreter's own prejudgments come into play. The more the other is "objectified," that is, the more his or her background gets explicated, the more the interpreter's own background comes into profile. What thus emerges is not a repetition of the primary constitution of a conscious self but the metareflexive attitude of an interpreting self that learns to see and understand itself *as such a conscious and symbolically mediated self*. The self thus draws on the mechanism of dialogical perspective taking in order to develop a higher cultural reflexivity, which is transformed toward a metareflexive self-understanding. The final stage is metareflexive because it transcends the usual reflexive self-understanding of the situated self and instead implies the consciousness of symbolic, cultural, and social structures that defines the taken-for-granted self-understanding. Accordingly, in the reflexive interpretations of the human and cultural sciences, understanding does not have the function of integration with regard to a symbolically mediated self but rather enables such a situated self a specific methodical self-alienation and self-distanciation from its own taken-for-granted beliefs and assumptions.

4. Yet we might now inquire about the precise relevance of this distinction between the primary symbolic self-constitution and the metareflexive attitude toward oneself as a symbolically constructed self. According to our argument, dialogical practices make the development of the reflexive self possible. However, the socialization into the linguistic medium allows in turn a more radical reflexivity that can thematize symbolic conventions as such. The interpretive space between the two dimensions of reflexivity makes an understanding of the impact of social power on self-constitution possible and yet avoids reducing the agent to a mere reproduction of existing identity schemes. By engaging in dialogical perspective taking, agents build up a sedimented store of symbolic assumptions and practical dispositions that "reflect," albeit unconsciously, the existing power structures of a given social and cultural context. Yet the fact that those habitualized schemes of meaning have been incorporated into the self through dialogical practices means that agents can transcend these identity schemes. The dialogical mechanism of taking the attitude of the other can be activated to break the spell of habitualized forms of self-understanding. Methodologically, the reconstruction of discursive rules and symbolic preconceptions, the ethnographic and ethnomethodological descriptions of more or less codified social and cultural practices, and the functional and structural analysis of the codes of larger social institutions and systems all have to be understood as developing the reflexive potential to thematize hidden and hitherto unrecognized processes of social meaning constitution. They allow the situated self to objectify essential aspects of its own cultural and social background, and thus to thematize how power has influenced the disclosure of meaning.[49]

5. The move from a reflexive and dialogical self to the position of critical reflexivity involves two steps. First, the self breaks its habitualized self-schemes by taking cultural perspectives of others and thereby distanciates herself from the taken-for-granted assumptions of her background. In a second step, this reflexive freedom is employed to take a more radical attitude of distanciation and to use linguistic reflexivity to represent the self in the context of social, cultural, and historical constellations. The newly won theoretical perspectives are thus seen as emerging from the dialogical reflexivity of perspective taking. At this final stage, we are now faced with the demand for a general social theory that can both explain how agents come to

adopt and internalize power-inculcated schemes of self-understanding and yet how the built-in reflexivity of language nonetheless allows for a critical reflexivity that enables situated transcendence. What we need is a *theory of symbolic self-constitution* that can analyze and distinguish the different components in the process of interpretive self-construction. Such a theory would have to show how the self comes to attach its intrinsic sense of identity to culturally and socially preformulated identity images, how it is led to identify and fuse with those "external" expectations and demands, and yet how the fact of symbolic mediation, due to its grounding in dialogical role taking, nonetheless allows for a reflexive and imaginative transcendence of those habitualized social meanings. Such a theory, of course, is beyond the scope of this chapter. Yet the methodological reflections presented here—which are interested primarily in delineating the scope of simulation and dialogical perspective taking in the human and social sciences—might nevertheless have pointed to its possible profile.[50]

Notes

1. For the simulation approach, see the following classic papers: Gordon 1995a; Goldman 1995a; Heal 1995a. For a critique of the theory theory, see especially Heal 1995b; 1996b; for a critique of formal-rational models, see Goldman 1995a, pp. 75–79.

2. By "immediate understanding" I mean a comprehension of meaning that does not require a reflective or explicitly interpretive effort but that simply grasps something to be—that is, to mean—such and such. It is thus understood as self-evident. My argument in the following section is based on the fact that symbolically and culturally mediated experiences can acquire the same sense of "immediacy" or "self-evidence" as supposedly natural or noncultural phenomena.

3. See the reference to such phenomena in Gordon 1995a; Goldman 1995b; see also the chapters by G. Vielmetter and S. Turner in this volume, both of whom identify those expressions as "starting points" for social interpretations.

4. See as representative Scheler 1923; Cassirer 1985, pp. 58–91.

5. It should be noted that in contrast to some simulation theorists, phenomenology conceives this interpretive immediacy as a symbolic relation and not a causal one. The phenomenologists emphasize that the natural expressions *signify* or *express* certain emotional states and thus represent a natural and nonconventional symbolic form in which something (the facial expression) stands for something else (the emotional state).

6. Scheler 1923, p. 21 (my translation); see also Cassirer (1985, p. 68), who states: "The expressive meaning attaches to the perception itself, in which it is apprehended and immediately perceived."

7. See Ekman 1973; 1980. Yet instead of seeing here nothing but an awkward confusion between conventional and universal body signs, we should rather realize that Scheler, in spite of himself, has actually discovered what we could call the semiotic law of the independence between the immediacy of meaning and the conven-

tional origin of form: *Whatever the real origin of an emotional bodily expression (whether biological, cultural, or social), its experience might come with exactly the same force of self-certainty and immediacy.*

8. See Ekman 1980; Ekman and Davidson 1994, especially pp. 5–47.

9. See Averill 1980; Averill 1994; Shweder 1994. For an approach that places the narrative construction of selfhood at the center of experience, and thus defines the significance of emotional experiences in relation to the biographical context, see Bruner 1990, pp. 99ff.

10. In the cross-cultural experiments, agents are presented with what researchers take to be pictorial prototypes of emotions, for instance, a smiling face, and then are asked to assign a linguistic label expressing an emotion, say, happiness, to the image. In order to reveal the assumedly universal meaning of such bodily expressed prototypes, contextual specifications as well as more detailed assignments such as frozen smile, play face, etc. are excluded. Agents are instead asked to stick to basic labels such as happiness, sadness, anger, etc.

11. To argue that the identification of one image (smiling face) with one term (happiness) actually reveals a truly universal core of an emotional experience—that is, that happy states are both experienced and expressed in the same manner and thus are understood immediately across cultures—commits the fallacy of forgetting its own procedure of abstractive decontextualization. That such happy faces express happiness might be just as absurd as the claim that the universal identification of a man and a women as a couple on a picture reveal the same experience of gender relations across all human cultures.

12. Shweder 1994, pp. 32, 38. See also Harré and Gillet 1994.

13. Robert Gordon 1995a, p. 103.

14. The advantage of this version of simulation is often seen in its high reliability with regard to predicting the behavior of other agents. By reconstructing the steps that lead to an empathetic identification with the other, I might first recall the extremely high success rate predicting my own behavior, then extend my own responses to imagined settings so as to preserve the reliability, and finally use myself in the place of the other to simulate what he or she might do in a certain situation. Note that (1) the reliabilism is based on the similarity between (psychic) subjects: I have to assume that the other reacts in the very same way, emotionally and motivationally, to that situation as I would; that (2) no discursive, cultural, or social factors enter so as to influence and distinguish my responses from that of the other, and that (3) the situation is somehow capable of directly influencing the emotional and motivational attitudes of myself as much as of the other. Accordingly, the reliabilist account of transpositional simulation is not based on "psychic similarity" between interpreter and agent alone; in order to work as an antitheoretical argument for social cognition (i.e., in order to show that I can truly claim to understand the other by simulating myself in her place), I also have to argue that *the situation affects me in a manner that is not significantly structured or mediated by propositional attitudes or symbolic mediations.* In other words, precisely because there is a level of (cognitively nonpenetrated) emotional and motivational responses to the environment, and because it is this level that has the major impact on how I—and anyone else—acts and reacts, I can rely on imagining myself in the situation of the other for understanding and predicting the other's behavior.

15. See Gordon 1995a, in which he mentions a discussion with Dennett concerning the fact that simulation often falls short of an adequate taking into account of the specific perspective of the other. From our perspective, it is this requirement that ultimately points to the insufficiency of a psychological grounding of simulation and requires us to see it as a thoroughly interpretive process.

16. See Gordon 1995b for "The Primacy of Total Projection," pp. 102–105.

17. The example is taken from Gordon 1995a.

18. We can see this situation as a standard context in which the basic emotion of anxiety is triggered. Since my friend and I are psychically similar, we will experience exactly the same emotional response to the environment.

19. Heidegger (1962), in *Being and Time,* and recently Hubert Dreyfus (1991), in his interpretations of Heidegger, strongly emphasize the hermeneutic dimension of experiencing something as something while at the same time denying that this as-structure is propositionally structured. For a critique of that position that emphasizes the equal importance of symbolic and conceptual structures for understanding, see Kögler 1996a.

20. See Gordon 1987. A hidden yet crucial assumption in the whole theory and its defense, Gordon is convinced, is that we do experience emotions prior to and uncontaminated by beliefs or propositional attitudes. While this, of course, is true of very young children and nonhuman primates, it remains to be seen whether the case can be plausibly made for reflexive forms of interpreting human agents: Is there a relatively independent and at the same time foundational function of emotions, which can thus be understood as a cognitive mode prior to conceptual disclosure and yet highly efficacious for understanding?

21. Emotions can, according to this scheme, be divided into factive and epistemic emotions—factive emotions relating to existing states and epistemic ones to anticipated conditions. The first imply that p in fact exists, the second that p be possible. Although this distinction captures the two basic modes of the aboutness relation, concerning the object of emotion, the full picture only emerges once we complement it with the distinction between positive and negative emotions. Positive emotions are connected with wish satisfaction, whereas negative ones relate to wish frustration. Gordon's conviction now is that with this scheme we can reconstruct all emotions as being causally connected to actual states of affairs, which are disclosed and evaluated in terms of basic pro or con attitudes.

22. This dovetails well with Edith Stein's phenomenological observation that true empathy is not directed at the emotional state of the other as such but requires an orientation at the object at which the other's emotional experience is directed; only thus can the full content be empathetically reexperienced. See Stein 1989 and her Husserlian treatment of empathy.

23. In a trivial sense, of course, I have to be able to identify certain objects via beliefs in order to have an emotional response to them, such as the fear that the stock market will crash, etc. Since Gordon wants to base emotional understanding on knowledge, however, he curtails the role of beliefs and assumptions with regard to emotional experience: "Explanation and prediction begin with a presumption of knowledge. This suggests, among other things, that a capacity to attribute *beliefs* (particularly, *false* beliefs) is not a prerequisite for attributing factive emotions" (Gordon 1987). It might be that Gordon's correct rejection of the need to possess

the *concept* of belief for emotions leads him to trivialize and ignore the relation of emotions to unreflective conceptual assumptions. Since emotions are immediately understood, that is, do not require the conscious mediation of a belief-attitude, they are also experienced as unmediated, that is, independent from cultural conceptions and influence. If Gordon would not make this assumption, his conception of "total projection" would lose its ground as the primary process for understanding.

24. Again, the example is taken—with a slight variation—from Gordon (1987), who uses "Dewey won the election."

25. For a similar argument concerning the codependency of beliefs and emotions, see Greenspan 1988.

26. For a social analysis that makes this case for "love," see Luhmann 1986; Stendhal 1975.

27. In any event, what is required for self-consciousness is a capability for self-identification that grasps the mental act *as its own act* and that does, accordingly, establish a self-relation through connecting the act and the acting self. In order to do so, the act has to be represented by the consciousness, and also be identified and "attributed to" the currently reflecting consciousness itself. This process, however possible, requires a medium in which the representation of the act (which can be a proposition, a feeling, a wish, a desire) can take place and thus allows for a connection to the active consciousness. If those conditions are given, we can speak of self-consciousness. It can be defined as the reflexive understanding of oneself as having or exercising certain acts. Yet if this is correct, we have to give up the assumption that self-consciousness has any immediate access to itself. Since the self-relation can only establish itself through a reflexive act, in which the act is related to a reflecting self, the relation is necessarily interpretive in nature. As we saw, such a process requires the representation of the act in some medium, which as such is not immediately given but demands the interpretive recognition of the medium *as the vehicle* of the self's expression.

28. This problem was a major concern for Mead (1934), who attempted to reconstruct the emergence of symbolic self-consciousness from presymbolic role taking. See also Kögler 1996c for a discussion of these claims, as well as the chapter by S. Turner in this volume.

29. The "world disclosure" concept is taken from Heidegger and designates a holistic and symbolically mediated understanding of phenomena in light of some more basic, usually implicit assumptions.

30. See the classic experiments presented by Wimmer and Perner 1983.

31. Gordon 1995a, pp. 67–71; and Goldman 1995b, who sees an "increase in imaginative flexibility" as the most plausible explanation.

32. Wimmer and Perner 1983; see also Stich and Nichols 1995a and the slightly revised position of Perner 1996.

33. See Perner 1993.

34. Perner 1993, p. 67.

35. This disability to represent something at this stage as belief, that is, the lack of the concept of belief, is what motivated simulation theorists to argue against the theoretical view of social cognition.

36. I see "role taking" as an innate capacity prior to conceptual or symbolic competence (which is supported by the fact of children's role-taking behavior or the "in-

tersubjective" behavior of animals, such as when dogs respond and anticipate each other's behavior). I understand "perspective taking" to be the capacity to construct the world or experience from the viewpoint of someone else (which does not imply that one can articulate and represent this viewpoint). Perspective taking thus depends on the symbolic medium of language, since it discloses the specific understanding of something as something. The developmental fact that children learn to take the *perspective* of another when they enter communicative practices will serve as important evidence for my following point.

37. See Harris 1996. Harris's suggestions seem to be based solely on empirical observation. He seems to be unaware of the long German tradition in dialogical thought, from Buber to Gadamer and Habermas. He also makes no explicit connection to Mead's similar concerns.

38. Gadamer 1989; see also Kögler 1996a, especially pp. 38–42.

39. Perner 1993.

40. This view could also explain an objection that Perner and Howes (1992) make against simulation theory. In a new experiment, they argue that on the simulation approach, children are not to be expected to have any difficulty with reflexive self-knowledge, since it implies no perspective taking. Yet empirically, children have just the same problems with attributing beliefs reflexively to themselves as to others. My approach can solve this problem, since the self-attribution of knowledge presupposes dialogical perspective taking, and thus is as difficult as the role taking vis-à-vis someone else.

41. Mead 1934; Kögler 1996c.

42. See Mead 1934.

43. I am suggesting that we have to develop an account of self-understanding that relates or mediates the dimensions of flexible and reflexive role taking (where the self creates herself imaginatively and is interpretively autonomous) and the already built-up schemes and constellations that define a more deeply engrained, underlying structure of disclosure (which are usually related to social contexts such as class, gender, or ethnicity). For some first steps in that direction, see Kögler 1997a; 1997b; as well as the other essays in the special issue of *Social Epistemology* on reflexivity and social background.

44. I have not explicitly taken up Jane Heal's position, partly because she avoids many of the pitfalls I am addressing in this chapter. Yet it seems that at this point even her position reveals some bias toward an acultural psychologism, since a shared orientation at co-cognition or toward the same subject matter would not by itself allow a reliable and adequate reconstruction of the other's beliefs and assumptions. My position emphasizes the need to thematize the relation between interpreter and interpretee in the process of understanding itself.

45. Simulation is usually invoked as an interpretive strategy that is based on the psychic similarity between agents. In this vein, it is assumed that the interpretive procedure should make the other look as similar to us as possible. Here, simulation theory concurs with the theoretical and the rationality-based approaches. But if it is true that there is no psychologically pure, culturally uncontaminated core of human experience, and if it is equally true that our "bedrock" experiential schemes are implicated in cultural, social, and historical constellations and processes, then a truthful and adequate interpretation of the other needs to give an account of how pre-

cisely our assumptions can be *mediated and negotiated* with her self-understanding without making similarity the basis or the goal of understanding. Instead of basing the interpretive process on an assumedly more fundamental dimension of similarity, the mechanism of dialogical perspective taking will itself determine what we share and where we differ. The extent to which we agree on the issues at stake, or with regard to what we engage in substantially diverse projects of existential self-understanding, cannot and should not be determined from the outset.

46. There is an inbuilt normativity in such a process of dialogical interpretation, since it requires the interpreter to take the self-understanding of the other agent structurally into account, and it equally asks from the interpreted self that it be open to the interpretations provided by the other. The interpreter has to acknowledge the self-understanding of the other, since the other is defined as a cosubject. That alone would require the recognition of the other's self-understanding *on moral grounds*, since we owe it to her (just as much as we would demand this in our case) to treat her as a reflective and knowledgeable agent. Yet there is also *a unique epistemic constraint* demanding the inclusion of the symbolic and cultural self-definitions of the other. This is so because the other self is emerging, just like the interpreter, from intersubjective cultural practices that define the scope of her self-understanding. Since it is *that meaning* that the interpretation is supposed to reconstruct, and since that meaning exists in a preconstructed, or preinterpreted, form, it is crucial that the modes of articulation of the other be taken into account without simply imposing our own standards. In fact, we have to acknowledge that the other is always the interpreter of our interpretations of his or her self-understandings. Yet precisely because the self-understanding of situated subjects is defined in such a culturally mediated sense, it is tied to a holistic background knowledge that can never be fully exhausted or transparently understood by the existing self alone, and thus it remains intrinsically open to anybody's interpretation. Because of this holistic situatedness, the self is never the absolutely privileged or only possible interpreter of herself but is rather, in order to trigger the process of dialogical self-communication, referred back to the interpreting voice of the other; it indeed requires that voice for the completion of its self-constitution as reflexive self.

47. For a more developed account of this process, including the difference between concepts—as shared bridgeheads—and conceptions—as the cultural and contextual constellations that define and "fill" those concepts for situated interpreters—see Kögler 1996a, especially pp. 159–178.

48. For positions emphasizing such a switch, see Habermas 1987; Gadamer 1989.

49. Our model can thus connect the methodology of reflexive self-interpretation to a host of studies and interpretive practices in critical social science and cultural studies. Those approaches precisely attempt to analyze the pervasive function of social power relations without the disempowerment of the potentially reflexive agent. As just one site collecting numerous such analyses, see Grossberg, Nelson, and Treichler 1992.

50. I would like to thank Jim Bohman, Ted Schatzki, and Karsten Stueber for their helpful comments.

Chapter Nine

The Importance of the Second Person: Interpretation, Practical Knowledge, and Normative Attitudes

JAMES BOHMAN

When they go smoothly, everyday acts of communication depend on the various complex capacities of speakers and hearers, such as the capacity to use words appropriately or to exchange perspectives with each other in co-ordinating actions. In order to communicate something to someone, speakers and hearers must, among other things, be able to adopt each other's point of view. More often than not, speakers of the same language share enough background assumptions that the detailed knowledge of how their perspectives diverge is unnecessary. In most cases, speakers know enough and have the capacity to fill in the rest so that interaction goes on more or less unproblematically. But when communication goes badly, the other person's point of view must be made explicit in interpretation. Interpretive social science employs these complex abilities (both explicit and implicit) that we use to understand others; it tries to see things through the other's point of view without necessarily assuming that it resembles our own. Under-standing the fact of divergence in self-interpretations is precisely the do-main of the ethnographer, who seeks to overcome the limits of our own perspectives and attitudes and thus to adopt (to the extent that it is possi-ble) "the native's point of view." The less this perspective is like ours the more difficult the ethnographic task becomes. More is demanded of the in-terpreter's communicative know-how, including abilities to reflect upon one's own assumptions and to see oneself from the other's perspective. Such an interpreter sees the epistemic importance of the second person.

As Clifford Geertz has argued in reflecting upon ethnographic field-work, access to the native's point of view is had only by offering "interpre-tations of self-interpretations." Such an interpreter adopts a particular intentional stance and attributes intentionality to others who already assign meanings to their own expressions and perform their actions for particular reasons they deem good or bad. What is distinctive about such social science is that it seeks to make explicit the meaningfulness of an action or expression. It does so not in the terms of some general theory (no matter how helpful or explanatory these may be) but in terms of the agent's own reasons, or at least how these reasons might seem to be good ones from the first-person perspective. As many anthropologists have noted, this requires a delicate epistemological balancing act. The social scientist cannot directly claim to understand agents better than they understand themselves, even when they seem most obviously deluded in their self-interpretation; nor can agents just speak for themselves, since for the most part the interesting cases are not self-interpreting from the point of view of the social scientist. This leaves the interpreter in a peculiar epistemic predicament: What started as the enterprise of seeing things from the other's point of view can at best approximate that point of view only by providing the best interpretation *for us* of how things are *for them*. As a matter of interpretive responsibility, there is no getting around the fact that ethnography or history is our attempt "to see another form of life in the categories of our own."[1] Particularly since the observational evidence for alternative interpretations is hardly ever decisive, the epistemic situation of the interpreter seems to be irredeemably a first-person rather than a third-person or even second-person affair.

One response to such a dilemma is to try to escape it. The other response is to embrace it while denying its skeptical implications. To do so requires grasping the full implications of the epistemic fact that all interpretations, no matter how well justified, depend on practical knowledge and attitudes. Practical knowledge does not appeal to neutral evidence that all must accept in determining the *best* interpretation of something. This lack of independent evidence is due to the fact that standards for interpretation are themselves matters for interpretation. Such a regress leads to the well-known problem of "the hermeneutic circle." This circular relation of interpretation and evidence does not logically exclude the possibility of showing that some interpretations are better than others. For many, however, it suggests that the best interpretation is only one that is best for us or for me. But this perspectival character does not adequately reconstruct the practical problem of interpretation. It is not *I* or *we* that must be satisfied; the interpretive situation is one in which an interpreter is interpreting someone else, who in turn can offer an interpretation of his own actions and the interpretation of the other's interpretations. The I who is an interpreter is a *you* as a participant in communication, and thus no account of the hermeneutic circle can do without the second person. Indeed, the point of my argument is that I do not simply adopt your point of view or even mine in offering an

adequate interpretation. Instead I do something that is much more complicated and dialogical: When I offer an interpretation of your actions or practices, I adopt the point of view that you are an interpreter of me. This is a
capacity or ability that can only be explicated as a form of practical knowledge from the second-person perspective.

In what follows I defend such a second-person perspective on interpretation as practical knowledge. The "second person" is important in two senses.
In the first sense it is important as an adjective describing the attitude or
stance that the interpreter adopts: that of me interpreting how you interpret
my interpretations. But the second person is also important as a noun phrase:
The presence of this other person herself is crucial to understanding the normative assessment of interpretation as practical knowledge. By this I mean
that interpretation is the practical knowledge by which we establish and
maintain relationships to others in dialogue or conversation. Interpretations
then can be judged in terms of their capacity to promote or inhibit such relations, primarily by mutual interpretation in dialogue. This approach con-
trasts with other methodologies that employ first- or third-person perspectives. Third-person accounts do not connect interpretation to a performative
attitude but rather to the attitude of an observer who has nothing to appeal
to but publicly available evidence such as behavioral regularities and patterns. Such interpreters impose significance on the data in terms of fit. First-
person accounts see the task of the interpreter as understanding what it is like
to be someone else, something that can be achieved through transforming
one's beliefs or desires by use of imagination, changing one's emotional states
by use of empathy or using other such abilities to modify one's own understandings. By contrast, second-person approaches see interpretation as dependent on the right sort of performative attitude typical of ordinary conversation and upon complex practical abilities to triangulate behavior,
intentions, and reference to the common world with which agents interact. It
does not take as its paradigm case radical interpretation or even cultural misunderstanding, but the vagaries and abilities required for ordinary conversation and dialogue. Pictures of radical interpretation, I submit, have held the
philosophical imagination on the nature of understanding captive. The full
appreciation of the importance of the second person offers the way out of the
recurrent dilemmas of interpretation, even in cases of interpretive failure.

Such an account, I argue, solves several recurrent epistemological dilemmas that have plagued interpretive social science and the account of the intentional stance in the philosophy of mind. After explicating the complex
practical capacities involved in interpreting the second person, I then turn
to debates in the philosophy of mind between simulation theory and the so-
called theory theory. I shall show that neither adequately captures the interpretive stance, since both are exclusively first- or third-person accounts. Finally, I propose the dialogical alternative to both these accounts and show

that it more properly explicates the form of practical knowledge and the normative attitudes aimed at by the interpretive social sciences. The result is a normative and pragmatic account of interpretation and its practical verification in dialogue. Such practical knowledge not only takes other's self-interpretations seriously but is constitutive of the normative attitudes of assessment on which dialogue is based. These attitudes of correctness, I suggest, have moral and political significance for how we interpret others.

1. The Performative Attitude of Interpretation: Pragmatism, Critical Theory, and Practical Knowledge

The epistemic difficulties of interpretation stem from the difference that taking agents' self-interpretations into account makes. In this respect, it is useful to distinguish not only among the interpretive perspectives mentioned above but also between two different interpretive situations. Consider, for example, an entry in an old-fashioned card catalog still found in some libraries. Here the interpreter reads the card and interprets it, such that the success of the interpretation is measured by finding the book. In this case, the interpreter simply *imposes* an interpretation on the card by making use of his or her practical knowledge of how to relate the numbers on the card to book locations in the stacks. The same may be said of the scales on a thermostat. Here the problem of interpretation only involves one interpreter, for whom such marks are meaningful practical guides. Now consider a speaker making the statement that "I will be in the coffee shop this afternoon." Such a remark could be taken in different ways: It could be just a description of the speaker's habits or it could be a promise to meet the hearer there. In this case a successful interpretation requires something more than simply imposing one's interpretation, given some practical know-how of certain conventions. Interpretive success will depend on taking the speaker's self-interpretation into account. Imposing a wrong interpretation will have clear consequences. At the very least, the speaker and hearer will not establish or maintain a social relationship should their independent self-interpretations fail to converge.

Given that we often do succeed in coordinating intentions, it seems then that agents do possess practical know-how of how to treat others as self-interpreters who are also interpreters of me. Even if interactions can fail (either tragically or comically), at the very least, when we see others as originators of their own intentionality we need to at least recognize that, unlike card catalogs and thermostats, other agents know what they are doing by interpreting their actions for themselves. The argument here is a familiar Davidsonian one: There is no independent way to predict beliefs on the basis of behavior or behavior on the basis of beliefs.[2] The logical entailment of beliefs and the practical implications of actions can then only be fixed by interpretations. But whose interpretations? Neither the interpreter's nor the observer's perspectives are sufficient to specify these opaque intentional contexts for others. Since actions therefore underdetermine the interpretations that may be assigned to them by third-person interpreters, there is no alternative than interpretations of agents' self-interpretations that can be settled only practically in ongoing dialogue and interaction.

Theories of many different sorts locate interpretation practically in acts and processes of communication and communication in turn as the exercise of a distinctive form of practical rationality. Like other such accounts of the practical knowledge put to use in interpretation, the theory of communicative action offers its own distinctive definition. In good pragmatist fashion, Habermas's definition is epistemic, practical, and intersubjective. For Habermas, rationality consists not so much in the possession of knowledge, and thus with the consistency and content of one's beliefs, but in "how speaking and acting subjects acquire and use knowledge."[3] Such a broad definition suggests that the theory could be developed through explicating the formal conditions of rationality in knowing and reaching understanding through language, and this task falls primarily on "formal pragmatics." The positive goal of such a theory is not only to provide a rich enough account of the structure of communicative action needed for a "comprehensive" theory of rationality that encompasses both its theoretical and practical uses; it must also be normative enough to be able to clarify the necessary conditions for its employment. One of the features of such practical knowledge is that it is available only in the "performative attitude," that is, the perspective of the interpreter trying to understand others as they employ their practical knowledge is also the perspective for reflection upon the possibility of successful interpretation.

I call any such account "pragmatic" because it shares a number of distinctive features with other views that see interpreters as competent and knowledgeable agents. It is pragmatic not only because it sees "saying something" as a performative act and thus a kind of doing (and also interpreting as itself a kind of doing in establishing and maintaining social relationships); it also takes up a position that classical pragmatism develops in different contexts, such as James's theory of truth as successful action or Peirce's account of inquiry and habits of action. Brandom has developed the central features of such a pragmatic and hence performative account of truth, at least two of which apply by analogy to the pragmatic theory of interpretation as practical knowledge.[4] The first is that interpreting is not merely describing something and hence is not merely a true description from the observer's point of view. This means that a pragmatic theory emphasizes the circumstances and consequences of the *act* of interpreting, what it does in establishing commitments and entitlements of the interpreter and the one interpreted, as well as its cognitive content as making claims about the meaning of other's speech and actions. Second, interpreting is performative in the sense that the interpreter takes up particular *normative* attitudes. These "normative attitudes" must be those of the interpreter. In interpreting one is expressing and establishing one's attitude toward a claim, such as when the interpreter takes it to be true, appropriate according to social norms, or correct or incorrect in its performance. But some of these attitudes are more complex than the usual analysis of pro-attitudes in belief-desire psychology allows. Some such attitudes are essentially two-person attitudes: The interpreter does not just express an attitude in the first person alone but rather incurs a commitment or obligation by interpreting what others are doing, by interpreting what they say as correct or true for themselves as well as those whom they are interpreting.

The adoption of this sort of attitude places the speaker and hearer in Sellars's "logical space of reasons." Each thereby imputes rationality to the actions or utterances of the other in a weakly normative sense. As Habermas puts it, the interpreter cannot understand the content of an utterance or the intention of an action unless she is "in the position to present to herself the reasons the speaker might be able to adduce" to defend the utterance or action. But this must be done in a normative and performative attitude because it is not the same thing for reasons to be good or correct and for them only to seem so to the interpreter: "The interpreter cannot present reasons to herself without judging them, without taking a positive or a negative position on them."[5] Thus the performative attitude is one of taking something to be valid or invalid and in this way acknowledging certain sorts of commitments that the interpreter and speaker are or are not entitled to have. To stand *hors de combat* and not to take a position is not to take up the appropriate attitude and thus not to interpret at all.

The interpreter only places herself in the space of reasons when she says why what is said is appropriate or inappropriate, correct or incorrect. But whose point of view does the interpreter occupy? That the normative attitude can only be the interpreter's (and not merely that of first-person expression or third-person observation) makes the pragmatic position "phenomenalist" in methodology on Brandom's view.[6] This may be a misleading term. It is not the interpreter taking the first-person perspective (as it might be in the case of the perceiver and the way things seem to her) but rather adopting the second-person perspective of interpreting something someone else says or does correctly or incorrectly. The speaker too takes up this same normative attitude in using an utterance to offer something to an interpreter to understand and thus sees herself from a distinctly second-person and normative perspective. The interpreter's normative attitude is thus *taking something to be true* from others and not merely *holding it to be true* by his own lights.

Such a pragmatic analysis of the normative attitude of interpretation appears to be rather intellectualistic, if not rationalistic. This objection would hit the mark if the interpreter took his stance in interpretation to be adequate by adopting a particular theory, say, a pragmatic theory of truth. But the interpreter is not employing a theory, which could only be done from a third-person perspective; taking up the normative attitude of the second person in interpretation is a matter of practical knowledge, a "knowing how" and not a "knowing that." While interpreters must be knowledgeable about what they are doing, their knowledge is implicit and need not be explicit, except in cases in which interpretation fails and no understanding ensues.

"Knowing how" does not identify a single sort of knowledge. There are many kinds of implicit knowledge with various degrees of accessibility to reflection. For example, the know-how of swimming or typing could be stated in a theory and made explicit; but such a theory is one that is reconstructed from the point of view of the observer, of the teacher or coach who wants to improve the techniques needed to impart or develop a skill that might not even require awareness of its exercise. Here textbook knowledge of kinematic efficiency alone is sufficient. The coach need not even have acquired the ability to have a fully adequate conception of what it is an ability to do.[7] By contrast, a pragmatic theory is a reconstruction of the speaker's and hence the interpreter's knowledge; it is the reconstruction of structure of a complex ability whose exercise is itself necessary to know fully what it is. Although some parts of this ability may be more like swimming (such as syntactic correctness), this reconstruction is one that makes explicit implicit know-how and, in making it explicit, never leaves the performative attitude. It is still reflective in that it makes available to the reflective performer how this ability can be used to acquire and use knowledge of others. Interpretive social science is practical knowledge, a science from within the second-person perspective and its normative attitude. What sort of knowledge does it use? It must be normative and reflexive, invoking implicit norms of correctness that are capable of being made explicit.

2. Interpretation as Practical Knowledge: Beyond Simulation Theory and Theory Theory

The current debate in the philosophy of mind between simulation theorists and theory theorists concerns precisely the nature of this implicit knowledge used in understanding. The debate is enjoined around two opposing views that place this practical ability at the opposite ends of a continuum. On the one hand, a theory could be the best way to reconstruct practical know-how. The practical ability involved in doing something could be very much like possessing an implicit theory, since what we are doing is very much like what theorists do, such as attempting to predict people's behavior on the basis of their past behavior. Since the theory is only implicit, a given interpreter may not be able to state it explicitly. Nonetheless, she is able to employ it when she performs operations at least analogous to theory formation, such as offer explanations or hypotheses. The implicitness of the theory relates to its method of acquisition over childhood and the vagueness of its generalizations as "rules of thumb."[8] We might then want to say that this account is consistent with taking up normative attitudes toward beliefs and desires when explaining them is ipso facto to see them as at least rationally consistent.

On the other hand, simulation theory denies the analogy to theoretical knowledge, however implicit. Rather, the prodigious ability that we employ in understanding and predicting properly what others are going to do is a first-person ability, the ability to "simulate the appropriate kind of practical reasoning" by engaging "a kind of pretend play" that transforms the agent into the other person.[9] Such a transformation is a first-person ability employed, for example, when predicting what others do by "deciding what I would do" in such a case, adjusting for relevant differences. In this case, the practical ability is more like swimming than theorizing, closer to the capacity for mimicking the direction of someone's gaze found already in young infants than to an implicit knowledge that can be reconstructed in a theory. Rather, "our primary competence with (intentional) content is of the 'know-how' variety and only the smallest part reflected in any theoretical 'know-that' of how the contents relate."[10] The debate is then one between third- and first-person approaches to the intentional. Although certain obviously empirical issues are at stake here, the debates may represent a false dilemma, especially if neither side identifies the proper attitude in which interpretive abilities of either sort are exercised.

In order to see the weaknesses of both first- and third-person approaches, it is important to examine why interpreters often get it wrong. We are often wrong in our first-person knowledge (whether singular or plural), so that lack of transparency is an unavoidable problem. When faced with interpreting others' behavior, we quickly run into the limits of first-person knowledge *simpliciter*. As Gordon rightly suggests for such failures of "total projection," interpreters then evoke contextual factors and even "conceptual adjustments" of first-person simulation to make actions and behavior intelligible, especially when large differences between the interpreter and the one whom is being interpreted make relevance a key issue to success.[11] This shift in perspective only postpones the problem, moving the interpreter from the first-person frying pan into the contextual fire and no closer to determining a standard of relevance. From a third-person perspective, it is indeterminate whether behavior follows some common rule or merely some regular idiosyncrasy. Third-person accounts face the same "gerrymandering problem" as made clear in the private language argument.[12] That is, it is always possible to interpret some behavior as related to many different and even incompatible contextual factors. Here simulation theory is caught in a circle. The appeal to contextual factors was supposed to overcome the limits of first-person knowledge, yet they in turn require first-person knowledge to supply some standard for determining their relevance. Such a standard of relevance must in the first instance be normative and is fixed by what is correct or incorrect for the intentional action being interpreted and not by making the person interpreted more rather than less like the interpreter. Certainly, third-person approaches have the corresponding opposite problem: In cases of interpretive failure the one being interpreted must be considered less like me and thus irrational, benighted, or some such derogatory judgment.

In order to surmount these difficulties, first-person and third-person approaches often turn to ideal theories of rationality typical of decision theory supplemented only by the abilities needed to understand the content of beliefs and desires. However, these theories are not normative in the right sort of way to guide interpretive know-how. Because they are not self-interpreting, third-person norms are not put in a practical enough way. Because they are cases of a pure ability, first-person performances of simulation are not normative enough. Neither tells us when we are correctly using the ideal theory, and both simply push interpretation proper back a step. The practical knowledge of the second person avoids this dilemma of first-person limits on the one hand and third-person indeterminacy on the other by taking up a distinctly normative attitude of assessing or treating the actions or speech of others as correct or incorrect. Adopting attitudes requires the practical ability to negotiate in dialogue between various social perspectives and not merely to enlarge or distance oneself from one's own or to adopt ideal or explanatory theories when first-person understanding fails. Theory theory and simulation theory are each caught on different horns of the same dilemma, which is overcome only by considering the practical abilities and normative attitudes involved in the full range of perspective taking.

Consider a related debate about the abilities needed to understand a language. Davidson attempts to reconstruct the practical ability of understanding a language in terms of T-sentences that the theorist constructs out of Tarski's Convention T; these are clearly not the theorems that speakers know but only represent the abilities of speakers by identifying all and only true sentences in a language. Dummett rightly objects that these sentences presuppose some practical knowledge of what it means for a sentence to be true and that practical knowledge is best manifested in the ability to justify an assertion when asked. The problem in this, as Dummett has recently noted, is that it pushes the speaker's knowledge in the direction of knowledge of an explicit theory. Indeed, Dummett now admits that his account only gets off the ground if the speaker's practical knowledge has "a substantial theoretical component."[13] When Davidson proposes his theory of rationality as a "unified account of speaking and acting," he pushes the analysis of this same practical ability in the opposite and equally unsatisfactory direction. The proper performative attitude of the interpreter (as modeled on the situation of radical interpretation or the absence of any background commonalties from which to start interpretation) is that of taking his or her own beliefs as a model; the proper normative attitude is that of "holding true" where the normative backing for this as assumption as necessary for interpretation is that our beliefs are largely true. Armed with this assumption, the interpreter can then use various ideal theories, such as decision theory or the probabilistic theory of induction, in order to establish what it is that rational agents should do, all things considered. The first-person perspective is for Davidson sufficient for "radical" interpretation provided it is undertaken in the normative attitude of "holding true."[14] This is an insufficient basis for interpretation, since, like simulation theory, it neither adopts the right attitude nor gives central importance to iterated, dialogical activity.

As in the case of simulation theory, Davidson wants to use his ability-based account of what speakers do in interpretation to trim the proliferation of transcendental arguments for the knowledge necessary for interpretation down to its most minimal form. The theory of truth elucidates this knowledge necessary for communication even if neither speaker nor hearer possesses explicit knowledge of the theory itself. The practical linguistic ability to interpret others regardless of mistakes replaces the explicit knowledge of the theory that represents it, but also other kinds of typical assumptions such as knowledge of a common language shared between speaker and interpreter. Successful communication does not even require "that any two speakers speak in the same way" (as the cases of malapropisms and slips of the tongue show) but only that the speaker intends to have his or her utterances interpreted in a particular way.[15] This intention seems to be simply an ability we must have for successful communication; explicit or shared knowledge is not a necessary presupposition for this intention to be carried out. The problem is once again that the performance is a first-person one. When communication fails and must be iterated, the speaker becomes a hearer who must adopt not only a different perspective but formulate his next contribution in light of new and different practical knowledge—the knowledge of a second person, who rejects the interpretation that the speaker gives of him or his beliefs and desires so that she may be understood.

Such intentions have a status, the peculiarity of which Davidson does not make sufficiently clear. The intention to be interpreted is not directly a first-person intention, even one about the other's intentions; it is already to adopt the normative attitude of the interpreter toward one's own communication. Thus Davidson has misidentified the normative attitude of interpretation; it is not "held to be true" but "taken to be true." This attitude is more complex than that of the speaker's intention or desire to be interpreted, but this intention is filtered through the normative attitude that appraises the correctness or incorrectness of that interpretation by a second person. As iterated (an interpretation of my own intention to be interpreted, and so on), it is already communication in a reflective normative attitude, whereby each adopts the perspective of the second person in order to judge communicative success. This ability is neither a purely practical ability like simulation nor is it merely the "knowing-that" of the theory theory.

When he argues for the irreducibility of the normative in taking the intentional stance, Davidson comes very close to formulating an alternative. But the interpreter is not a theorist armed with an ideal theory of rationality that is constitutive of being able to interpret someone's behavioral regularities as intentional at all. The interpreter does not use a theory at all, but practical knowledge of how to employ and attribute normative attitudes in the second person. Davidson poses the problem of radical interpretation as a way to understand the adequacy of interpretation by using the analogy of a field linguist armed with no knowledge of some language other than his own beliefs. These are insufficient, since even if he is to employ these resources, he must already know how to take up normative attitudes that are not his own but those of a second person who judges the adequacy of his interpretations.

3. The Normative Attitude of the Interpreter: A Dialogical Account

Interpreting from a third-person point of view entails observing the other's behavior for regularities or patterns that can be explained by underlying dispositions. But if this were all that the interpreter has at her disposal, we could not determine the sort of regularity that such behavior exhibits. Interpreters on this account are not able to distinguish between habits and rule following. As many have argued following Wittgenstein's private language argument, rule following is radically indeterminate from the third-person perspective, since the interpreter cannot identify how it is correct to go on simply on the basis of observing dispositions.[16] The attitude of the first person is more promising. In the case of radical interpretation, in which the speaker does not share a common language or practices, the interpreter can simply hold his or her own beliefs constant: "My" largely true beliefs are a guide to "their" beliefs. This normative attitude allows the interpreter to circumvent the problem of evidence in triangulation, whereby we cannot understand an action qua action or have evidence of an interpretation of it independent of the attribution of beliefs and desires.

The problem with this solution is that this sort of normative attitude is ultimately parasitic on another if it is to be of any practical use: the second-person attitude of taking others' statements to be true or correct. How does this attitude avoid the problem of indeterminacy, since we cannot assume that the speaker's normative attitudes are simply identical to ours as a constitutive condition for interpretation as in the first-person case? This problem is acute in the case of interpretive social science and history, which often has as its subject matter how the normative attitudes and beliefs of speakers of other cultures or texts of the distant past are very different from our own. Since rationality is constitutive of our being able to interpret others at all, divergence in belief is explained as error or as irrationality.[17] Davidson's narrowly first-person approach allows no other options.

Suppose we admit, pace Davidson, that such differences in beliefs not only exist but are salient to social scientific and historical understanding. Here the interpreter cannot avoid the problems of the hermeneutic circle, that interpretation always takes place within a background of largely unthematic beliefs and traditions. The problem is similar to the one Davidson has pointed out for the observer: The interpreter can only interpret in light of his particular attitudes in which something can be evidence for him at all. Without taking up my own normative attitudes, I cannot identify whether something is a good reason or correct application of a rule or not. Should the other speaker say or do something that does not make sense from within my normative attitudes, interpretation simply fails and I have to switch to some other third-person observer or explanatory attitude. But if my attitude and thus my rationality is constitutive of interpretation, then we have drawn the limits of interpretation too tightly and no appeal to independent evidence will overcome this indeterminacy. The problem is not to identify some special source or type of evidence that establishes "the fact of the matter" about what the other thinks or does. This means that discovering the right evidence is not the solution to indeterminacy but rather interpreting in the right performative attitude.

From the indeterminacy of interpretation, many have drawn skeptical conclusions about the possibility of interpretive knowledge. I have argued elsewhere that such skeptics commit two forms of the transcendental fallacy: They confuse formal and empirical conditions of interpretation as well as limiting and enabling constraints.[18] They see the hermeneutic circle as establishing determinate limits on establishing the truth of interpretation, since there is no evidence available to the interpreter outside of the holistic background assumptions of any hermeneutic circle. The skeptic asks the wrong sort of question. Rather than identify general epistemic limits on understanding others from any point of view, the hermeneutic circle establishes limits of theoretical knowledge in this enterprise in the absence of a basis for evidence independent of any interpretation. This is not a problem closer to the practical end of the continuum of practical knowledge.

So far in my argument, raising the problem of indeterminacy has been useful in establishing what interpretation is not. It is now time to say what it is as a form of practical knowledge: It is a form of practical knowledge in the normative attitude that establishes possible knowledge about norms and the normative dimensions of actions and performances. It is knowledge of the normative from within the normative attitude. As the attitude of the second-person interpreter, it is knowledge that is manifested in interaction and in dialogue and is to be measured in terms of the success of dialogue and communication. That ongoing dialogue establishes that the interpreter attempts to offer interpretations of the normative attitudes of others that are ones that they could in principle accept. This requires that we view interpretation very differently as a second-person form of knowledge. The question is not, What evidence makes one interpretation better than the other? It is rather, What are better interpretations able to do? They are able to establish relations of obligation and commitment.

The normative attitudes of the second person are neither true descriptions nor self-expressive claims. Rather, they are assessments that become explicit only in actual dialogue. By treating what others are saying as true or taking them to be correct or incorrect in their performance, the interpreter establishes nothing more than the possibility of more and perhaps better interpretations and thus the possibility of future dialogue or interpretive exchange. Gadamer puts this in a practical way: "Every interpretation establishes the possibility of a relationship with others."[19] Such a relationship could only be established in the normative attitude. Gadamer goes on to say that these relationships institute obligations, since "there can be no speaking that does not bind the speaker and the person spoken to."[20] In seeing others either as making claims that interpreters could treat as true or as being guided by norms that could be ones that the interpreter could accept, the interpreter accepts a second-person perspective. Competent interpreters and communicators thus possess the practical knowledge that is manifested in the ability to establish and maintain just such normatively guided interaction and social relationships. It is the implicit know-how of establishing normative relations, the ability to open up or close off various practical possibilities with others with whom we are engaged in the process of mutual interpretation or of reaching understanding. This ability is not that of imposing an interpretation on others' actions or speech given the available evidence. Establishing social relations of this sort is a matter of finding terms that each interpreter can accept and, in so accepting, also maintain the social relationship and its obligations. Thus the interpretive situation is always a social relation between at least two inter-preters, *each* of whom must adopt the attitude of the second person.

This practical and second-person account of understanding suggests that certain debates about interpretation need to be reformulated. The debate between Habermas and Gadamer is best seen in light of their basic agree-ment that "all understanding is reaching understanding" or that "under-standing an expression is to know how to use it to reach understanding."[21] It is thus not fundamentally a debate about tradition and its authority on the one hand and social scientific and critical explanations such as the cri-tique of ideology on the other—the conflict between the need for a first-person plural or the "we" perspective of the internal participant and that of a third-person perspective of the external critic. It is rather about correc-tives needed to expand the normative attitudes of the second-person per-spective. Certainly, it is sometimes necessary to invoke the standards of the community; at other times it is necessary to refer to features of the situation of interpretation that may affect its practical possibilities. The real problem is the role of reflection in the context of interpretation. Reflection estab-lishes the possibility of epistemic improvement even when know-how can-not be transformed into theoretical knowledge, since it is the means by which we make explicit and thus come to accept or reject the practical con-sequences of the interpretations that we offer of others.

Because of the practical, dialogical, and contextual character of under-standing in the second-person perspective, Gadamer thinks that "the power of reflection" is seriously limited. In becoming an object of reflection, he ar-gues, "a limit does not thereby cease to be a limit."[22] This may be true for some limitations described in the third-person perspective, such as histori-cal or social facts about the knowledge available to a specific generation. Instead of following out the methodological insights of his own model of the noninstrumental practical knowledge manifested in "genuine conversa-tion," Gadamer instead analyzes interpretation with the methodologically incompatible notion of the first-person plural authority of the substantive truths of tradition and the practical knowledge of their expert application.[23] For this reason, he argues that all interpretation is necessarily "self-interpretation" or explication in a first-person plural sense. When ap-plied to the interpretation of others, Gadamer's argument fails to distin-guish various sorts of conditions for practical know-how, indeed to distin-guish between its factual and empirical conditions, which may or may not be reflectively available to us and "at our free disposal," and general, nor-mative constraints of adopting the second-person perspective and its atti-tudes. Such constraints might be limits if the know-how of interpretation is not a pure practical ability like swimming or typing; but as the act of mak-ing explicit the normative constraints of creating and maintaining social re-lationships in dialogue, interpretation has more than merely factual conditions for its employment. It is precisely in cases of interpretive failure that we begin first by asking about normative conditions that refer to the social relations established by acts of interpretation that may violate the normative constraints on interpretive dialogue. To the extent that these constraints can be made explicit and the violations of interpretive norms shown to be incorrect according to the relevant normative attitudes, interpretation can be epistemically improved by dialogue. We would expect no less from a science of the normative undertaken in the normative attitude.

The antiepistemological character of such "ontological" and first-person plural notions such as prejudice and traditions leads to an underestimation of the methodological importance of dialogue normatively conceived. As in the theory theory–simulation theory debate, the Habermas-Gadamer debate revolves around complementary errors. While Gadamer thinks that implicit practical knowledge cannot ipso facto be normative, Habermas argues for the normative status of norms on the model of explicit rules. As in the theory theory–simulation debate, both sides appeal to forms of practical knowledge at the extreme ends of the continuum between implicitness and explicitness. While Gadamer's account of the second-person perspective so lacks normative structure that he must search for some normative authority for interpretation outside of it in traditions, Habermas's pragmatic account tends to rely too heavily on the analogy to explicit rules in developing its normative dimension. He has thought of its theoretical reconstructions as making explicit the know-how needed for raising and redeeming of the validity claims that guide our speech and communicative interaction. His approach uses formal pragmatics philosophically to reflect upon norms and practices that are already explicit in justifications in various sorts of argumentation, or second-order communication. Such reflection has genuine practical significance in yielding explicit rules governing discursive communication (such as Alexy's rules of argumentation), which in turn can be used for the purpose of designing and reforming deliberative and discursive institutions.[24] It is easily overlooked that such rules are only part of the story; they make explicit and institutionalize norms that are already operative in all correct language use.

Such implicit norms of well-formed and communicatively successful utterances are not identical with the explicit rules of argumentation. Here Habermas has been misled by modeling formal pragmatics on Chomsky's reconstruction of linguistic competence in a generative grammar of explicit rules governing how we actually use language. Besides the problem of the regress of rules, which Wittgenstein and Brandom have shown to be unavoidable for the intellectualism of Kantian explicit rules, such an approach is insufficient to see how norms are operating in practice, whatever their rational status. If such explicit rules are said to guide practices in light of the rational reconstruction of speaker's knowledge, it is impossible to avoid a vicious regress of rules; other rules would then have to be shown to be part of a speaker's knowledge necessary to apply them.[25] Habermas's own admission that formal pragmatics is only "indirectly legislative" already takes us away from Kant's jurisprudential analogy between the necessary conditions of rationality and explicit rules. The theory of the misuse of practical know-how in dialogue (Habermas's theory of "distorted communication") makes no sense without rejecting this analogy: Its norms are implicit in practice, not just in a speaker's general know-how.[26]

Although such implicit norms expressed in practice are open to the cognitive revision that could result from making them explicit, they are not the same as such explicit rules, nor are they captured in a normative account of explicit or discursive justification. Such norms are implicit in conditions for communicative success and are discovered by explicating how complete utterances are formed and receive uptake from others. Formal pragmatic analysis not only moves upward from intuitive know-how to explicit norms that might guide our discursive practices; it also moves downward in reflection to the implicit normative conditions of communicative success. Such a downward reconstruction proves its critical and practical significance in showing how power and other asymmetries operate to distort communication and violate the implicit norms of everyday communicative practice. Such a reconstructive science is thus not only critical; it also provides a way to explicate the implicit understandings on which explicit interpretations and justifications are based. In this way the two directions of analysis are interrelated. As the examples of democratic norms indicated, the institutionalization of explicit rules demands reflection on the conditions implicit in linguistic and communicative practices that promote or inhibit their operation in everyday life practice. In this way, such institutional norms create conditions that promote mutual understanding by connecting them to implicit norms of practices. Reconstructing such practical know-how by which agents take up performative attitudes and are able to coordinate their goals with others is thus also the main task of the social scientist who interprets the norms implicit in practices; the task of the participant-critic in the democratic public sphere is, when necessary, to change them in order that participants can better exercise their practical abilities in the normative attitudes of the second person.[27] Interpretive social science has a related but different role. It discloses the enabling and limiting conditions of our practical know-how in normatively demanding dialogues with those whose normative attitudes are very different from our own and with whom we have not yet established an interpretive and hence normatively constrained social relationship, often because we have not exercised our practical abilities properly.

On this basis, it might be thought possible to reconstruct a version of the ideal of objectivity. One such argument that starts from the idea of interpretation as based in practical knowledge and normative attitudes was recently put forth by Brandom, whose phenomenalist and second-person approach to normative attitudes I have followed to a certain point. But the step from normative attitudes to objectivity that he takes, I would argue, makes him fall back to the position of Davidson's first-person account of interpretation, even as he seems to go beyond him to the second person. Brandom's basic idea is that objectivity can be introduced into an account of normative attitudes through various social perspectives that are "a matter of perspectival form and not of non-perspectival or cross-perspectival content."[28] In order to interpret what someone says *de dicto,* it must employ a *de re* description of the content of the statement or claim. Thus we may say of Ptolemy that "he believed of the elliptical orbit of the planets that their lack of circularity could be explained by epicycles." Speakers may employ other similar locutions to make the formal objectivity of perspectives manifest in interaction.

But from what perspective is the interpreter able to employ *de re* locutions such as "of the elliptical orbit of the planets"? It is not some objective, or third-person, perspective. Since that observer perspective succumbs under the gerrymandering problem, the only possibility is that it is from *my* perspective. Thus this account of objectivity inserts a first-person perspective back in precisely when norms fail to adjudicate the correct perspective. In doing so, it falls back into a version of the same dilemma apparent in the debate between simulation theory and theory theory. *Either* the interpreter takes up his own first-person perspective in such description (which merely clashes rather than converges) *or* the interpreter adopts some third-person on which both somehow converge (but which is not the attitude of either one of them). This sort of objectivity is, however, not consistent with the normative attitude of interpretation and ought to be rejected for the same reasons that pertain to Davidson's first-person account. There is then no other "objective" attitude of interpretation than the normative attitude of the second person and the obligations that it entails.[29] I conclude by proposing a more consistent and pragmatic alternative to norms of objectivity inspired by Mead's conception of the Generalized Other.

4. Conclusion:
Interpretation and the
Normativity of the Human Sciences

Interpretation is based on a complex practical ability, a know-how that is certainly permeable by reflection and modifiable by theoretical knowledge and explicit norms. Philosophical accounts of interpretation have tended to misidentify this ability or to identify all of its constraints with some feature of it. All interpretation, it is said, is "simulation," "prediction," or the application of a historical tradition; interpretation is said to be "evaluation," "thick description," "self-understanding," or "making sense of others in one's own symbol system." Interpretation is always explication of norms, but not in the sense of the substitution of one expression of a rule for another or of giving rules for applying rules. Rather, it makes explicit norms that are implicit in practices and performances, and as explication it requires the capacity to use the very practical knowledge it seeks to make explicit. This know-how must be rich enough and interpretive practices developed and self-referential enough for the interpreters themselves (and not just theorists) to be able to say how their practices employ basic normative attitudes (correctly or incorrectly). Such know-how is exercised in a particular performative attitude in a specific context of interaction: in the normative attitude of the second person, an attitude that is primarily manifested in the ability to establish and maintain social relationships of dialogue and to explicate the conditions for such relationships themselves. Interpretations and expression are taken to be correct and incorrect according to attitudes of commitment and entitlement rather than explicit rules.

This argument therefore suggests the importance of the second person in interpretation in all the ambiguity of the phrase. It is the normative attitude of the second person in which interpretations are explicated and to whom they are expressed. But the second person is unavoidable in the literal sense: It is the other person to whom our interpretation is responsible and by whom it is judged adequate or inadequate. This judgment is implicit in the very acts of response that establish, maintain, and sometimes change the normative terms of a social relationship. George Herbert Mead tried to capture the distinction inherent in the second-person perspective by distinguishing between "the alter" and "the Generalized Other." The specific other is the literal second person, our interpretation of which establishes the possibilities of a social relationship. But this is always mediated by the Generalized Other, not in the sense of the we of the community in which this takes place but the normative attitudes in which we undertake such judgments of adequacy or correctness. Indeed, it is this normative attitude that trumps even the consensus of the community, the fallible collective self-interpretation of a community that can only be problematized in the second person by the other who does not share this we perspective but is a potential member. It is for the sake of those second persons that interpretive social science teaches us to "judge and feel capaciously" and, as Geertz also reminds us, thereby overcome the "comforts of merely being ourselves."[30] Because of this role of the second person that explication is not merely stating what is given in a linguistic expression in terms of another but rather clarifies our practical knowledge.

I have argued that the practical significance of interpretation is found in the way that any interpretation opens up possibilities of social relationships and dialogue. It is here that we are to best find normative criteria of adequacy. That is why interpretive social science is a morally and epistemically worthwhile enterprise that helps us explicate the norms implicit in our interpretive practices. In so doing, we often come to see their limits when we fail to meet our obligations as defined by second-person normative attitudes of interpretation. These attitudes cannot be eliminated and still make use of such practical knowledge. Interpretation cannot then be naturalized, even if we look to cognitive science or sociology to explain how norms are acquired or how they function in specific contexts. For this reason, the interpretive social sciences are a form of practical knowledge just as Aristotle envisioned "political science" or Mill the "moral sciences" or Dewey "cooperative and democratic inquiry." Their proper task is to be the sciences of normative attitudes done in the normative attitude of interpretation.[31]

Notes

1. Geertz 1973b, pp. 16–17; the epistemic predicament of contextual interpretation is discussed in Bohman 1991, pp. 132ff.

2. On this point, see Rosenberg 1988, p. 44f. If appeals to the self-interpretations of others are to be epistemologically respectable, they must solve this problem of the lack of independent evidence for them.

3. Habermas 1984, p. 11.

4. Brandom 1988, pp. 79ff.

5. Habermas 1984, p. 132.

6. Brandom 1988, pp. 80ff. These attitudes are (properly) taking to be true and treating as true. "A pragmatic phenomenalist account of knowledge will accordingly investigate the social and normative significance of acts of attributing knowledge. The account of taking-true is what makes possible such a way of thinking about knowledge claims" (p. 83).

7. Dummett calls such abilities as swimming "pure practical abilities." See Dummett 1995, p. x.

8. See Davidson 1980, pp. 238–239. For an explicit defense of the theory theory as a reconstruction of implicit knowledge, see Fodor 1995, pp. 109–122. The essays in this volume make it clear that empirical evidence does not solve the dispute about the status of such abilities.

9. On this conception of simulation, see Gordon 1995a. Gordon more recently emphases simulation as a "hot methodology" that transforms the self, not the projection or inference, from oneself to another. See Gordon 1996a, pp. 12ff. Both formulations concern "pure practical" abilities that are biologically based in our genetic endowments.

10. Heal 1996b, p. 78.

11. See, for example, Gordon 1995a, pp. 106ff. Here Gordon distinguishes "partial" from "total" projection and attempts to show various ways of adjusting our imaginative capacities in cases of first-person failure.

12. For a treatment of this general problem for all regularity theories (whether formulated in first- or third- person terms) and its origins in Wittgenstein, see Brandom 1994, pp. 28ff.

13. Dummett 1995, p. x.

14. Davidson 1986, pp. 134ff. "A good place to begin is with the attitude of holding a sentence is true or of accepting it as true" (p. 135).

15. Davidson 1994, p. 311. The intention to communicate is thus a "reflexive intention" in Grice's sense. See Grice 1957, pp. 377–388. For an argument that the meaning of an utterance must be "self-identifying" rather than dependent on the speaker's intention, see Habermas 1992, pp. 65ff. Habermas points out a regress problem in order to establish the basis of meaning in linguistic structure rather than intentionality. This issue bears directly upon what it means for a speaker to know how to use a language.

16. See, among others, Kripke 1982, pp. 37ff.; Brandom 1994, pp. 28ff. Brandom argues that naturalistic theories succumb to this same gerrymandering problem (pp. 208ff.).

17. Here I mean that Davidson's approach to interpretation is ensnared on the dilemma common to first-person methods. It permits only two options in case of failure: in the first person to consider the reasons to be irrational or to shift to the third person in order to explain the error causally in terms of circumstances. For how this Davidsonian argument could motivate "frank ethnocentrism," see Rorty 1991b, pp. 333ff. For a criticism of these transcendental arguments, see Bohman and Kelly 1996, pp. 181–200.

18. Bohman 1991, pp. 133–139.

19. Gadamer 1989, p. 397.

20. Gadamer 1989, p. 397.

21. Gadamer 1989, p. 180; Habermas 1995, pp. 67ff.

22. This is a constant theme in Gadamer's criticism of Enlightenment reason. See Gadamer 1989, pp. 234, 276, 301, 342.

23. On this point, see Kögler 1996a, pp. 144ff. According to Kögler, for Gadamer, "substantive identity—the agreement on basic assumptions in the sense of shared truth—becomes a criterion for the acceptance of the other" (p. 147).

24. Habermas 1996, p. 230; Alexy's rules of argumentation include the following: "speakers may not contradict themselves"; "different speakers may not use the same expression with different meanings"; "every speaker must assert what he believes"; "every competent speaker may participate in the discourse"; "everyone is permitted to express their attitudes, question any assertion, etc."; "no speaker may be prevented from speaking due to internal or external coercion." Similarly, Habermas claims that accepting such procedural conditions for discourse "is tantamount to implicitly acknowledging U" (his explicit principle of moral justification that "all those affected" must be able to accept a norm). See Habermas 1995, p. 93. What we implicitly acknowledge in practice is not some explicit rule, although it could be made explicit as a practical norm. On an attempt to see legal argumentation in terms of explicit rules of justification, see Alexy 1989. This approach succumbs to the regress of rules argument discussed below.

25. First formulated by Wittgenstein against the overly intellectualist account of rule following as always requiring explicit knowledge of rules, "the regress of rules argument" has many implications. See Brandom 1994, pp. 18–30. Brandom shows that the Kantian conception of norms that have legislative force always treats them as explicit rules: On this account, a performance is correct or incorrect only in rela-

tion to some explicit rule, and "acts are liable to normative assessments insofar as they are governed by propositionally explicit prescriptions, prohibition and permission" (p. 19). Habermas succumbs to this Kantian temptation in discussing the usefulness of formal pragmatics and in this way sees them as modeled on explicit principles. I have shown here how implicit norms can be used critically, albeit indirectly. Explicit norms developed from formal pragmatics could become the basis for a normative moral or political theory in wide reflective equilibrium; the analysis of implicit norms could form the basis for critical social inquiry into normative practices.

26. On this view of the critical theory of distorted communication as based on an account of communication as a practical ability with implicit norms, see Bohman, "Formal Pragmatics as a Critical Theory," in *Perspectives on Habermas*, ed. L. Hahn (Indianapolis: Open Court, forthcoming).

27. On the role of perspectives in critical, public communication, see Bohman 1996, chaps. 3–4.

28. Brandom 1994, p. 600.

29. I leave for another occasion the discussion of whether this normativity is deontic or prudential. It would be deontic if it were based in particular interpretive obligations; it would be prudential if the norms were based on the desire to achieve the goal of communication. I hold that such norms are deontic and not merely prudential, but the difference is not relevant for my epistemological purpose here.

30. Geertz 1986, pp. 122–123. For a further discussion of the inadequacy of ethnocentrism as an unavoidably first-person plural perspective in interpretation and the source of postmodern skepticism about interpretation, see Bohman 1991, pp. 142–145. Here I still thought of the answer to such "us versus them" skepticism only in terms of the problem of evidence for judging better or worse interpretations rather than in terms of practical verification found in establishing and maintaining social relationships.

31. I would like to thank Paul Roth, Karsten Stueber, Bert Kögler, and Jason Murphy for their helpful comments.

Chapter Ten

The Object of Understanding

PAUL A. ROTH

Silence, the absence of signals, is itself a signal. . . . To say that it is im-possible to communicate is false; one always can. To refuse to commu-nicate is a failing; we are biologically and socially predisposed to com-munication, and in particular to its highly evolved and noble form, which is language.

—Primo Levi

It would be equally wrong to announce the glorious news that all mankind—all speakers of a language, at least—share a common scheme and ontology. For if we cannot intelligibly say that schemes are different, neither can we intelligibly say that they are one.

—Donald Davidson

What is the object of understanding? Answers to this question can be (philosophically) simple or complex, depending on the meaning given the term "object." Construing "object" as "goal" or "purpose" permits a philosophically simple answer. For that reading carries no presumption that there is some discrete thing or process to theorize about. Thus "to satisfy one's curiosity" suffices to answer the initial question.

But the simple answer might seem far too simple. Real understanding, the thought may be, is not a question of what satisfies an individual's cu-riosity but rather an issue of whether one correctly grasps *the* meaning. From this perspective arises a second, quite complex reading of the open-ing question. The object of understanding (purposively construed) be-comes a true or correct description of the associated object. This reading posits a fact of the matter to understanding and makes it something to the-orize about.[1]

Disputes regarding the objectivity of historical explanation involve in fact arguments over the plausibility of each of these different readings—the simple and the complex.[2] In particular, the simple reading is held too simple to underwrite claims to truth or objectivity for historical explanations. Efforts to vouchsafe the scientific status of historical explanation traditionally urge either the complex reading just noted or a formalist account of explanation. But efforts to tie the scientific status of history (or any other discipline) to some model or other of explanation have proven futile and do not concern me here.

Ironically, as challenges to the scientific status of narrative historical explanation have receded from the philosophical scene, disputes regarding the objectivity of such explanations have come more to the fore among those countenancing them. The focus of the debate is whether the past is an object that (true) narratives represent or whether narratives create (as in explicitly fictional works) coherent views but do not represent some independent object—The Past. The former view I dub "narrative realism," the latter "narrative antirealism." On the narrative realist view, narrative explanations correctly explain when representing the past *wie es eigentlich gewesen*. In this respect, claims to objectivity by narrative realists assume the complex reading.

Two sorts of defense of narrative realism predicated on the determinacy of "the object of understanding" can be found in the literature. These theories couch their metaphysics of understanding either in terms of the constraints the world imposes on our efforts at systematic understanding or with regard to claims about the structural interrelation of intention, action, and narrative.

Regarding the former, Michael Levine and Jeff Malpas take it that events are like natural kinds, and true histories are true because they depict these and how they are connected.[3] The latter view, found in the work of David Carr, takes a more explicitly idealist position with regard to the object of understanding.[4] For Carr, the object of understanding is constituted by the intentional structure of action. Moreover, the intentionality of actions entails that they possess a narrative structure.

Both types of theories presume that our understanding of historical actions is right or wrong (true or false). Levine, Malpas, and Carr defend the assumptions basic to a traditional "scientific" conception of history: "(1) They accepted a correspondence theory of truth holding that history portrays people who really existed and actions that really took place. (2) They presupposed that human actions mirror the intentions of the actors and that it is the task of the historian to comprehend these intentions in order to construct a coherent historical story."[5] I examine their views in turn, detailing the way in which each relies on a complex reading of "object of understanding" to underwrite narrative realism.[6] As I hope to show, their accounts of understanding are not made plausible either through appeal to historical practice or a priori argument.

1. Historical Realism: A View from Nowhere

What could it mean to say that historians can, as Levine and Malpas urge, "tell it like it was"? According to these authors, "realism with respect to the past means not only that the past existed but that past actuality is an objective reality discoverable in principle as it was. It is the metaphysical assumption needed to suppose that one can 'tell it like it was.'"[7] Their argument has two steps. The first seeks to establish the metaphysical assumption that "reality" has an inherent narrative structure. By this they mean that there is a determinate historical past consisting of distinct types of events interrelated in a specific way. The second step maintains that proper methods of historical inquiry so constrain narrative representations of this historical reality that proper narratives conform to this object of understanding, that is, correctly represent The Past.

What underwrites the metaphysical assumption? Central to their discussion here is Arthur Danto's well-known "thought experiment" of an Ideal Chronicler (IC) and the corresponding Ideal Chronicle. The IC, Danto imagines, writes down everything that happens as it happens. Would the corresponding chronicle, Danto asks, constitute a type of observational database on which to predicate claims to historical knowledge?

Danto posits the experiment to test the hypothesis of the possibility of a *complete* and definitive factual record of the past.[8] Danto argues that any effort at an Ideal Chronicle fails because there will be true descriptions of a particular moment or event that cannot be known true at that time. One example is: "The Thirty Years War began in 1618." Even an IC cannot record every description true of what happens when it happens.

Levine and Malpas believe that such incompleteness does not tell against the metaphysical assumption of an independent record of the past. Their goal is to chart a *via media* for realism, which, on the one hand, avoids the demand for completeness that Danto imputes to such idealizations and, on the other hand, repudiates narrative antirealist positions (such as my own) in which the event structure that we find is only the one we put there.[9] Their arguments for this realism consist of efforts to show the incoherence or implausibility of Danto's position and my own. I examine these arguments in turn.[10]

Regarding Danto, they believe that he sins against historical realism by making the structure of the IC too conceptually austere. Danto's Ideal Chronicler does not observe, as Levine and Malpas think, a genuine realist must. They complain that Danto misjudges the character of what a chronicler chronicles because he ignores the fact that events are temporally extended. For an Ideal Chronicle to constitute an observational analog for historical theorizing, it must, Levine and Malpas insist, incorporate descriptions of observed acts that extend beyond what is available to observation at any given moment. For, they charge, by supposing the IC chronicling only moment to moment, Danto's way of posing the hypothesis denies any possibility of coherence to the imagined chronicle. The metaphysical picture Levine and Malpas propose provides a basis for historical truth not by having the chronicle depict a complete record but by having it account for how happenings actually interconnect.

> [Danto] conceives of the Ideal Chronicle as a purely observational account of the past, which stands to historical narrative much as observational evidence stands to theory. Yet . . . the organisational structure embodied in narrative is to be found not only in history, but in even the most basic descriptions of events as well. Danto's account is thus mistaken in its insistence on excluding all temporal or narrative descriptions from the chronicle, for if one removes the narrative structure from the events, then one also removes their temporal structure and, perhaps, even their character as events.[11]

Theirs could be called a "causal realism" about The Past. Events have a brute temporal and causal structure, one that is also an incipient narrative structure.

It is this allegedly base level and ineliminable narrative structure of events that provides the independent factual basis for establishing the objectivity of historical explanations. For if the notion of an Ideal Chronicle is coherent, they claim, then it entails incorporation of an Ideal Narrative—a particular way of interrelating events. And the notion of an Ideal Chronicle, they maintain, is coherent.

For example, suppose a pitcher in a baseball game throws a curve ball. Noting the pitcher's movements at each instant would not, I take Levine and Malpas to be contending, necessarily be to record the event "the throwing of the curve ball." On the Levine-Malpas view, that event was "present" in the structure of the act from the outset. There is one event—a pitch—that is temporally and causally extended. Correct descriptions at a moment transcend the moment, that is, incorporate or anticipate an indefinite number of earlier and later events in being properly described at a time T.

But matters are even more complex on the Levine-Malpas view than this. In an earlier essay (Roth 1988), I used a fictional example drawn from the film *Rashomon* to raise doubts about the notion of the "same" event, and so of a single causal order for historical explanation. The varying narratives offered by characters in that film could not be summed because inconsistent; they could not be chosen between because empirically equivalent. Levine and Malpas flatly deny that there are such situations: "Not all descriptions will be allowed because not all can be true. Either the wife was raped or she was not raped. Perhaps something other than rape occurred."[12] We are not told whose criteria are determinative of what type of event each event is, but clearly some criteria are. The Ideal Chronicler is also to be an Absolute Judge.

Cases such as these are taken to establish that in order to chronicle correctly, the Ideal Chronicle must look beyond the horizon of the present. If the IC is held unable to look beyond the present, then Danto's thought experiment leads only to a paradox. For, to the extent that the horizon of observation is restricted to the moment, events remain unperceived. Yet expanding the horizon embeds a narrative/temporal element within the chronicle. So the chronicle must anticipate the future or it cannot chronicle the present.[13]

One might well wonder about their easy linking of "narrative structure," "temporal structure," and "event structure." For not all (or, one suspects, even most) events are ipso facto narratives, especially in the sense relevant to historical explanation—the presenting of a causal explanation. Consider again the pitcher's pitch. This surely is an event, but it is just as surely not a narrative. The statement "the pitcher threw a curve" is not a story, much less an explanation. Actions may have a beginning-middle-end structure, but this is not sufficient to give acts a narrative (or explanatory) structure.[14]

Now a way to try to save the point that Levine and Malpas appear to want to make would be to argue that, at the observational level, what one sees is the action—the throwing of the curve ball. Thus, for an Ideal Chronicle to be an observational analog to perceptual data in epistemology, it must record the facts one observes just as, for example, one observes whole objects—apples—and not red patches of such and such a shape from which one infers the existence of an apple. But this argument does not prove enough in the sense that there is still no narrative structure to be found in the perceived action. It proves too much insofar as it would license multiple descriptions of how the sequences of behavior are perceived, some of which deny the temporal structure Levine and Malpas seem to believe is necessary. For unlike apples and red patches, there are individuals—for example, baseball naïfs—who will just perceive the discrete behaviors and be "blind" to the action. So where the enthusiast sees a particular act—the pitch of the curve ball—the untutored sees unconnected sequences.

The above considerations suffice to show why it is simply false to declare, as Levine and Malpas do, that Danto's way of posing the task of the IC is incoherent. For that argument depends on the assertion that the IC cannot record without including a specific temporal or narrative structure. But nothing said as yet shows that observational reports must honor some one particular description over another. Yet a necessary temporal structure, in their sense, is there only under a particular description of the act.

The fact that some descriptions require temporal structures but others do not raises questions, in addition, about what would make the IC *ideal*. Imagine an IC taking a steadfastly third-person view of the behaviors and goings-on, for example, of an alien ethnographer with no prior knowledge of any characteristic human action. Perhaps there is a methodological mandate *not* to assume the native's way of describing matters.[15] All Levine and Malpas do is beg the question against Danto's IC by insisting upon a descriptive stance favorable to their conclusion. In short, they establish no necessary entailment from an Ideal Chronicle to an Ideal Narrative (or any narrative) structure. Nothing they adduce by way of argument or example establishes that incorporating anticipatory temporal or narrative structure is a necessary condition to the very idea of an Ideal Chronicle. In consequence, even if their notion of an Ideal Chronicle is coherent, it does not entail a narrative form. Hence, their metaphysical claim remains unfounded.

Turning from their arguments against Danto to those addressed to me, my worry regarding the notion of an IC was not the incompleteness of descriptions but their "theory-ladenness." My challenge, in other words, was not to the capacity to chronicle, but the possible meaning of "ideal." If the term was meant to connote an analog to "the given" for perceptual knowledge, then, I claimed, no such ideal is possible. In this regard, my position challenges Levine and Malpas's second premise, namely, that the methods of inquiry suffice to constrain narrative representations to conform to the object of understanding.

Levine and Malpas begin by conceding that my arguments provide grounds "for the claim that *event descriptions* are not 'natural' entities." But, they wonder, "what justifies the apparent slide from talk of event-descriptions to talk of plain events?" As they note, my position "is justified only on the assumption that there are no events apart from their description, but this is exactly the point at issue."[16] To illustrate the weakness of what they take to be my position, Levine and Malpas offer the following example of the distinction between events and event-descriptions.

> For, of course, no chronicle, ideal or not, contains events in other than a very loose sense—chronicles, stories, histories, and narratives contain, not events, but event-descriptions. In the same way a list of objects in Smith's briefcase . . . does not contain the objects it lists . . . but only descriptions of those objects or terms referring to this. This simple distinction (for the abandonment of which Roth provides no argument) is what makes possible our claim that different event-descriptions may nevertheless describe the same event. It is also what makes possible the further claim that while there are many ways in which events can be truly described, and so many true narratives, they are all constrained and contained by the same historical past.[17]

Levine and Malpas are surely correct to note that the distinction between "events" and "event-descriptions" is one that is crucial to their argument.[18] But I would have thought it obvious that my case turns on no such simple-minded confusion between words and objects. At issue, rather, is how object positing schemes connect to the world.

My worry in the article they cite concerns how one infers from a theory of how the world is divided (into events or whatever) to conclusions about what the structure of the world is *an sich*. I complain that there is no warrant licensing an entailment from one—the descriptions given by historians, for example—to the other—conclusions regarding what there must be. What I say of events (in another passage they quote) is that "they are not known to be of nature's making rather than of ours."

My twist on Danto's ingenious idea is to argue that if an IC is to supply *Protokollsätze* for historians, what the thought experiment actually reveals is the "theory-ladenness" of such erstwhile observations. Even an Ideal Chronicler cannot record in History's Own Vocabulary. There is no isolating what one takes to be true statements about events from other beliefs because to designate an experience as an event is just to have organized it in a certain way. *There is no "ideal" with regard to describing how the pitcher pitches; there are just different levels at which observing such a person will be influenced by other information one possesses or lacks.* My argument warns against the "myth of the given" with regard to historical knowledge.

Ironically and surprisingly, Levine and Malpas appear to endorse the view sketched above, that is, that even an IC could not record in History's Own Vocabulary. "The sense in which our stories correspond, or fail to correspond, to the world—the sense in which they do or do not 'tell it like it was' or 'like it is'—is not a sense which warrants the idea of the past as some untheorised given."[19] But what then licenses the view that some historian's account or other connects in some special "objective" way to events?

They maintain that three types of constraints—evidential, experiential, theoretical (formal)—keep potential disagreements about matters historical within "manageable limits."

> But while there is no absolute standard that would have us prefer one set of identity conditions for events or one mode of event description, such conditions and modes of description are nevertheless not just up for grabs. They are embedded in and dictated by our location in the encompassing causal-historical nexus of persons and other things. . . . Indeterminacy is always kept within manageable limits by the constraints imposed by principles of theory construction, existing bodies of knowledge, and so forth.[20]

What results, they claim, is "an objective unity of historical practice." In consequence, there is "the idea of the single Chronicle to which all historical research can be seen as contributing. They [historians] should approach it (ideally) asymptotically." The Ideal Chronicle represents a "regulative ideal" by which "to tell a story which connects the facts in the right way."[21]

The "sameness" of the world in which everyone operates constitutes the key constraint, on the Levine and Malpas view, to what historians can say about it. Indeed, the constraint is sufficient, on their view, to justify the Peircian view of history they allude to when they speak of historical researchers who construct various (true) historical narratives collectively approaching (historical) truth asymptotically over time.[22] They purport to find their metaphysical proof in the historical pudding, in the consensus surrounding the ways in which people "actually do" individuate events and construct histories.

Are there good reasons to expect the sort of Peircian chronicle imagined by Levine and Malpas? Two sorts of reasons might be given: formal, regarding how events must be specified, and material, regarding the evidence available to support any proposed narrative. But there are, as a matter of fact, no formal conditions in place that do the job. Scientific method leaves underdetermination in place.[23] Indeed, historical practices, past and present, generate the problems of interpretation under discussion.[24] There is no basis in fact or in theory for the contention that historical research does or eventually must result in the sort of convergence they hypothesize. The suggestion by Levine and Malpas that historical research actually exhibits the qualities they celebrate is at best jejune.

The following two cases illustrate that formal and material conditions are not determinative in historical practice. The first involves debates over the question of how scientists decide in favor of one view as opposed to another in cases of experimental conflict. Contrasting accounts of the sorts of factors that are determinative of the conclusions scientists reach can be found, for example, in Andrew Pickering's *Constructing Quarks,* on the one hand, and Peter Galison's *How Experiments End,* on the other. Pickering and Galison offer competing explanations of the reasons for the shift within the high-energy physics community to quantum chromodynamics. Pickering infamously declares that "in principle, the decisions which produce the world are free and unconstrained. They could be made at random, each scientist choosing by the toss of a coin at each decision point what stance to adopt."[25] Galison, in opposition to this "the calculus of interests explains all" view of scientists' choices, protests that at least some scientists do not appear to choose conclusions in this fashion. [26] But matters are more complicated than this. For, Galison observes, given the normative question at issue—ought scientists to have been persuaded by the evidence available to them—the norms deemed relevant will vary from group to group. He observes that "by now it should be no surprise that criteria that satisfy people *inside* an experiment can differ from those used by scientists (or philosophers) judging from the outside."[27] There is no summing of these narratives; they are inconsistent.

Is there a "master" perspective, an "ideal" account regarding how the facts connect? But what would count in this case as "telling it like it was"? Grasping at metaphysical straws does not allow Levine and Malpas to construct an argument that, in the proliferation of actual accounts, there *must* be one that constitutes "telling it like it was," which connects the facts in "the" right way. As the *Rashomon* case also suggested, there is no warrant for the view that facts must always be determinative in the manner Levine and Malpas require.

A second example concerns a debate surrounding the historical significance and understanding of the Holocaust that went on in the mid-1980s (in the shadow of the *Historikerstreit*).[28] The particular dispute instructive for our purposes was between a prominent German historian of Nazi period, Martin Broszat, and a distinguished Israeli historian, Saul Friedländer.[29] Broszat argues for the priority of a history of the period 1933–1945 that does not center on the madness of the Nazis and the crimes they committed. Rather, he urges, the focus should be on the underlying "normalcy" of everyday life during this period.

> The German historian too will certainly accept that Auschwitz—due to its singular significance—functions in retrospection as the central event of the Nazi period. Yet qua scientist and scholar, he cannot readily accept that Auschwitz also be made, after the fact, into the cardinal point, the hinge on which the entire factual complex of historical events of the Nazi period turns.[30]

Broszat's suggestion, in short, is that without trying or intending to minimize the horror or criminality of the Nazi regime, good portions of the history of Germany for the period in question could be told, as it were, without reference to that regime. "Historicization" means, in this context, situating German history from 1933 to 1945 within a larger narrative than the frame demanded by the political realities of that period.

Friedländer vehemently protests against the acceptability of this way of structuring the narrative. One cannot, he insists, speak of the "normalcy" of this era. He will grudgingly allow talk only of the "perception of normalcy." For Friedländer, "this 'historicization' . . . could mean not so much a widening of the picture, as a *shift of focus*."[31] Friedländer goes on to observe that, inter alia, claims of the "normalcy" of everyday life for this period cannot be fused with that of its victims.[32]

> This type of perspective necessarily will differ considerably from that belonging to another group—and above all from the perspective of the victims. Almost by definition, we have differing emphases, differing foci in the general descriptions of that epoch. What might be viewed as a kind of "fusion of horizons" is not in sight.[33]

The horizons of the "ordinary German" and that of the victims of the Nazi regime cannot be "fused," though each could tell true narratives—one of normalcy, one of extraordinary horrors. Friedländer believes that a moral choice underlies choice of narrative strategy here. But no one imagines that there is some master narrative giving the God's-eye view of the master race. There are only competing, conflicting perspectives to choose among.

The two examples consist of cases in which the conflicts are between contemporaries, and the evidence is not what is in dispute. I have gone into such detail because, in the face of claims such as those made by Levine and Malpas, all one can do is consider actual cases and ask whether their hypothesis regarding an Ideal Chronicler's "view from nowhere" makes any sense. Whatever they mean by their appeal to the "same" world or to whatever they imagine the "norms" of historical research to be, the constraints on interpretation do not function as they contend. Neither material nor formal factors lead to anything like convergences of interpretation or even the reasonable expectation of such convergences. The view from nowhere required for the Levine and Malpas conception of an object of understanding remains not just undefined but indefinable.

2. Narrative Realism: A Myth of the Given

But there is a different account of the objectivity of understanding, which, it might appear, does not rely on misplaced confidence in the necessity of description or the constraining effects of method and evidence. This would be a structuralist account that locates the unity of events in the intention guiding the action. Intention structures action, and this structure constitutes the touchstone for correct understanding. Like Levine and Malpas, David Carr wants to reject any suggestions that "our experience of life does not itself necessarily have the form of narrative, except as we give it that form by making it the subject of stories."[34] For, Carr protests, the alleged bifurcation between lived experience and narrative structure is "totally false."[35]

The asserted discontinuity between experience and narrative is thoroughly mistaken, Carr argues, because acts necessarily have a narrative structure: "Narrative activity . . . is a constitutive part of action."[36] That is, insofar as the lives people lead consist of actions (intentionally directed behavior), these lives possess by virtue of that fact an intrinsic coherence that provides a narrative structure. In turn, this very narrative structure constitutes an object of understanding for historians, at least with regard to constituting the "actual" meaning of the experience for an agent. "Narrative, in our view, lies in the objects of historical research, not merely in its own manner of writing about these objects."[37] Although Levine and Malpas cite Carr with approval,[38] Carr's own metaphysical assumption argues only for a narrative structure inhering in the intention-action linkage.

Carr's argument is disarmingly straightforward. Our intentions give various bits of our behavior a special unity and coherence. Acts, on this view, transcend the moment; they refer both backward and forward in time. As with Levine and Malpas, Carr maintains that to observe an action is to see the connectedness of movements over time.

But if one grants only the capacity for action, then, Carr believes, this entails that narrative structure is an intrinsic part of lived experience. Agents are authors; they construct the story of their lives.

> The essence of deliberative activity is to anticipate the future and lay out the whole action as a unified sequence of steps and stages, interlocking means and ends. . . . My point is simply that action seems to involve, indeed quite essentially, the adoption of an anticipated future-retrospective point of view on the present. . . . What I am saying, then, is that we are constantly striving, with more or less success, to occupy the story-tellers' position with respect to our own lives. . . . Such narrative activity, even apart from its social role, is a constitutive part of action, and not just an embellishment, commentary, or other incidental accompaniment.[39]

The extended temporal structure of action suffices to imbue action with a narrative structure—to make it a causally connected sequence that explains what one is doing and why. For Carr, the inference is immediate; the structure of action is a narrative structure.

> Lives possess a narrative structure prior to any explicit telling. That is, lives are not organized by a process of articulating what was done, but merely in the living.
>
> Furthermore, narrative structure refers not only to such a play of points of view but also to the organizational features of the events themselves. . . . We maintain that all these structures and organizational features pertain to everyday experience and action whether or not the narrative structure or the act of narrative structuring takes the form of explicit verbalization.[40]

Carr plausibly takes his central contentions to be undeniable, namely, people plan, people act, and their actions are (often enough, anyway) in rough accord with such intentions and plans. But, Carr maintains, this is all that is needed to establish that narrative structure is not made but found; not imposed on lives but borrowed "from their source."[41]

Discontinuity theorists (Carr's term for those who see a "discontinuity" between the lived and the narrated) imagine that one occupies the storyteller's position vis-à-vis action only retrospectively. That is why Carr suggests they maintain that stories are not lived but told. But according to Carr, the mistake of discontinuity theorists is basic, residing in a failure to understand the nature of lived experience. For what they somehow miss is the fact that all of us "are constantly striving, with more or less success, to occupy the story-teller's position with respect to our own actions."[42] By virtue of occupying the position of the narrator of our own stories, we are also able to be the explainers of our own actions. On Carr's account, we can explain ourselves retrospectively because we prospectively author our acts. Intentionality provides an intrinsic narrative structure, making possible an explanation of what was done and why.

If Carr is correct, the claims made by discontinuity theorists must be directly contrary to their own experience. But what then could ever have prompted discontinuity theorists like Mink or White to claim otherwise, that is, that stories are not lived but told?

Some philosophical history regarding the notion of explanation is needed here. Narratives were held (by theorists of explanation such as Hempel or Nagel) not to be proper scientific explanations because scientific explanations required laws (or high probability generalizations). Laws were taken to be the engine of explanation because they are critical to explanatorily "connecting" particular happenings by allowing the deducibility of the *explanandum* from the *explanans*. Historians, in contrast, often explain by telling a story that provides reasons or circumstances particular to a certain time and place. What appears to link the reasons given or circumstances cited to the event to be explained is the filter of the historian (and that person's audience) rather than, as scientific explanation was taken to require, taking initial conditions as triggering law-governed connections. Given this understanding of what science is and what explanation requires, to explain by a narrative is not to explain at all.

The terms of the original critique presumed the only inferential license certified for scientific explanation required laws, and so narratives failed as explanations. Discussion of "narrative form as a cognitive instrument" (Mink's phrase) arises explicitly in reaction to demarcation criteria for scientific explanation that ascribe nonexplanatory status to (narrative) historical explanation. The salient point is that the debate about the legitimacy of narrative explanation is one of how to understand its logical form, and so the licensing of inferential/causal connections.

What is ironic is that as challenges to the scientific status of narrative waned, debate revived and intensified among narrativist theorists regarding the objectivity of narrative explanations.[43] For the status of the assumption of "the past" as an independent object of understanding—"the past" as constituting an independent and knowable realm of investigation—has increasingly been viewed as problematic. The evolution of debate in historiography has been from a confidence in the historian's ability to provide an account of the past *wie es eigentlich gewesen* to the view of the historian as a novelist manqué.[44] Histories on this view are more made than found.

What led narrative antirealists to deny the assumption of the past as some fixed object that a historian may hope to reconstruct or re-create? One central issue here involves the different sort of empirically equivalent stories qua explanations that can be mounted in narrative dress. As Hayden White[45] emphasizes, there is no fact of the matter to questions of narrative *type*, for example, "can the Holocaust only be portrayed as a tragedy?"[46] White's analyses of the tropes by which narratives may be constructed offer striking evidence for his claim that the choice of the "mode of emplotment" is not constrained by facts but is the historian's doing.

Moreover, when Mink argues for narrative form as a cognitive instrument, he is arguing for it as a form of explanation that is on all fours with the very different type of theoretical explanation familiar from the natural sciences. Narrative, his suggestion goes, is just one of the basic ways that creatures with cognitive faculties like ours have of organizing and representing information for ourselves. "Narrative form as it is exhibited in both history and fiction is particularly important as a rival to theoretical explanation or understanding. Theory [a formalized natural scientific account] makes possible the explanation of an occurrence only by describing it in such a way that the description is logically related to a systematic set of generalizations or laws."[47] Just as a scientific theory lets us pick out from experience what is relevant to the causal chain given what we are interested in explaining, so too a narrative represents a selective identification and construction of a causal story.

Mink, White, and others assume that narratives are "constructed" just as explanations in science are "constructed," that is, against a background of beliefs that already inform investigators in a general way what could possibly count as a cause. Narrative antirealism considered from this perspective takes familiar form as a type of Quinean/Duhemian holism, a mode of theorizing about experience in which "experience" is mediated through a background of other beliefs. So conceived, the voice of narrative in the conversation of humankind, for Mink and others, is one that speaks through a theoretically informed understanding of how the world works.

However, discussion of narrative as a form of explanation raises, as Mink so clearly recognizes, the problem of narrative form all over again, albeit in somewhat different dress than the problem took in the debate noted earlier. For even if one grants with Mink (and the narrative realists) that narratives explain, there emerges an interesting and important *disanalogy* between narrative and more familiar forms of scientific explanation. It is this. The clear reason to favor formalization in accounts of theory structure and explanation is that what makes for "good" or "proper" deductive connections is well-known and understood. But there is no correspondingly well-articulated account specifying the "proper" form of a narrative explanation. Mink puts it this way:

In the critical philosophy of history, narrative has increasingly come to be re-garded as a type of explanation different from and displacing scientific or "covering-law" explanation of actions and events. But one result has been the emergence of problems not even recognized before. There is, for example, the problem of explicating how a narrative structure determines what is or is not relevant to it; this problem has no analogue in the explication of the structure of theories.[48]

No formal criterion for narrative structure stands as an analogue to deriv-ability in formal models of scientific explanation. The problem is not that narrative fails a test imposed by some nonnarrative criterion for licensing causal connections. Rather, the issue is that it has none of its own to offer.

This absence of any clear criterion for "correct" narrative structure—for specifying licit means of "inferring" one event from another—helps moti-vate the antirealist view. For if the question of what defines an acceptable narrative inference has no general answer, then within "accepted" narrative histories there is, in White's apt phrase, an "embarrassment of plot." What dictates the plot structure—the way matters connect—must, it seems, come from the mind of the historian and the culture of which that person is a part. What else constrains or makes plausible narrative structure? In this respect, narrative explanations owe their credibility to how experience is conceptualized and/or theorized. They yield "the odor of the ideal."[49] An-swers to the question of "how things connect" appear to be a function of a historian's imaginative abilities, narrativizing skills, and cultural resources.

In Carr's writing the discontinuity theorists seem to view life as a kind of buzzing, booming cacophony until narratives are overlaid *(ex post experi-entia)* on them.[50] But Carr's efforts to position narrative antirealism as a re-ductionist foil to his more authentic "holistic" account of lived experience are completely misplaced. What happens, rather, is that Carr confuses dis-continuity theorists' puzzlement with why we accept some narratives and not others with the claim that our lives lack structure for us. But he has matters exactly backward. Carr's appeal to the "self-evidence" of explana-tions of actions is part of the problem with which antirealists start, not the discovery of a solution.

The epistemological positions are thus the opposite of what Carr claims. For it is Carr who stakes out a foundationalist position with his claims for the privileged explanatory positions of agents. The point at issue, which Carr just misses, is how to understand what informs the structuring of a narrative so that it is open to rational debate and evaluation. It is at this point—discerning what licenses the linkages that a narrative imputes—that the real debate begins.

Taken as a debate on the legitimate structure of a narrative explana-tion, what is to be made of Carr's challenge to discontinuity theorists? What drives Carr's argument to the conclusion that Mink and others are operating with a "totally false distinction"[51] is the asserted necessary structural link between the intentionality of action and its narrative form. For Carr, this structural connection is assured by the very meaning of the notion of action. Action is by definition intentional, and intentionality is the glue uniting behaviors into actions and actions into lives with narrative structures.

Carr takes the inference from action to narrative structure to be immediate, a consequence of what it means to be an agent. It appears to require no more than to acknowledge that we can explain the actions because we authored them. But we no longer need be gulled by this argument. Its very transparency creates a question instead of supplying an answer. How does the prospective structure of action fit with narrative structure qua explanation? Do intentions always or necessarily explain actions?

Consider, in this regard, what Carr's view seemingly implies with respect to the question of whether one can learn from experience what one's intentions are (or were). Can reflection on experience reveal that we were just wrong or mistaken in our assessment of our own prior intentions? Surely the general answer here is yes. Yet Carr's a priori argument appears to have the odd consequence that we cannot learn about ourselves from experience. For learning about ourselves from experience requires that there would have to be just a contingent connection between what we take, at any given moment, our intentions to be and what, upon reflection, we see that they more likely were. But Carr clearly holds that the agent must hold the narrator's perspective on her own life and that this perspective explains the agent's actions. Yet only if one allows for a discontinuity between intention and action is learning about oneself from experience possible.

Carr is not simply unclear but quite possibly inconsistent regarding the question of the extent to which an agent's status as narrator of his or her own life—a point on which he repeatedly and emphatically insists—is compatible with the revisability of accounts. We may rewrite the past, he acknowledges, in the light of new experience.

> It may indeed be true that historical research will often penetrate to causal connections among events and actions (particularly psychological or economic connections) which were hidden from the historical agents themselves. But this is not to deny that these agents lived in a narrative fashion; it is just to say that *their* story of what they were doing must be revised or indeed replaced by a better one.[52]

But he fails to consider how this possibility impacts his claims that agents necessarily occupy the narrator's role with regard to their own actions. "Better" in this passage concerns the relative assessment of "causal connections." Recall that for Mink the issue is narrative as a theorized form of explanation and the inferential connections within a narrative so conceived. But if that is so, Carr surrenders the very point in contention by declaring that *"their* (i.e., agents') story of what they were doing must be revised or indeed replaced by a better one." For Carr reinserts the key discontinuity— that between the explanation of a narrator and that of an agent—which he previously claimed to deny. By allowing the agent's intentions to go one way and the causes of action another, Carr renders otiose his key claim that the narrative structure of action is a consequence of agency.

So far, I have only challenged Carr's "continuity" claim, that is, the alleged explanatory link of intention to action and the implications of this for narrative structure. But there is a still more general problem with Carr's conception of the relation of action and narrative. This is the fact that it is simply false to claim as he does that it is a necessary feature of experience that one finds a narrative unity in it.

How can one assess Carr's claim that, in general, life is experienced as having a narrative structure? Since historical explanation is the immediate focus, let us take a biography as one case study. Consider, in this regard, Gitta Sereny's justly celebrated biography of Franz Stangl.[53] Sereny documents Stangl's march through the Nazi hierarchy of extermination, from his early position as a "middle manager" in the T–4 eugenics program to his efficient overseeing of Treblinka (where about 1.2 million Jews were gassed in a seventeen-month period). Much of this account is in Stangl's own terms, based on the author's extensive interviews with him.

How does Stangl see the evolution of his own career and his role in the various programs of death in which he participated? Well, for example, Stangl explains his decision to accept the position in the T–4 program in terms of wishing to avoid working under someone he disliked. Similar sorts of explanations are provided for his actions in assuming the post at Treblinka as well. There was no plan; there was no intention to become overseer of the most efficient death camp in history. Options were offered, decisions were made, posts were accepted—one damn thing after another. Stangl lives a chronicle, not a narrative.

Stangl explains his actions in terms of what he needed to do to provide for his family, advance his career, or avoid working under difficult superiors. But his succession of positions does not, in his view, constitute a narrative, an explanation in the form of a story. His "narrative" is one of frustrated ambition; what he wanted was to become a combat officer. In any case, "wanting a career" provides neither for an anticipation of what Stangl did nor even, as he admits, an explanation of his particularly heinous actions.

In Stangl's case, his conversations with Sereny led to a highly dramatic moment. He died of heart failure less than a day after the conversation Sereny records.

"My conscience is clear about what I did myself," he said, in the same stiffly spoken words he had used countless times at his trial, and in the past weeks, when we had always come back to this subject, over and over again. But this time I said nothing. He paused and waited, but the room remained silent. "I have never intentionally hurt anyone, myself," he said, with a different, less incisive emphasis, and waited again—for a long time. For the first time, in all these many days, I had given him no help. There was no more time. He gripped the table with both hands as if he was holding on to it. "But I was there," he said then, in a curiously dry and tired tone of resignation. These few sentences had taken almost half an hour to pronounce. "So yes," he said finally, very quietly, "in reality I share the guilt. . . . Because my guilt . . . my guilt . . . only now in these talks . . . now that I have talked about it all for the first time." . . . He stopped.

He had pronounced the words "my guilt"; but more than the words, the finality of it was in the sagging of his body, and on his face.

After more than a minute he started again, a half-hearted attempt, in a dull voice. "My guilt," he said, "is that I am still here. That is my guilt."[54]

"Now that I have talked about it all for the first time." Stangl arrives at an eleventh-hour reassessment of his actions. He had cast himself as a character amid events not in his control, to which he could only react. When matters are not in one's control, one cannot bear responsibility for what happens. But that is the account Stangl comes to believe is false. He learns (or finally admits) something about himself not previously acknowledged.

Stangl's case is a particularly dramatic one, involving events and actions that seemingly defy explanation. But the philosophical points here are quite general. For one, there is a sharp discordance between what wants explaining—the willingness to aid and abet the murder of over a million people whom he had no particular reason to murder—and the self-ascribed actions of the individual. Simply put, the intentions fail to come close to explaining the actions.[55] Second, and contrary to the type of entailment relationship that Carr claims must exist between action and narrative, while Stangl's life is replete with actions of one sort or another, it lacks, in his telling of it anyway, any narrative quality. It is a chronicle of events he lives through.

The explanatory structure, if such there is, is invisible to him. For him, life is a series of postings and tasks, not a story lived out. The structure of some greater intentions—to advance his career, to keep out of trouble, to protect his wife and children from the hardships of the war—which Stangl ascribes to himself do not yield *in advance* any anticipation of his actions. From the fact that an act is intentional, it does not follow (i.e., is in no sense entailed) that the intention "explains" the action in terms of giving an understandable reason for it. It does not even give it narrative structure in some looser sense of "narrative." There is no story, no plot, no unfolding of a coherent picture forged by intentions and consequent actions.

Consider in this regard Christopher Browning's stunning portrait of German execution squads in Poland[56] based on archived interviews with members of the squads. One is hard-pressed in this, as in other cases of Holocaust historiography, to locate either an individual or a "collective" intention (whatever that is)[57] to, for example, effect a "Final Solution." Browning's reserve policemen are, as Browning stresses, ordinary men and not ideologues or hard-bitten anti-Semites. Why did they kill? Browning ultimately adverts to Milgram-like explanations of behavior, explanations notably devoid of any straightforward linking of individual intentions with the actions to be explained. If, in Stangl's case, intentions are not explanatory of the actions, in Browning's study what explains, if anything does, is the apparent absence of intentions (or the will) to do otherwise. Yet, in all cases, one is looking at actions—voluntary behavior. Carr's claims to the contrary notwithstanding, there is simply no inconsistency as a matter of experience or of logic in ascribing both agency and a nonnarrative structure to experience.

A final point is that the owl of Minerva takes flight only at dusk. Prospectively, one may have hopes, but only retrospectively does one know enough to fashion a story: that is, whether the intentions, plans, goals, or ambitions one says one has, the reasons one claims for actions, are in fact the reasons that plausibly explain one's actions are learned, if at all, in retrospect. The notions of self-fulfilling prophecies, self-defeating actions, false consciousness, unconscious motives, and so on are all testimony to the generally recognized disjunction between how people may characterize what they are doing and what is taken to be the explanation of what is being done, or even what their intentions "really" are.

Carr's failure to consider actual historical cases leaves it to a priori argument to show that life is narrativized in the living. But examination of actual cases confutes any claim of this sort; the link Carr asserts must be there simply is not. Intentions do not necessarily explain or provide narrative structure to individual actions. Moreover, appeals to intentions must be weighed against other factors even in the explanation and assessment of individual actions. In addition, self-understanding characteristically alters over time, as Stangl's case dramatically illustrates. What "actually" happened takes different shapes on different tellings, even for the individual whose life it is. It is a symptom of the problem with narrative, not its cure, to boldly declare that intentions "explain" actions. The a priori entailment between intention, action, and narrative structure does not obtain. The disanalogy Mink stresses between narrative and scientific explanation underscores the fact that for the latter cases but not the former we have a well-informed theoretical understanding of which factors to favor as causes.

Because Carr commits himself a priori to the "transparency" of intentions as the causes of actions, he blinds himself to the actual complexity of linking intentions to explanations. Carr imagines the dispute to reside in what in fact all parties in this debate take for granted—narratives as a nonreductive mode of explanation—and takes for granted what is in fact problematic—knowledge of what shapes and informs our imputed understanding of the causes of action, for ourselves or others.

3. Historical Naturalism:
Dualisms Lost, the World Regained

My strategy for undermining philosophic distinctions between types of science has been to argue that there is no good reason to believe that meanings (and related notions) are something fixed, settled, or determinate, objects to be retrieved by diligent investigation. My pluralism reflects my skepticism regarding the existence of determinate demarcation criteria that give a universal, fixed meaning to "scientific method" or "rational inquiry."[58] Thus, on my view, the sciences cannot be divided by kinds (e.g., natural versus social, hard versus soft) based on essentially differing ends of inquiry (explanation versus understanding) or essentially differing methods (nomothetic versus ideographic).

My naturalism together with my critiques of "meaning realism"[59] have, some claim, the unintended consequence of reinvigorating the alleged distinction between the *Geisteswissenschaften* and *Naturwissenschaften*. This would be ironic inasmuch as this is a distinction I took these critiques (including those in the first two sections) to undercut. Does, in fact, the strategy animating the criticisms rehearsed in the first two sections ultimately reinforce a distinction I seek to reject?

The problem arises for me, the suggestion goes, because my rejection of meanings has not been thoroughgoing enough. The problem is this: Skepticism regarding meaning is justified, on my view, because there are no reasons legitimating the assumption of such objects to theorize about. However, I make no parallel sort of criticisms of object-positing schemes in the natural sciences. That is, the objects of natural science are, on the Quinean view to which I subscribe, underdetermined but not indeterminate. But what makes objects of one sort a less fit subject of speculation than objects of the other? *How, in other words, can I deny theories of understanding their objects and yet hold that there is no distinction between the* Geisteswissenschaften *and* Naturwissenschaften? Insofar as the social sciences aim at "objects of understanding" and I claim that there are no such objects, I have seemingly posited a metaphysical distinction in kind while denying a methodological one.

Joseph Rouse presses this apparent puzzle regarding my position with particular force and clarity. Rouse charges that a residual empiricism in my account of Quinean indeterminacy engenders the unwanted consequence from my view that "the difference between theories about the publicly available world, and theories about meanings, conforms to the difference between the natural and social sciences."[60] Rouse proposes a revision in my account that he believes preserves my argument for the indeterminacy but invokes no invidious metaphysical distinctions between types of sciences.

The account of Quinean indeterminacy I put forward and Rouse endorses sees indeterminacy as a result of the fact that all there is to meaning must be in the public sphere. There are intersubjectively available cues, there are interpretations, but there is nothing to meaning "beyond" evidence and interpretation, no "fact of the matter" to which evidence and interpretation points, so to speak.

Exactly where my argument goes off track, on Rouse's view, is when I infer from the centrality of intersubjectivity to the conclusion that appeals to the world have some special evidentiary status that appeals to meaning cannot. My argument licensing this inference is predicated on the "paradox of language learning," that is, the problem of how, given holistic assumptions about evidence and meaning, it is possible to learn language.[61] The paradox focuses on what I take to be the "purest" case of Quinean radical translation, namely, an infant learning his or her first language, for an infant has no prior theory to serve as a basis for forming genuine or analytical hypotheses. Translation thus proceeds against the most minimal background of beliefs. And if the language–world relation is holistic, then the paradox arises straightforwardly. Infants are observed learning language only a sentence or term at a time, but, *ex hypothesi,* sentences and terms, in isolation from the larger language/theory of which they are a part, have no meaning. So learning language under these circumstances would seem an impossible task. But, of course, most infants do. Hence the apparent paradox.

I suggest (following Quine) that the resolution to the paradox resides in some initial way of cuing utterances with the environment. Specifically, the paradox is only resolved because some initially learned sentences serve a function akin to the one Quine attributes to observation sentences. Thus it is that infants, though lacking a prior theory, nevertheless succeed in coordinating with teachers certain sounds or gestures and shared features of the environment. It would otherwise be inconceivable how they could enter the web of belief.[62]

But, Rouse contends, my argument here is tantamount to assigning special ontological status to a "shared" environment. Rather, there are only conventions for making oneself understood. "Social practice and public world are inextricable, and this is what Roth's argument from the conditions for language learning should once again teach us. . . . The ability to correlate utterances and the surrounding world is constitutive of their being utterances at all."[63] Although I draw the moral that the natural and social sciences must share a common explanatory focus, Rouse reads this as a privileging of the domain usually associated with the natural sciences—the object domain—over that usually associated with the social sciences—meaning or understanding. By allowing a fact of the matter to one but not the other, the unwanted divide allegedly creeps into my epistemological account.

If there is no prior domain of meanings, Rouse suggests, then there is no prior domain of objects either. Rouse's "practices" account, to the contrary, would have it that "there is no fact of the matter about who is a competent speaker of language, beyond determining whom other speakers (themselves of contestable identity) will recognize as competent speakers."[64] Rouse concludes that the objects of all domains are by-products of social circumstances and interactions.

This conclusion, in turn, leads Rouse to maintain that what is explanatorily basic of communication is the fact that, from the outset, it is a relation of those in positions of unequal power. "Language learning is a form of social interaction which does not occur between social equals. . . . There is no publicly available check on the correctness overall of the teachers' utterances (it is important here that the role of the teacher is filled collectively by those whose speech the learner seeks to master for herself)."[65] *Relations of unequal power fill the role in Rouse's account that appeal to general environmental cues occupies in mine.* Power relations ground his theory of meaning.

Are appeals to notions of "social practices" in general and power relations in particular explanatory of how communication is achieved?[66] By way of assessing whether or not Rouse's invocation of social practices for explanatory purposes is compelling, a key issue is whether an appeal to practice resolves "the paradox of language learning." For Rouse, however the infant learns, the power differential in the teacher-learner relation must somehow account for that infant's entering wedge into language.

> Yet [it] is also unacceptable to take that shared environment as securing a domain of "objective evidence" in any sense that would escape negotiation; the identification of evidence within that shared environment, along with its employment for the sake of furthering the practices of inquiry, is an ineliminable social activity that cannot be fixed by any determinate fact of the matter, whether physiological or behavioral.[67]

That is, while I allow only the study of intersubjectively available environmental cues for purposes of legitimate explanation and evidence, Rouse for his part allows only socially mediated negotiations to be explanatory of what there is. Rouse would explain any shared world on the basis of relations of power and the associated practices. We differ, in short, with regard to what to take as explanatorily basic. Indeed, Rouse reacts to the paradox by assimilating the natural sciences to the social.

By way of illustrating a question about Rouse's power approach to meaning, consider Victor Klemperer's powerful and arresting diary of his life as a Jew in Nazi Germany.[68] One might take Klemperer's situation as a type of paradigm of powerlessness. Klemperer can only "bear witness," that is, record what he experiences and observes. He occupies an observer's role to his own life precisely because he has ceased to be able to structure it or explain what is going on.

Klemperer's case bears on Rouse's position in the following way. If Rouse is correct, then such severe asymmetries in power relations should, it seems, determine what meanings both parties impute to experience inasmuch as, in Rouse's view, power relations are determinative of meaning. But this is not what we find happening. If Rouse was right, I am suggesting, tensions and problems experienced by Klemperer (or imagined by Orwell in *1984)* ought not to occur. Granted, Klemperer (or Orwell's Winston) is not an infant, but what applies to an infant should apply, mutatis mutandis, to adults. But it is precisely because we identify the distorting effects of power and contrast them against other sorts of experience that the notion of meaning cannot be fully cashed out in terms of power relations as Rouse suggests.

On my account, language remains keyed to a shared environment, and it is on this shared environment that all inquiry should focus in order to have a fact of the matter. My naturalism represents favoritism not among *types* of objects—physical versus mental—but in the order or direction of explanation—public versus private, social versus individual. My naturalism has latter notions in each pair explained in terms of the former, and this because naturalism in its turn is constrained by meaning holism. It is not, as Rouse imagines, that I give to natural science a domain of objects I deny to the social sciences. A naturalized epistemology need not privilege any particular domain of objects or methods as paradigmatic but is free to draw from all disciplines. Naturalism leaves open the question of what to recognize as a science.

Thus, in the end the difference between Rouse and me is not that I divide the sciences by kind according to domain but that I naturalize all inquiry and thus explain both domains—social and natural—relative to a shared world. The charge that I traffic in a privileged domain of objects can be seen as misplaced, for my notion of "shared environment" is metaphysically empty. On my account, the notion of sharing can only be cashed out intratheoretically, and our current best way of understanding "sharing" is empirical. But this latter claim I view as itself contingent, and so open to revision.

We seek understanding. But from this it does not follow that there is a thing to be sought—the object of understanding.[69]

Notes

1. Since one way of defining "understanding" might be "the recovery or appreciation of meaning," it should come as no surprise to discover, as I argue, that the notion of understanding is as "myth eaten" as the notion of meaning. The views of understanding criticized in this essay parallel thFe "unchallenged assumptions" of theory of meaning that Hilary Putman identifies (1975, p. 219).

2. Throughout I speak of understanding as a mode of explanation. The tradition of contrasting explanation and understanding presumes a certain notion of scientific explanation, specifically one that stipulated the citing laws as a condition of explanation. "Understanding" connoted offering just reasons peculiar to and only operative within particular contexts. But reasons without laws did not qualify as an explanation. While acknowledging that types of explanation differ with regard to what is formally necessary to establish a causal connection, I find no reason now to exclude understanding from the domain of explanation.

3. Levine and Malpas 1994, hereafter cited as L&M; Levine 1991, hereafter cited as L.

4. The following works by Carr are considered: Carr 1986a; 1986b; 1985.

5. Iggers 1997, p. 3. The alternatives represented by these authors are not mutually exclusive. The primary difference is that for Carr, the structure is provided by the intentions of agents, but the source of event structure in L&M includes Carr's views but seems to encompass some type of agent-independent conception as well.

6. In an earlier essay (Roth 1988), I argued against what I there termed the "metaphysical objection" to taking narrative as a legitimate mode of historical explanation. The core of this objection as I then imagined it held that narrative form was not open to verification, and so narrative could not be an appropriate mode for historical explanations. Although I replied to the objection in that article, I have since become aware of ways in which my reply is incomplete. Other important variants of the metaphysical assumption remained untouched. These are my focus below.

7. L&M, p. 154.

8. First published in 1965 in Danto's *Analytical Philosophy of History;* the book has been republished in a revised edition, Danto 1985. See, for example, Danto 1985, pp. 148–149 on the Ideal Chronicler and the Ideal Chronicle.

9. L&M criticize a number of the antirealist arguments that I offer. Most puzzling is their dismissal of my argument from the underdetermination of theories. The puzzle here is in their reason for dismissing it. They agree that theories "will always be underdetermined by the evidence" (p. 164) but they go on to claim that such theories "could well be treated as simply translations of each other, in which case there is no reason to treat them as incompatible" (p. 164). They cite Quine as their authority for the suggestion that underdetermined theories are intertranslatable (p. 164 n. 28). Yet Quine, even in the sources L&M cite, takes underdetermination as a problem only because it can engender logical incompatibility between theories despite their being empirically equivalent. That competing theories cannot always or even characteristically be treated as translations of one another,

that is, are logically incompatible, is stressed by Quine in the very passage (Quine 1960) cited by L&M. Incompatibility arises because empirical equivalence does not ensure sameness of meaning for terms in the theories. Quine considers the point L&M raise, only to reject it. "It may be protested that when two theories agree thus in point of all possible sensory determinants they are in an important sense not two but one" (p. 78). But this "protest" is *not,* as Quine goes on to make clear, one he accepts. He does not accept it because of "its glibness on the topic of meaning." For given the "empirical slack" between available evidence and imputed meaning, *ex hypothesi* there is no fact of the matter regarding which of two incompatible meanings is to be deemed correct. The question of whether or not there is an additional problem here regarding indeterminacy of translation (and I believe, following Quine, that there is) need not be answered in order to see that L&M simply misread Quine regarding the necessary reconcilability of empirically equivalent theories.

10. L&M also charge that failure to ascribe the requisite sort of realism to events leads into some "anti-realist metaphysic," which would leave one unable, in their view, to distinguish between, for example, Holocaust denial and its alternatives. "Without such a notion [as an ideal chronicle], or some correlate, one is left without any notion of error in history; without any possibility of distinguishing historical fact from historical fiction; without any chance of distinguishing correct recollection from false" (p. 162). No argument is provided as to why the only alternatives are either a realist metaphysics of history or a complete inability to distinguish error or falsehood. Moreover, this way of posing the alternatives surely is false. Clearly, antirealists can have notions of error, and they discern error in the usual way, for example, on the basis of the available evidence. Metaphysical issues go one way, epistemic go another. In what follows, I concern myself only with arguments that are raised in support of their metaphysical claims.

11. L&M, p. 161.

12. L&M, p. 170; L, p. 236.

13. L&M, p. 161.

14. An example would be to contrast the nonnarrative statement "the king died and then the queen died" with the narrative "the king's dying caused the queen to die." Narrative requires something more than a sequence of acts or events; whatever else narrative requires, there must be some linking of the events. Otherwise random sequences would count as narratives. For example, water dripping from a faucet has a temporal order but no narrative one. Regarding narrative and time, consider the following example (owing to Hemingway, I believe) of a mininarrative: "For Sale. Baby shoes. Never used." So temporal sequencing is neither necessary nor sufficient for a narrative.

15. This is a standard ethnographic strategy in the sociology of science. See, for example, Woolgar and Latour 1986.

16. L&M, p. 165.

17. L&M, p. 166. L&M sometimes draw succor and support for their position by their reading of Davidson's critique of the scheme-content dichotomy. Their understanding of this argument is tendentious. I try to state their position throughout without making Davidson's interpretation the issue between us.

18. As to the question of whether my argument ignores the distinction between events and their descriptions, and indeed confuses the latter with the former, the reading here imputed by L&M is belied by one of the very passages they quote (p. 164 n. 27): "My point about putative 'ideal events' . . . is that treating such events as objects independent of our object (and event) positing scheme of things runs afoul of what we know about the relation of evidence to theory." As I would have hoped this remark makes clear, the point I emphasize throughout my essay is that the objects to which our *theory* of the world commits us cannot be assumed to have some theory-independent standing. I confess that I slip between expressing the point as a theory-evidence question and as a language-world question. But in moving between "theory" and "language" in this way, I thought I was helping myself to be a familiar enough identification, and so too the corresponding issue between how we describe matters and how matters stand seen subspecie *aeternitatus*. Although this assumes a type of holism regarding language/theories, this holism is one that Quine and Davidson share. L&M seem content enough with a Davidsonian view here. In short, the issue between L&M and myself, I would have said, is one regarding the basis for imputing theory-independent status to a type of theoretical entity—an event. I do not see how my argument trades in so coarse a confusion as that between terms and the objects to which the terms refer.

19. L&M, p. 167.

20. L&M, p. 167; see also pp. 168–169.

21. L&M, pp. 170–171.

22. The argument of Levine's paper "Historical Anti-Realism" repeats the convergence argument found in L&M, including the reasons for rejecting my *Rashomon* example, discussed below. The earlier paper also insists that I fail to give due weight to "conditions of material adequacy" (p. 234), by which I understand Levine to intend what the later paper refers to as the "constraints" on theory construction. Although I do not discuss the earlier paper directly, I take my replies to the later paper to suffice, since all of Levine's arguments reappear in that later paper.

23. For an elaboration of how little is to be achieved by appeals to "scientific method," see Roth 1996.

24. Excellent accounts of the sort of disputes, past and ongoing, that wrack the historical profession can be found in Novick 1988; Wise 1980.

25. Pickering 1984, pp. 405–406.

26. See, for example, Galison 1987, p. 258.

27. Galison 1987, p. 260.

28. This provides yet another case study for those who, like L&M, argue for the convergences among historical narratives without attending to actual historiographical disputes. See, for example, Maier 1997. The controversies that interest me here have nothing to do with so-called revisionist positions or efforts at Holocaust denial, views I can only regard with contempt. Rather, vexed and fascinating conflicts persist concerning how to explain the massive complicity of people in and out of the Nazi Party, Germans and non-Germans alike, in the systematic killing. A sense of the nature, depth, and complexity of this controversy, which often enough is not a dispute about any matter of fact, can be gleaned from Moses 1998; Berenbaum and Peck 1998 (especially the articles by Christopher Browning and Daniel

Goldhagen). For a good survey of generic problems of interpretation, see Marrus 1989.

29. One reason for looking at the Broszat-Friedländer exchange, rather than the *Historikerstreit* proper, is that the sort of political allegiances that clouded much of the debate in the *Historikerstreit* are not central here. No one suggests that Broszat is motivated by a lack of antipathy for the Nazis or blinded by nationalist aspirations for West Germany. Thus this dispute is far more "academic" in tone and nature. References are from Broszat and Friedländer 1988.

30. Broszat, in Broszat and Friedländer 1988, p. 103.

31. Friedländer, in Broszat and Friedländer 1988, pp. 123, 104; also 106–107.

32. Obviously, similar questions might be raised regarding U.S. history in the pre–civil rights era. One might ask, following MacIntyre, whose normalcy, which narrative?

33. Friedländer, in Broszat and Friedländer 1988, p. 125.

34. Mink 1987, p. 187.

35. Carr 1986b, p. 125; 1986a, p. 61.

36. Carr 1986b, p. 125.

37. Carr 1986a, p. 177; see generally pp. 168ff.

38. L&M, pp. 159ff.

39. Carr 1986b, pp. 125, 126; 1986a, p. 62.

40. Carr 1986a, pp. 62, 49–52, 90–91; 1985, p. 121.

41. Carr 1985, p. 121.

42. Carr 1986a, p. 61.

43. The publication of White 1973 marks the moment when narrative antirealism becomes a philosophical force in historiography.

44. Consider, in this regard, Georg Iggers's apposite comment: "The idea that objectivity in historical research is not possible because there is no object of history has gained increasing currency." Iggers 1997, p. 9. See, relatedly, Berkhofer 1997.

45. For a helpful overview and elaboration of White's views, see Kannsteiner 1993.

46. Criticisms of White on just this point, that is, the "correctness" of alternative emplotments of the history of the Holocaust, can be found in Friedländer 1992. See especially the essays by Perry Anderson, Christopher Browning, Carlo Ginzburg, Martin Jay, and Hayden White.

47. Mink 1987, p. 185.

48. Mink 1987, p. 187.

49. Hayden White, "The Value of Narrativity in the Representation of Reality," in White 1987, p. 21.

50. Carr 1986a, pp. 65–66.

51. Carr 1986a, p. 61.

52. Carr 1986a, p. 177. See also p. 99.

53. Sereny 1983.

54. Sereny 1983, p. 364, ellipses in the original.

55. Henry Friedländer, author of the authoritative study of the executions of more than 70,000 Aryans carried out in the T–4 program, remarks, "When all is said and done, I am still unable to fathom why seemingly normal men and women were able to commit such extraordinary crimes. Neither ideology nor self-interest is

a satisfactory explanation for such behavior" (H. Friedländer, "The T–4 Killers," in Berenbaum and Peck 1998, p. 249). Consider the following quotes cited in Browning 1992, garnered from interviews with German reservists who had participated in bloody mass shootings in Poland. "Truthfully I must say that at the time we didn't reflect about it at all. Only years later did any of us become conscious of what had happened then. . . . Only later did it first occur to me that it had not been right" (p. 72). Compare this with the following explanation. "I made the effort, and it was possible for me, to shoot only children. It so happened that the mother led the children by the hand. My neighbor then shot the mother and I shot the child that belonged to her, because I reasoned with myself that after all without its mother the child could not live any longer" (p. 73). Both remarks, each in its own way, poses a chilling counterbalance to Carr's readiness to connect intention and action, on the one hand, and explanation and narrative, on the other. For the intentions seem either irrelevant to efforts at understanding ("we didn't reflect," "only years later did any of us becomes conscious") or opaque to normal capacities for understanding (the "reason" rationalizing the shooting of children). It is Browning who thematizes, narrativizes, and attempts to explain the actions of those involved. None of this is done by the agents themselves.

56. Browning 1992.

57. But see Carr 1986a, pp. 149ff. Carr's curious and totally unargued positing of a "collective consciousness" regarding the explanation of action is one of the stranger facets of his fundamentally implausible views regarding the connection of intention and explanation. However, it is a recognized consequence of the tradition within which Carr writes and has well-known political implications as well. See, for example, David Cooper, "*Verstehen,* Holism, and Fascism," in O'Hear 1996.

58. See Roth 1996, p. 48 n. 20.

59. Roth 1996; 1987.

60. Rouse 1991, p. 446.

61. See Roth 1987, pp. 21ff.

62. However, when speculation begins regarding which sentences these are, I no longer believe (contrary to Quine) that we can pick out just which sentences played this role and say exactly how they abetted the initial learning process.

63. Rouse 1991, p. 451.

64. Rouse 1991, p. 453.

65. Rouse 1991, p. 449.

66. One worry is whether or not practice-based explanation ultimately leads back to a domain of mental objects. The basis for this worry regarding the notion of practices is best developed in Turner 1994.

67. Rouse 1991, p. 463.

68. Klemperer 1998.

69. I wish to thank Jim Bohman, Brian Fay, Lynn Hankinson Nelson, and Karsten Stueber for helpful comments on earlier drafts of this chapter.

Chapter Eleven

Reenactment as Critique of Logical Analysis: Wittgensteinian Themes in Collingwood

SIMON BLACKBURN

In putting together Collingwood and Wittgenstein, I am conscious of court-ing misunderstanding. So far as I know neither influenced the other in the least. Although Collingwood mentions Moore and Russell quite frequently, he virtually never mentions Wittgenstein, and he never discusses any spe-cific doctrine, even of the earlier work of Wittgenstein. It is only the later work of Wittgenstein, of which Collingwood can have known nothing, that betrays significant similarities. Equally the only recorded mention of Collingwood by Wittgenstein I can find is a typically unflattering exclama-tion Drury reports him as having made, on learning that "Collingwood of Oxford" was one of the electors to Moore's Cambridge Chair.

More importantly their work is antithetical in a very deep sense, for what is at stake is nothing less than what philosophy is, and how it is to be done. The question is how philosophy relates to its history, and whether it can be done without it. Collingwood stands firmly on one side of this issue—so much so that today I am talking of one career of his, while his other career, as a Roman and British historian, must go unsung. He was steeped not only in historical method but in the history of the philosophy and the history of thought about nature. He is unquestionably the most acute English histo-rian of philosophy of this century. Nobody can read *The Idea of Nature*, still less the *Idea of History*, without admiring the penetration with which Collingwood understood the history of Western science and philosophy; the former book seems to me to stand alongside E. J. Dijkterhuis's *The*

Mechanization of the World View as the best study there is of the evolution of classical mechanics in the seventeenth century.

A large part of Collingwood's critique of analytical philosophy stems from his dislike of its unhistorical nature. It is possible to be a good scientist, at the cutting edge, with little or no historical sense. But when we understand history properly, it is not at all obvious that the same is true of philosophy, although it is part of the credo of analytical philosophy that it is. History of philosophy is not antiquarianism, or the scissors-and-paste knowledge of Locke's likely predecessors or word counts in Aristotle. This kind of study exists as a slightly downscale curriculum option of no great interest to contemporary practitioners, just as history of physics might exist alongside physics as something for retirement or bedtime. Instead Collingwood sees thought as something that is essentially historically embodied: The idea of a worthwhile philosophy with no reflection on its own historical situation would be a contradiction. We can understand where we are only by understanding our own historical embedding. We have to understand how we got here, and the thoughts of those who would wish us to have got somewhere else.

In doing history properly we reenact the thoughts—meaning the problems and the concepts with which they were met—that are found in the evolution of scientific and philosophical activity, and it is by these means, and these means only, according to Collingwood, that we understand where we are. As Hegel claimed, there is no self-understanding got by gazing inward. Understanding ourselves philosophically means comparing ourselves to others, placing our own concepts and concerns in their historical development. For Collingwood, therefore, there is no split, of the kind that has been made much of in recent philosophy, between treating historical philosophers as great but unlearned contemporaries and treating them as historical material: In all the important respects, the past lives in the present and the present cannot be understood without it.

Wittgenstein's whole conception of philosophy, both in its earlier and later periods, is entirely unhistorical. His concern is with the possibility of thought, truth, and meaning, and with the question of what a language, or a mind or a world, is that such things are possible. His conception of the investigation is thus entirely a priori. The *Tractatus* is describing the preconditions for the possibility of any language; the *Investigations*, while at least embedding language in the activity of its users, remains sublimely indifferent to any historical aspect of that activity. The *Tractatus* attempts to describe what is common to all languages, actual and possible. But likewise, the famous builders whose activities start the later work could equally be in ancient Egypt or modern New York. By contrast, Collingwood's conception of metaphysics saw it as an entirely historical subject, a subject in which argument, proof, and truth are not the field but only a historical understanding of the presuppositions of particular ages. Wittgenstein cheerfully admits to never having read either Hume or Aristotle, and his awareness of the historical development of the problems on which he worked, or the tools he used to work on them, is minimal. With one exception, which I shall come to presently, he presents philosophy as if it were a subject that only accidentally had a history. In this, as I say, even in the later work, he is still at one with the ruling ethos of "analytical philosophy," standing as Kant to Collingwood's Hegel.

1. The Critique of Logical Positivism

A nonhistorical philosophy has to think of its methods as either purely a priori or as continuous with those of unhistorical science. Collingwood entirely mistrusted the first route, and in this he anticipates a large part of modern criticism of the a priori. He writes of Kant that he mistook the historical accidents of seventeenth- and eighteenth-century physics for conditions to be satisfied by any possible physics, and in his *Autobiography* he writes of his contemporaries: "One heard them maintaining the 'axiomatic' or self evident character of doctrines . . . which had first been propounded by very adventurous thinkers, at risk of their own liberty and life . . . and had become part of every educated European's beliefs only after long and fanatical propaganda in the eighteenth century."[1] Attributing an a priori status to any conceptual investigation is an illusion, fostered by failing to realize the contingent, historical evolution of the concepts that form its topic. But equally, the scientific paradigm for such an investigation fails as badly, although to understand why Collingwood, as well as Wittgenstein, thought this we must first turn to his philosophy of mind.

Ryle, Collingwood's successor, was famous for his exorcism of "the ghost in the machine," or in other words his hostility to treating the problems of mind and body as if they concerned the relation of two things, one bodily and physical and the other ghostly. Ryle did not notice that Collingwood preceded him: "The problem of the relation between body and mind is a bogus problem which cannot be stated without making a false assumption . . . for man's body and mind are not two different things. They are one and the same thing, man himself as known in two different ways."[2] The priority does not lie with a metaphysics or an ontology of mind: mind and its place in nature. It lies with understanding the two different epistemologies, that is, the way we know about people's minds, as opposed to the way we know other things about them. The only serious question is the relationship between the sciences of matter—physics, chemistry, and physiology, and knowledge of mind, which in Collingwood means history. To understand mind and its place in nature means first understanding mind and its place in mind. Collingwood calls this epistemology a theory of history, but it is what we with less dignity call a theory of folk psychology. He is quite clear that it is not only concerned with the remote past: "If it is by historical thinking that we re-think and so rediscover the thought of Hammurabi or Solon, it is in the same way that we discover the thought of a friend who writes us a letter, or a stranger who crosses the street," and, he adds, our own thoughts of ten years or five minutes ago.[3]

The twist is that history is autonomous, so that properly speaking there is no science of mind, although there can be sciences of some mental events. As I see it, Collingwood has three interlocking reasons for this doctrine. The first is that to study a person in respect of mental features is to study the person's own self-understanding, and that means the concepts under which she puts herself and her actions—the concepts that determine her plans, his activities and thoughts. The second is that understanding these concepts is not an atomistic project, a matter of finding individual elements of a person, perhaps written in the brain, connected by scientific law with other elements. It is an essentially holistic enterprise that needs to draw on the wider knowledge of the person's human context. These reasons will find echoes in much contemporary philosophy of mind, for example, in the writings of both Davidson and Dennett. The third reason is by far the most distinctive, and it is far harder to pin down. Roughly, it sees psychological understanding as akin to deliberation. Just as when I deliberate I am not in the business of simply predicting my future behavior, so when I come to understand why you acted as you did I am not concerned to place you in a lawlike causal network but to see the point of your doings. In the modern jargon, rationalizing you is a distinct normative activity, not reducible to seeing your behavior just as part of what generally happens, part of a scientifically repeatable pattern. But the modern rediscovery of this idea only plumbs half of it. It treats theorizing under a normative umbrella still as an instance of theorizing, only as one invoking slightly different constraints from the usual. Collingwood went further, and shortly I shall try to say why and how. None of this implies that persons are anything more than the complex physical or physiological systems we know them to be, but it does imply that psychological description of them is description in a different and independent mode.

To explore these themes further, I turn to Collingwood's deep hostility to analytical philosophy. All philosophy is concerned with the nature of thought. Analytical philosophy is a special way of pursuing that concern. It conceives of the data in terms of particular propositions, thought of as complexes of concepts. These propositions are those furnished, usually, by science, mathematics, or common sense. The task of analysis is to "lay bare" what exactly is meant by such propositions, by revealing the perhaps hidden constituent concepts out of which the proposition is constructed.

Propositions have several properties. They are true or false, and they imply or are implied by other propositions. It is the business of a theory of truth to investigate the first property, and of logic to investigate the second. Analytical philosophy was made possible by the extraordinary success of logic, since Frege and Russell, at charting the forms of valid inference and the functional structures, within sentences, that are apparently responsible for them. Finding the hidden structure, and finding what makes for valid or invalid argument thus go hand in hand. But so, apparently, does the theory of truth: Logic, as Quine puts it, chases truth up the tree of grammar. Unfortunately, analytical philosophy has been less successful at producing a theory of truth, or even at agreeing what form such a theory ought to take. The *Tractatus* was the last great substantive theory of truth conforming to the analytical view of the proposition. After it the inclination has been to withdraw from any substantive view of truth at all, and to try not to mourn the loss. Logic rules on alone.

But within this rosy garden there lurks a worm. Propositions have a threefold life. They are not only true and false, and not only the objects of logic. They are also the objects of thought, and it is our relation to them that defines the content of our thought. The central problem of philosophy of logic is understanding how to hold together this triple aspect. The crucial locus of this problem at the beginning of the century—the aspect that dominated Moore and Russell and their wrestlings with the legacy of idealism—was to preserve the objectivity of the proposition, or in other words to free it from the taint of being something purely mental, purely subjective, and to protect its capacity to provide a vehicle for objective truth and knowledge. This requires some distinction between the objective concepts that constitute a proposition and the swirl of subjectivity out of which we are supposed to grasp them. The problem is to give any credible theory of this relation. Frege himself sketches what is necessary to entering the logical paradise: objective concepts, or senses, and objective relations between them, each capable of being "grasped" by the right kind of mind. The most notable result of Frege's determination to free these denizens of paradise from any essential human contamination is the doctrine of the unsaturatedness of the concept—a property that conveniently enables such things to tie together with others to make up a judgment quite without any contribution, any activity or involvement, of someone making the judgment. The history of Russell and Moore's rejection of Hegel, and particularly of the battles over internal relations, is largely a history of objectivists trying to worm their way past the problem of providing for the unity of the proposition, without relying on a subjective activity of the mind. The end of this line is of course Wittgenstein's *Tractatus*, in which the disappearance of mental activity from the power of the proposition to mirror reality is finally complete.

Once the self-standing proposition is allowed as the primary object of philosophical enquiry, its logical structure is ready for analysis. The process is analogous to that whereby a chemist might discover the structure of a material; hence the eventual doctrine of logical atomism. The enquiry is purely internal, and the techniques of analysis require only logic to operate. Logic thus becomes the centerpiece of the philosopher's display, the central fact about the self-standing proposition being its logical structure and its logical links with others. Fundamentalist analytical philosophers therefore believe either in the a priori analysis of timeless conceptual structures or, in a less pure or "naturalized" form, believe in an investigation continuous with that of science into the cognitive and hence logical structures underlying mind and language. History has nothing to do on either model.

At its purest, then, the logician's paradise is a kind of abstraction in which all relations of sense are necessary and timeless. In this paradise live eternal concepts and eternal problems to which they give rise—mind, matter, number, causation, natural law—and anybody who enters it can discuss the same problems in the same way with other inmates—Plato, Aristotle, Descartes, Kant. Obviously such an idea is not empirically given but represents a theoretical overlay free from the historical flux, mess, and muddle that determines our actual use of language. The logician's paradise is only useful, even in theory, if we can get through its doors and establish relations with the timeless propositions that inhabit it. The big question is how anything made of clay gets through these doors.

Why does Collingwood think that Russellian logic needs substituting by what he called a logic of question and answer, and how would this differ? The question is whether the self-standing proposition and its logic is a legitimate object of either a priori or scientific study. It is here that the reflexive nature of thought, the first argument mentioned above, strikes. The question is whether it is an illusion, exactly parallel to the illusion Kant found it the rational psychology of Descartes, to suppose that we can abstract the elements that make the framework of all our thought and turn them into objects of a priori or scientific study, given that in any such study we are bound to remain relying on them. We cannot escape using categories of thought as we study elements of thought, and the understanding we rely on will determine our whole conception of the investigation. Thus if Russell or Frege came to the study of the proposition with a distinctive requirement of logical form and objectivity of sense, modern writers on content such as Fodor or Churchland come with an equally definite concept of representation and reduction; others perhaps rely on shady legacies of positivism, innocently talking of "manifestation" and "experience" as points at which paradise comes down to earth.

The next element I see in Collingwood picks up a common theme in his predecessors F. H. Bradley and H. H. Joachim. This is the importance of realizing that any indicative sentence, such as might express a proposition of classical logic, is embedded in a context that itself plays an essential role in creating the proposition expressed. For Joachim—to whose work on truth Collingwood always refers with the greatest respect—the context is the wider framework of scientific theory. Joachim preceded Quine in his contempt for the idea that a body of knowledge is a "sum, aggregate, collection or class of single truths, each of which is what it is in its singleness. . . . It is as if one were to treat the Choral Symphony as a collection of beautiful sounds, Othello as an aggregate of fine ideas, or a picture by Rembrandt as a sum of colours and lines."[4] Individual sentences retain their significance only so long as they are not severed from the context, the whole that alone forms a determinate unity of significance. This is now a relative commonplace of the philosophy of mind and meaning, but its implications are less well understood. In particular since a fact is what makes a proposition true, if the single proposition is a secondary abstraction from an entire body of thought, the single fact becomes a secondary abstraction from an entire, wholly particular, slice of reality. Then the task of retaining a satisfactory conception of truth obviously becomes formidable.

The reintroduction of context as an essential determinant of the proposition has far-reaching consequences. The chemical model of analysis depends, as I have said, on logical atomism: The self-standing proposition presents itself to the logical eye, and techniques of analysis break open its constitution. Whereas on a holistic model, there is no principled limit to the sources that might have to be tapped to understand a proposition. We need to know about its external surroundings as much as its internal structure: The model becomes not so much the analytical chemist as, again, the historian, telling us where we are by retracing the steps by which we got there. We understand a proposition not by revealing its internal structure but by revealing its place in a whole form of life.

Under a holistic model our relationship to propositions changes profoundly. The prospects for a science of thought dim considerably. There can be no generalizations of the form that whenever people think thus and so they act thus and so, since everything will depend upon an entire matrix, which will not be open to historical duplication. The way in which a thinker moves upon accepting a proposition, either intellectually in terms of finding implications or actively in the sense of finding something that it prompts him to do, can vary without end, depending upon the other elements of his thought. To use an analogy from the theory of chaos, a full psychology will resemble a system whose evolution could never be predicted, not because it is inherently indeterministic but because there could be no such thing as identifying its original state with sufficient accuracy. In natural systems such as the atmosphere this is because of necessary limitations of measurement; in a psychology it is because the impact of one proposition depends upon the unknowably complex context provided by all the others believed to be true to different degrees, or desired to be true with different strengths. It is here that the first blow against a scientific approach to mind is made: Collingwood gleefully accepts the destructive consequences for the positivist sciences of sociology and anthropology. It is a central plank in his claim for the autonomy of history. In a modern setting he might equally gleefully have exposed the destructive consequences for functionalism, or the claim that we understand people by seeing their behavior as the typical outcome of states defined by their typical causes and typical effects—for in Collingwood no such states have any part in our knowledge of thought.

2. The Objectivity of Thought

Collingwood is of course living dangerously. For the other casualty seems to be the objectivity of content, or any useful concept of the shared sense of a single sentence; yet the legitimacy of this very notion is the foundation of any notion of thought at all. Understanding cannot melt back into the flux of transient experience, and Collingwood indeed draws back from this abyss. Although he is sometimes charged with idealism, he is in fact as positive as any follower of Frege, and for the same reasons, that we have to acknowledge the objectivity of thought. In *The Principles of Art* he stresses the contrast between thought and feeling that arises because thought must have as its object things knowable to more than one person and to the same person on more than one occasion. He gives the same message in *The Idea of History*. He is not forthcoming, however, on the means whereby this constraint is met. In particular we should notice that he never turns to the stabilizing conventions of public language as a possible source of the solution. In this he is notably at odds with Wittgenstein's approach, repeated by innumerable followers, although, as I now show, this may not be to his disadvantage.

Tutored by his work in archaeology and history, Collingwood stresses one element of "the context," the element being the question to which a sentence is supposed to provide an answer. Once more we are not to think of the single indicative sentence as a moderately self-sufficient vehicle of propositional content. In this rejected picture the unit of thought, that which is either true or false, is a kind of logical "soul" whose body is the indicative sentence. Whereas, according to Collingwood, not only he but Bacon and Descartes, Plato and Kant had all seen that the true "unit of thought" was not the proposition but something dialectically much more complex in which the proposition served as answer to a question—a question, furthermore, that arises only in some specific historical context. Even Joachim's holism leaves us with the conception of a proposition abstracted out from a total theory, and this theory can be thought of statically, in terms of a total body of sentences expressing some scientific theory or the results of some investigation, whereas Collingwood's stress on questions makes it plain that in his view a proposition cannot be abstracted from anything static. It needs a process, an ongoing activity that takes problems, asks questions, and eventually suggests answers, for any property of truth or falsehood to gain a purchase. Truth only emerges from a *deliberation,* a process that, in his own terms, obeys a principle of minimum time. The parallel with the later Wittgenstein is here immediate, if we remember his view that understanding only exists in the context of a form of life and his remark that a rule cannot be something that is obeyed only once.

Nobody can dispute the brilliance with which Collingwood proceeds to derive a lesson of historical and exegetical methodology from this thought. It follows that you cannot tell whether a proposition is true or false unless you can know what question it was intended to answer, "but also that a proposition which in fact is true can always be thought 'false' by any one who takes the trouble to excogitate a question to which it would have been the wrong answer. . . . And a proposition which in fact is significant can always be thought meaningless by any one who convinces himself that it was intended as an answer to a question which, if it had really been intended to answer it, it would not have answered at all, either rightly or wrongly."[5] Finding the question involves historical inquiry and obviously involves considerable knowledge of the writer's intellectual context. And, as Collingwood drily remarks, if a writer is a classic the question has probably been forgotten, for if the answer he gave was generally acknowledged to be right, people would stop asking the question and begin asking the next question that arose.

We can see that if he is right to insist on the dynamic situation as central to the identification of the objective content of thought, then he is also right to mistrust a simple appeal to language to do the same job. Collingwood sums up his view by pointing out that language is an abstraction from discourse, which is the *activity* (my italics) by which a man means anything. "One does not first acquire a language and then use it. To possess it and to use it are the same."[6] The priority is clear, Wittgensteinian, correct, and often ignored.

What rapidly emerges is that shared language is no empirical solution to the problem, for it requires as much of an act of *historical* thinking to see people as sharing a language as it does to see them as sharing a thought. This is, I believe, sadly ignored by those who think that after Frege, philosophy of language has somehow superseded epistemology as the foundation of philosophy. We can go further: Appeal to shared "grammar" or shared language is not a sufficient determinant of sense if the stabilizing conventions simply show us deeming each other to be related to the same thoughts for the purposes of rubbing along, unless we also hold that the objectivity of thought can spring out of this mutual ceremonial. But in relation to the past it is obvious that the policy of deeming someone who uses the same words to mean what we now mean by them is at best unwise and at worst downright silly. For Collingwood genuine interpretation must emerge from intelligent reenactment, which means knowing enough of the subject's context to know what *must have been the thing to think* in his circumstance, in order to perform the actions he did perform.

All this is true enough, and well worth saying in the climate of a positivism in which facile criticism flourished, uninformed by an intelligent appreciation of what historical philosophers—the despised metaphysicians—were trying to do. But what is its impact on classical logic? Collingwood does not suggest, for instance, that the law of contradiction is threatened because a sentence taken as an answer to one question might say something true, and as an answer to a different question say something false. If this is so, it merely expresses two different propositions. But then it seems that the doctrine of the proposition is flexible enough to accommodate his point. In Russell or Frege propositions do not in fact stand to sentences as souls to bodies: Different sentences may have the same sense, and the same sentence may have a different sense, and will do if ellipsis, ambiguity, or various forms of context dependence arise. Collingwood's own example of context dependence bears out the classical response: Someone may say that the contents of a box form one thing, and also say that they form many things, but there is no contradiction if the first question were how many sets of chessmen the box contained, and the second was how many chess pieces. Ironically, of course, the theory of counting needed here was first developed by Frege and is a cornerstone of the Frege-Russell logic Collingwood takes himself to be attacking. Yet the same example has been put forward recently by Hilary Putnam in a quixotic attempt to persuade us of the relativity of truth to modes of "world-making."[7]

But this is not his real target. Collingwood is clearly not interested in a different "logic" in the sense in which intuitionism, or even relevance logic, or erotetic logic, provides an alternative system of inferential procedures to classical two-valued logic. He is using the term in the same sense as Wittgenstein when he said, "The basic evil of Russell's logic, as also of mine in the Tractatus, is that what a proposition is is illustrated by a few commonplace examples, and then pre-supposed as understood in full generality."[8] Wittgenstein was not ushering in a deviant formal logic, and had no interest in doing so, but he was of course turning his back on the whole early conception of the proposition as a logical picture of a state of affairs—the *Tractatus* solution to the problem of entering paradise.

There is indeed one consequence for formal logic. Collingwood believes that in any system of thought there will be some propositions that do not arise in answer to a question, but themselves form an absolute presupposition of the whole system of inquiry. They function as if they were a priori, although not actually having that status. These will be neither true nor false, but not because of any failure in the indicative sentence that expresses them to have a sense. Wittgenstein was similarly puzzled by the status of propositions that form the riverbed within which inquiry runs, or the hinge upon which everything else swings, and he comes close to denying that they can be regarded as true, if only because we cannot well understand what it would be to regard them as false. But neither Collingwood nor Wittgenstein actually puts the contrast they have in mind to much work, and neither is interested in any change in formal logic that might be suggested.

3. Determining Mental Content
Through Reenactment

We might now pause to consider a likely objection to Collingwood. Granted, it may be said, that "holism" as represented by Joachim and Quine needs a hearing; nevertheless, it does not help its cause to introduce "the question" as a separate element in the formation of meaning, that is, in the crystallization of determinate content for a sentence. For "questions" are on the same side of the problem as propositions. To ask something definite is as much of a feat as to say something definite; to know what someone in some historical setting was asking may be as hard as to know what he was saying. To consider this objection we need to apply Collingwood's own method for a moment and ask more closely what he was trying to do by stressing the importance of the question as a determinant of inquiry.

The great problem is that of explaining what it is that invests signs with meaning, this being whatever makes the difference between the mere shuffling of noises and letters on the one hand, and thought on the other. With thought comes correctness and incorrectness, truth and falsity, and it is in thought that we are related to the logician's propositions and their relations. If our thought has one content it will be correct to say one thing faced with new and potentially divisive cases; if it has a different content it will be correct to say something different; if there is no determinacy of content there will be freedom to pursue either answer. If that is the question, the solution that for thought to be possible the noises and letters must occur as answers to a question, handsomely begs it. For it presupposes that we are already satisfied that some previous episode counted as the asking of a determinate question, and that is a feat no less dependent on thought than the expressing of a proposition. We do not suppose that parrots express propositions, but we do not suppose that they ask questions either.

Of course, this objection applies equally to Joachim or Quine, construed as dealing with the same problem. A lifeless noise is not animated purely by being surrounded by many more of the same. And saying that it occurs as an element of a theory is introducing a term that presupposes thought and intention. The point is not always so obvious. The big question is the central concern of the *Philosophical Investigations* and indeed much of the later work of Wittgenstein. He himself favors the introduction of words like "practice" and "technique." Language mastery is thought of as the mastery of a technique, and it is because his belief that he is operating a technique is supposed to be a sham that the would-be private linguist is unmasked in the famous central polemic. But Wittgenstein is in danger of falling into the same trap, since a technique, as opposed to a movement, is usually something adopted in pursuit of an end that an agent can represent to himself. And conceiving of an agent as doing that is already seeing him as a thinker and planner.

We can see the point like this. If the problem is the big one, it is a condition of its solution that we find an unmoved mover, an uncontentful content giver. It is this requirement that was infringed alike by invoking embedding in a theory, or answering of an antecedent question. But citing technique is not necessarily any better. Technique arises in connection with goals, aims, and purposes. And we should not presume that we know how these are possible, what their presence consists of, if we are still at a stage in which we cannot give any theory of propositional content. It is perhaps most obvious where this shoe pinches if we consider animals or infants. Where the attribution of contentful thought remains moot, so does the issue of whether behavior is genuinely purposeful or genuinely governed by a technique. So it appears that even if Collingwood's stress on the complex of question and answer cannot by itself amount to an answer to the big question, neither can other better-received suggestions.

The problem is perhaps more visible if we consider not how content arrives at all but how it is made determinate, given that it exists. In other words, given that a subject is saying something, how is it fixed exactly what senses his words on this occasion bear? Bare mention of technique, use, or custom is of little help. Suppose there arises a "hard case" or problem of determining correct application of some term to a new circumstance: A determinate technique might enable us to insist on only one answer, but where cases are hard and answers disputed, there is no way of falling back and identifying just one such technique. It is as hard to identify the authority as it is to identify its answer.

It is here that history comes into its own. It is indeed part of a good answer that we need to look at the problematic, the question that use of a concept purports to answer, and the theoretical backdrop of the conversation. Collingwood's questions arise in connection with the same element of technique, or the solving of (nonlinguistic) problems. His proudest examples of his methodology come when he tries to discover what thoughts lie behind an action by asking what problem needed solving. What was Nelson trying to do at Trafalgar, or Hadrian in building his wall? All understanding of what was thought on an occasion is historical understanding, a matter of identifying the activities, the problems and practices and techniques for solving them, of the agents.

Both thinkers therefore offer us a highly modified view of the proposition. To the analyst propositions carve all reality. In any circumstance and under any possibility they will be determinately true or false. But nothing arising in the rooted activities of human beings will have this range. No tool invented to solve a particular problem will be indiscriminately applicable in other situations and circumstances. Truth and falsity and weapons for dealing with them will have to be hammered out if and when they arise (it is ironic therefore that there exists a substantial industry of enlisting Wittgenstein in particular on behalf of legal, ethical, and other "realisms"). Although Wittgenstein and Collingwood may seem to be at one here, it is notable, as I have said, that for Wittgenstein there is little mention of the historical setting within which activities and techniques gain their existence. The idea that his actors will only be visibly doing things in the light of a historical understanding of their position achieved only from inside a "home" point of view is no part of his thought and in this, it seems to me, Collingwood has the edge.

Collingwood is at least clear that we do enter some holistic version of paradise, and I have said a little about his method of arriving. For us the problem of mind and its place in nature is certainly not one, as it was for Kant, of nature and its place in mind. It is mind that has become problematic, and nature is where it must be found; our knowledge of nature is the standard that a proper epistemology of mind needs to imitate. In David Lewis's terms, we don't just want to know how we determine what other people think but how the world determines what we and the others equally think. Yet for Collingwood to know what someone is thinking, it is never sufficient to conduct an "objective" investigation modeled on either observation or theory in natural science. There is no telling what you think except by thinking for myself the same thought, reliving the problem as you saw it and the reenacting the process with which you met it. Natural science and its methods will not certify that a subject thinks such and such; so to describe him is to place him in an essentially normative space, one defined by reasons, implications, and an overall principle of rationality. The similarity between two people who think the same is thus invisible to science. They need not use the same words, since they may speak different languages; they need not behave in the same way, since they may have different beliefs and desires; they need not have the same images or the same neural organization. In the theory of thought there is no unmoved mover—no method except rethinking the same thought for understanding this common property.

There are now three suggestions to compare. We might understand what people think by observation, by theory, or by this kind of dramatic reenactment. These proposals are not necessarily incompatible, but the third at least has to fight for a place in the partnership. In this hermeneutic picture, mind is placed in mind but not scientifically, not in nature. Now if thought is invisible to science, and science alone tells us what there is, then the gates not only of the analyst's paradise but even of any downscale suburb slam shut. This is Quine's conclusion. For him, description of what people think and believe and desire is not a way of limning the true nature of the world. Instead it is partaking in what he calls, unconsciously echoing Collingwood, an "essentially dramatic idiom." The trouble is that tough-minded seekers after truth have no patience with dramatic idiom. Many are therefore left promoting skepticism about thought and truth: the elimination of propositional attitude psychology. These thinkers follow the "theory" paradigm. Psychological description of people, it is said, formed part of an old theory of behavior, but like all old theories it is vulnerable to obsolescence as newer models come along. In this case the newer model promises to be computational, with computations exercised not on thoughts but on "sentences in the head." The mind becomes a syntactic engine whose workings can be understood, like the transitions of state of a digital computer, without invoking any conception of the content, nor the truth or falsity, of the arrays of machine code it transforms. But Collingwood has an argument against any such position that has also recently been rediscovered: It must be an absolute, nonnegotiable presupposition of any inquiry into mind that its subject matter is real. For otherwise we face a pragmatic self-refutation: The sayings of those who would deny it are not, by their own doctrines, to be construed as genuine denials, for so interpreting them is going beyond the only reality they want to acknowledge.

It is here that the contrast between reenacting deliberation and just theorizing really has its home. Similarly, when I deliberate, I am not predicting what I shall think but trying to think. Thus when I interpret you by reliving your position and wondering what to think, I am not primarily theorizing about you but instead wondering what is to be thought, and therefore must have been thought, in your situation. This is what it is to "make your words my own." But deliberation is not optional to us as human beings. There is indeed an artificial, alienated, second-order stance in which I can wonder whether I ever really think, or whether all that happens is that words and images go through my head, while behavior independently takes place. But this is not a second-order reflection that can coexist with real problems, real decisions, and real actions, nor with the modes of thinking inevitably forced upon me by the need to cope with the world. Thinking is not optional, and using beliefs and desires is not a potentially optional piece of theorizing but part and parcel of thinking itself. I can, of course, refuse to embrace *you* as someone in the same kinds of situation and with the same kinds of resource to meet it: refuse to treat you as a rule follower or insider. But this would be mere psychopathology.

It may be objected that in the dramatic story my own first-person certainties are given too much of a foundational status. Some would say that we have learned from Wittgenstein that third-person and first-person psychology are, in essence, in the same boat. Treating you as a rule follower, as an insider, is then much the same as treating myself as one. But in any sense in which this is true, it does not differentiate Wittgenstein from Collingwood. Collingwood's account of self-consciousness is forthright:

> The child's discovery of itself as a person is also its discovery of itself as a member of a world of persons. . . . The discovery of myself as a person is the discovery that I can speak, and am thus a persona or speaker; in speaking I am both speaker and hearer; and since the discovery of myself as a person is also the discovery of other persons around me, it is the discovery of speakers and hearers other than myself.[9]

So it is not as if the self-understanding Collingwood demands is the outcome of prior observation of oneself or theorizing about oneself. If it were, skepticism about my own beliefs and meanings would get a foothold that, in spite of Quine, and Kripke's Wittgenstein, it cannot have. And incidentally, Wittgenstein too understood well that "my own relation to my own words is wholly different from other people's":[10] It is the whole source of his fascination with Moore's paradox.

Nevertheless the tradition of humane studies that follows Wittgenstein ignores these hints and copes differently with the problem. It realizes that the attitude that psychological interpretation, or history, is just science done on a macroscopic scale was anathema to Wittgenstein just as much as Collingwood. So, ignoring the dramatic option, it goes for the observational: Our thoughts are said to be manifested in our behavior, manifested to the suitable perceiver, who then sees what we think and mean, just as she can see our emotions in our face or hear the sadness of a musical phrase. In Dummett's expression of this idea the slogan "meaning is use" is even taken to imply that meaning is observable use, conjuring up the vision of the professor of physics required to display his understanding of nature to an audience that can only gape. The restriction is an unmotivated legacy of positivism: All that we can properly get from the slogan is that understanding is capable of being exercised in our activities, not that it is manifested to anyone at all, except to those capable of reliving it—of making the words their own. If there is any virtue in the observational direction it must lie not in simply appropriating the vocabulary of perception to what on the face of it need not be a perceptual matter. It is rather the message that nothing else can be done. Mind is seen by mind; it is even constituted by mutual relationships, but there is no independent perspective from which its relationship to nature is to be understood.

Partisans of the "theory" paradigm are unimpressed. They point out, rightly, that nothing is gained by mentioning observation as if it were usefully distinguishable from theory. Of course, when I hear your words, I spontaneously know what you said, and if I have reason to trust you, I spontaneously believe you. But this is spontaneously applying what is in fact a theoretical terminology—one given its identity and its point by different theses that govern our understanding of others. And in this crucial point the theorists are right. It does not matter that it sounds odd to say that the principles of common understanding form a theory. The question is whether a person is only equipped to know what others think in virtue of a capacity, call it perceptual or not, that uses data in accordance with theoretical principles. And once this is the question, there is no contest.

It might be said that in an analogous manner the computational processes underlying the interpretation of the visual scene are not processes that we perform but processes that the adapted brain performs for us. However, this model is slightly misleading. Whatever computations underlie normal visual perception are hidden from us. In the jargon, they amount to subcognitive states; my brain deals magnificently with the bombardment of photons, but I myself have no control over the process. Whereas processes of interpretation are frequently highly self-conscious, the feats of understanding required to see what Homer means or to get inside the mind of a four-year-old or to see what Cezanne was trying to do are feats that are not performed for us by hard wiring. They are things we do, well or badly, with imagination, with learning, and often with difficulty. We might end up saying that we "see" each other's meaning and thought, but a purely perceptual model only disguises the feats of understanding necessary for us to do any such thing.

The rival pictures of the epistemology are, on the one hand, that our thoughts are detected by suitably tuned receivers, either perceptually or via some inchoate theory, and, on the other hand, that there is an element of reenactment, of projection into another's situation, in understanding. It is not at all obvious that these views are in competition, but it seems to me clear that the dramatic model either wins or at least deserves a senior partnership. This, to repeat, is because of the inexorability of the "home case": the impossibility of taking a coherent rational stance to the world that is not conducted in terms of deciding on truth or falsity, what to believe, and what to desire. It is, in the end, because of this inexorability that we are not just theorizing when we enter into the intentional stance but, as Kant almost certainly saw, doing something much more intimately connected with the very possibility of thought itself.

We end, indeed, with a picture of mind as visible only in the perspective of a like-minded interpreter. This has an element highly reminiscent of Kant. Kant's Copernican revolution solved the problem of access to the world by making the world essentially ours: The understanding is the author of the experience in which its objects are found. This stroke proved too bold for most readers, and the century following Kant was preoccupied with avoiding it. It sounds less bad to us to say that the understanding is the author of the understanding it can find in others, which is the hermeneutic turn we are here entered upon. It had better sound less bad because no modern thinker known to me has offered a stable way of saying anything better.

Conclusion

I will now draw back from these deep themes and close by reflecting on the different standing of Collingwood and Wittgenstein. For in saying a little to resurrect Collingwood, I have not intended to bury Wittgenstein the man but only perhaps Wittgenstein the god. When I came to write this lecture a friend said that I might with more justice have called it Collingwoodian themes in Wittgenstein. But when I looked in the *Philosophers Index* there were as I expected hundreds of entries indexed under Wittgenstein but just four under Collingwood. Obviously this tells us that we are not nowadays interested in philosophy of art or of history. But, if I am right in drawing the comparisons I have done, I think it tells us something else about academic sociology. Collingwood, it is true, can alienate sympathy by his brusque, no-nonsense tone; by comparison Wittgenstein's dedication to the difficulties of mining his material has proved to have an irresistible moral and aesthetic resonance. But I think there is something still further, and perhaps less healthy, that determines our allegiances. Collingwood wrote disparagingly of aesthetic individualism, which "conceives a man as if he were God, a self-contained and self-sufficient creative power whose only task is to be himself and to exhibit his nature in whatever works are appropriate to it."[11] He could almost have had in mind Wittgenstein's parade of utter self-absorption in his own quest, for instance, his indifference to other philosophers, particularly the living pragmatist and holistic tradition that surrounded him. The one case in which Wittgenstein concedes that a historical understanding is necessary to reading him relates to his own history, when he says magisterially that his later philosophy can only be seen in the right light by contrast with and against the background of his own old way of thinking. We like romantic grandeur, and we collaborate all too readily in the self-image of the lone genius, solitary on his peaks of thought; it spares us the labor of reading and understanding other philosophers. Nor was Wittgenstein short of the emotional armaments commonly used to ensnare disciples, and these included completely ignoring the pragmatic, holistic, and hermeneutic traditions surrounding him. In ignoring them too we fail to understand the history of modern philosophy and for that matter Wittgenstein as we should; instead we painfully set about rediscovering paths already trodden.

Notes

This paper is a lightly edited version of a talk given in honor of Collingwood's centenary in Oxford in 1989. I stand by much of it, although some things I might put differently now. I have not attempted to incorporate mention of more recent work on empathy and simulation. I am grateful that in spite of this the editors have encouraged me to place it in this volume.

1. Collingwood 1939, p. 65.
2. Collingwood 1942, sec. 2, pp. 10–11.
3. Collingwood 1946, p. 219.
4. Joachim 1906, p. 102.
5. Collingwood 1939, p. 38.
6. Collingwood 1938, p. 250.
7. See, for instance, Putnam 1987.
8. Wittgenstein 1980, vol. 1, sec. 48.
9. Collingwood 1938, p. 248.
10. Wittgenstein 1958, p. 192.
11. Collingwood 1938, p. 316.

References

Abel, Theodore. 1948. "The Operation Called *Verstehen.*" *American Journal of Sociology* 54, 211–218. Reprinted in *Understanding and Social Inquiry,* edited by Fred Dallmayr and Thomas McCarthy. Notre Dame, Ind.: Notre Dame University Press.

Adorno, Theodore W., et al. 1982. *The Authoritarian Personality.* New York: Norton.

Alexy, Robert. 1989. *A Theory of Legal Argumentation: The Theory of Rational Discourse as a Theory of Legal Justification.* Oxford: Oxford University Press.

Alston, William. 1989. *Epistemic Justification.* Ithaca, N.Y.: Cornell University Press.

Anscombe, G. E. M. 1957. *Intention.* Oxford: Basil Blackwell.

Apel, Karl-Otto. 1967. *Analytic Philosophy of Action and the Geisteswissenschaften.* Dordrecht: D. Reidel.

Apel, Karl-Otto, et al. 1971. *Hermeneutik und Ideologiekritik.* Frankfurt: Suhrkamp Verlag.

Averill, James R. 1980. "Emotion and Anxiety: Sociocultural, Biological, and Psychological Determinants." In *Explaining Emotions,* edited by Amelie O. Rorty. Berkeley: University of California Press.

Averill, James R. 1994. "In the Eyes of the Beholder." In *The Nature of Emotions,* edited by Paul Ekman and Richard Davidson, 7–14. Oxford: Oxford University Press.

Baldwin, James Mark. [1895] 1906. *Mental Development in the Child and the Race.* 3d ed. Reprint, Darby, Pa.: Darby Books/Fairfield, N.J.: A. M. Kelley, 1966.

Barley, Nigel. 1986. *The Innocent Anthropologist.* New York: Viking Penguin.

Berenbaum, M., and A. J. Peck, eds. 1998. *The Holocaust and History: The Known, the Unknown, the Disputed, and the Reexamined.* Indianapolis: Indiana University Press.

Berg, George. 1992. "A Connectionist Parser with Recursive Sentence Structure and Lexical Disambiguation." In *AAAI–92: Proceedings of the Tenth National Conference on Artificial Intelligence.* Cambridge: AAAI Press/MIT Press.

Berkhofer, Robert F., Jr. 1997. *Beyond the Great Story.* Cambridge: Harvard University Press.

Bohman, James. 1991. *New Philosophy of Social Science: Problems of Indeterminacy.* Cambridge: MIT Press.

Bohman, James. 1996. *Public Deliberation: Pluralism, Complexity, and Democracy.* Cambridge: MIT Press.

Bohman, James. Forthcoming. "Formal Pragmatics as a Critical Theory." In *Perspectives on Habermas,* edited by L. Hahn. Indianapolis: Open Court.

Bohman, James, and Terrence Kelly. 1996. "Rationality, Intelligibility, and Comparison: The Rationality Debates Revisited." *Philosophy and Social Criticism* 22, 1, 181–200.

Bonjour, Laurence. 1985. *The Structure of Empirical Knowledge.* Cambridge: Harvard University Press.

Brandom, Robert. 1988. "Pragmatism, Phenomenalism, Truth Talk." In *Midwest Studies in Philosophy,* edited by P. French, T. Uehling, and H. Wettstein, 12, 75–93. Minneapolis: University of Minnesota Press.

Brandom, Robert. 1994. *Making It Explicit: Reasoning, Representing, and Discursive Commitment.* Cambridge: Harvard University Press.

Broszat, Martin, and Saul Friedländer. 1988. "A Controversy about the Historicization of National Socialism." *New German Critique* 15, 85–126.

Browning, Christopher. 1992. *Ordinary Men: Reserve Police Battalion 101 and the Final Solution in Poland.* New York: HarperCollins.

Bruner, Jerome. 1990. *Acts of Meaning.* Cambridge: Harvard University Press.

Carr, David. 1985. "Life and the Narrator's Art." In *Hermeneutics and Deconstruction,* edited by H. Silverman and D. Ihde. Albany: SUNY Press.

Carr, David. 1986a. *Time, Narrative, and History.* Indianapolis: Indiana University Press.

Carr, David. 1986b. "Narrative and the Real World: An Argument for Continuity." *History and Theory* 25, 118–131.

Carruthers, Peter, and Peter Smith, eds. 1996. *Theories of Theories of Mind.* Cambridge: Cambridge University Press.

Cassirer, Ernst. 1985. *Philosophy of Symbolic Forms.* Vol. 3. New Haven: Yale University Press.

Cherniak, Christopher. 1986. *Minimal Rationality.* Cambridge: MIT Press.

Churchland, Paul A. 1979. *Scientific Realism and the Plasticity of Mind.* Cambridge: Cambridge University Press.

Collingwood, Robin George. 1938. *The Principles of Art.* Oxford: Clarendon.

Collingwood, Robin George. 1939. *An Autobiography.* Oxford: Clarendon.

Collingwood, Robin George. 1942. *New Leviathan; or, Man, Society, and Barbarism.* Oxford: Clarendon.

Collingwood, Robin George. 1946. *The Idea of History.* Oxford: Clarendon.

Cook, Gary A. 1993. *George Herbert Mead: The Making of a Social Pragmatist.* Urbana: University of Illinois Press.

Cooper, David. 1996. "*Verstehen,* Holism, and Fascism." In *Verstehen and Humane Understanding,* edited by Anthony O'Hear. Cambridge: Cambridge University Press.

Danto, Arthur. 1965. *Analytical Philosophy of History.* Cambridge: Cambridge University Press.

Danto, Arthur. 1985. *Narration and Knowledge.* New York: Columbia University Press.

Darwin, Charles. 1988. *The Expression of Emotions in Man and Animals.* New York: Oxford University Press.

Davidson, Donald. 1963. "Actions, Reasons, and Causes." *Journal of Philosophy* 60, 685–700. Reprinted in Donald Davidson. 1980. *Essays on Actions and Events.*

Davidson, Donald. 1980. *Essays on Actions and Events*. Oxford: Oxford University Press.

Davidson, Donald. 1984. *Inquiries into Truth and Interpretation*. Oxford: Clarendon.

Davidson, Donald. 1985. "Incoherence and Irrationality." *Dialectica* 39, 345–354.

Davidson, Donald. 1986. "Radical Interpretation." In *Inquiries into Truth and Interpretation*, 125–140. Oxford: Oxford University Press.

Davidson, Donald. 1987. "Problems in the Explanation of Action." In *Metaphysics and Morality*, edited by Philip Pettit et al., 35–49. Oxford: Oxford University Press.

Davidson, Donald. 1994. "Structure and Content of Truth." *Journal of Philosophy* 87, 279–328.

Davies, Martin, and Tony Stone, eds. 1995a. *Folk Psychology*. Oxford: Blackwell.

Davies, Martin, and Tony Stone, eds. 1995b. *Mental Simulation*. Oxford: Blackwell.

Dennett, Daniel. 1987. *The Intentional Stance*. Cambridge: MIT Press.

Devitt, Michael. 1993. "A Critique of the Case of Semantic Holism." *Philosophical Perspectives* 7, 281–306.

Dilthey, Wilhelm. 1927. *Gesammelte Schriften*. Leipzig: B. G. Teubner.

Dilthey, Wilhelm. 1977a. "Ideas Concerning a Descriptive and Analytic Psychology." In *Descriptive Psychology and Historical Understanding*. The Hague: Martinus Nijhoff.

Dilthey, Wilhelm. 1977b. "The Understanding of Other Persons and Their Life-Expressions." In *Descriptive Psychology and Historical Understanding*. The Hague: Martinus Nijhoff.

Dilthey, Wilhelm. 1981. *Der Aufbau der geschichtlichen Welt in den Geisteswissenschaften*. Frankfurt: Suhrkamp Verlag.

Dilthey, Wilhelm. 1982a. *Gesammelte Schriften*. Vol. 5, *Die Geistige Welt*. Stuttgart: B. G. Teubner Verlagsgesellschaft.

Dilthey, Wilhelm. 1982b. *Gesammelte Schriften*. Vol. 7, *Der Aufbau der Geschichtlichen Welt in den Geisteswissenschaften*. Stuttgart: B. G. Teubner Verlagsgesellschaft.

Dilthey, Wilhelm. 1989. *Introduction to the Human Sciences*. Vol. 1 of *Selected Works*. Edited by Rudolf A. Makkreel and Frithjof Rodi. Princeton: Princeton University Press.

Dilthey, Wilhelm. 1996. "The Rise of Hermeneutics." In *Hermeneutics and the Study of History*, edited by Rudolf A. Makkreel and Frithjof Rodi. Vol. 4 of *Selected Works*. Princeton: Princeton University Press.

Dray, William. 1957. *Laws and Explanation in History*. Oxford: Clarendon.

Dreyfus, Hubert. 1980. "Holism and Hermeneutics." *Review of Metaphysics* 34, 3–23.

Dreyfus, Hubert. 1991. *Being-in-the-World*. Cambridge: MIT Press.

Dreyfus, Hubert, and Paul Rabinow. 1983. *Michel Foucault: Beyond Structuralism and Hermeneutics*. Chicago: University of Chicago Press.

Dummett, Michael. 1995. *The Seas of Language*. Oxford: Oxford University Press.

Eisenberg, Nancy, and Janet Strayer, eds. 1987. *Empathy and Its Development*. Cambridge: Cambridge University Press.

Ekman, Paul. 1973. "Cross-Cultural Studies of Facial Expressions." In *Darwin and Facial Expression,* edited by Paul Ekman. New York: Academic Press.

Ekman, Paul. 1980. "Biological and Cultural Contributions to Body and Facial Movement in the Expression of Emotions." In *Explaining Emotions,* edited by Amelie Rorty, 73–101. Berkeley: University of California Press.

Ekman, Paul. 1993. "Facial Expression of Emotion." *American Psychologist* 48, 384–392.

Ekman, Paul, and Richard Davidson. 1994. *The Nature of Emotions.* Oxford: Oxford University Press.

Ekman, Paul, and W. V. Friesen. 1971. "Constants Across Culture in the Face and Emotion." *Journal of Personality and Social Psychology* 17, 124–129.

Elgin, Catherine Z. 1996. *Considered Judgment.* Princeton: Princeton University Press.

Ellis, Hayden. 1998. "Face Values." *Times Higher Education Supplement,* May 15.

Evans-Pritchard, Edward. 1937. *Witchcraft, Oracles, and Magic Among the Azande.* Oxford: Oxford University Press.

Fingarette, Herbert. 1972. *Confucius: The Secular as Sacred.* New York: Harper and Row.

Fodor, Jerry. 1983. *The Modularity of Mind: An Essay in Faculty Psychology.* Cambridge: MIT Press.

Fodor, Jerry. 1987. *Psychosemantics.* Cambridge: MIT Press.

Fodor, Jerry. 1995. "A Theory of the Child's Theory of Mind." In *Mental Simulation,* edited by Martin Davies and Tony Stone, 109–122.

Fodor, Jerry, and Ernest Lepore. 1992. *Holism: A Shopper's Guide.* Oxford: Blackwell.

Follesdal, Dagfinn. 1979. "Hermeneutics and the Hypothetico-Deductive Method." *Dialectica* 33, 319–336.

Foucault, Michel. 1978. *History of Sexuality.* Vol. 1. New York: Random House.

Foucault, Michel. 1979. *Discipline and Punish: The Birth of the Prison.* New York: Pantheon.

Foucault, Michel. 1985. *The Use of Pleasure.* New York: Pantheon.

Frank, Manfred, ed. 1990. "Einleitung des Herausgebers." In *Schleiermacher: Hermeneutik und Kritik,* 7–67. Frankfurt: Suhrkamp Verlag.

Friedländer, Saul, ed. 1992. *Probing the Limits of Representation.* Cambridge: Harvard University Press.

Gadamer, Hans-Georg. 1989. *Truth and Method.* New York: Crossroad.

Gadamer, Hans-Georg. 1990. "Reply to my Critics." In *The Hermeneutic Tradition,* edited by Gayle Ormiston and Alan Schrift, 273–297. Albany: SUNY Press.

Galison, Peter. 1987. *How Experiments End.* Chicago: University of Chicago Press.

Geertz, Clifford. 1973a. *The Interpretation of Cultures.* New York: Basic.

Geertz, Clifford. 1973b. "Thick Description." In *The Interpretation of Cultures,* 3–30. New York: Basic.

Geertz, Clifford. 1986. "The Uses of Diversity." *Michigan Quarterly Review* 23, 122–123.

Geertz, Clifford. 1995. "Culture Wars." *New York Review of Books* 42, November 30, 4–6.

Goldman, Alvin I. 1992. "In Defense of Simulation Theory." *Mind and Language* 7, 104–119. Reprinted in *Folk Psychology,* edited by Martin Davies and Tony Stone. Oxford: Blackwell.

Goldman, Alvin I. 1993a. *Philosophical Applications of Cognitive Science.* Boulder: Westview.

Goldman, Alvin I. 1993b. "The Psychology of Folk Psychology." *Behavioral and Brain Sciences* 16, 15–28.

Goldman, Alvin. 1995a. "Interpretation Psychologized." In *Folk Psychology,* edited by Martin Davies and Tony Stone, 185–208. Oxford: Blackwell.

Goldman, Alvin. 1995b. "Empathy, Mind, and Morals." In *Mental Simulation,* edited by Martin Davies and Tony Stone, 74–99. Oxford: Blackwell.

Goldman, Alvin. 1995c. "In Defense of Simulation Theory." In *Folk Psychology,* edited by Martin Davies and Tony Stone, 191–206. Oxford: Blackwell.

Goldman, Alvin. 1996. "Simulation and Interpersonal Utility." In *Mind and Morals,* edited by Larry May, Marilyn Friedman, and Andy Clark, 181–198. Cambridge: MIT Press.

Gopnik, Alison, and Andrew Meltzoff. 1997. *Words, Thoughts, and Theories.* Cambridge: MIT Press.

Gopnik, Alison, and Henry Wellman. 1995. "Why the Child's Theory of Mind Really *Is* a Theory." In *Folk Psychology,* edited by Martin Davies and Tony Stone, 232–258. Oxford: Blackwell.

Gordon, Robert M. 1987. *The Structure of Emotions.* Cambridge: Cambridge University Press.

Gordon, Robert M. 1995a. "Folk-Psychology as Simulation." In *Folk Psychology,* edited by Martin Davies and Tony Stone, 60–73. Oxford: Blackwell.

Gordon, Robert M. 1995b. "Simulation Without Introspection from Me to You." In *Mental Simulation,* edited by Martin Davies and Tony Stone, 53–67. Oxford: Blackwell.

Gordon, Robert M. 1995c. "The Simulation Theory: Objections and Misconceptions." In *Folk Psychology,* edited by Martin Davies and Tony Stone, 100–122. Oxford: Blackwell.

Gordon, Robert M. 1996a. "'Radical' Simulationism." In *Theories of Theories of Mind,* edited by Peter Carruthers and Peter Smith, 11–21. Cambridge: Cambridge University Press.

Gordon, Robert M. 1996b. "Sympathy, Simulation, and the Impartial Spectator." In *Mind and Morals,* edited by Larry May, Marilyn Friedman, and Andy Clark, 165–180. Cambridge: MIT Press.

Grandy, Richard. 1973. "Reference, Meaning, and Belief." *Journal of Philosophy* 70, 439–452.

Greenspan, Patricia. 1988. *Emotions and Reasons.* London: Routledge.

Grice, H. P. 1957. "Meaning." *Philosophical Review* 66, 377–388.

Grossberg, Larry, Cary Nelson, and Paula Treichler, eds. 1992. *Cultural Studies.* London: Routledge.

Grünbaum, Adolf. 1976. "The Duhemian Argument." In *Can Theories Be Refuted?,* edited by Sandra Harding. Dordrecht: Reidel.

Habermas, Jürgen. 1971. *Knowledge and Human Interest.* Boston: Beacon.

Habermas, Jürgen. 1984. *Theory of Communicative Action*. Vol. 1. Boston: Beacon.

Habermas, Jürgen. 1987. *Theory of Communicative Action*. Vol. 2. Boston: Beacon.

Habermas, Jürgen. 1988. *The Logic of the Social Sciences*. Translated by Shierry Weber Nicholson and Jerry Stark. Cambridge: MIT Press.

Habermas, Jürgen. 1990. "The Hermeneutic Claim to Universality." In *The Hermeneutic Tradition*, edited by Gayle Ormiston and Alan Schrift, 245–272. New York: SUNY Press.

Habermas, Jürgen. 1992. "Toward a Critique of the Theory of Meaning." In *Postmetaphysical Thinking*, 58–87. Cambridge: MIT Press.

Habermas, Jürgen. 1995. "Discourse Ethics: Notes on a Program of Philosophical Justification." In *Moral Consciousness and Communicative Action*, 43–115. Cambridge: MIT Press.

Habermas, Jürgen. 1996. *Between Facts and Norms*. Cambridge: MIT Press.

Haney, Craig, Curtis Banks, and Philip Zimbardo. 1973. "Interpersonal Dynamics in a Simulated Prison." *International Journal of Criminology and Penology* 1, 69–97.

Hansen, Chad. 1998. "The Zhuangzi (Chuang Tzu): 'In the Social World: Is Anything Left of Lao-Zhuang Daoism?'" http://www.hku.hk/philodep/ch/mind.htm#concept.

Harré, Rom, and Grant Gillet. 1994. *The Discursive Mind*. Thousand Oaks, Calif.: Sage.

Harris, Paul. 1989. *Children and Emotion: The Development of Psychological Understanding*. Oxford: Blackwell.

Harris, Paul. 1992. "From Simulation to Folk Psychology." *Mind and Language* 7, 120–144. Reprinted in *Folk Psychology*, edited by Martin Davies and Tony Stone. Oxford: Blackwell.

Harris, Paul. 1996. "Desires, Beliefs, and Language." In *Theories of Theories of Mind*, edited by Peter Carruthers and Peter Smith, 200–220. Cambridge: Cambridge University Press.

Heal, Jane. 1994. "Simulation vs. Theory Theory: What Is at Issue?" In *Objectivity, Simulation, and the Unity of Consciousness*, edited by Christopher Peacocke, 129–144. Proceedings of the British Academy 83. Oxford: Oxford University Press.

Heal, Jane 1995a. "Replication and Functionalism." In *Folk Psychology*, edited by Martin Davies and Tony Stone, 45–59. Oxford: Blackwell.

Heal, Jane. 1995b. "How to Think About Thinking." In *Mental Simulation*, edited by Martin Davies and Tony Stone, 33–52. Oxford: Blackwell.

Heal, Jane. 1996a. "Simulation and Cognitive Penetrability." *Mind and Language* 11, 44–67.

Heal, Jane. 1996b. "Simulation, Theory and Content." In *Theories of Theories of Mind*, edited by Peter Carruthers and Peter Smith, 75–89. Cambridge: Cambridge University Press.

Heal, Jane. 1998. "Co-cognition and Off-line Simulation. *Mind and Language* 13, 477–498.

Heidegger, Martin. 1962. *Being and Time*. New York: Harper and Row.

Heil, John. 1992. "Believing Reasonably." *Nous* 26, 47–62.

Heil, John, and Alfred Mele, eds. 1995. *Mental Causation.* Oxford: Clarendon Press.

Hempel, Carl. 1965. *Aspects of Scientific Explanations.* New York: Free Press

Henderson, David. 1993. *Interpretation and Explanation in the Human Sciences.* Albany: SUNY Press.

Henderson, David. 1994a. "Epistemic Competence." *Philosophical Papers* 23, 139–167.

Henderson, David. 1994b. "Conceptual Schemes After Davidson." In *Language, Mind, and Epistemology,* edited by G. Preyer et al. Dordrecht: Kluwer Academic Publishers, 171–197.

Henderson, David. 1995. "Simulation Theory Versus Theory Theory: A Difference Without a Difference in Explanations." *Southern Journal of Philosophy*, 34, Suppl., 65–93.

Henderson, David, and Terence Horgan. Forthcoming. "Iceberg Epistemology." In *Philosophy and Phenomenological Research.*

Henderson, David, and Terence Horgan. Forthcoming. "Practicing Safe Epistemology."

Hesse, Mary. 1974. *The Structure of Scientific Inference.* London: Macmillan.

Hesse, Mary. 1980. *Revolutions and Reconstructions in the Philosophy of Science.* Brighton, U.K.: Harvester.

Hiley, David, James Bohman, and Richard Shusterman. 1991. *The Interpretive Turn.* Ithaca: Cornell University Press.

Hirsch, E. D., Jr. 1967. *Validity in Interpretation.* New Haven: Yale University Press.

Hollis, Martin. 1970a. "The Limits of Irrationality." In *Rationality*, edited by Brian Wilson, 214–220. New York: Harper and Row.

Hollis, Martin. 1970b. "Reason and Ritual." In *Rationality*, edited by Brian Wilson, 221–239. New York: Harper and Row.

Hollis, Martin. 1972. "Witchcraft and Winchcraft." *Philosophy of Social Science* 2, 89–103.

Hollis, Martin, and Stephen Lukes, eds. 1982. *Rationality and Relativism.* Cambridge: MIT Press.

Horgan, Terence. 1997. "Connectionism and the Philosophical Foundations of Cognitive Science." *Metaphilosophy* 28, 1–30.

Horgan, Terence, and John Tienson. 1990. "Soft Laws." *Midwest Studies in Philosophy* 15, 256–279.

Horgan, Terence, and John Tienson. 1994. "A Nonclassical Framework for Cognitive Science." *Synthese* 101, 305–345.

Horgan, Terence, and John Tienson. 1995. "Connectionism and the Commitments of Folk Psychology." *Philosophical Perspectives* 9, 127–152.

Horgan, Terence, and John Tienson. 1996. *Connectionism and the Philosophy of Psychology.* Cambridge: MIT Press.

Horkheimer, Max. 1987. "Autorität und Familie in der Gegenwart." In *Gesammelte Schriften 5*, 377–395. Frankfurt: Fischer Verlag.

Horkheimer, Max, and Theodore W. Adorno. 1996. *Dialectic of Enlightenment.* New York: Continuum.

Hoy, David, and Thomas McCarthy. 1994. *Critical Theory.* Oxford: Blackwell.

Humphreys, Paul. 1989. *The Chances of Explanation.* Princeton: Princeton University Press.

Iggers, Georg 1997. *Historiography in the Twentieth Century: From Scientific Objectivity to Postmodern Challenge.* Hanover, N.H.: Wesleyan University Press.

Jay, Martin. 1973. *The Dialectical Imagination: A History of the Frankfurt School and the Institute of Social Research, 1923–1950.* Boston: Little, Brown.

Joachim, Harold H. 1906. *The Nature of Truth.* Oxford: Clarendon.

Kannsteiner, Wulf. 1993. "Hayden White's Critique of the Writing of History." *History and Theory* 32, 273–295.

Kessler, Hubert. 1941. "Basic Factors in the Growth of Mind and Self: Analysis and Reconstruction of G. H. Mead's Theory." Ph.D. diss., University of Illinois.

Kim, Jaegwon. 1993. *Supervenience and Mind.* Cambridge: Cambridge University Press.

Kim, Jaegwon. 1996. *Philosophy of Mind.* Boulder: Westview.

Kim, Jaegwon. 1998. *Mind in a Physical World.* Cambridge: MIT Press.

Kitcher, Philip. 1992. "The Naturalist Returns." *Philosophical Review* 101, 53–114.

Klemperer, Victor. 1998. *I Will Bear Witness: A Diary of the Nazi Years.* New York: Random House.

Kögler, Hans Herbert. 1994. *Michel Foucault: Ein anti-humanistischer Aufklärer.* Stuttgart: J. B. Metzler Verlag.

Kögler, Hans Herbert. 1996a. *The Power of Dialogue.* Cambridge: MIT Press.

Kögler, Hans Herbert. 1996b. "The Self-Empowered Subject: Habermas, Foucault, and Hermeneutic Reflexivity." In *Philosophy and Social Criticism,* 22, 13–44.

Kögler, Hans Herbert. 1996c. "Symbolic Self-Consciousness. Rethinking Reflexivity After Mead and Semiotics." In *Studies in Symbolic Interactionism,* 20, 193–223.

Kögler, Hans Herbert. 1997a. "Alienation as Epistemological Source: Reflexivity and Social Background After Mannheim and Bourdieu." In *Social Epistemology,* 141–164. London: Taylor and Francis.

Kögler, Hans Herbert. 1997b. "Reconceptualizing Reflexive Sociology: A Reply." In *Social Epistemology,* 223–250. London: Taylor and Francis.

Kögler, Hans Herbert. 1999. "Kritische Hermeneutik des Subjekts: Cultural Studies als Erbe der Kritischen Theorie." In *Widerspenstige Kulturen: Cultural Studies als Herausforderung,* edited by Karl Hörnig and Rainer Winter. Frankfurt: Suhrkamp Verlag.

Kripke, Saul. 1982. *Wittgenstein on Rules and Private Language.* Cambridge: Harvard University Press.

Leach, Edward. 1967. "Virgin Birth." In *Genesis as Myth and Other Essays,* 85–112. London: Cape.

Levine, Michael. 1991. "Historical Anti-Realism: Boethian Historians Tell Their Story." *Monist* 74, 230–239.

Levine, Michael, and Jeff Malpas. 1994. "'Telling It Like It Was': History and the Ideal Chronicle." *Australasian Journal of Philosophy* 72, 151–172.

Lipps, Theodor. 1979. "Empathy, Inner Imitation, and Sense-Feelings." In *A Modern Book of Esthetics,* edited by Melvin Rader. 5th ed. New York: Holt, Rinehart, and Winston.

Little, Daniel. 1991. *Varieties of Social Explanation.* Boulder: Westview.

Louch, A. 1966. *Explanation and Human Action.* Berkeley: University of California Press.

Luhmann, Niklas. 1986. *Love as Passion: The Codification of Intimacy.* Cambridge: Harvard University Press.

Lukes, Stephen. 1970. "Some Problems About Rationality." In *Rationality,* edited by Brian Wilson, 194–213. New York: Harper and Row.

Lukes, Stephen. 1982. "Relativism in Its Place." In *Rationality and Relativism,* edited by Martin Hollis and Stephen Lukes, 261–305. Cambridge: MIT Press.

MacIntyre, Alasdaire. 1986. "The Intelligibility of Action." In *Rationality, Relativism, and the Human Sciences,* edited by J. Margolis, M. Krausz, and R. M. Burian, 63–80. Dordrecht: Martinus Nijhoff.

Maier, Charles S. 1997. *The Unmasterable Past: History, Holocaust, and German National Identity.* Cambridge: Harvard University Press.

Makkreel, Rudolf A. 1992. *Dilthey: Philosophy of the Human Studies.* Princeton: Princeton University Press.

Marrus, Michael. 1989. *The Holocaust in History.* New York: Meridian.

May, Larry, Marilyn Friedman, and Andy Clark, eds. 1996. *Mind and Morals.* Cambridge: MIT Press.

Mead, George Herbert. 1934. *Mind, Self, and Society.* Chicago: University of Chicago Press.

Melden, A. 1961. *Free Action.* London: Routledge and Kegan Paul.

Meltzoff, Andrew. 1995. "Understanding the Intentions of Others." *Developmental Psychology* 31, 838–850.

Meltzoff, Andrew, and Alison Gopnik. 1993. "The Role of Imitation in Understanding Persons and Developing a Theory of Mind." In *Understanding Other Minds: Perspectives from Autism,* edited by S. Baron-Cohen, H. Tager-Flusberg, and D. J. Cohen, 335–366. Oxford: Oxford University Press.

Meltzoff, Andrew, and Keith Moore. 1983. "Newborn Infants Imitate Adult Facial Gestures." *Child Development* 54, 702–709.

Milgram, Stanley. 1963. "Behavioral Study of Obedience." *Journal of Abnormal and Social Psychology* 67, 371–378.

Mink, Louis O. 1987. *Historical Understanding.* Edited by B. Fay, E. O. Golob, and R. T. Vann. Ithaca: Cornell University Press.

Moses, A. D. 1998. "Structure and Agency in the Holocaust: The Case of Daniel Jonah Goldhagen." *History and Theory* 37, 194–219.

Nagel, Thomas. 1979. *Mortal Questions.* Cambridge: Cambridge University Press.

Nagel, Thomas. 1986. *The View from Nowhere.* Oxford: Oxford University Press.

Needham, Rodney. 1972. *Belief, Language, and Experience.* Chicago: University of Chicago Press.

Neurath, Otto. 1973. *Empiricism and Sociology.* Dordrecht: D. Reidel.

Nietzsche, Friedrich. 1982. *Daybreak: Thoughts on the Prejudices of Morality.* Cambridge: Cambridge University Press.

Nisbett, Richard, and L. Ross. 1980. *Human Inferences: Strategies and Shortcomings of Social Judgment.* Englewood Cliffs, N.J.: Prentice-Hall.

Nisbett, Richard, and Timothy Wilson. 1977. "Telling More Than We Can Know." *Psychological Review* 3, 231–259.

Novick, Peter. 1988. *That Noble Dream.* Cambridge: Cambridge University Press.

Obeyesekere, Gananath. 1992. *The Apotheosis of Captain Cook.* Princeton: Princeton University Press.

O'Hear, Anthony, ed. 1996. *Verstehen and Humane Understanding*. Cambridge: Cambridge University Press.

Ormiston, Gayle, and Alan Schrift. 1990. *The Hermeneutic Tradition: From Ast to Ricoeur*. Albany: SUNY Press.

Passmore, John. 1962. "Explanation in Everyday Life, in Science, and in History." *History and Theory* 2, 105–123.

Peacocke, Christopher, ed. 1994. *Objectivity, Simulation, and the Unity of Consciousness*. Proceedings of the British Academy 83. Oxford: Oxford University Press.

Perner, Josef. 1993. *Understanding the Representational Mind*. Cambridge: MIT Press.

Perner, Josef. 1996. "Simulation as Explicitation of Prediction-Implicit Knowledge About the Mind: Arguments for a Simulation-Theory Mix." In *Theories of Theories of Mind*, edited by Peter Carruthers and Peter Smith, 90–104. Cambridge: Cambridge University Press.

Perner, Josef, and Deborah Howes. 1992. "'He Thinks He Knows.'" *Mind and Language* 7, 72–86. Reprinted in *Folk Psychology*, edited by Martin Davies and Tony Stone. Oxford: Blackwell.

Peters, R. S. 1958. *The Concept of Motivation*. London: Routledge and Kegan Paul.

Pickering, Andrew. 1984. *Constructing Quarks*. Chicago: University of Chicago Press.

Pollack, Jordan. 1990. "Recursive Distributed Representations." *Artificial Intelligence* 46, 77–105.

Popper, Karl. 1957. *The Poverty of Historicism*. London: Routledge and Kegan Paul.

Premack, David, and Guy Woodruff. 1978. "Does the Chimpanzee Have a Theory of Mind?" *Behavioral and Brain Science* 4, 515–526.

Putnam, Hilary. 1975. *Mind, Language, and Reality*. Cambridge: Cambridge University Press.

Putnam, Hilary. 1987. *The Many Faces of Realism*. La Salle: Open Court.

Pylyshyn, Z. 1984. *Computation and Cognition*. Cambridge: MIT Press.

Quine, W. V. O. 1960. *Word and Object*. Cambridge: MIT Press.

Quine, W. V. O. 1963. "Two Dogmas of Empiricism." In *From a Logical Point of View*. 2d ed. New York: Harper and Row.

Quine, W. V. O. 1971. "Ontological Relativity." In *Ontological Relativity and Other Essays*. 2d ed. New York: Columbia University Press.

Quine, W. V. O. 1986. "Reply to Hilary Putnam." In *The Philosophy of WV Quine*, edited by L. E. Hahn and P. A. Schilpp. La Salle, Ill.: Open Court.

Quine, W. V. O. 1992. *Pursuit of Truth*. Rev. ed. Cambridge: Harvard University Press.

Risjord, Mark. Forthcoming. *Woodcutters and Witchcraft*. Albany: SUNY Press.

Rorty, Amelie, ed. 1980. *Explaining Emotions*. Berkeley: University of California Press.

Rorty, Richard. 1979. *Philosophy and the Mirror of Nature*. Princeton: Princeton University Press.

Rorty, Richard. 1983. "Method and Morality." In *Social Science as Moral Inquiry*, edited by N. Haan, 155–176. New York: Columbia University Press.

Rorty, Richard. 1991a. "Inquiry as Recontextualization: An Anti-Dualist Account of Interpretation." In *The Interpretive Turn,* edited by David Hiley, James Bohman, and Richard Schusterman, 59–80. Ithaca: Cornell University Press.

Rorty, Richard. 1991b. "Pragmatism, Davidson, and Truth." In *Objectivity, Relativism and Truth: Philosophical Papers* 1, 126–150. Cambridge: Cambridge University Press.

Rosaldo, Renato. 1984. "Grief and a Headhunter's Rage: On the Cultural Force of Emotions." In *Text, Play, and Story: The Construction and Reconstruction of Self and Society,* edited by S. Plattner and E. M. Bruner. 1983 Proceedings of the American Ethnological Society.

Rosenberg, Alexander. 1995. *The Philosophy of Social Science.* Boulder: Westview.

Roth, Paul A. 1978. "Paradox and Indeterminacy." *Journal of Philosophy* 75, 347–367.

Roth, Paul A. 1984. "Critical Discussion: On Missing Neurath's Boat: Some Reflections on Recent Quine Literature." *Synthese* 61, 205–231.

Roth, Paul A. 1987. *Meaning and Method in the Social Sciences.* Ithaca: Cornell University Press.

Roth, Paul A. 1988. "Narrative Explanation: The Case of History." *History and Theory* 27, 1–13.

Roth, Paul A. 1989. "How Narratives Explain." *Social Research* 56, 449–478.

Roth, Paul A. 1996. "Will the Real Scientists Please Stand Up?" *Studies in the History and Philosophy of Science* 27, 43–68.

Rouse, Joseph. 1991. "Indeterminacy, Empirical Evidence, and Methodological Pluralism." *Synthese* 86, 443–465.

Ruben, David-Hillel. 1990. *Explaining Explanation.* London: Routledge.

Sahlins, Marshall. 1995. *How the "Natives" Think About Captain Cook, for Example.* Chicago: University of Chicago Press.

Salmon, Wesley. 1989. "Four Decades of Scientific Explanation." In *Scientific Explanation: Minnesota Studies in the Philosophy of Science,* edited by P. Kitcher and W. Salmon, 13: 3–219.

Schatzki, Theodore R. 1996. *Social Practices: A Wittgensteinian Approach to Human Activity and the Social.* New York: Cambridge University Press.

Scheler, Max. 1923. *Wesen und Form der Sympathie.* Bern München: Francke.

Schleiermacher, Friedrich. 1977. *Hermeneutics: The Handwritten Manuscripts.* Atlanta: Scholars.

Schutz, A. 1962. *Collected Papers.* The Hague: Nijhoff.

Schutz, A. 1967. *Phenomenology and the Social World.* Evanston, Ill.: Northwestern University Press.

Searle, John. 1969. *Speech Acts.* Cambridge: Cambridge University Press.

Searle, John. 1979. "Literal Meaning." In *Expression and Meaning,* 117–136. Cambridge: Cambridge University Press.

Searle, John. 1989. *Intentionality.* Cambridge: Cambridge University Press.

Searle, John. 1995. *The Construction of Social Reality.* New York: Free Press.

Sereny, Gitta. 1983. *Into That Darkness.* New York: Vintage.

Shweder, Richard. 1994. "'You're Not Sick, You're Just in Love.' Emotion as an Interpretive System." In *The Nature of Emotions,* edited by Paul Ekman and Richard Davidson, 32–44. Oxford: Oxford University Press.

Smith, Peter K. 1996. "Language and the Evolution of Mind Reading." In *Theories of Theories of Mind,* edited by Peter Carruthers and Peter Smith. Cambridge: Cambridge University Press.

Smolensky, Paul. 1990. "Tensor Product Variable Binding and the Representation of Symbolic Structures in Connectionist Systems." *Artificial Intelligence* 46: 159–216.

Smolensky, Paul. 1995. "Connectionist Structure and Explanation in an Integrated Connectionist/Symbolic Cognitive Architecture." In *The Philosophy of Psychology: Debates on Psychological Explanation,* edited by C. MacDonald and G. MacDonald, 2: 357–394. Oxford: Blackwell.

Spiro, Melford. 1968. "Virgin Birth, Parthenogenesis, and Physiological Paternity: An Essay in Cultural Interpretation." *Man,* n.s. 3, 242–261.

Stegmüller, Wolfgang. 1988. "Walther von der Vogelweide's Lyric of Dream-Love and Quasar 3C 273." In *Hermeneutics versus Science,* edited by J. Connolly and Th. Keutner, 102–152. Notre Dame, Ind.: Notre Dame University Press.

Stein, Edith. 1989. *On the Problem of Empathy.* Washington, D.C.: ICS Publishers.

Stein, Edward. 1996. *Without Good Reason: The Rationality Debate in Philosophy and Cognitive Science.* Oxford: Clarendon.

Stendhal. 1975. *Love.* London: Penguin Classics.

Stich, Stephen. 1990. *The Fragmentation of Reason.* Cambridge: MIT Press.

Stich, Stephen, and Shaun Nichols. 1992. "Folk Psychology: Simulation or Tacit Knowledge?" *Mind and Language* 7, 35–71.

Stich, Stephen, and Shaun Nichols. 1995a. "Folk Psychology: Simulation or Tacit Theory." In *Folk Psychology,* edited by Martin Davies and Tony Stone, 123–158. Oxford: Blackwell.

Stich, Stephen, and Shaun Nichols. 1995b. "Second Thoughts on Simulation." In *Mental Simulation,* edited by Martin Davies and Tony Stone, 87–108. Oxford: Blackwell.

Stich, Stephen, and Shaun Nichols. 1997. "Cognitive Penetrability, Rationality, and Restricted Simulation." *Mind and Language* 12, 297–326.

Stueber, Karsten. 1993. *Donald Davidsons Theorie Sprachlichen Verstehens.* Frankfurt: Anton Hain.

Stueber, Karsten. 1994a. "Understanding Truth and Objectivity: A Dialogue Between Donald Davidson and Hans Georg Gadamer." In *Hermeneutics and Truth,* edited by Brice Wachterhauser, 172–189. Evanston: Northwestern University Press.

Stueber, Karsten. 1994b. "Practice, Indeterminacy, and Private Language: Wittgenstein's Dissolution of Scepticism." *Philosophical Investigations* 17, 15–36.

Stueber, Karsten. 1997a. "Psychologische Erklärungen im Spannungsfeld des Interpretationismus und Reduktionismus." *Philosophische Rundschau* 44, 304–328.

Stueber, Karsten. 1997b. "Holism and Radical Interpretation: The Limitations of a Formal Theory of Meaning." In *Analyomen 2,* edited by Georg Meggle, 290–298. Berlin: de Gruyter.

Tarde, Gabriel de. 1903. *The Laws of Imitation*. Translated from the 2d French edition by E. C. Parson. New York: Henry Holt.

Taylor, Charles. 1964. *The Explanation of Behavior*. London: Routledge and Kegan Paul.

Taylor, Charles. 1980. "Understanding in Human Science." *Review of Metaphysics* 34, 3–23.

Taylor, Charles. 1985. "Interpretation and the Sciences of Man." In *Philosophy and the Human Sciences: Philosophical Papers 2*, 15–57. Cambridge: Cambridge University Press

Thagard, Paul, and Richard Nisbett. 1983. "Rationality and Charity." *Philosophy of Science* 50, 250–267.

Turner, Stephen. 1994. *The Social Theory of Practices*. Chicago: University of Chicago Press.

Vielmetter, Georg. 1998. *Die Unbestimmtheit des Sozialen: Zur Philosophie der Sozialwissenschaften*. New York: Campus.

Von Wright, Georg Henrik. 1971. *Explanation and Understanding*. Ithaca: Cornell University Press.

Weber, Max. 1949. *The Methodology of the Social Sciences*. New York: Free Press.

Weber, Max. 1978. *Economy and Society: An Outline of Interpretive Sociology*. 3 vols. Edited by Guenther Roth and Claus Wittich. Berkeley: University of California Press.

Wellman, Henry. 1990. *The Child's Theory of Mind*. Cambridge: MIT Press.

White, Hayden. 1973. *Metahistory*. Baltimore: Johns Hopkins University Press.

White, Hayden. 1987. *The Content of the Form*. Baltimore: Johns Hopkins University Press.

Wierzbicka, Anna. 1998. "Angst." *Culture and Psychology* 4, 161–188.

Wilson, Brian, ed. 1970. *Rationality*. New York: Harper and Row.

Wimmer, Heinz, and Josef Perner. 1983. "Beliefs About beliefs: Representation and Constraining Function of Wrong Beliefs in Young Children's Understanding of Deception." *Cognition* 13, 103–128.

Winch, Peter. 1958. *The Idea of a Social Science and Its Relation to Philosophy*. London: Routledge and Kegan Paul.

Winch, Peter. 1964. "Understanding a Primitive Society." *American Philosophical Quarterly* 1, 307–324. Reprinted in *Rationality*, edited by Brian Wilson, 78–111. New York: Harper and Row.

Winch, Peter. 1972. *Ethics and Action*. London: Routledge and Kegan Paul.

Wise, Gene. 1980. *American Historical Explanations*. 2d rev. ed. Minneapolis: University of Minnesota Press.

Wittgenstein, Ludwig. 1958. *Philosophical Investigations*. 3d ed. Translated by G. E. M. Anscombe. Englewood Cliffs, N.J.: Prentice-Hall.

Wittgenstein, Ludwig. 1977. *On Certainty*. Translated by Denis Paul and G. E. M. Anscombe. Oxford: Blackwell.

Wittgenstein, Ludwig. 1980. *Remarks on Philosophical Psychology*. Oxford: Basil Blackwell.

Woolgar, Steve, and Bruno Latour. 1986. *Laboratory Life*. Princeton: Princeton University Press.

Zimbardo, Philip. 1972. "Pathology of Imprisonment." *Society* 9, 4–9.

About the Editors and Contributors

Simon Blackburn is the Edna J. Koury Distinguished Professor of Philosophy at the University of North Carolina, Chapel Hill. He was Fellow and tutor in philosophy at Pembroke College, Oxford, from 1970 to 1990, and editor of *Mind* from 1984 to 1990. His books include *Spreading the Word* (Clarendon, 1984), the *Oxford Dictionary of Philosophy* (Oxford University Press, 1994), *Ruling Passions* (Clarendon, 1998), and *Think* (Oxford University Press, 1999).

James Bohman is Danforth Professor of Philosophy at St. Louis University. His publications include *New Philosophy of Social Science: Problems of Indeterminacy* (MIT Press, 1991) and *Public Deliberation: Pluralism, Complexity, and Democracy* (MIT Press, 1996). He edited, with David Hiley and Richard Shusterman, *The Interpretive Turn* (Cornell, 1991) and, with Tom McCarthy and Kenneth Baynes, *After Philosophy: End or Transformation?* (MIT Press, 1987). He has authored numerous articles on problems of interpretation and explanation in the social sciences.

Robert M. Gordon is professor of philosophy at the University of Missouri, St. Louis. He has been a Fellow of the American Council of Learned Societies and the National Endowment for the Humanities. His work on the relation between emotions and cognition has appeared in the *Philosophical Review*, the *Journal of Philosophy*, the *American Philosophical Quarterly*, and in a book, *The Structure of Emotions* (Cambridge University Press, 1987). He has published extensively on simulation theory. His contributions to simulation theory can be found in Davies and Stone (1995a; 1995b) and Carruthers and Smith (1996).

David Henderson is associate professor of philosophy at the University of Memphis. He is author of *Interpretation and Explanation in the Human Sciences* (SUNY Press, 1993) and editor of *Explanation in the Human Sciences* (Southern Journal of Philosophy, 1996). He publishes widely in the areas of philosophy of social science (including simulation theory) and epistemology.

Terence Horgan is professor of philosophy and William Dunavant University Professor at the University of Memphis. He has published numerous articles (many collaborative) in metaphysics, philosophy of mind, philosophy of psychology, philosophy of language, metaethics, and epistemology. He is coauthor (with John Tienson) of *Connectionism and the Philosophy of Psychology* (MIT Press, 1996).

Hans Herbert Kögler is associate professor of philosophy at the University of North Florida. He has published two books in the fields of interpretive and social theory: *Michel Foucault: Ein anti-humanistischer Aufklärer* (Metzler Verlag, 1994) and *The Power of Dialogue: Critical Hermeneutics After Gadamer and Foucault* (MIT Press, 1996). He has also authored the target essay in a special issue of *Social Epistemology* ("New Directions in the Sociology of Knowledge," 1997) and numerous articles in hermeneutics, philosophy of language, and social philosophy.

Rudolf A. Makkreel is Charles Howard Candler Professor of Philosophy and chair of the department at Emory University. He is the author of *Dilthey: Philoso-*

pher of the Human Studies (Princeton University Press, 1975, 1992) and *Imagination and Interpretation in Kant: The Hermeneutical Import of the Critique of Judgment* (University of Chicago Press, 1990), and the coeditor of Dilthey's *Selected Works* (vol. 1, *Introduction to the Human Sciences*, 1989; vol. 4, *Hermeneutics and the Study of History*, 1996; vol. 5, *Poetry and Experience*, 1985; Princeton University Press). He publishes widely on hermeneutics, aesthetics, Kant, and Dilthey and is currently at work on two books, one on philosophy and hermeneutics, the other on interpretation and historical judgment. He was the editor of the *Journal of the History of Philosophy* from 1983 to 1998.

Paul A. Roth is professor and chair of the Department of Philosophy at the University of Missouri, St. Louis. He is the author of *Meaning and Method in the Social Sciences* (Cornell University Press, 1987) as well as numerous articles in epistemology and the philosophy of the social sciences. He is also coeditor of the *Guidebook to the Philosophy of Social Science* (Blackwell, forthcoming).

Theodore R. Schatzki is associate professor of philosophy and codirector of the Committee on Social Theory at the University of Kentucky, Lexington. In 1997–1998, he was a visiting scholar at the Max Planck Institute for the History of Science in Berlin, Germany. He is author of *Social Practices: A Wittgensteinian Approach to Human Activity and the Social* (Cambridge University Press, 1996) and coeditor of a number of anthologies, among them *Postmodern Contentions: Epochs, Politics, and Space* (Guilford Press, 1993) and *Objectivity and Its Other* (Guilford Press, 1995). He is author of numerous articles on Wittgenstein, action theory, social philosophy, and continental thought.

Karsten R. Stueber is associate professor of philosophy at the College of the Holy Cross. He is the author of *Donald Davidson's Theorie Sprachlichen Verstehens* (Anton Hain, 1993) and coeditor of *Philosophie der Skepsis* (utb, 1996). He has published various articles on Wittgenstein, the philosophy of language, epistemology, and philosophy of mind, and he is a member of the advisory board for the journal *Facta Philosophica*.

Stephen Turner is graduate research professor of philosophy at the University of South Florida. He has taught at Virginia Tech, the University of Notre Dame, and Boston University, and has been Honorary Simon Visiting Professor at the University of Manchester, as well as a Fellow of the Swedish Collegium for Advanced Study in the Social Sciences and the National Endowment for the Humanities. His books include, among others, *Sociological Explanation as Translation* (California University Press, 1980), *Max Weber and the Dispute over Reason and Value* (with Regis Factor; Routledge, 1984), *The Search for a Methodology of Social Science* (Boston Studies in the History and Philosophy of Science, 1986), *Max Weber: The Lawyer as Social Thinker* (with Regis Factor; Routledge, 1994), and *The Social Theory of Practices* (University of Chicago Press, 1994). His articles have appeared in such journals as the *American Philosophical Quarterly* and the *American Sociological Review*.

Georg Vielmetter has taught philosophy at the Free University of Berlin. He is the author of *Die Unbestimmtheit des Sozialen: Zur Philosophie der Sozialwissenschaften* (Campus, 1998) as well as articles on epistemology, philosophy of social science, and political philosophy. At the moment he works as a managing consultant.

Names Index

Adorno, Theodor W., 42–43
Alexy, R., 236, 241(n24)
Apel, Karl-Otto, 40–41, 168, 209
Aristotle, 149, 172
Averill, James, 100(n18)

Baldwin, James Mark, 107
Barley, Nigel, 92
Bernstein, Richard, 35
Blackburn, Simon, 53–54, 270–288
Bohman, James, 52, 222–242
Bradley, F.H., 275
Brandom, Robert, 226, 236, 238,
    241(nn16, 25)
Broszat, Martin, 251–252
Browning, Christopher, 260, 268(n55)

Carr, David, 244, 252–253, 256–261,
    265(n5), 268(n55), 269(n57)
Cassirer, Ernst, 37, 197–198
Cherniak, Christopher, 152
Chomsky, Noam, 57(n53), 116
Collingwood, Robin George, viii, 5–6,
    17–19, 53, 55(nn6,9), 165,
    270–287

Danto, Arthur, 30–31, 245–249
Darwin, Charles, 100(n18), 118(n10)
Davidson, Donald, 16–17, 21, 58(n60),
    62–66, 80(nn5, 6), 150–152,
    230–232, 241(n17), 266(n17),
    273
Dennett, Daniel, 95, 97, 218(n15), 273
Dijksterhuis, E.J., 270–272
Dilthey, Wilhelm, viii, 5, 22, 25–29, 50,
    59(nn76,77,80,82), 100(n20),
    105, 165, 182–192
Dray, William, viii, 14–15, 62
Dreyfus, Hubert, 218(n19)
Dummett, 230–231, 240(n7),
    284

Ekman, Paul, 100(n18)
Evans-Pritchard, Edward, 20, 141(n5),
    157–159

Fodor, Jerry, 55(n14), 101(n28),
    125–126
Foucault, Michel, 44
Friedländer, Henry, 268(n55)
Friedländer, Saul, 251–252

Gadamer, Hans-Georg, viii, 2, 29–31,
    39, 46, 58(n71), 60(n91), 158,
    163, 234–236, 241(n23)
Galison, Peter, 250
Geertz, Clifford, 112, 165–166, 168,
    222–223
Goethe, Johann Wolfgang von, 58(n71)
Goldman, Alvin I., 9, 12, 37, 49,
    55(n20), 56(n36), 117(n4), 121,
    147–148, 154, 161(n9), 175–177,
    180(n21), 181, 204
Gopnik, Alison, 7
Gordon, Robert M., 9, 10–12, 37, 47,
    55(nn20,23), 62–82, 84, 88,
    99(12), 155, 169–170, 175, 177,
    181–182, 191–192, 200–203,
    218(nn20,21,23), 229,
    240(nn9,11)
Grandy, Richard, 22
Grice, Paul, 58(n67), 241(n15)

Habermas, Jürgen, 35, 40–41, 44–46,
    226–227, 235–237,
    241(nn15,24,25)
Hansen, Chad, 118(n14)
Harris, Paul, 208, 220(n37)
Heal, Jane, 9–12, 48–49, 56(n25),
    123–126, 129–130, 146–148,
    146(n7), 155–156, 160(n2),
    169–172, 176, 180(nn12,21),
    220(n44)

Subject Index